Robes, Romans, and Rituals

in First Corinthians

Dissertationes Theologicae Holmienses
Dissertations from University College Stockholm
www.ehs.se/dth

Main editor:
Thomas Kazen

Editors:
Petra Carlsson Redell
Joel Halldorf
Jonas Ideström
Susanne Wigorts Yngvesson

No. 9

Aldar Nõmmik

Robes, Romans, and Rituals in First Corinthians

Paul and the Conflict over Head-Coverings

WIPF & STOCK · Eugene, Oregon

Robes, Romans, and Rituals in First Corinthians: Paul and the Conflict over Head-Coverings

Dissertation presented at University College Stockholm to be publicly examined in Room 219–220 at Åkeshovsvägen 29, Bromma, January 17, 2025, at 13:00, for the degree of Doctor of Philosophy in Theology (Biblical Studies: New Testament). The examination will be held in English.

Faculty examiner: Richard E. DeMaris, Senior Research Professor, Valparaiso University
Supervisor: Thomas Kazen, Professor of Biblical Studies, University College Stockholm
Assistant supervisor: Rikard Roitto, Associate Professor of Biblical Studies, New Testament, University College Stockholm

Abstract

This thesis offers a novel interpretation of 1 Cor 11:2–16 in light of the Roman ritual practice of *capite velato*—a custom of covering the head with a garment during prayer, sacrifice, and divination. It traces linguistic and conceptual links between ancient descriptions and depictions of *capite velato* and 1 Cor 11:2–16, and demonstrates that this ritual gesture must have been familiar to Paul and his Corinthian interlocutors. With the aid of cognitive science of religion, this thesis explores the possible reasons for and implications of Paul's instructions on this Roman custom in First Corinthians. It argues that 1 Cor 11:2–16 preserves a clash of values between Paul and his addressees in regards to the correct procedure and efficacy of prayer and accessing of divine knowledge: some in Corinth had begun to argue that for the sake of uniformity, all members of the Christ association, including married women of all cultures, should strip their heads of everything when in prayer or when seeking divine knowledge to match the appearance of Roman men whom Paul had asked not to pray with garments over the head. In response to this, Paul found a way to argue that praying with a garment over the head is only shameful for men, but the same does not apply for women, and so women can keep their head-coverings and hair accessories on during prayer and prophecy. While these instructions may have been intelligible to the original readers, later interpreters of Paul, who had no knowledge of the *Sitz im Leben* that prompted 1 Cor 11:2–16, misunderstood and misappropriated Paul's instructions in this passage, mistakenly believing Paul to have been solely concerned with a faction of rebellious women in the Corinthian congregation. These assumptions have dominated the readings of 1 Cor 11:2–16, but this thesis offers an alternative interpretation that builds on a more accurate understanding of ancient customs and ideals related to ritual head-coverings.

Kläder, romare och ritualer i Första Korinthierbrevet:
Paulus och konflikten om huvudbonader

Akademisk avhandling presenterad vid Enskilda Högskolan Stockholm för disputation i sal 219–220, Åkeshovsvägen 29, Bromma, 17 januari 2025 kl. 13.00, för teologie doktorsexamen i bibelvetenskap med inriktning mot Nya testamentet. Disputationen kommer att äga rum på engelska.

Opponent: Richard E. DeMaris, Senior Research Professor, Valparaiso University
Handledare: Thomas Kazen, professor i bibelvetenskap, Enskilda Högskolan Stockholm
Bitr. handledare: Rikard Roitto, docent och högskolelektor i bibelvetenskap, Nya testamentet, Enskilda Högskolan Stockholm

Sammanfattning

Denna avhandling erbjuder en ny tolkning av 1 Kor 11:2–16 i ljuset av den romerska rituella praktiken *capite velato* – sedvänjan att täcka huvudet med ett klädesplagg när man bad, offrade och spådde. Studien spårar språkliga och konceptuella samband mellan antika beskrivningar och avbildningar av *capite velato* och 1 Kor 11:2–16, samt visar att denna rituella gest måste ha varit bekant för Paulus och hans korinthiska samtalspartners. Med hjälp av kognitiv religionsvetenskap undersöks möjliga orsaker till och konsekvenser av Paulus instruktioner beträffande denna romerska sedvänja i Första Korinthierbrevet. Avhandlingen hävdar att 1 Kor 11:2–16 speglar en värdekonflikt mellan Paulus och hans adressater gällande korrekt procedur, bönens effekt och sättet att få tillgång till gudomlig kunskap. Somliga i Korinth hade börjat hävda att för enhetlighetens skull behövde alla medlemmar i Kristusgruppen, inklusive gifta kvinnor från alla kulturer, ta av sig allt de hade på huvudet när de bad eller sökte gudomlig kunskap, för att motsvara utseendet hos de romerska män som Paulus hade bett att inte be med klädesplagg över huvudet. Som svar på detta fann Paulus ett sätt att argumentera för att det är skamligt för män att be med ett plagg över huvudet, men att detsamma inte gäller för kvinnor, och att kvinnor därför kan behålla sina huvudbonader och håraccessoarer på under bön och profetia. Även om dessa instruktioner kan ha varit begripliga för de ursprungliga läsarna har senare uttolkare av Paulus, som inte hade någon kunskap om den *Sitz im Leben* som föranledde 1 Kor 11:2–16, missförstått och missbrukat Paulus instruktioner i detta avsnitt, och felaktigt trott att Paulus enbart bekymrade sig över en grupp upproriska kvinnor i den korinthiska församlingen. Dessa antaganden har länge dominerat läsningen av 1 Kor 11:2–16, men denna avhandling erbjuder en alternativ tolkning som bygger på en mer korrekt förståelse av antika seder och ideal relaterade till rituella huvudbonader.

Enskilda Högskolan Stockholm

Enskilda Högskolan Stockholm erbjuder utbildningsprogram i mänskliga rättigheter och demokrati, samt i teologi/religionsvetenskap. Högskolan grundades 1993 genom en sammanslagning av utbildningsinstitutioner med rötter från 1866, hette tidigare Teologiska högskolan, Stockholm, och har tre avdelningar: Avdelningen för mänskliga rättigheter och demokrati, Avdelningen för religionsvetenskap och teologi, samt Avdelningen för östkyrkliga studier. Forskarutbildningen i Bibelvetenskap bedrivs inom inriktningarna Gamla testamentets/Hebreiska bibelns exegetik respektive Nya testamentets exegetik. Utbildningen är både bred och djup, och innefattar bland annat filologiska, historiska, litterära, teologiska, socialvetenskapliga, ideologikritiska och hermeneutiska perspektiv.

University College Stockholm

University College Stockholm offers programmes in Human Rights and Democracy and in Theology / Religious Studies. The university college was founded in 1993 through a merger of educational institutions with roots dating back to 1866, is also known as Stockholm School of Theology, and has three departments: the Department of Human Rights and Democracy, the Department of Religious Studies and Theology, and the Department of Eastern Christian Studies. The doctoral programme in Biblical Studies provides specialisations in Old Testament/Hebrew Bible exegesis and New Testament exegesis. The programme offers both breadth and depth, and includes among other things philological, historical, literary, theological, and hermeneutical perspectives, as well as perspectives from social science and ideological criticism.

Wipf and Stock Publishers
199 W 8th Ave, Suite 3
Eugene, OR 97401

Robes, Romans, and Rituals in First Corinthians
Paul and the Conflict over Head-Coverings
By Nõmmik, Aldar
Copyright © 2025 by Nõmmik, Aldar All rights reserved.
Softcover ISBN-13: 979-8-3852-5982-3
Hardcover ISBN-13: 979-8-3852-5983-0
eBook ISBN-13: 979-8-3852-5984-7
Publication date 7/31/2025
Previously published by Enskilda Högskolan Stockholm, 2025

This edition is a scanned facsimile of the original edition published in 2025.

*In loving memory of my grandparents,
Theodor Voldemar Viirsalu (1912–2006) and
Raely Viirsalu (1934–2020), who taught me to read.*

Acknowledgments

I wish to acknowledge the invaluable support of those who helped make this dissertation possible. My deepest thanks go to my advisors, Prof. Thomas Kazen and Dr. Rikard Roitto, who have guided me every step of the way—especially Thomas, whose mentorship has turned into a meaningful friendship and who has gone above and beyond to ensure the timely completion of this project.

Many thanks also to all my other colleagues at EHS for the many insightful comments throughout the process of writing this thesis. I especially want to highlight the role of Dr. Carl Johan Berglund, who has been immensely helpful in the final stages of this project with formatting, style, and content.

Many other biblical scholars in the various institutions in Norway and Sweden—and particularly Prof. Cecilia Wassen—have provided thorough critiques of my ideas, which have raised the quality of this work significantly. Thank you.

I also have many wonderful friends to thank for enhancing the quality of my life in so many ways and for challenging me to think deeper. But I am especially grateful to Judson, who has been a constant supporting presence in my life for the past five years, and to Janek for his indispensable and enjoyable companionship on my research trip to Greece and Italy to document *capite velato*.

I am also much indebted to my parents and my sisters for being the sort of family presence in my life that many dream of but never get to experience.

And last, but by no means least, my wife and life companion, Laura, whose unexplainably courageous willingness to switch the blue skies, fresh fruit, and warm sunshine of California for the grey skies and long winters of Estonia, only for me to write a book that very few will ever care to read in full, has made this all possible. This, and the two—and counting—wonderful children that you have brought into this world and are so lovingly raising! I cannot thank you enough.

Tallinn in November 2024
Aldar Nõmmik

Contents

Acknowledgments 9
Contents 11
Figures 17
Abbreviations 19
Introduction 21
    Overview of the Thesis 23
    Theory and Method 25
    Terminology 27
    Presuppositions and Biases 28

1. From Greek Customs to Roman Rites 29
    1.1 John Chrysostom 30
    1.2 Jewish Customs as Source of Conflict 32
        1.2.1 John Lightfoot 32
        1.2.2 Johann Lorenz von Mosheim 33
        1.2.3 Johann David Michaelis 34
        1.2.4 Analysis 35
    1.3 Misbehaving Women as Paul's Sole Concern 36
        1.3.1 Gustav Billroth 36
        1.3.2 Hermann Olshausen 37
        1.3.3 Heinrich August Wilhelm Meyer 37
        1.3.4 Charles Hodge 38
        1.3.5 Frédéric Louis Godet 39
        1.3.6 Archibald Robertson and Alfred Plummer 39
        1.3.7 Stefan Lösch 40
        1.3.8 Elisabeth Schüssler Fiorenza 41
        1.3.9 Dennis Ronald MacDonald 41
        1.3.10 Gerd Theissen 42

	1.3.11 David E. Garland	43
	1.3.12 Joseph A. Fitzmyer	43
	1.3.13 Benjamin A. Edsall	44
	1.3.14 Gordon D. Fee	45
	1.3.15 Analysis	45
1.4	The Length or Style of Hair as the Subject Matter	55
	1.4.1 Abel Isaksson	55
	1.4.2 James B. Hurley	57
	1.4.3 Jerome Murphy-O'Connor	58
	1.4.4 Marlis Gielen	59
	1.4.5 Kirk R. MacGregor	60
	1.4.6 Philip B. Payne	60
	1.4.7 Torsten Jantsch	61
	1.4.8 Analysis	62
1.5	Ritual Transvestism as Paul's Enemy	67
	1.5.1 Catherine Kroeger	68
	1.5.2 Birgitte Graakjær Hjort	68
	1.5.3 Gillian Townsley	68
	1.5.4 Analysis	69
1.6	Roman Rites as Background to 1 Cor 11:2–16	70
	1.6.1 Richard Oster	71
	1.6.2 Cynthia L. Thompson	71
	1.6.3 David W. J. Gill	72
	1.6.4 Ben Witherington III	73
	1.6.5 Bruce W. Winter	73
	1.6.6 Mark Finney	74
	1.6.7 Cynthia Long Westfall	75
	1.6.8 Analysis	76
1.7	Conclusion	79
2.	**Having a Garment Down from the Head**	**81**
2.1	What Do We Mean by *capite velato*?	82
	2.1.1 The Outer Garment as Head-Covering	82
	2.1.2 The Garment of *capite velato*	88
2.2	*Capite velato* in the Roman Epics and Histories	91
	2.2.1 *Capite velato* and Aeneas	91
	2.2.2 *Capite velato* and Mopsus	94
	2.2.3 *Capite velato* and Numa	94

    2.2.4 *Capite velato* and Attus Navius...97
    2.2.5 *Capite velato* and Camillus 99
    2.2.6 *Capite velato* and the College of *Fetials* 100
    2.2.7 *Capite velato* and the Decii 101
    Excursus: A Covered Head and the Murder of Tiberius Gracchus............ 103
    2.2.8 *Capite velato* and Lucius Vitellius.. 105
    2.2.9 *Capite velato* and Vespasian and Titus 105
    2.2.10 *Capite velato* and Hadrian..106
2.3 *Capite velato* in Plays, Satires, and Other Works 107
    2.3.1 *Capite velato* in Plautus 107
    2.3.2 *Capite velato* in Lucretius 108
    2.3.3 *Capite velato* in Varro 109
    2.3.4 *Capite velato* in Plutarch...109
    2.3.5 *Capite velato* in Juvenal 111
2.4 Summary of the Literary References to *capite velato* 112
2.5 *Capite velato* as a Symbol of Augustan Propaganda.......................................112
    2.5.1 Ara Pacis Augustae 113
    2.5.2 Statues of Augustus in Rome, Corinth, and Beyond...........................116
    2.5.3 *Capite velato* and Livia 123
    2.5.4 The Altars of the *vicomagistri* 125
    2.5.5 Augustus Honored in Pompeii and Corinth 128
2.6 *Capite velato* and Augustus's Successors 131
    2.6.1 *Capite velato* and the Julio-Claudian Dynasty 131
    2.6.2 *Capite velato* and the Nerva-Antonine Dynasty 136
2.7 *Capite velato* and Domestic Religion 141
2.8 Summary of the Selected Archaeological Evidence.. 145
2.9 Conclusion..149

3. Whoever Prays or Prophesies 151
3.1 Head-Coverings in the Context of Prayer 152
    3.1.1 Roman Prayers 153
    3.1.2 Prayer in the Letters of Paul 154
    3.1.3 Prayer in 1 Cor 11:2–16.. 163
3.2 Head-Coverings in the Context of Prophesying 164
    3.2.1 "Prophesying" in the Letters of Paul 164
    3.2.2 1 Cor 12–14 and the Definition of "Prophesying"................................176
    3.2.3 "Prophesying" in Philo and Josephus...180
    3.2.4 The Relationship between Prophesying and Divination.................... 188

3.2.5 Divination in the Letters of Paul 196
3.2.6 "Prophesying" in 1 Cor 11:4–5 201
3.3 Conclusion 203

4. *Capite velato*, Human Cognition, and Group Dynamics 205
4.1 *Capite velato* and Cognitive Science of Religion 206
    4.1.1 What Do We Mean by "Ritual"? 207
    4.1.2 Modes of Religiosity Theory: Overview 211
    4.1.3 *Capite velato* and Modes of Religiosity Theory 213
    4.1.4 Ritual Form Theory: Overview 216
    4.1.5 *Capite velato* and Ritual Form Theory 216
    4.1.6 Rituals and the Hazard-Precaution System 217
    4.1.7 *Capite velato* and the Hazard-Precaution System 218
    4.1.8 Costly Signaling Theory: Overview 219
    4.1.9 *Capite velato* and Costly Signaling Theory 221
4.2 CSR Theories and 1 Cor 11:2–16 222
    4.2.1 The Make-Up of First-Century Corinth 223
    4.2.2 The Make-Up of the Corinthian Christian Congregation 226
    4.2.3 The Venue of Prayer, the Venue of Prophecy 230
    4.2.4 *Capite velato* and Shame 236
4.3 Conclusion 241

5. Shame on Christ, Shame on Man, and Shame on Woman 243
5.1 Opening Praise of the Corinthians (1 Cor 11:2) 244
5.2 Hierarchy of Heads: Foundational Premise (1 Cor 11:3–6) 248
    5.2.1 "Of Every Man the Head is Christ" and *capite velato* 250
    5.2.2 "The Head of Woman is the Man" and *capite velato* 252
    5.2.3 Summary 263
5.3 Because of Creation: First Supportive Argument (1 Cor 11:7–10a) ... 264
5.4 "Because of the Angels" (1 Cor 11:10b) 270
    5.4.1 "The Angels" as "the Watchers" 271
    5.4.2 "The Angels" as Guardians of Worship 273
    5.4.3 "The Angels" as Creators or as Guardians of Creation Order ... 275
    5.4.4 "The Angels" as Spies or Messengers 277
    5.4.5 "The Angels" as Mediators 279
    5.4.6 Summary Analysis 280

5.5 "Nevertheless": Paul's Qualification (1 Cor 11:11–12) 281
5.6 Analogy from Nature: Second Supportive Argument (1 Cor 11:13–15) 282
5.7 Example of Others: Third Supportive Argument (1 Cor 11:16) 286
5.8 Conclusion 287

6. Women as Scapegoats 289
6.1 The Letter of 2 Corinthians 289
6.2 The Letter to the Romans 293
6.3 The Household Codes and the Pastoral Epistles 294
6.4 Valentinians according to Irenaeus 298
6.5 Theodotus according to Clement of Alexandria 301
6.6 Clement of Alexandria 302
6.7 Tertullian 305
6.8 Origen 311
6.9 *Dialogue between a Montanist and an Orthodox* 311
6.10 John Chrysostom 314
6.11 Conclusion 315

7. Conclusions 317

Bibliography 323
Ancient sources 323
Literature 327

Index of Ancient Literature 347

Index of Modern Authors 359

Index of Subjects 365

Figures

All figures are photographs taken by the author.

Figure 1.1. A statue of a priestess of Isis 54
Figure 1.2. A statue of Isis 54
Figure 1.3. Bust of Demeter 55
Figure 2.1. A funerary statue of a togatus man 89
Figure 2.2. Ara Pacis panel of Aeneas's inaugural sacrifice 115
Figure 2.3. Ara Pacis panel of Aeneas's inaugural sacrifice 116
Figure 2.4. Ara Pacis panel of Augustus in procession 117
Figure 2.5. Ara Pacis panel of Augustus in procession 117
Figure 2.6. Ara Pacis panel of Agrippa and Livia in procession 118
Figure 2.7. Ara Pacis panel of Antonia Maior and Minor in procession 118
Figure 2.8. Ara Pacis panel of augurs and quindecemviri in procession 119
Figure 2.9. Ara Pacis panel of the college of septemviri in procession 119
Figure 2.10. Capite velato statue of Augustus from Corinth 120
Figure 2.11. Capite velato statue of Augustus from Corinth 121
Figure 2.12. Map of the ancient city of Corinth 122
Figure 2.13. Capite velato statue of Augustus from Rome 122
Figure 2.14. Capite velato statue of Augustus from Rome 123
Figure 2.15. A bronze statue of Livia praying 124
Figure 2.16. A bronze statue of Livia praying 125
Figure 2.17. A bronze statue of Livia with raised hands 125
Figure 2.18. An altar in Pompeii depicting *capite velato* 129
Figure 2.19. An altar in Pompeii depicting *capite velato* 130
Figure 2.20. A statue of Eumachia, a Pompeiian priestess 131
Figure 2.21. Capite velato bust of Marcellus 132
Figure 2.22. Capite velato statue of Tiberius 133
Figure 2.23. Capite velato bust of Claudius 134
Figure 2.24. Capite velato bust of Nero from Rome 135

Figure 2.25. Capite velato bust of Nero from Corinth 135
Figure 2.26. Capite velato statue of Hadrian 138
Figure 2.27. A relief of Marcus Aurelius pouring libation 139
Figure 2.28. A relief of Marcus Aurelius pouring libation 141
Figure 2.29. A wall-painting in the House of Placidus in Pompeii 142
Figure 2.30. A wall-painting in the House of Vettii in Pompeii 143
Figure 2.31. A wall-painting in the House of Vettii in Pompeii 143
Figure 2.32. A wall-painting from an unnamed house in Pompeii 144
Figure 2.33. A statuette of a *genius capite velato* 146
Figure 2.34. A statuette of a *genius capite velato* 146
Figure 2.35. A statue of a female in the act of offering 147
Figure 2.36. A statue of a female in the act of offering 148
Figure 5.1. A statue of Pudicitia 256

Abbreviations

Abbreviations follow *The SBL Handbook of Style: For Biblical Studies and Related Disciplines,* second edition (Atlanta: SBL, 2014). In addition to this, the following abbreviations are also used.

Ab urbe cond.	Livy, *Ab urbe condita* (*History of Rome*)
Hesiod	Lucian, *A Conversation with Hesiod*
Hist. Aug.	Historia Augusta
Hist. Rom.	Dio Cassius, *Historiae romanae* (*Roman History*)
JSRNC	*Journal for the Study of Religion, Nature and Culture*
SCJ	*Stone-Campbell Journal*

Introduction

> In its present form this is hardly one of Paul's happier compositions. The logic is obscure at best and contradictory at worst. The word choice is peculiar; the tone, peevish.[1]

The above characterization of 1 Cor 11:2–16 by Robin Scroggs from 1972 has often been echoed in subsequent biblical scholarship on this passage. It has repeatedly been pointed out that the text is confusing and incoherent, and that it does not easily align with Paul's value system as expressed elsewhere in his writings. Scholars have struggled to understand the pericope's purpose in its original context, as well as its implications for modern times. As a result, some biblical scholars have deemed this passage a non-Pauline interpolation and interpreted it as such.[2] And some others have proposed that in 1 Cor 11:2–16, ideas belonging to Paul are mixed with ideas from his Corinthian interlocutors—that is, that Paul quotes or describes the Corinthian positions on certain issues regarding proper conduct during praying and prophesying, and then refutes them. Thus, ideas that sound inconsistent with the views of the "authentic Paul" are attributed to the Corinthians, while the more acceptable ideas are attributed to Paul.[3] In both cases, Paul is absolved of having made the sort of statements that are deemed off-putting or offensive.

---

[1] Robin Scroggs, "Paul and the Eschatological Woman," *JAAR* 40 (1972): 297.
[2] William O. Walker, Jr., "1 Corinthians 11:2–16 and Paul's Views regarding Women," *JBL* 94 (1975): 94–110; Lamar Cope, "1 Cor 11:2–16: One Step Further," *JBL* 97 (1978): 435–36; G. W. Trompf, "On Attitudes Towards Women in Paul and Paulinist Literature: 1 Corinthians 11:3–16 and Its Context," *CBQ* 42 (1980): 196–215; William O. Walker, Jr., "The Vocabulary of 1 Corinthians 11.3–16: Pauline or Non-Pauline?" *JSNT* 35 (1989): 75–88; Christopher Mount, "1 Corinthians 11:3–16: Spirit Possession and Authority in a Non-Pauline Interpolation," *JBL* 124 (2005): 313–40.
[3] Alan Padgett, "Paul on Women in the Church: The Contradictions of Coiffure in 1 Corinthians 11:2–16," *JSNT* 20 (1984): 69–86; Lucy Peppiatt, *Women and Worship at Corinth: Paul's Rhetorical Arguments in 1 Corinthians* (Eugene, OR: Cascade Books, 2015).

Neither solution is convincing, however. We have no text-critical evidence that points to 1 Cor 11:2–16 being a later interpolation. Nor does the vocabulary or syntax in this passage point in that direction.[4] It is also very uncharacteristic for Paul to extensively quote or describe the position(s) of his addressees—while he indeed at times quotes back his interlocutors' catchphrases (cf. 1 Cor 7:1; 10:23), these rarely exceed the length of a few words.[5] It takes special pleading to argue that the text is a dialogue rather than a continuous monologue, and none of the scholarly efforts to demonstrate the dialogical nature of the passage have been convincing thus far. If we allow excisions of entire passages from the received corpus of Paul's authentic letters—or if we allow the chopping up of entire passages into statements of Paul and statements of others—solely on the basis that some things do not sound like Paul to our ears, then the entire enterprise of Pauline scholarship is in danger of becoming a Marcionite exercise of creating a Paul in whatever image we fancy. Thus, without sufficient evidence pointing to the contrary, we must take 1 Cor 11:2–16 as authentically and entirely Pauline and work from the premise that it was addressed to a select group of individuals residing in Corinth in the middle of the first century CE, and that it responded to a specific situation and was therefore intended to be intelligible to its very first readers.

While interpreting 1 Cor 11:2–16 from this premise is admittedly not an easy task, it will become evident in this thesis that most of the perceived problems and incoherencies in this passage that biblical scholarship has traditionally highlighted have more to do with our own presuppositions, biases, and lack of knowledge regarding first-century customs, values, ideas, and ethics than with anything else. I propose in the pages that follow that Paul's arguments in 1 Cor 11:2–16 take on an element of coherency and logic if they are read in the context of a Roman ritual gesture of covering the head with the edge of an outer garment during certain acts of devotion that Paul's contemporaries widely practiced. As Chapter 1 will demonstrate, I am not the first to read 1 Cor 11:2–16 from this perspective. However, what I offer here is the most comprehensive interpretation of 1 Cor 11:2–16 from the above premise to date, and I also propose a novel solution to what has proved to be the most challenging issue for those interpreters who have argued for the

---

[4] Extensive criticisms of the interpolation theories in regards to 1 Cor 11:2–16 can be found in several standard biblical commentaries on 1 Cor, but see also, Jerome Murphy-O'Connor, "The Non-Pauline Character of 1 Corinthians 11:2–16?" *JBL* 95 (1976): 615–21.

[5] See also, Torsten Jantsch, "Einführung in die Probleme von 1Kor 11,2–16 und die Geschichte seiner Auslegung," in *Frauen, Männer, Engel: Perspektiven zu 1Kor 11, 2–16*, ed. Torsten Jantsch (Göttingen: Neukirchener, 2015), 7.

relevance of this Roman ritual gesture on 1 Cor 11:2–16: why does Paul discourage men from praying and prophesying with a covered head, but encourages women to do the opposite, even though in Roman religion, both men *and* women worshiped with a covered head? Here is an overview of my thesis.

Overview of the Thesis

In Chapter 1, I discuss the most common interpretive frameworks through which 1 Cor 11:2–16 has been read throughout history, and I demonstrate their inadequacy in dealing with the various elements of the text. I particularly criticize those approaches that have dominated biblical scholarship on this passage in the last century: a) that Paul in 1 Cor 11:2–16 only chastises certain rebellious women in the Corinthian congregation, and b) that Paul criticizes men's and women's hairstyles and hair lengths. I show, however, that there is merit in the suggestion that 1 Cor 11:2–16 addresses a certain Roman ritual head-covering practice known as *capite velato*, although I point out that some important issues have not been satisfactorily dealt with in this line of interpretation (as discussed above), a situation which I set out to remedy in the remainder of the thesis.

In Chapter 2, I present and analyze all of the literary references to *capite velato* that I have been able to gather from ancient sources. I also present and analyze a sizable collection of portrayals of this gesture on monuments, statues, statuettes, altars, and paintings from the time of Augustus to the end of the second century CE. I demonstrate that covering the head with an outer garment during sacrifice, prayer, and divination was a widespread and important custom of the Romans at the time of Paul and that Paul and his addressees in Corinth would have been familiar with it, as depictions of this ritual gesture were also exhibited in prominent places in first-century CE Corinth. Furthermore, I point out that there are linguistic links between 1 Cor 11:2–16 and certain contemporaneous Greek descriptions of *capite velato*. I conclude, then, that this custom is the most likely subject matter of 1 Cor 11:2–16.

In Chapter 3, I highlight that Paul shows concern with covered and uncovered heads only in the context of "praying or prophesying" (cf. 1 Cor 11:4–5). I argue that this specificity has not been appreciated enough in biblical scholarship. I demonstrate, for example, that the term "prophesying" should be understood in the Pauline corpus as a general reference to activities through which divine (fore)knowledge was sought in antiquity: oracular reading of scriptures; marvel, dream, and vision interpretation; casting of lots; and so on. There is thus overlap between what the ancients understood as "divination" and what Paul understood as "prophecy." Considering, then, that Paul's contemporary Romans prayed and sought divine knowledge with covered heads, Paul's concern with head-coverings only in the context of "praying or prophesying" can be explained in light of this. I argue that 1 Cor 11:2–16 is the only text in the authentic letters of Paul where Paul shows any interest in any formularies, postures, or appearances related to praying and prophesying, whereas for the ancient Romans, such things were of paramount concern. I conclude, therefore, that 1 Cor 11:2–16 preserves a clash of values between Paul's way of thinking about prayer and how to access divine knowledge and the Roman way of thinking about these matters, which centered on the ritual gesture of covering the head with an outer garment.

In Chapter 4, I begin to probe the possible reasons why Paul came to address this Roman ritual gesture in his letter to the Corinthian Christians. With the aid of cognitive science of religion, I demonstrate that participation in and observation of ritual performances and non-performances greatly affects individual cognition and social relationships. I argue that the various theories about rituals predict the performance of *capite velato* to have been an excellent cultural device for promoting social cohesion and traditional values in Roman society and its non-performance to have been unthinkable for the majority of Roman citizens at the time of Paul. This is crucial because, as I show, there was an influential Roman presence in first-century Corinth and in the congregation of Christ-followers located there. I argue, then, that Paul's association of men's covered heads with shame in the context of praying and prophesying (cf. 1 Cor 11:4) would have been heard by those with affiliations to Rome as a radical statement calling for a complete alteration to one's lifestyle, including the severing of meaningful and vital social relationships, which is why its implementation would not have been a straight-forward matter.

In Chapter 5, I present an exegetical study of 1 Cor 11:2–16 in order to discover the most reasonable *Sitz im Leben* that could best explain Paul's convoluted arguments in this passage in light of the perspectives gained in Chapters 2–4. I hypothesize that during his initial stay in Corinth, Paul discouraged the performance of *capite velato*, but that after he had left Corinth, the implementation of his instructions caused a conflict. Some questioned Paul's authority and reasoning, while others took Paul seriously and began to argue that for the sake of uniformity, no one should have anything on their heads or in their hair whenever they prayed or accessed divine (fore)knowledge. This development, however, caused great concern for those women (and their husbands) for whom covering the head with outer garments and veils symbolized their faithfulness to their husbands and longevity of their marriages. 1 Cor 11:2–16 should therefore be read as Paul's response to these developments: on the one hand, Paul defends his initial instructions not to perform *capite velato* but, on the other hand, he also protests against those who were taking his traditions in this regard to the extreme. In this passage, Paul's primary argument is rooted in the idea that men and women have different metaphorical heads and so they accrue and distribute shame and honor differently in regards to what they do with their physical heads. For this reason, while it is shameful for men to cover their heads with outer garments during praying and prophesying, it is not so for women. Therefore, women do not need to be stripped of their head-coverings and hair accessories during these activities simply to match men's appearances. Rather, women must have the right to adorn their heads in a way that reflects their own honor, the honor of their male relations, and the honor of the mediating angels. A completely uncovered head on a woman is not appropriate for Paul precisely because it brings shame to all parties involved.

In Chapter 6, I explore why the earliest surviving interpretations of 1 Cor 11:2–16 do not recognize *capite velato* as a contextual background for this passage. I argue that by the time of the first surviving engagements with the text of 1 Cor 11:2–16 (about a century after its composition), the original *Sitz im Leben* was no longer known. Instead, certain interpretive layers had been added, significantly altering how the text was understood, which then obscured the original intent behind Paul's instructions. For instance, the deutero-Pauline letters known as Ephesians and 1 Timothy reworked some of the concepts that Paul had made use of in 1 Cor 11:2–16 to argue for the complete subjugation and silence of women. Furthermore, some early readers altered the wording of 1 Cor 11:10, so that this verse came to be read as Paul's command for women to wear (facial) veils, even though this reading does not occur in the early manuscript tradition. As a result of these changes, increasingly more interpreters understood the original problem in Corinth that 1 Cor 11:2–16 addresses to have been about Corinthian women overstepping their God-ordained limits, a perspective that has dominated the interpretations of this passage ever since.

Theory and Method

The main aim of this study is to understand a particular text within its historical context. To achieve this, I employ such tools that biblical scholarship at large finds helpful and appropriate in close reading of ancient texts. I have scoured databases of ancient Greek and Latin literature for texts that appear relevant to what I consider to be the subject matter of 1 Cor 11:2–16 (I do not claim to have found them all). I have translated most of the relevant Greek sources myself but in regards to Latin sources, I have placed more trust in the translations already available, while also utilizing the ever more powerful AI translation tools for analysis and comparison. I have also searched the databases for relevant archaeological material and have documented many of the finds in person during visits to museums and archaeological sites in Greece and Italy. Furthermore, I have also immersed myself in modern studies on human cognition in relation to religion and rituals, applying these insights to my analysis of ancient literary and material sources. All of this informs my exegesis of 1 Cor 11:2–16, which follows the standard exegetical works on biblical texts.

My work is not governed by a single theoretical framework. However, I do incorporate various theories from the field of cognitive science of religion in my close reading of ancient texts and in my analysis of archaeological remains. I do so because I believe that 1 Cor 11:2–16 addresses a particular ritual gesture, and since cognitive scientists of religion have hypothesized that the performance and non-performance of rituals affect human cognition and human relationships, their theories need to be taken into account in the interpretation of 1 Cor 11:2–16. As Brett Maiden explains,

> if we step back and consider the course of human history and evolution, the past few thousand years is too short a time for human cognitive architecture to have undergone substantial change, and therefore contemporary cognitive findings and theoretical insights offer not just cross-cultural but also transhistorical relevance. An up-to-date view of the mind may, then, help bridge the gap between ancient and modern minds and thus render ancient religious texts and phenomena a little less distant, a little less alien.[6]

Thus, a theory about human cognition and social relationships that is based on the observation of modern ritual performances and non-performances should also hold some relevance in the study of ancient rituals. And in Chapter 4, I argue precisely for this in relation to the ancient Roman ritual gesture of covering the head with an outer garment during acts of devotion. My work, therefore, contributes to the growing body of literature in biblical scholarship in which the cognitive sciences are given a place of prominence.

---

[6] Brett E. Maiden, *Cognitive Science and Ancient Israelite Religion: New Perspectives on Texts, Artifacts, and Culture*, SOTSMS (New York: Cambridge University Press, 2020), 4.

Terminology

In this work, I use designations such as (early) Christians, congregation or congregants, community, gathering, assembly, Christ association, Christ-believers, Christ-followers, and similar terms interchangeably. I realize that each of the above terms carries its own set of issues in regards to the clarity of what is being described.[7] I am fully aware that whatever social network Paul had established in Corinth was not at the time of his correspondence with it a rigid organization with clear boundaries and with a neatly defined identity. I do not claim, therefore, that any of these terms were self-identifications of a well-defined group. However, for the sake of brevity and stylistic variety, I use all of the above terms interchangeably to refer to a network of individuals in first-century Corinth who had in some way been impacted by Paul's message about "Christ crucified" (cf. 1 Cor 2:2) or by his "demonstration of the Spirit and of power" (cf. 1 Cor 2:3), and who regularly gathered in each other's homes (cf. 1 Cor 11–14).[8] I count in this network also those

---

[7] In the so-called "Paul within Judaism" perspective, inappropriateness of the designation "Christian" for Paul or for Paul's congregants is particularly highlighted. E.g., Anders Runesson, "The Question of Terminology: The Architecture of Contemporary Discussions on Paul," in *Paul within Judaism: Restoring the First-Century Context to the Apostle*, ed. Mark D. Nanos and Magnus Zetterholm (Minneapolis: Fortress Press, 2015), 53–78. I understand the concerns of these scholars and am sympathetic to them, but I do not think it necessary to "retire" the term "Christian" altogether in Pauline scholarship. I believe that the term can still be made use of, if we keep in mind what "Paul within Judaism" scholarship has taught us.

[8] Paul himself addresses 1 Cor "to the *ekklēsia* of God in Corinth, (to) the ones sanctified in Christ Jesus, (to the) called saints, together with all who invoke the name of our lord Jesus Christ" (τῇ ἐκκλησίᾳ τοῦ θεοῦ τῇ οὔσῃ ἐν Κορίνθῳ, ἡγιασμένοις ἐν Χριστῷ Ἰησοῦ, κλητοῖς ἁγίοις, σὺν πᾶσιν τοῖς ἐπικαλουμένοις τὸ ὄνομα τοῦ κυρίου ἡμῶν Ἰησοῦ Χριστοῦ ἐν παντὶ τόπῳ, 1 Cor 1:2). There is, however, debate about the precise meaning of ἐκκλησία, which is why I have chosen to transliterate it here rather than translate it. The anachronistic "church" is rightly no longer the standard translation of ἐκκλησία in biblical scholarship, but alternative translations also pose challenges, since it is difficult to determine what connotations Paul has in mind with the usage of ἐκκλησία. For instance, some suggest that we should define ἐκκλησία based on its usage in the LXX, while others argue for the significance of Greco-Roman associations as background. See, for example, Paul Trebilco, "Why Did the Early Christians Call Themselves ἡ ἐκκλησία?" *NTS* 57 (2011): 440–60; George H. van Kooten, "Ἐκκλησία τοῦ θεοῦ: The 'Church of God' and the Civic Assemblies (ἐκκλησίαι) of the Greek Cities in the Roman Empire; A Response to Paul Trebilco and Richard A. Horsley," *NTS* 58 (2012): 522–48; G. K. Beale, "The Background of ἐκκλησία Revisited," *JSNT* 38 (2015): 151–68; Richard Last, "*Ekklēsia* outside the Septuagint and the *Dēmos*: The Titles of Greco-Roman Associations and Christ-Followers' Groups," *JBL* 137 (2018): 959–80. This debate

individuals who were not personally acquainted with Paul and those whose involvement or commitment was only tangential.

Similarly, when I use terms like "Jew," "Jewish," or "Judaism," I do not have in mind a well-defined religion, movement, ideology, ethnicity, geographic area, social network, political affiliation, or the like. But for the purposes of my arguments in this thesis, I employ these terms in a broad sense and without prejudice in reference to individuals, writings, groups, or institutions whose identities appear to us in hindsight in some way meaningfully tied to the history of a specific geographical area—Jerusalem and its vicinity; to the cult of the temple in Jerusalem; to the Torah; or to the "house of David."

Presuppositions and Biases

No academic work is free of bias and this study is no exception. However, it would be impossible for me to list here all the factors that have shaped my approach to ancient texts. While my academic journey has allowed me to confront many of my presuppositions and biases, I remain ignorant of or obstinate about much still. That said, I must acknowledge what is most relevant here: unlike many readers of biblical literature, I do not share the presupposition that Paul (or any other biblical writer for that matter) was divinely inspired. Consequently, I do not believe that anything Paul wrote should be regarded as a divine message for contemporary generations. While I do appreciate the endeavor of seeking relevance and applicability of ancient texts for modern times—I resonate with the sentiment that "those who cannot remember the past are condemned to repeat it"—I do not therefore believe there is a true or correct or divinely mandated way to go about it. I have, therefore, little interest in whether or how 1 Cor 11:2–16 is applied in the context of modern households or Christian congregations, the preoccupation with this text of much of the readership. My primary interest in this research is to understand 1 Cor 11:2–16 in its historical context. And in this regard, I am convinced that there *is* a better way to read this passage than what has been suggested so far.

---

is ongoing, so we cannot be more precise here than to say that there was a network of individuals in Corinth that Paul had in mind when writing 1 Cor, but the exact nature and (self-)identity of this group remains elusive. Thus, throughout this work, I use the terms listed above with this caveat in mind.

1. From Greek Customs to Roman Rites

History of Interpretation of 1 Corinthians 11:2–16

Throughout history, 1 Cor 11:2–16 has attracted considerable attention among Christians due to its subject matter. However, the main interest for most readers of 1 Cor 11:2–16 has been the relevance of this passage for one's everyday life and how the text should be applied in the context of Christian gatherings. We see this most clearly in the writings of some of the first surviving interpreters of this pericope, such as Clement of Alexandria and Tertullian (see Chapter 6). Yet, even some early readers (such as John Chrysostom at the end of the fourth century CE) occasionally paused to consider the historical circumstances that could have given rise to 1 Cor 11:2–16. In more recent centuries, interest in the historical background of Paul's arguments in this text has grown exponentially, driven by the hermeneutical shift toward the historical-critical method of studying the NT compositions. Yet, no consensus has emerged in scholarly circles regarding the *Sitz im Leben* that could have prompted Paul to write 1 Cor 11:2–16, and this text is therefore still considered one of the most difficult Pauline passages to make sense of (see Introduction).

In this chapter, I review the leading proposals that biblical scholars have advanced regarding the historical circumstances behind 1 Cor 11:2–16 and I do so in chronological order. I begin with John Chrysostom's fourth-century suggestion that Paul addresses certain Greek customs prevalent in first-century Corinth that had influenced the Corinthian Christians. Next, I examine a hypothesis popular in biblical scholarship especially in the seventeenth and eighteenth centuries, which proposes that Paul was concerned with certain contemporaneous Jewish customs which the Corinthian Christians practiced. Following this, I provide an overview of scholarly works that argue that despite the mention of men's covered heads in 1 Cor 11:2–16, the passage is solely focused on addressing the problematic behavior of the Corinthian women—a conviction that has dominated the readings of this passage for the past two centuries. I then discuss a theory developed in the mid-twentieth century which suggests that 1 Cor 11:2–16 does not address head-coverings at all, but is about the length of hair and hairstyles for both men and women. After that I look at interpretations which consider Dionysiac ritual cross-dressing as a background to 1 Cor 11:2–16, and finally, I analyze the most recently developed proposal that certain Roman head-covering rites should be taken as Paul's focus in 1 Cor 11:2–16. As I go along, I critique most of these proposals for failing to adequately account for the available evidence regarding the appearances of men's and women's heads in antiquity and for not giving due consideration to Paul's language and grammar in 1 Cor 11:2–16. However, I conclude the chapter with a submission that a particular Roman ritual gesture known as *capite velato* is the most likely candidate for the subject matter of 1 Cor 11:2–16, although I point out that there are some serious challenges with this line of interpretation that have not been adequately addressed.

Before proceeding, it is important to note that while the following overview of the history of interpretation regarding this passage is fairly extensive, it is not exhaustive. Given that 1 Cor 11:2–16 has been subject to many treatments from various scholarly and non-scholarly circles throughout the years, not all readings of the passage can be included here. For the purposes of the following analyses, I have selected hypotheses that I believe are representative of interpretations that specifically address the nature of the customs that Paul is concerned with in 1 Cor 11:4–5.

1.1 John Chrysostom

John Chrysostom (ca. 347–407 CE) is, to my knowledge, the first surviving interpreter of 1 Cor 11:2–16 to provide a more thought-out suggestion as to what may have occurred in the Corinthian congregation that prompted Paul to pen this passage. However, since Chrysostom deals with this pericope in his sermon series on 1 Cor, his primary aim in discussing this text is to impart on his parishioners some practical advice on how to live faithfully as Christians. As a result, Chrysostom's remarks about the historical background of 1 Cor 11:2–16 are made in passing and do not have much bearing on his overall arguments. Therefore, I will not delve into Chrysostom's overall exegesis here; my main concern is with the casual observations Chrysostom makes about the historical circumstances that may have led Paul to write 1 Cor 11:2–16.

Chrysostom imagines that in the Corinthian congregation at the time of Paul, women prayed and prophesied without head-coverings and with bare heads (ἀνακεκαλυμμέναι καὶ γυμνῇ τῇ κεφαλῇ), while men grew their hair long (ἐκόμων) due to their time spent in philosophy and "enwrapped" their heads (περιεβάλλοντο τὰς κεφαλάς) during prayer and prophecy because such practices were in line with contemporaneous Greek customs (ὅπερ ἑκάτερον Ἑλληνικοῦ νόμου ἦν).[1] According to Chrysostom, Paul disapproved of all of this because a covered head on a woman was a God-given symbol of subjection, while a bare head (including short hair) on a man a God-given symbol of ruling. To appear otherwise was to "demolish good order and the commandment of God, and to overstep boundaries set for each" (τὴν εὐταξίαν συγχέοντες, καὶ τὴν τοῦ θεοῦ διαταγήν, καὶ τοὺς οἰκείους ὑπερβαίοντες ὅρους).[2]

Leaving aside Chrysostom's interpretation of Paul's response to the Corinthian congregation for the moment, we must consider whether there is any merit in Chrysostom's suggestion that the Corinthians' misbehavior was influenced by certain Greek customs of the day. While there is indeed some evidence that certain men who had espoused particular strands of philosophy grew their hair long as a sign of devotion (e.g., Aulus Gellius, *Noct. att.* 9.2), this was by no means a universal practice among philosophers, nor was it exclusive to the Greeks. Furthermore, there is no evidence that it was a Greek custom for men to "enwrap" their heads during prayer. On the contrary, available evidence suggests that covering the head during certain devotional acts was actually a Roman practice, as will be demonstrated more thoroughly in the next chapter. Thus, it seems that in his sermon, Chrysostom does not rely on factual knowledge, but to a large degree invents a background scenario for rhetorical and homiletical purposes. Perhaps Chrysostom simply assumed that the Corinthian congregation at the time of Paul was composed mainly of local Greeks—a reasonable but ultimately indefensible hypothesis in light of what we now know about the make-up of Corinth in the first century CE (see Chapter 4 and Chapter 5)—and surmised therefore that the unseemly behavior must have stemmed from local Greek customs of the day. Whatever the case, the bottom line is that Chrysostom's suggestion regarding the customs that Paul addresses in 1 Cor 11:2–16 does not have much evidence to support it.

Before moving on from John Chrysostom's hypothesis, however, let us briefly return to his interpretation of Paul's response to the Corinthian situation, as it aptly illustrates the exegetical challenges that much of subsequent Western scholarship has faced in providing a *Sitz im Leben* for 1 Cor 11:2–16. In the midst of his explanation that Paul required women to be covered of the head as a symbol of

---

[1] John Chrysostom, *Hom. 1 Cor.* 26 (PG 61:213a).
[2] John Chrysostom, *Hom. 1 Cor.* 26 (PG 61:216b-c). The translations provided for primary sources are mine unless otherwise noted.

subjection, and men to have short hair and uncovered heads as a symbol of ruling (see above), Chrysostom realizes that this assertion does not align easily with the text itself in which Paul's concern with head-coverings seems to be solely within the context of praying and prophesying (and not with the appearances of men and women in general). Yet, through some exegetical maneuvering (the tracing of which is not necessary here), Chrysostom finds a way to conclude that what Paul actually required was for women to be covered at all times (not just during praying and prophesying) and for men to always have short hair, but that the command for men to be uncovered of the head was only applicable during praying and prophesying and not otherwise.[3]

Chrysostom's awareness here that any hypothesis regarding the Corinthian situation behind 1 Cor 11:2–16 must account for why Paul specifically mentions praying and prophesying as contexts for improper behavior regarding head-coverings is commendable, despite his exegesis not meeting modern standards. Much of subsequent Western scholarship has often overlooked the specific activities of praying and prophesying in its reconstructions of the Corinthian *Sitz im Leben*, as we shall see. Nevertheless, this appreciation for Chrysostom's awareness notwithstanding, his overall hypothesis—that certain Greek customs were the cause of trouble that Paul addresses in 1 Cor 11:2–16—can be dismissed without much difficulty, since there is very little evidence to support it.

1.2 Jewish Customs as Source of Conflict

During the seventeenth and eighteenth centuries in particular, many biblical scholars turned to the study of ancient (and more contemporary) Jewish customs in an effort to shed light on the various biblical passages. In this section, we examine some of the scholars from that time period who also engaged with 1 Cor 11:2–16 and whose hypotheses regarding this passage continued to be influential well into the twentieth century.

1.2.1 John Lightfoot

John Lightfoot (1602–1675) is renowned for his extensive engagement with rabbinic literature and it comes as no surprise, then, that his commentary on 1 Cor 11:2–16 is informed by mainly the rabbinic sources. Lightfoot finds in the Talmud and in the works of Maimonides (an influential twelfth-century Torah scholar) references to a practice of Jewish men going to prayer with a covered head as a

---

[3] John Chrysostom, *Hom. 1 Cor.* 26 (PG 61:217a-b).

token of their ashamedness in the presence of God. He also finds that the Talmud and Maimonides forbade women to appear in public with a bare head.[4] Lightfoot believes that it is these Jewish customs that are at the heart of the issues addressed in 1 Cor 11:2–16. Lightfoot suggests that in Corinth at the time of Paul, Christian men had retained the Jewish custom of appearing with a head-covering during prayer, while the Christian women had abandoned the Jewish custom of veiling themselves. These women, Lightfoot argues, believed that their beauty exempted them from appearing in the presence of God with a covered head out of shame.[5] Yet, according to Lightfoot, Paul reproves both groups—men for keeping the Jewish custom of covering the head during prayer, because it was deemed by him dishonorable in a Christian context, and women for neglecting the Jewish custom of covering the head, because their uncovered heads and faces gave the devil an opportunity to tempt the Christian men (especially the ministers) into sin.[6]

1.2.2 Johann Lorenz von Mosheim

Johann Lorenz von Mosheim (1693–1755), a prominent German church historian and exegete, offers a similar interpretation to John Lightfoot regarding 1 Cor 11:2–16, emphasizing the role of ancient Jewish customs in Paul's argument. Like Lightfoot, von Mosheim contends that part of the issue within the Corinthian Christian community stemmed from the practice of Jewish men covering their heads during prayer as per the traditions of the synagogue. Von Mosheim proposes that this was a problem because the local Greek men were accustomed to worshiping with a bare head (contra John Chrysostom) and did not want to succumb to the Jewish practices.[7] Concerning the issue with women's appearances, on the other hand, von Mosheim suggests that the Jewish women appeared bareheaded during Christian services because this is how they had worshiped in the synagogues where they sat in a separate section from men and thus did not need to cover their heads as no man could see them. When these Jewish women attended the Christian gatherings in the like manner, however, they drew the ire of the Greek women who were in the habit of carefully covering their faces out of modesty whenever outside

---

[4] John Lightfoot, "The Harmony, Chronicle, and Order, of the New Testament," in *The Whole Works of the Rev. John Lightfoot, D.D.*, ed. John Rogers Pitman (London: J. F. Dove, 1822), 3:243–44.

[5] Lightfoot, "The Harmony," 244.

[6] Lightfoot, "The Harmony," 244.

[7] Johann Lorenz von Mosheim, *Erklärung des Ersten Briefes des heiligen Apostles Pauli an die Gemeinde zu Corinthus* (Flensburg: Korten, 1762), 479.

of their homes.⁸ In this dispute, according to von Mosheim, Paul sided with the Greeks because he was sensitive to the customs of the local land and did not want the Christian congregation to be in disrepute.⁹

1.2.3 Johann David Michaelis

Johann David Michaelis (1717–1791), another German biblical scholar of the same period, aligns with Lightfoot and von Mosheim in arguing that one part of the problem in the Corinthian congregation was that the Jewish men had introduced there a head-covering practice familiar from the synagogue. However, Michaelis expands on this premise with a more intricate hypothesis concerning the situation that could have given rise to 1 Cor 11:2–16. Michaelis suggests that the Jewish men had learned this behavior of covering the head (and the face) during praying and reading of the scriptures from contemporary Roman men who participated in certain of their religious ceremonies with a covered head out of fear of observing bad omens. The Jewish men then introduced this practice into the Christian congregation to the chagrin of the Greek men who, according to Michaelis, never covered their heads and thus considered such a behavior superstitious.[10]

When addressing the inappropriate behavior of the Corinthian Christian women, however, Michaelis diverges from both Lightfoot and von Mosheim in that Michaelis does not think that any of the Jewish customs were responsible for issues that Paul addresses regarding women. Rather, Michaelis suggests that the behavior of prophesying with an uncovered head and disheveled hair was introduced into the congregation by certain Greek women who, although otherwise scrupulously covered, would have been allowed and even encouraged to uncover during certain festivities in honor of the Greek deities.[11] Michaelis posits that while these women might have believed this manner of prophesying to be equally fitting in the worship of the Christian deity, Paul found such behavior unacceptable and rightly prohibited it.[12]

---

[8] Von Mosheim, *Erklärung*, 479.

[9] Von Mosheim, *Erklärung*, 479–81.

[10] John David Michaelis, *Introduction to the New Testament*, 4th ed., trans. Herbert Marsh (London: Rivington, 1823), 4:58–59.

[11] Michaelis, *Introduction*, 59–60.

[12] Michaelis, *Introduction*, 60.

1.2.4 Analysis

All the aforementioned interpreters—Lightfoot, von Mosheim, and Michaelis—operate under the assumption that Jewish men at the time of Paul wore head-coverings whenever in prayer and during the reading of scriptures since there is evidence of this practice in some rabbinic material. This idea that rabbinic sources can illuminate biblical texts since they describe practices current at the time of the biblical writers held sway in certain parts of biblical scholarship well into the twentieth century and is by no means singular to the above three scholars. However, as the twentieth century progressed, increasing number of biblical scholars began to voice their concerns regarding the uncritical use of rabbinic material in interpreting biblical texts. It is now commonly held among exegetes of 1 Cor 11:2–16 that while it is theoretically possible that Jewish customs mentioned in the rabbinic material may have had their origins at the time of the biblical writers, there is no direct evidence that Jewish men in Paul's day covered their heads during prayer.[13] As such, the relevance of this rabbinic custom for understanding 1 Cor 11:2–16 is highly questionable. Moreover, the idea that Jewish women uncovered their heads during Christian worship either because they were unashamed of their beauty in God's presence, as Lightfoot suggests, or because they were accustomed to doing so in the synagogue, as von Mosheim argues, also lacks any substantial evidence. As such, the hypotheses of Lightfoot (that Paul remonstrated against Jewish customs) and von Mosheim (that Paul sided with the Greeks in their disapproval of Jewish customs) lack sufficient historical support. And by extension, any modern interpretation that depends on similar assumptions about ancient Jewish practices fails to provide a compelling framework for understanding the *Sitz im Leben* behind 1 Cor 11:2–16.

That being said, Michaelis's hypothesis merits a more serious consideration here. Even though Michaelis (like Lightfoot and von Mosheim) argues that the Jewish practice of men covering their heads during prayer was part of the problem in Corinth, he does not imply that this practice was a Jewish invention. Rather, Michaelis believes that the Jews learned the custom from the Romans and subsequently introduced this *Roman* custom into the Christian congregation. Michaelis's keen observation that Paul's contemporary Romans covered their heads during certain religious activities and that it may have some bearing on 1 Cor 11:2–16 is way ahead of his times as we shall see. However, for some reason, Michaelis felt the

---

[13] The first clear references to the practice of Jewish men covering their heads during prayer appear very late in the rabbinic material. E.g., Gordon D. Fee, *The First Epistle to the Corinthians: Revised Edition*, NICNT (Grand Rapids: Eerdmans, 2014), 560 n. 67.

need to introduce Jewish middlemen into the picture to make his hypothesis more believable, even though there is no good reason why Roman converts themselves could not have directly introduced such a custom into the Christian gatherings as more recent biblical scholars have argued (see section 1.6).

As far as the issue of women's behavior is concerned, here Michaelis's suggestion is also ahead of his times, since this idea that women uncovered their heads and disheveled their hair during Christian gatherings due to the influence of certain Greek mystery cults and festivals became one of the more prominent theories in twentieth-century biblical scholarship on this passage (see below). I will address the weaknesses of this proposition more thoroughly below (see sections 1.3.15 and 1.5.4), so it does not need to detain us here. What remains to be said about Michaelis, however, is that regardless of his visionary interpretation of 1 Cor 11:2–16, the overall hypothesis that he proposes is far too complex to be probable. He imagines that there was on the one level a conflict between Greek men and Jewish men regarding Roman practices, and on another level a dispute between Greek women and the rest of the congregation (including Paul) about certain Greek practices and that somehow Paul managed to address it all in one paragraph. As I will argue in what follows, more likely scenarios can be reconstructed that provide a clearer explanation of the *Sitz im Leben* of 1 Cor 11:2–16 and that align better with the textual evidence.

1.3 Misbehaving Women as Paul's Sole Concern

The interpretations of 1 Cor 11:2–16 that we have encountered so far have tried to provide a *Sitz im Leben* in which Paul's instructions to both men and women would make sense. Much of the scholarship on this passage in the nineteenth and twentieth century, however, either completely ignored Paul's instructions to men not to pray and prophesy with a covered head in their hypotheses or dismissed such instructions as hypothetical and not relevant to any real situation in the Corinthian congregation at the time of Paul. In this section, we discuss the views of a number of such interpreters whose sole focus concerning this passage has been to highlight the (mis)behavior of the *female* addressees of Paul's letter.

1.3.1 Gustav Billroth

Gustav Billroth (1808–1836), a German philosopher of religion, argues in his commentary on 1 Cor that Paul's comments in 1 Cor 11:2–16 regarding men had nothing to do with any real situation in the Corinthian congregation at the time of Paul. Billroth believes that all Christian men participated in the gatherings of the congregation with a bare head anyway, because an uncovered head was a symbol of freedom among the Greeks and Romans. Thus, Paul's instructions to men in this passage should be taken as simply a statement of fact about how things were regarding the Christian men.[14] For Billroth, the only real problem that Paul addresses in 1 Cor 11:2–16 concerns certain Christian women who flouted contemporary (Greek) customs by uncovering their heads in the congregation because they also wanted to appear free.[15]

1.3.2 Hermann Olshausen

Hermann Olshausen (1796–1839), a German theologian contemporary with Billroth, likewise cannot fathom that the Corinthian Christian men would have participated in any improper head-covering practices that required Paul's intervention. Olshausen suggests that Paul's comments about men in 1 Cor 11:2–16 are there "only by way of antithesis" to "elucidate the meaning" of instructions given to women.[16] The only actual problem that Paul addresses in 1 Cor 11:2–16, according to Olshausen, is that certain Christian women, in their pursuit of "unlimited liberty," had abandoned the customary practice of covering their heads and faces.[17] Olshausen believes that Paul found this problematic because a covered head (and face) on a woman was a symbol of authority that a husband had over his wife, a token of womanly modesty, and necessary for avoiding "unlawful excitement" in the Christian gatherings.[18]

1.3.3 Heinrich August Wilhelm Meyer

Heinrich August Wilhelm Meyer (1800–1873) was a German Protestant exegete and is well known for his commentaries on the NT. Although in his exegesis of 1 Cor 11:2–16, Meyer discusses ancient head-covering practices of Jewish and Roman men, he nevertheless concludes that these have no bearing on the *Sitz im Leben* of the Corinthian congregation at the time of Paul. Meyer believes that the Corinthian Christian men did not engage in any such head-covering practices that required Paul's correction. Rather, Paul's comments about men should be taken as

---

[14] Gustav Billroth, *A Commentary on the Epistles of Paul to the Corinthians*, trans. W. Lindsay Alexander (Edinburgh: Thomas Clark, 1837), 1:266–68, 272.

[15] Billroth, *A Commentary*, 266, 268.

[16] Hermann Olshausen, *Biblical Commentary on St Paul's First and Second Epistles to the Corinthians*, trans. John Edmund Cox (Edinburgh: T&T Clark, 1851), 173–74.

[17] Olshausen, *Biblical Commentary*, 172.

[18] Olshausen, *Biblical Commentary*, 172.

"a plea of privilege for the men" meant to "prepare the way for the censure next to be passed upon the women."[19] According to Meyer, the specific behavior that required Paul's censure involved certain married women who had begun removing their head-coverings—tokens of a husband's authority over his wife—in the house churches.[20] Meyer suggests that this situation arose due to two primary factors: first, an overextension of the boundaries of "the principle of Christian liberty," and second, the "greater laxity of Hellenic ideas about female dress" gaining in influence among the congregants.[21]

1.3.4 Charles Hodge

Charles Hodge (1797–1878), an influential American theologian and long-serving principal of Princeton Theological Seminary, likewise argues in his commentary on 1 Cor that Paul's comments regarding men in 1 Cor 11:2–16 do not address any actual situation in Corinth. According to Hodge, "men are mentioned only for the sake of illustrating the principle."[22] And this "principle," as Hodge understands it, is that "women should conform in matters of dress to all those usages which the public sentiment of the community in which they live demands."[23] Hodge believes that covering the head was especially important for women in Corinth at the time of Paul because it was considered a symbol of subjection and modesty. Any woman who flouted this custom openly renounced modesty and her husband's authority over her. It is for this reason, Hodge argues, that Paul insisted on the practice of women wearing head-coverings in the Corinthian congregation.[24] In all of this, however, Hodge fails to suggest any reason for why the Corinthian Christian women would have wanted to remove their head-coverings in the first place. He simply assumes this behavior occurred without exploring the motivation behind it.

---

[19] Heinrich August Wilhelm Meyer, *Critical and Exegetical Handbook to the Epistles to the Corinthians*, ed. William P. Dickson, trans. D. Douglas Bannerman (Edinburgh: T&T Clark, 1877), 1:318.

[20] Meyer, *Critical and Exegetical Handbook*, 321.

[21] Meyer, *Critical and Exegetical Handbook*, 322.

[22] Charles Hodge, *An Exposition of the First Epistle to the Corinthians* (New York: Robert Carter & Brothers, 1874), 208.

[23] Hodge, *An Exposition*, 205.

[24] Hodge, *An Exposition*, 205.

1.3.5 Frédéric Louis Godet

The Swiss theologian Frédéric Louis Godet (1812–1900) is also well aware of the various men's head-covering practices contemporary to Paul, but he does not think it probable that the Corinthian Christian men would have engaged in such practices in the land of the Greeks where worship by men was conducted bare-headed.[25] Godet believes that men are only mentioned in 1 Cor 11:2–16 "to bring out by contrast that which alone is becoming in the woman."[26] The real problem in Corinth, according to Godet, was that certain women, inspired by Paul's teaching that in Christ there is neither male nor female, began worshiping with a bare head just like the Christian men were doing.[27] This behavior was disapproved by Paul because he did not think it proper for women to speak at all during the gatherings (cf. 1 Cor 14:34–35), but on the rare occasion when they happened to utter a prayer or a prophetic utterance, they needed all the more to appear inconspicuous by wearing a veil, a symbol of modesty and dependence.[28]

1.3.6 Archibald Robertson and Alfred Plummer

Archibald Robertson and Alfred Plummer likewise contend that the Corinthian Christian men did not engage in any inappropriate head-covering practices, but that Paul's comments about men's head-coverings were only included for the sake of highlighting the inappropriate behavior of the women.[29] This inappropriate behavior, according to Robertson and Plummer, was the removal of *facial* coverings during public worship. Robertson and Plummer suggest that this rebellious act may have been inspired by certain beliefs that the Corinthian Christian women held: for example, that "distinctions of sex were done away in Christ"; that it was no longer appropriate to wear the "mark of servitude" in worship; or that Paul "was in favor of the emancipation of women."[30] Alternatively, Robertson and Plummer entertain the idea that the Corinthian women simply wanted to remove

---

[25] Frédéric Louis Godet, *Commentary on St. Paul's First Epistle to the Corinthians*, trans. A. Cusin (Edinburgh: T&T Clark, 1890), 2:104–5, 113.

[26] Godet, *Commentary*, 113.

[27] Godet, *Commentary*, 105.

[28] Godet, *Commentary*, 117.

[29] Archibald Robertson and Alfred Plummer, *A Critical and Exegetical Commentary on the First Epistle of St Paul to the Corinthians*, 2nd ed. (Edinburgh: T&T Clark, 1914), 229.

[30] Robertson and Plummer, *A Critical and Exegetical Commentary*, 230.

their veils out of necessity as it was too difficult for them to speak in the congregation with something covering the mouth.[31]

1.3.7 Stefan Lösch

The interpreters we have examined so far in this section at least acknowledge the comments Paul makes about men's head-coverings in 1 Cor 11:2–16, even though they dismiss these as irrelevant for the reconstruction of the *Sitz im Leben* of the Corinthian congregation at the time of Paul. We now discuss certain works in which Paul's instructions to men are simply ignored. In these interpretations, the sole focus is on the attempt to explain the behavior of the Corinthian women whom Paul addresses, without any clarification regarding Paul's comments about men's head-coverings. One of such works is that of Stefan Lösch. In his treatment of 1 Cor 11:2–16, Lösch expresses his dissatisfaction with the hypotheses of some of the above scholars who suggest that women took their head-coverings off as part of some emancipation movement. Lösch himself does not think it to have been a very probable cause of the unrest that Paul addresses in 1 Cor 11:2–16.[32] Instead, Lösch proposes that the Corinthian Christian women prayed and prophesied without a veil and with loose hair because they had been accustomed to doing so in the Greek mystery cults which were very popular in the area at the time. Lösch bases his argument mainly on an inscription found in the Greek city of Andania dated to first century BCE which includes regulations about the cult of Demeter and Kore. Among other things, the inscription (in Lösch's interpretation of it) orders the female participants in certain rituals to appear without a veil and with loose hair.[33] Lösch believes that this way of worshiping had become so common for women in Corinth and in the surrounding areas that when these women became Christians they thought it the only right way to worship the Christian god.[34] Paul, however, was wary about allowing heathen practices into the Christian community and called on the Christian women to pray and prophesy in a traditional Jewish manner—with covered heads—as it best symbolized the true relationship between husband and wife.[35]

---

[31] Robertson and Plummer, *A Critical and Exegetical Commentary*, 230.

[32] Stefan Lösch, "Christliche Frauen in Corinth (1 Cor. 11, 2–16): Ein neuer Lösungsversuch," *TQ* 127 (1947): 225–30.

[33] Lösch, "Christliche Frauen," 236–41.

[34] Lösch, "Christliche Frauen," 246–47.

[35] Lösch, "Christliche Frauen," 251–61.

1.3.8 Elisabeth Schüssler Fiorenza

Elisabeth Schüssler Fiorenza likewise ignores Paul's comments concerning men's head-coverings in 1 Cor 11:2–16 and focuses solely on explaining the behavior of the women. Schüssler Fiorenza suggests that the main issue Paul addresses in this text is not so much about women's head-coverings as it is about how they display their hair. Schüssler Fiorenza believes that the Corinthian Christian women let their hair down (and loose) because this is how they had been used to worshiping in the cult of Isis which was popular also in Corinth at the time.[36] These women, according to Schüssler Fiorenza, continued to worship in like manner in the Christian congregation because they considered their newfound "devotion to Sophia-Spirit" analogous to the Isis cult since "Isis was also said to have made the power of women equal to men."[37] In her later work on this passage, Schüssler Fiorenza adds that "disheveled hair and head thrown back were typical for the maenads in the cult of Dionysos, in that of Cybele, the Pythia at Delphia, [and] the Sibyl" and that "such ecstatic frenzy in oriental cults was a highly desirable spiritual phenomenon and a mark of true prophecy."[38] Paul, however, insisted on these women to keep their hair pinned up during worship (in a manner of contemporary Jewish women) since, among other things, loose hair had a rather different meaning in the Jewish-Christian context familiar to Paul—that of uncleanness.[39]

1.3.9 Dennis Ronald MacDonald

With Dennis Ronald MacDonald we return to the line of scholars who, despite acknowledging Paul's comments about men's head-coverings in 1 Cor 11:2–16, reject them as irrelevant for understanding what was going on in the Corinthian congregation that required Paul's intervention. MacDonald, for example, simply does not think there to have been any reason for men to cover their heads during the occasions of Christian worship in Corinth.[40] As far as the behavior of women

---

[36] Elisabeth Schüssler Fiorenza, "Women in the Pre-Pauline and Pauline Churches," *USQR* 33 (1978): 159. James Dunn follows essentially a similar line of reasoning in his take on the passage. See, James D. G. Dunn, *The Theology of Paul the Apostle* (Grand Rapids: Eerdmans, 1998), 590.

[37] Schüssler Fiorenza, "Women in the Pre-Pauline and Pauline Churches," 159.

[38] Elisabeth Schüssler Fiorenza, *In Memory of Her: A Feminist Theological Reconstruction of Christian Origins*, tenth anniversary edition (New York: Crossroad, 1994), 227. A similar argument can be found in Richard A. Horsley, *1 Corinthians*, ANTC (Nashville: Abingdon Press, 1998), 154.

[39] Schüssler Fiorenza, *In Memory of Her*, 228.

[40] Dennis Ronald MacDonald, *There Is No Male and Female: The Fate of a Dominical Saying in Paul and Gnosticism* (Philadelphia: Fortress Press, 1987), 84.

is concerned, MacDonald disagrees with those scholars who suggest that some form of emancipation movement was responsible for the removal of head-coverings. MacDonald argues that since Paul only mentions the activities of praying and prophesying as contexts for the disagreeable behavior, it would not make much sense for the Corinthian women to pursue freedom by removing their head-coverings only during these moments.[41] Thus, in his interpretation, MacDonald seeks to explain why the Christian women removed their head-coverings only at the time of praying and at the time of prophesying, while remaining otherwise covered. MacDonald suggests that they did so because, inspired by their reading of Gen 1–3, they wished to demonstrate their authority over the angels during ecstatic worship (that is, when angels were present).[42] In the words of MacDonald:

> It would therefore appear that the Corinthian order of creation was: (1) God; (2) the pneumatic, sexually unified *Urmensch*, who, by dint of the image of God, enjoyed hegemony over the spirit world; (3) the psychic, sexually divided human made out of clay according to Gen 2:7, no longer in God's image and therefore not sovereign over angels; and (4) Eve, whose fall women mourn by wearing veils. If this is more or less their interpretation of Genesis 1–3, their return to the divine image might well have been symbolized by women's removing their veils. They compensated for Eve's sin by climbing a rung on the ladder of being, by reuniting the primordial androgyne, and thereby enjoying "authority because of the angels."[43]

According to MacDonald, 1 Cor 11: 7–10 suggests that Paul did not share this reading of Gen 1–3, but instead held the belief that women must dress in a socially approved fashion by donning a veil which had been mandated by God in the act of creation.[44]

1.3.10 Gerd Theissen

Gerd Theissen also maintains that the only real problem addressed in 1 Cor 11:2–16 pertains to the behavior of women in the Corinthian congregation. According to Theissen, Paul "attacked" the head-covering practices of men "only hypothetically and prophylactically."[45] At the same time, however, Theissen defends the scholarly view that it was the women's desire for emancipation which drove them to pray and prophesy without head-coverings—and by "head-covering" Theissen

---

[41] MacDonald, *There Is No Male and Female*, 91.
[42] MacDonald, *There Is No Male and Female*, 92.
[43] MacDonald, *There Is No Male and Female*, 95.
[44] MacDonald, *There Is No Male and Female*, 104.
[45] Gerd Theissen, *Psychological Aspects of Pauline Theology*, trans. John P. Galvin (Edinburgh: T&T Clark, 1987), 168.

means here specifically the practice of drawing one's mantle over the head.[46] According to Theissen, a bare head on a woman would have been most problematic for Paul precisely during praying and prophesying (regardless of how she dressed otherwise), because in Paul's understanding, a covered head on a woman served an important apotropaic function against "sexual fantasies" (of men and of angels) and it also "stabilize[d] the differentiation of sex roles."[47]

1.3.11 David E. Garland

David Garland is also of the opinion that in 1 Cor 11:2–16, Paul is exclusively concerned with the behavior of women and that his instructions about men's head-coverings are included in order only to more sharply highlight the problematic behavior of the Corinthian Christian women.[48] However, contrary to several of the above scholars, Garland does not think that this issue arose in Corinth due to some form of emancipation movement. Rather, Garland suggests that the "fuzzy boundary between home and the house church" may have been the underlying cause of conflict regarding women's head-coverings, as women felt comfortable participating in the house churches in a manner they appeared in their own homes—with heads uncovered.[49] Paul, however, disapproved of such an appearance because of his conviction that an uncovered head on a woman publicly shamed her husband (or the head of household). In Garland's view, Paul therefore required women to be covered of the head also in the house churches in a manner customary for respectable Jewish and Greek women, in order to keep the honor of the family intact and to prevent women from being "ogled as sex objects during worship."[50]

1.3.12 Joseph A. Fitzmyer

Joseph A. Fitzmyer is yet another scholar to argue that the behavior of women was the sole problem in the Corinthian congregation that prompted Paul to pen 1 Cor 11:2–16. Although Fitzmyer acknowledges that Roman men worshiped with a covered head at the time of Paul, he does not think this practice to be relevant for what

---

[46] Theissen, *Psychological Aspects*, 160–61, 165–67.
[47] Theissen, *Psychological Aspects*, 170–74.
[48] David E. Garland, *1 Corinthians*, BECNT (Grand Rapids: Baker Academic, 2003), 507–8; 517.
[49] Garland, *1 Corinthians*, 507.
[50] Garland, *1 Corinthians*, 509–10, 520–22.

Paul is addressing in 1 Cor 11:2–16.[51] According to Fitzmyer, the Corinthian Christian men were not involved in any inappropriate head-covering practices that required Paul's intervention—Paul refers to men's behavior only hypothetically to make his main point about women "by contrast."[52] Fitzmyer supports this view by noting the disproportionate attention Paul gives to women in this passage—that is, Paul has more things to say about women than men—which leads Fitzmyer to conclude that Paul's sole concern here must be with women's head-coverings.[53] However, Fitzmyer expresses uncertainty in regards to the possible reasons why Corinthian Christian women wished to remove their head-coverings and also in regards to the exact nature of the head-covering that Paul has in mind in 1 Cor 11:2–16.[54] Despite this ambiguity, Fitzmyer concludes that an uncovered head on a woman (particularly if married) must have been disgraceful at the time of Paul and is the reason for Paul's involvement in the matter.[55]

1.3.13 Benjamin A. Edsall

Like Fitzmyer, Benjamin Edsall also argues that Paul's extended comments about women in 1 Cor 11:2–16, in comparison to his briefer comments about men, indicate that the passage is concerned only with the behavior of women. Edsall especially highlights 1 Cor 11:13, in which Paul challenges the Corinthian congregation to decide for themselves whether it is appropriate for women to pray uncovered, as signaling the subject matter of the whole pericope.[56] Edsall argues that it was customary for Greek, Roman, and Jewish women during this period to cover their heads with an outer garment whenever they were outside of their homes or in the presence of unrelated males.[57] The Corinthian Christian women, however, began uncovering their heads during praying and prophesying because, inspired by Paul's teaching that in Christ there is neither male nor female, the congregation thought that women now had "the same status as men."[58] In Edsall's view, Paul opposed this application of his teaching because he was convinced that an

---

[51] Joseph A. Fitzmyer, *First Corinthians: A New Translation with Introduction and Commentary* (New Haven: Yale University Press, 2008), 412.

[52] Fitzmyer, *First Corinthians*, 405, 413.

[53] Fitzmyer, *First Corinthians*, 405–6.

[54] Fitzmyer, *First Corinthians*, 406–7.

[55] Fitzmyer, *First Corinthians*, 413.

[56] Benjamin A. Edsall, "Greco-Roman Costume and Paul's Fraught Argument in 1 Corinthians 11.2–16," *JGRChJ* 9 (2013): 138.

[57] Edsall, "Greco-Roman Costume," 139.

[58] Edsall, "Greco-Roman Costume," 144–45.

uncovered head on a woman brought shame on her husband or on her father and was thus not appropriate for the worship setting.[59]

1.3.14 Gordon D. Fee[60]

Gordon D. Fee, like many other scholars encountered in this section, argues that Paul's comments about men's head-coverings in 1 Cor 11:2–16 are concerned only with a "hypothetical situation" and included merely for the sake of "setting up his argument with the women."[61] Yet, Fee is unsure of the precise nature of this head-covering that Paul refers to in 1 Cor 11:2–16, although he does suggest that it must have been "some kind of external covering" (rather than a reference to the length or style of hair, for example).[62] Despite this ambiguity, Fee concludes that wearing a head-covering must have been a customary practice for women at the time and its removal associated with shame—perhaps due to "some kind of breakdown in the distinction between the sexes"—for which reason Paul was keen for the Christian women not to remove it during worship.[63] Fee proposes that the Corinthian Christian women may have begun removing their head-coverings during praying and prophesying because of their theological outlook. That is, taking cue from Paul's own teachings, these Christian women of Corinth could have considered themselves *"pneumatikoi"*—those already "arrived in the Spirit"—for which reason they began "acting as those who would be 'like the angels,' among whom sexual distinctions do not exist."[64]

1.3.15 Analysis

This list of scholars who, in their reconstructions of the Corinthian situation, either ignore Paul's instructions about men's head-coverings in 1 Cor 11:2–16 or dismiss them as hypothetical or irrelevant could be extended further. However, we have gained a representative overview of the various hypotheses these scholars

---

[59] Edsall, "Greco-Roman Costume," 139–41, 145.

[60] Gordon Fee's commentary on 1 Corinthians was first published in 1987, with a revised edition released in 2014. In my chronological presentation of the material, I refer to Fee's 2014 revised commentary on 1 Cor 11:2–16, even though there are minimal differences between the 1987 and 2014 editions.

[61] Fee, *First Corinthians: Revised*, 557, 560.

[62] Fee, *First Corinthians: Revised*, 561–63.

[63] Fee, *First Corinthians: Revised*, 549, 561–63.

[64] Fee, *First Corinthians: Revised*, 549.

hold.⁶⁵ All of these interpretations are united in their aim of explaining the misbehavior of the Corinthian women—and only the women—whom Paul addresses in 1 Cor 11:2–16. But is the assumption that only women misbehaved in the Corinthian congregation in relation to head-coverings warranted? When we set Paul's instructions concerning men and women in 1 Cor 11:2–16 side by side, for example, it seems that Paul's comments about men are as complete as those about women:

Man	Woman
Christ is the head of every man (v. 3)	Man is the head of woman (v. 3)
Man must not pray or prophesy covered (v. 4)	Woman must not pray or prophesy uncovered (vv. 5–6)
Man is not obligated to be covered, because… (v. 7a)	Woman ought to have authority over the head, because… (v. 10)
Man is the image and glory of God (v. 7b)	Woman is the glory of man (v. 7c)
Man was not made from woman nor created for woman (vv. 8–9)	Woman was made from man and created for man (vv. 8–9)
In the Lord, neither man without woman…	…nor woman without man (v. 11)
Nature teaches that long hair is disgraceful on a man (v. 14)	Nature teaches that long hair is a woman's glory (v. 15)

Table 1.1: Side-by-side comparison of Paul's arguments regarding men and women in 1 Cor 11:2–16.

The above table demonstrates that Paul follows a similar pattern of argumentation for men as for women. In the introduction he gives each a place in the hierarchy of heads, then specifies for both what is shameful in praying and prophesying, then gives reasons for why this is so from Gen 1–3 concerning both, and concludes with an analogy from nature regarding the length of hair also for both. Thus, the line of argument concerning men is in its essentials as complete as the line of argument concerning women, so why should one be considered to address a hypothetical scenario and the other a real one?⁶⁶

---

⁶⁵ But see also, for example, F. F. Bruce, *1 and 2 Corinthians* (repr., Grand Rapids: Eerdmans, 1984), 104–5; Lone Fatum, "Image of God and Glory of Man: Women in the Pauline Congregations," in *Image of God and Gender Models in Judaeo-Christian Tradition*, ed. Kari Elisabeth Børresen (Oslo: Solum Forlag, 1991), 70–86; Craig S. Keener, *Paul, Women and Wives: Marriage and Women's Ministry in the Letters of Paul* (Peabody, MA: Hendrickson, 1992), 19–69; Mark C. Black, "1 Cor. 11:2–16 – A Reinvestigation," in *Essays on Women in Earliest Christianity*, ed. Carroll D. Osburn (Joplin, MO: College Press, 1993), 1:191–218.

⁶⁶ See also, Gillian Townsley, *The Straight Mind in Corinth: Queer Readings across 1 Corinthians 11:2–16* (Atlanta: SBL Press, 2017), 57–61.

1.3 Misbehaving Women as Paul's Sole Concern 47

Some of the above scholars argue that on several points Paul extends his explanation concerning women when he does not do so for men (e.g., 1 Cor 11:4 vs 1 Cor 11:5–6), and count it as a reason to hold that in the case of men he addresses a hypothetical situation and in the case of women a real one. However, such a conclusion is not warranted by the given premise—that one thing requires more explanation than the other does not mean that one is real and the other is not. Rather, it may simply reflect that one side of the argument is less self-explanatory than the other—but as much real—and thus in need of extended reasoning.[67] And as will be demonstrated in the following chapters, Paul's phrase κατὰ κεφαλῆς ἔχων (lit., "having down from the head") in association with "praying or prophesying" as in 1 Cor 11:4 would have been immediately grasped by any contemporary man or woman who had either participated in Roman worship, had observed public or private acts of Roman worship, or had visited any public place such as a forum, a market place, or the precincts of a Roman temple, whereas the idea of ἀκατακάλυπτος ("uncovered") in association with women's heads as in 1 Cor 11:5 was a much more complex issue all across the board (see Chapter 5). In this context, therefore, it is rather expected that Paul would extend his arguments regarding women but not regarding men and as such, the comparative brevity of comments about men cannot be taken as proof that only women caused the kind of trouble that required Paul to author 1 Cor 11:2–16.

However, as part of their argument that Paul's extended comments about women suggest that it was only the women that caused trouble in Corinth regarding head-coverings, the above scholars especially highlight 1 Cor 11:13. In this verse, Paul challenges the Corinthians to judge among themselves whether it is appropriate for a woman to pray uncovered, and it is then taken as an indication that women praying without head-coverings was the only real problem that the whole passage addresses. Yet again, however, such a conclusion is not warranted by the premise. That Paul challenged the Corinthians to decide amongst themselves regarding women's praying postures does not necessarily mean that this was the sole issue. It may suggest only that the argument regarding women was the more

---

[67] This is how David S. du Toit, for example, understands the brevity of verse 4 in relation to the more extended argument of verses 5–6: "Das bedeutet, dass die These von V. 4 unstrittig war—Paulus führt sie ein und rechnet mit allgemeiner Zustimmung—, während die Feststellung in V. 5 die Streitsache markiert, sodass sie ausführlich begründet werden muss." David S. du Toit, "Status und Anstand als Schlüssel zum Verständnis von 1Kor 11,2–16: Argumentationslogische und sozialgeschichtliche Überlegungen," in *Frauen, Männer, Engel: Perspektiven zu 1Kor 11,2–16*, ed. Torsten Jantsch (Göttingen: Neukirchener, 2015), 77.

controversial or the less self-explanatory one of the two lines of argument of 1 Cor 11:2–16, as discussed above. Thus, I remain unconvinced by this reasoning that the more verbose the argument, the more real the situation, and that brevity is a sign of the hypothetical.

However, even if we concede on this point and take Paul's admonition that men ought not to pray or prophesy "covered" as concerning a hypothetical situation, it does not follow that we can then dismiss this comment as irrelevant to what was going on in the Corinthian congregation at the time of Paul. As will become evident in the following chapters, the Roman practice of covering the head with the edge of an outer garment during certain devotional acts—such as prayer, divination, and sacrifice—was so ubiquitous and pervasive at the time of Paul that it is incredible to think that there is no connection here to 1 Cor 11:4. At the very least, such known head-covering practices associated with devotion require a thorough investigation because Paul's argument in 1 Cor 11:2–16 that it is shameful for women to pray or prophesy "uncovered" seems to be anchored in his conviction that it is shameful for men to pray and prophesy "having down from the head." Thus, regardless of whether the Corinthian Christ-followers (men or women) themselves prayed with a head-covering or not, it is certain that some men (and women) in Corinth at the time did, and that this must have been known to the Corinthian Christ-believers as well. This context must then be accounted for in any interpretation of 1 Cor 11:2–16.

The hypotheses examined in this section aptly demonstrate that disregarding Paul's instructions concerning men's head-coverings in 1 Cor 11:4 leads only to confusion about what head-covering practice Paul has in mind for women in 1 Cor 11:5. As noted above, several scholars confess that they are simply unsure about what custom Paul is referring to. There is a general lack of agreement about whether we are dealing with a Jewish, Greek, or Roman custom and whether Paul is referring to a facial veil, head veil, mantle, cap, or some other form of head-covering. Although some scholars confidently claim that whatever the custom in question, it must have been common for all or most of the women at the time, the evidence suggests that head-coverings for women (in any culture) were not as ubiquitous as these interpreters make them out to be (as Theissen rightly admits[68]). And there is even less evidence to support the position espoused by several of the above scholars that a head-covering (of whatever nature) symbolized in general a woman's subjection to her husband (see Chapter 5).

---

[68] Theissen, *Psychological Aspects*, 158–61.

1.3 Misbehaving Women as Paul's Sole Concern 49

This uncertainty surrounding the custom itself then leads to further confusion about why the Corinthian Christian women would have wanted to break with it specifically during praying and prophesying. The most popular opinion of the above scholars is that it had something to do with an emancipation movement, but this idea that women were otherwise happy to don head-coverings except during the moments of public prayer and prophesying when they suddenly felt compelled to take a stand for freedom by rejecting this custom seems hardly credible. Some scholars try to get around this problem by employing terms such as "worship" or "ecstatic worship" as substitutes for Paul's "praying or prophesying" to enlarge the window of opportunity for women's behavior but this is not being true to the text of 1 Cor 11:2–16 itself in which Paul specifically and only refers to the activities of praying and prophesying as contexts of his instructions. If Paul had intended to refer more broadly to the gathering of Christ-followers or to the worship of the Christian god, he had the vocabulary available for him to do so as the immediately following passages in 1 Cor suggest (see also Chapter 4). Thus, if we take Paul's terminology in 1 Cor 11:2–16 seriously, Paul ties the issue of head-coverings exclusively to the acts of praying and prophesying and not to the public worship or gathering in general. As such, the emancipation hypothesis is insufficient as it does not satisfactorily explain why the Corinthian Christian women would have wanted to remove their head-coverings specifically and only during praying and prophesying or why it was a problem for Paul specifically and only then and at no other time. The alternative theories, such as that the Corinthian Christian women abandoned their head-coverings in order to demonstrate their authority over the angels (so MacDonald) or to appear as angels (so Fee), fall short for the same reason: they do not satisfactorily explain why only the activities of praying and prophesying are in focus in 1 Cor 11:2–16.

However, a bit more needs to be said here about the hypothesis already entertained by Michaelis (see section 1.2.3) and later developed by Lösch, Schüssler Fiorenza, and others, which suggests that the Christian women of Corinth removed their head-coverings because this is how they had been used to worshiping in the popular mystery cults of the day. In this line of interpretation, the act of prophesying is particularly highlighted as often conducted by women participants with uncovered heads and with flowing hair. This hypothesis, therefore, offers a more plausible explanation for why the Corinthian Christian women would have wanted to uncover their heads or unloose their hair particularly during certain activities but not at other times.

However, there are several issues with this line of interpretation that make it unlikely that 1 Cor 11:2–16 addresses the sort of behavior that the Christian neophytes had acquired through their acquaintance with popular mystery cults. First, the defining feature of mystery cults was to hold whatever was going on secret from the uninitiated and, in some cases, even from certain initiated members, and membership in these cults was not accessible for everyone.[69] Thus, a lot of the ancient reports on the activities of mystery cults may be based on nothing more than hearsay or worse, they may be outright fabrications, and the accounts may be purposefully hostile or, at the very least, unflattering.[70] Portraying women as behaving wildly or irrationally in religious rituals (particularly if secret) was a rhetorical trope that many ancient male authors employed.[71] Thus, given the limited access of these authors to firsthand knowledge and the potential for exaggerations or even fabrications, we cannot claim with much confidence that women participated in these mystery cults exactly in a manner these sources, which mostly come from uninitiated and biased male authors, describe.

Second, while there are indeed entries in the ancient sources that mention loose or disheveled hair in connection to activities akin to prophesying and praying—such as the oft-cited "chants of praise" that a woman is tasked with performing for Isis with unbound hair in Tibullus (*Elegiae*, 1.3.29–32)—this appearance is by no means exclusive to these two activities. For example, in Juvenal's description of the "mysteries of the Good Goddess," the maenads (i.e., the female followers) toss about their loose hair while they howl at the sound of the flute (Juvenal, *Sat.* 6.314–319); in Livy's account of (someone else's description of) the origins of the Bacchic mysteries, women dishevel their hair and rush to the river Tiber to dip their burning torches in the water, while it is the men who prophesy with violent shakings (Livy, *Ab urbe cond.* 39.13.8–14); and in Ovid's description of a celebration of the

---

[69] E.g., Rubina Raja, "Ancient Sanctuaries," in *The Oxford Handbook of Early Christian Ritual*, ed. Risto Uro et al. (Oxford: Oxford University Press, 2019), 143–44; Michael E. Stone, *Secret Groups in Ancient Judaism* (New York: Oxford University Press, 2018), 45, 49; Alice Clinch, "Ecstasy and Initiation in the Eleusinian Mysteries," in *The Routledge Companion to Ecstatic Experience in the Ancient World*, ed. Diana Stein, Sarah Kielt Costello, and Karen Polinger Foster (New York: Routledge, 2022), 314.

[70] See, for example, Philip Harland's discussion of how the Roman historian Livy portrays the Dionysiac mysteries in his writings. Philip A. Harland, *Dynamics of Identity in the World of the Early Christians: Associations, Judeans, and Cultural Minorities* (New York: T&T Clark, 2009), 169–72.

[71] E.g., Jill E. Marshall, *Women Praying and Prophesying in Corinth: Gender and Inspired Speech in First Corinthians* (Tübingen: Mohr Siebeck, 2017), 167.

Bacchic mysteries, certain women commit a murder while their hair is in disarray (Ovid, *Metam.* 3.690-731). The common theme in these accounts is that those who participated in certain mysteries were believed to be possessed by the god(s) and for this reason exhibited the sort of behavior that others deemed mad (cf. also Herodotus, *Hist.* 4.79.3-4). The image of women with disheveled hair was thus used by these ancient (uninitiated male) authors to amplify the perceived madness associated with the rites of the mysteries. To suggest, as Schüssler Fiorenza does, that such an appearance was much sought after by women specifically during praying or prophesying at the time of Paul overstates the case.[72] Rather, disheveled hair seems to have been a feature of "mad" behavior during certain religious celebrations in general (if we are to believe the reports) and as such, occasionally also during praying and prophesying, but not exclusively so. Therefore, ancient descriptions of mystery cults do not sufficiently explain why Paul specifically highlights praying and prophesying in his discussion about covered and uncovered heads.

Third, there is significant variance in our literary and material sources concerning how the mysteries were celebrated and how the prophetesses or priestesses in these cults (such as the ones highlighted by Schüssler Fiorenza) behaved or appeared (even in honor of the same god or goddess), depending on location and time period.[73] Thus, in some cases, female initiates, participants, prophetesses, and

---

[72] Besides, the inscription regarding the Rule of the Andanian Mysteries, upon which Lösch bases his entire argument (see section 1.3.7), addresses the appearance of women only during certain processions and not during praying or prophesying specifically nor during worship in general. Furthermore, in addition to forbidding women from wearing headbands and braided hair during these processions, the regulations also prohibit the wearing of gold, make-up, shoes (unless made from the skins of sacrificial animals), and expensive garments. See, Alicia J. Batten, "Neither Gold nor Braided Hair (1 Timothy 2.9; 1 Peter 3.3): Adornment, Gender and Honour in Antiquity," *NTS* 55 (2009): 484-85. Thus, these regulations concerning women's processional appearances do not primarily focus on women's uncovered heads or on their unbraided hair. Rather, the emphasis is on modest displays, and women not wearing headbands nor braided hair is only one aspect of this. In contrast, the focus of 1 Cor 11:2-16 is exclusively on the appearance of heads, with no mention of other forms of adornment.

[73] See, for example, Ross Shepard Kraemer, *Her Share of the Blessings: Women's Religions Among Pagans, Jews, and Christians in the Greco-Roman World* (Oxford: Oxford University Press, 1992), 38-41; Sarah Iles Johnston, "Mysteries," in *Religions of the Ancient World: A Guide*, ed. Sarah Iles Johnston (Cambridge: Harvard University Press, 2004), 98-105. Jorunn Økland has traced specifically how the ritual practices of the cult of Demeter and Kore in Corinth changed quite a bit between the first century BCE and the second century CE based on the available archaeological evidence. Jorunn Økland, *Women in Their Place: Paul and the Corinthian Discourse of Gender and Sanctuary Space*, JSNTSup 269 (New York: T&T Clark, 2004), 79-92.

priestesses are described or depicted as wearing head-coverings, such as veils, mantles, wreaths, or the like in their participation of the aforementioned mysteries or in their worship of the associated gods and goddesses such as Isis (see figure 1.1), Demeter and Kore, or Dionysos.[74] Notably, the goddesses Isis and Demeter themselves are also often depicted with a head-covering on (see figures 1.2 and 1.3). Furthermore, in some places and at certain time periods, the participation in the mysteries such as that of Dionysos was outright banned.[75] We cannot claim with any certainty, therefore, that most women in Corinth during the 50s CE were so accustomed to praying and prophesying without head-coverings and with loose hair that they knew no other manner of worship. The available evidence simply does not support such a conclusion.

This is not to argue that the Corinthian Christian women could not have been influenced by the mystery cults or other religious rites practiced by the Greeks, Romans, or others.[76] On the contrary, it is highly probable that the Corinthian

---

[74] A well-known example of this comes from the second-century CE Roman novelist Apuleius. In his novel *Metamorphoses*, Apuleius describes a procession of initiates into the cult of Isis at Kenchreai (situated roughly 10 km east of ancient Corinth). The female initiates wear clear head-coverings (veils) over their moisturized hair (*illae limpido tegmina obvolutae madidos crines*), while the male initiates are described as having completely shaved heads (*Metam.* 11.10). Apuleius also describes other participants in this procession and their appearances are not uniform: some wear garlands on their heads, while others seemingly do not don any head-coverings at all. Although this is a fictional account of something that may have never occurred in reality – or that Apuleius himself may not have experienced—it does illustrate that, in terms of head appearances, the cult of Isis was not solely associated with women's wild or unbound hair. See also, Theissen, *Psychological Aspects*, 163–64; Marshall, *Women Praying and Prophesying*, 167; Linda L. Belleville, "Κεφαλή and the Thorny Issue of Headcovering in 1 Corinthians 11:2–16," in *Paul and the Corinthians: Studies on a Community in Conflict; Essays in Honour of Margaret Thrall*, ed. Trevor J. Burke and J. Keith Elliott (Boston: Brill, 2003), 219.

[75] Kraemer, *Her Share of the Blessings*, 43–44.

[76] Some scholars argue that the alleged behavior exhibited in the mystery cults was inherently incompatible with the Christian teachings, and for that reason could not have found its way into the Christian congregations. E.g., Anthony C. Thiselton, *The First Epistle to the Corinthians: A Commentary on the Greek Text*, NIGTC (Grand Rapids: Eerdmans, 2000), 831. However, this perspective reflects an obvious bias that elevates Christianity to a morally superior position over other forms of religion. This assertion in itself does not provide sufficient evidence to dismiss the possibility that the Corinthian congregants could have engaged in behaviors incompatible with Paul's teachings or offensive to modern Christian sensibilities. It is well worth keeping in mind that Paul himself reprimanded the Corinthian congregation for tolerating behavior that, in his view, was not even "named among the nations" (1 Cor 5:1). We have, therefore, no basis for

Christians at the time of Paul had close contacts with such ideas and behaviors that were (later) deemed "pagan" (see also Chapter 4). However, to claim that the majority of the Christian women in Corinth had been so used to praying and prophesying without head-coverings and with loose hair that they continued to do so in the worship of the Christian god is to selectively compile evidence from a long time-span and a large geographical area, while ignoring contrary evidence. It seems more likely that while loose hair may have occasionally accompanied such activities as praying or prophesying in certain cults, such an appearance on a woman in worship was by no means universal. It is thus unlikely that 1 Cor 11:2–16 addresses the issue of Christian women discarding their head-coverings and loosening their hair during praying or prophesying due to the influence of mystery cults.

There is yet another fundamental problem with the hypotheses we have encountered in this section: for some reason men as a group are absolved of all the blame in these reconstructions of the Corinthian situation, while women are deemed collectively the guilty party as if the men were simply innocent and uninvolved bystanders in the conflict between Paul and the misbehaving women. Cynthia Long Westfall, however, has insightfully pointed out that in many of the (ancient and modern) veiling cultures it is often the men who are the instigators for the removal of head-coverings, while the majority of women (at least initially) remain resistant to the changes.[77] It is indeed highly unlikely that the Corinthian Christian men as husbands, sons, fathers, clients, patrons, slaves, slaveholders, or neighbors of these Christian women in Corinth would have had no involvement whatsoever in this state of affairs (whether as instigators or otherwise). Thus, in any interpretation of 1 Cor 11:2–16 this needs to be accounted for but the above scholars have to a large degree failed to do so.

Taking all of the above into consideration, it seems that in order to make sense of Paul's instructions about women's head-coverings in 1 Cor 11:2–16, Paul's comments about men's head-coverings require much closer attention than has been provided by the scholars discussed in this section.

---

assuming that practices deemed "pagan" or "unchristian" could not have been adopted by those who claimed allegiance to Paul, Apollos, Peter, or Christ (cf. 1 Cor 1:12).

[77] Cynthia Long Westfall, *Paul and Gender: Reclaiming the Apostle's Vision for Men and Women in Christ* (Grand Rapids: Baker Academic, 2016), 28–29.

Figure 1.1 (left): A statue of a priestess of Isis from the second century CE that stood on a street corner in Rome. The markings on the lip and the position of the hands suggest that the original statue portrayed the priestess playing a double flute, indicating her participation in an Isiac celebration. The priestess's head is covered with a garment. Museo Nazionale Romano, Palazzo Altemps, inv. 128073.

Figure 1.2 (right): A statue of Isis from the second century CE depicts the goddess with her head covered by a garment, although her crown and part of her hair remain visible. This is how Isis is often portrayed in Roman art. Museo Archeologico Nazionale di Napoli, inv. 6370.

Figure 1.3: Bust of Demeter, dated to the first half of the second century CE, depicts the goddess with a covered head, while her crown and part of her hair remain visible. Museo Nazionale Romano, Palazzo Altemps, inv. 8596.

1.4 The Length or Style of Hair as the Subject Matter

In the previous section we encountered certain interpretations of 1 Cor 11:2–16 that were more focused on how the hair on women was arranged than on the issue of head-coverings. This idea that Paul's concern in 1 Cor 11:2–16 was rather with hair than with head-coverings gained ascendancy in biblical scholarship in the middle of the twentieth century. In this section, we will examine the views of those scholars who argue that the subject matter of the whole of 1 Cor 11:2–16 is hair (on both men and women) and not head-coverings.

1.4.1 Abel Isaksson

The thesis of Abel Isaksson may perhaps be identified as the catalyst of the movement in biblical scholarship that came to regard 1 Cor 11:2–16 as Paul's response to certain inappropriate hairstyles (not head-coverings) in the Corinthian congregation that the Christian men and women were displaying.[78] Isaksson argues that the phrases κατὰ κεφαλῆς ἔχων in 1 Cor 11:4 and ἀκατακαλύπτῳ τῇ κεφαλῇ in 1 Cor 11:5 are not references to "covered" and "uncovered" heads, as biblical scholarship has traditionally understood them to be, but are rather references to "long hair" and "loose hair" respectively. Isaksson points out, for example, that the phrase κατὰ κεφαλῆς ἔχων in 1 Cor 11:4 lacks a direct object for the verb ἔχω ("have"), and so traditional scholarship has completed the phrase with words that actually do not appear in 1 Cor 11:2–16 itself—such as τὸ κάλυμμα ("veil") or τὸ ἱμάτιον ("garment"). However, since Paul does speak of the inappropriateness of long hair on a man in this passage (cf. 1 Cor 11:14), Isaksson finds that "long hair" must then also be the missing object of the verb ἔχω in 1 Cor 11:4. Thus, Isaksson argues that the verse should read as follows: each man who prays or prophesies having long hair hanging down from the head shames his head.[79] Concerning the phrase ἀκατακαλύπτῳ τῇ κεφαλῇ in 1 Cor 11:5, however, Isaksson proposes that this must correspond to the Hebrew phrase רֹאשׁ פָּרוּעַ, which according to Isaksson means "having loose hair hanging down," since in translating רֹאשׁ פָּרוּעַ in Lev 13:45 and Num 5:18, the LXX uses either the adjective ἀκατακάλυπτος ("uncovered") or the verb ἀποκαλύπτω ("uncover").[80]

In his thesis, Isaksson does not offer any suggestions in regards to what may have motivated the Christian men of Corinth to grow their hair long. He does, however, offer two possible explanations as to what may have prompted the

---

[78] Five years after the publication of Isaksson's thesis, a short study by William J. Martin on mainly the interpretation of 1 Cor 11:6 appeared in a collection of essays presented to F. F. Bruce on his 60th birthday. In this study, Martin also presents the idea that 1 Cor 11:2–16 is concerned with hair and not with head-coverings. He seems to do so independently of Isaksson as he portrays no awareness of Isaksson's earlier work on the passage. Martin's main thesis is that there were certain women in the Corinthian congregation who had for one reason or another cut their hair short, and so in 1 Cor 11:6, Paul is instructing the congregation that those short-haired women may remain so for the time being, but if they feel ashamed about it, they should grow their hair long again. William J. Martin, "1 Corinthian 11:2–16: An Interpretation," in *Apostolic History and the Gospel: Biblical and Historical Essays Presented to F. F. Bruce on His 60th Birthday*, ed. W. Ward Gasque and Ralph P. Martin (Grand Rapids: Eerdmans, 1970): 231–41. Given that Martin deals with the reasons why he thinks 1 Cor 11:2–16 is concerned with hair more in passing than in any depth, his short study has not received the same attention in scholarship as the hypotheses of Isaksson and Hurley (see below).

[79] Abel Isaksson, *Marriage and Ministry in the New Temple: A Study with Special Reference to Mt. 19.13–12 [sic] and 1. Cor. 11.3–16* (Lund: C.W.K. Gleerup, 1965), 166.

[80] Isaksson, *Marriage and Ministry*, 166.

Corinthian Christian women to pray and prophesy with loose hair. One of the reasons, according to Isaksson, may have been associated with an intense eschatological expectancy. That is, the prophetesses of Corinth may have viewed themselves as brides of Christ at the time of the messianic wedding and thus unbound their hair "like the Jewish bride on her wedding day."[81] And secondly, Isaksson suggests (following Lösch) that these prophetesses may have been accustomed to worshiping with loose hair due to their previous association with certain pagan ceremonies in which such a display of hair was customary.[82] Isaksson concludes that regardless of the motivations for this behavior, Paul in 1 Cor 11:2–16 admonishes the male prophets to exercise their tasks in Christian worship with short hair and the female prophetesses to do so with bound hair in a manner of Jewish married women—a custom which had prevailed in all the other early Christian churches—since loose hair on a woman brought shame on her husband, a scenario unacceptable to Paul.[83]

1.4.2 James B. Hurley

James B. Hurley essentially follows the same line of reasoning as Isaksson regarding whether Paul in 1 Cor 11:2–16 addresses hairstyles or head-coverings. Like Isaksson (but in greater detail), Hurley argues that the incomplete phrase κατὰ κεφαλῆς ἔχων in 1 Cor 11:4 should be supplemented with ἡ κόμη ("hair") from 1 Cor 11:14–15 as the implied direct object of the verb ἔχω, and that the phrase ἀκατακαλύπτῳ τῇ κεφαλῇ in 1 Cor 11:5 should be taken as corresponding to the Hebrew רֹאשׁ פָּרוּעַ ("loosed hair" in Hurley's translation) based on how the LXX translates Lev 13:45 and Num 5:18.[84] Additionally, Hurley relies on 1 Tim 2:9 (in which women's "gold-braided hair" is discussed) to argue that women in general did not wear head-coverings to the Christian gatherings at the time.[85] Based on these arguments, Hurley suggests that the situation in Corinth was such that, after Paul's departure, the Corinthian Christian women, who normally pinned up their hair, began to loosen their hair during worship, while the Christian men began to pin up their hair in a style that women traditionally wore. These men and women did so because they

---

[81] Isaksson, *Marriage and Ministry*, 169.

[82] Isaksson, *Marriage and Ministry*, 169

[83] Isaksson, *Marriage and Ministry*, 166–69.

[84] James B. Hurley, "Did Paul Require Veils or the Silence of Women? A Consideration of I Cor. 11:2–16 and I Cor. 14:33b–36," *WTJ* 35 (1973): 198–99. Hurley appears to be aware of Isaksson's work on this passage, but oddly only references him in a single footnote and this in a section that deals with a side issue (Hurley, "Did Paul Require Veils?" 195 n. 13).

[85] Hurley, "Did Paul Require Veils?" 199–200.

believed (based on Paul's own teachings) that "the gospel, consistently carried through, allows no distinction between man and woman."[86] Paul, however, was opposed to this practice because he believed that men brought shame on themselves and on Christ by displaying feminine hairstyles, and that women brought shame on themselves and on their husbands by loosening their hair, because loosed hair at the time was associated with adultery.[87]

1.4.3 Jerome Murphy-O'Connor

Jerome Murphy-O'Connor follows both Isaksson and Hurley in arguing that the subject matter of the whole of 1 Cor 11:2–16 is hair rather than head-coverings. Murphy-O'Connor especially draws attention to the fact that the preposition κατά with a genitive (as in 1 Cor 11:4) denotes downward motion and therefore fits well with the description of long hair falling down from the head. While Murphy-O'Connor recognizes that such a grammatical construct could also be used in reference to a mantle over the head, he finds this unlikely in the case of 1 Cor 11:4 since he believes that Paul should in principle have had nothing against men wearing head-coverings because he had been used to the tradition of Judean priests wearing turbans.[88] According to Murphy-O'Connor, 1 Cor 11:2–16 rather suggests that Paul was disturbed by the Corinthian Christian men arranging their long hair in an elaborate manner, since this way of displaying hair was at the time associated with "homosexuality."[89] The problem with the Corinthian Christian women for Paul, however, was the opposite: they had failed to arrange their hair in a manner appropriate for women at the time—bound up and wrapped around the head—

---

[86] Hurley, "Did Paul Require Veils?" 200–202.

[87] Hurley, "Did Paul Require Veils?" 202–3.

[88] Jerome Murphy-O'Connor, "Sex and Logic in 1 Corinthians 11:2–16," *CBQ* 42 (1980): 483–85. In a follow-up article on the same passage, Murphy-O'Connor relates how it had been brought to his attention after the publication of his initial article that the Romans used to cover their heads with a garment during worship, and that this custom could have some bearing on the interpretation of 1 Cor 11:2–16. However, Murphy-O'Connor rejects the relevance of this Roman ritual for understanding 1 Cor 11:2–16, reiterating his earlier argument that, in principle, Paul should not have had anything against men wearing head-coverings due to his upbringing. In this later article, therefore, Murphy-O'Connor distances himself from the possibility that the grammatical construct κατὰ κεφαλῆς ἔχων in 1 Cor 11:4 could reference a head-covering, asserting that "it can only refer to long hair." Jerome Murphy-O'Connor, "1 Corinthians 11:2–16 Once Again," *CBQ* 50 (1988): 267–68.

[89] Murphy-O'Connor, "Sex and Logic," 485–88.

and went about with disorderly hair.⁹⁰ The overall issue, therefore, was that the Christian men in Corinth appeared "'unmasculine' in a highly specific sense" (i.e., as "homosexuals") and that the Christian women appeared "'unfeminine' in a very generic sense."⁹¹ According to Murphy-O'Connor, such a situation in Corinth arose due to the influence of over-realized eschatology. That is, the believers there were certain that they "belonged entirely to the new age" and for this reason "felt free to blur the distinction between the sexes."⁹²

1.4.4 Marlis Gielen

Marlis Gielen likewise argues that hair, not head-coverings, is in focus in 1 Cor 11:4–5. However, unlike Isaksson and Hurley, Gielen does not think that LXX Lev 13:45 and Num 5:18 can lend support for such a view, since in Gielen's reading, ἀκατακάλυπτος and ἀποκαλύπτω retain the literal meaning of "uncover" also in these texts and do not take on the connotation of "dishevel."⁹³ For Gielen, the strongest support for reading 1 Cor 11:4–5 as referencing hair comes from the rest of 1 Cor 11:2–16 itself, particularly from 1 Cor 11:5b–6 and 1 Cor 11:14–15 in which hair is discussed in association with shame. Gielen proposes, then, that since 1 Cor 11:4 and 1 Cor 11:5 appear in an antithetical relationship, as do 1 Cor 11:14 and 1 Cor 11:15, the antithesis of the latter verses should inform how the antithesis of the former verses should be read. That is, given that Paul considers long hair a woman's glory but a man's shame (1 Cor 11:14–15), the reverse must also be true—short hair is a man's glory and a woman's shame—and so in 1 Cor 11:4–5, Paul must be saying that it is shameful for women to pray and prophesy with *short* ("uncovered") rather than disheveled hair (contra Isaksson and Hurley) and for men to do so with long hair ("having down from the head").⁹⁴ However, Gielen suggests that Paul's comments regarding men only describe a hypothetical scenario, and that the real problem in Corinth was that the Christian women had taken Paul's teaching that in Christ there was "no male and female" (cf. Gal 3:28) to mean that there was only

---

⁹⁰ Murphy-O'Connor, "Sex and Logic," 488–90. See also, Murphy-O'Connor, "1 Corinthians 11:2–16 Once Again," 268–69.

⁹¹ Murphy-O'Connor, "Sex and Logic," 489.

⁹² Murphy-O'Connor, "Sex and Logic," 490.

⁹³ Marlis Gielen, "Beten und Prophezeien mit unverhülltem Kopf? Die Kontroverse zwischen Paulus und der korinthischen Gemeinde um die Wahrung der Geschlechtsrollen-symbolik in 1Kor 11, 2–16," *ZNW* 90 (1999): 228–30.

⁹⁴ Gielen, "Beten und Prophezeien," 231–35.

male and that this required them to appear as male.⁹⁵ To this, then, Paul responded emphatically that gender distinctions continue to exist also in the new order.⁹⁶

1.4.5 Kirk R. MacGregor

Kirk R. MacGregor follows Murphy-O'Connor in arguing that κατὰ κεφαλῆς ἔχων in 1 Cor 11:4 refers to long hair which Paul found problematic on men due to the association that such an appearance had with "homosexuality."⁹⁷ Regarding the appearance of women that Paul found problematic, however, MacGregor suggests that it had to do with short hair rather than disorderly hair, since 1 Cor 11:4 and 1 Cor 11:5 seem to be in an antithetical relationship and the more natural opposite of long hair is short hair.⁹⁸ According to MacGregor, ancient women with short hair were "lesbians" and thus the whole of 1 Cor 11:2–16 should be taken as Paul's prohibition of "homosexuality."⁹⁹ MacGregor claims that "homosexual" behavior, which had found its inspiration in over-realized eschatology, was a major problem in the Corinthian congregation at the time of Paul that Paul then combated in 1 Cor 11:2–16 as well as in several other passages.¹⁰⁰

1.4.6 Philip B. Payne

Philip B. Payne points out that in 1 Cor 11:4, Paul connects κατὰ κεφαλῆς ἔχων with shame, and since it was not shameful for Romans nor Jews of Paul's day to wear head-coverings in religious contexts, Paul cannot be addressing head-coverings in this passage.¹⁰¹ Payne argues that men wearing long hair, however, was considered disgraceful by Paul (and his contemporaries), particularly if the hair was done up in a manner of women's hair due to its association with "homosexuality," and thus, 1 Cor 11:4 must be a reference to long hair.¹⁰² In regards to 1 Cor 11:5, on the other hand, Payne claims that this verse must be addressing loose hair on a woman and not the uncovering of the head, because an uncovered head on a woman was not considered shameful in either Greek, Jewish, or Roman culture, whereas loose

---

[95] Gielen, "Beten und Prophezeien," 235–37.

[96] Gielen, "Beten und Prophezeien," 237–38.

[97] Kirk R. MacGregor, "Is 1 Corinthians 11:2–16 a Prohibition of Homosexuality?" *BSac* 166 (2009): 206–7; 210–13.

[98] MacGregor, "Is 1 Corinthians 11:2–16 a Prohibition?" 207.

[99] MacGregor, "Is 1 Corinthians 11:2–16 a Prohibition?" 213–14.

[100] MacGregor, "Is 1 Corinthians 11:2–16 a Prohibition?" 214–15.

[101] Philip B. Payne, *Man and Woman, One in Christ: An Exegetical and Theological Study of Paul's Letters* (Grand Rapids: Zondervan, 2009), 141–42.

[102] Payne, *Man and Woman*, 142–44.

hair on a woman was considered disgraceful in all these cultures.[103] Payne contends that most women in these societies wore their hair pinned up on the head, and that the only context in which the hair was deliberately let loose was in the Dionysiac cult.[104] Payne suggests, then, that the Dionysiac cult, which was popular in Corinth at the time of Paul, must have influenced the Christian women to let their hair down and loose during Christian worship.[105] Paul, however, was against this practice, because in the Jewish culture loose hair on a woman was associated with adultery, and because in the Dionysiac cult it accompanied (sexual) debauchery and promiscuity.[106]

1.4.7 Torsten Jantsch

In his interpretation of 1 Cor 11:2–16, Torsten Jantsch relies on many of the arguments we have already encountered in this and in the previous section (1.3) to demonstrate that in 1 Cor 11:2–16 Paul addresses an issue related to the arrangement of hair. Jantsch notes, for example, that 1 Cor 11:2–16 does not mention a κάλυμμα ("veil") or ἱμάτιον ("garment"), which we would expect if veils or head-coverings were the subject of discussion. Instead, given the numerous references to hair in the passage, Jantsch finds it more likely that hair is in focus.[107] Regarding the phrase κατὰ κεφαλῆς ἔχων, for example, Jantsch claims that a covered head in the context of religious acts was not associated with shame among Jewish or Roman men, making it "absolutely astonishing" ("gar erstaunlich") that Paul would have made

---

[103] Payne, *Man and Woman*, 149–69.

[104] Payne, *Man and Woman*, 151, 162–64. In essence, Payne's argument follows a similar line of reasoning in regards to the subject matter of 1 Cor 11:2–16 that Wolfgang Schrage (with whom Payne engages) had presented in an earlier work. However, unlike Payne, Schrage does not commit to the possibilities that he presents (such that long hair on men was associated with "homosexuality" or that mystery cults were to blame for the women's behavior of loosening their hair during worship). Thus, I will not conduct a separate assessment of Schrage's work here, even though some of his suggestions seem to have influenced subsequent scholarship on this passage. See, Wolfgang Schrage, *Der erste Brief an die Korinther (1 Kor 6,12–11,16)*, EKKNT 7/2 (Düsseldorf: Benziger, 1995), 490–96; 504–7.

[105] Payne, *Man and Woman*, 169–71. Payne argues that Paul's "praying or prophesying" in 1 Cor 11:4–5 should not be taken as a reference to particular activities, but as representative of the whole of the worship experience. Payne, *Man and Woman*, 149–50.

[106] Payne, *Man and Woman*, 165–66, 169 – 71.

[107] Torsten Jantsch, "Die Frau soll Kontrolle über ihren Kopf ausüben (1Kor 11,10): Zum historischen, kulturellen und religiösen Hintergrund von 1Kor 11,2–16," in *Frauen, Männer, Engel: Perspektiven zu 1Kor 11, 2–16*, ed. Torsten Jantsch (Göttingen: Neukirchener, 2015), 100–103.

that connection.¹⁰⁸ Consequently, Jantsch concludes that it must be long hair that Paul considers shameful for men to pray and prophesy with, although Jantsch is quick to point out that since men in antiquity generally did not wear long hair, Paul only addresses a hypothetical scenario regarding men.¹⁰⁹ In Jantsch's reading, the only real problem that 1 Cor 11:2–16 addresses is Corinthian Christian women loosening their hair during ecstatic prophesying, a behavior these women had adopted from their previous cultic engagements (Jantsch follows Lösch and Schüssler Fiorenza here).¹¹⁰ Jantsch argues that this reading is supported by LXX Lev 13:45 and Num 5:18 in which the ἀκατακάλυπτος word group—normally employed in Greek literature with the meaning of "uncover"—also conveys the meaning of "disheveled hair" ("ungeordnetes, wirres und zerzaustes Haar tragen").¹¹¹ And in 1 Cor 11:2–16, then, Paul uses the ἀκατακάλυπτος language with the latter meaning in mind. Jantsch concludes, therefore, that Paul's response of 1 Cor 11:2–16 calls on the Corinthian women to control their hair during ecstatic worship for the sake of the attendant angels, who serve as guardians of pure and orderly worship of God (cf. 1 Cor 11:10).¹¹²

1.4.8 Analysis

All of the hypotheses discussed in this section are built on the premise that the phrases κατὰ κεφαλῆς ἔχων in 1 Cor 11:4 and ἀκατακαλύπτῳ τῇ κεφαλῇ in 1 Cor 11:5 are not references to the wearing or not wearing of physical head-coverings—such as veils, mantles, or caps—but that they describe how hair is arranged on the head. Thus, before we can analyze the various hypotheses regarding the Corinthian situation proposed by these scholars, it is necessary to first examine whether the phrases κατὰ κεφαλῆς ἔχων and ἀκατακαλύπτῳ τῇ κεφαλῇ can be read in a way that these interpreters have suggested.

The absence of a direct object for the verb ἔχω in the phrase κατὰ κεφαλῆς ἔχων in 1 Cor 11:4 is indeed strange. Typically, when ἔχω accompanies κατὰ κεφαλῆς in ancient literature, the phrase is completed with a direct object such as τὸ ἱμάτιον

---

¹⁰⁸ Jantsch, "Die Frau," 104–8.
¹⁰⁹ Jantsch, "Die Frau," 108, 120.
¹¹⁰ Jantsch, "Die Frau," 126–28.
¹¹¹ Jantsch, "Die Frau," 117–19.
¹¹² Jantsch, "Die Frau," 128–44.

1.4 The Length or Style of Hair as the Subject Matter 63

(see Chapter 2 for examples).¹¹³ Without such a direct object, 1 Cor 11:4 reads that "it is shameful for a man to pray or prophesy having something down from the head," leaving it to anyone's imagination to figure out what that something could be. In principle, then, long hair can function as that "something," since it hangs in a downward motion from the head. However, as Murphy-O'Connor acknowledges (see section 1.4.3), the same could be said about a garment, for example, since this also hangs down from the head if placed upon it. Indeed, there are a number of examples in ancient Greek literature in which κατὰ κεφαλῆς is used with some verb (such as ἔχω) to describe a head covered by a garment (see Chapter 2). However, we possess no examples in which the phrase κατὰ κεφαλῆς with ἔχω is completed with the word "hair."¹¹⁴ Thus, while the phrase κατὰ κεφαλῆς ἔχων on its own in no way determines whether the reference is to long hair or to a head-covering, the available examples of how κατὰ κεφαλῆς is used in ancient literature (particularly in relation to ἔχω) suggest that it would have been more probably understood to refer to a garment placed over the head than to long hair.

The above scholars argue, however, that the context of 1 Cor 11:4 itself provides the missing direct object for the verb ἔχω, since only a few verses later Paul states that long hair on a man is disgraceful (1 Cor 11:14). It is especially pointed out that the phrase ἡ κόμη ἀντὶ περιβολαίου δέδοται ("hair has been given instead of a wrap-around") in 1 Cor 11:15 indicates that the subject matter of the whole passage is hair and not head-coverings. However, as I will argue more thoroughly in Chapter 5, these verses do not lend themselves to be read in this way. Given their placement within Paul's argument, it seems more likely that Paul provides here an analogy from "nature" (ἡ φύσις) to bolster his stance that during praying and prophesying men and women can appear differently in relation to head-coverings. That is, Paul demonstrates that since it is natural for men and women to have different lengths of hair throughout the course of their lives, so it should be acceptable for men and

---

¹¹³ See also, Preston T. Massey, "The Meaning of κατακαλύπτω and κατὰ κεφαλῆς ἔχων in 1 Corinthians 11.2–16," *NTS* 53 (2007): 522. However, as A. Philip Brown II points out, Massey is not very careful with how he presents the primary evidence and this at times confuses the matter more than it clarifies. See, A. Philip Brown II, "Chrysostom and Epiphanius: Long Hair Prohibited as Covering in 1 Corinthians 11:4, 7," *BBR* 23 (2013): 369–71.

¹¹⁴ Philip Brown has tried to argue to the contrary, but there is a major flaw in his argument. While Brown demonstrates that the verb ἔχω can take the noun κόμη ("long hair") as its direct object, he fails to provide a single example in which κόμη and ἔχω together complete κατὰ κεφαλῆς. Brown II, "Chrysostom and Epiphanius," 372–73. It is one thing to say "to have long hair," which is a well-attested phrase, but it is another matter entirely to say "to have long hair down from the head," a construction not attested in the available sources.

women to dress their heads differently during praying and prophesying (see Chapter 5). In any case, while "long hair" is indeed mentioned in the same passage as κατὰ κεφαλῆς ἔχων, it nevertheless does not appear in the immediate context, and there are enough layers of argument between the two to suggest that it is not self-evident they should be merged into one sentence.

To strengthen the argument that 1 Cor 11:2–16 is about hair and not about head-coverings, however, several of the above scholars insist that Paul would have had no reason to find head-coverings on men in religious contexts problematic due to his own Jewish heritage in which priests wore turbans, and the fact that Romans did not consider it shameful to cover their heads during certain religious rituals. This, however, is fallacious reasoning. That Jewish priests wore turbans at the time of Paul (if true) has no bearing whatsoever on whether Paul would have found this or some other head-covering custom problematic in the context of his congregations' worship practices. Similarly, that Romans did not find covering of the head shameful in *their* rituals does not say anything about whether Paul would have considered covering *his* head shameful in worshiping the divine.[115] As will be demonstrated in the following chapters, there were plenty of reasons for Paul to find men wearing head-coverings during praying and prophesying problematic. Thus, the above argument in no way demonstrates that κατὰ κεφαλῆς ἔχων should only be taken as a reference to long hair and not to head-coverings.

In regards to the phrase ἀκατακαλύπτῳ τῇ κεφαλῇ, the argument of most of the above scholars runs as follows: the Hebrew phrase פָּרוּעַ רֹאשׁ refers to loosed or disheveled hair and since this phrase is translated in LXX Lev 13:45 as ἡ κεφαλὴ αὐτοῦ ἀκατακάλυπτος ("his head uncovered") and in LXX Num 5:18 as ἀποκαλύψει τὴν κεφαλήν ("he uncovered the head"), then the adjective ἀκατακάλυπτος must also include the meaning "disheveled" for Paul, and conversely, the verb κατακαλύπτω must include the meaning "properly arranged." The above line of reasoning, however, is fallacious. The Hebrew phrase פָּרוּעַ רֹאשׁ does not translate directly to "loose hair" or "disheveled hair" or the like. Its literal translation is

---

[115] To give a modern example, there are many religious officials (Christian or otherwise) who perform their public religious duties wearing certain head-coverings. For them to do so is in general acceptable to the spectators. If, however, a lay person appears in the same manner (e.g., participates in Christian worship with a replica of a papal mitre), it would likely be considered mockery. Similarly, there are many contexts (religious or otherwise) in which wearing a baseball cap backward is an acceptable form of dress, but praying from the pulpit in this manner would be considered inappropriate and offensive in many Christian churches across the globe. It is the *context*, not the head-covering itself, that determines whether a particular appearance is shameful or not.

something like "head let go," in a sense of "letting something have free, unrestrained course to move or act."¹¹⁶ The meaning of the Hebrew phrase is therefore ambiguous, and Lev 13:45 and Num 5:18 themselves offer little to no help in clarifying what exactly is being referenced. An examination of the rabbinic engagement with the biblical texts in which רֹאשׁ פָּרוּעַ features—the rabbis were particularly interested in Num 5:18—reveals that there was a lack of agreement among the later readers of the Hebrew Scriptures regarding the meaning of this phrase. Some rabbis considered it to reference only the unbinding or unloosening of hair (e.g., m. Sotah 1:5); some believed that it described only the removal of a head-covering (e.g., Gen. Rab. 7:8; b. Ketub. 72a.19 - 72b.1; Midr. Num. Rab. 9:16); yet some others that it alluded to both actions at the same time—the removal of a head-covering and the loosening of hair (e.g., t. Sotah 3:1; Sifre Num. 11 on 5:18); and some simply employed the phrase without explaining what they meant by it (e.g., m. Ketub. 2:1; m. B. Qam. 8:6; b. Sanh. 58b.13; t. Sotah. 5:5).

The above shows that some readers of the Torah understood רֹאשׁ פָּרוּעַ only in a sense of "uncover," making it highly unlikely that when the LXX translators chose the Greek words with the meaning of "uncover" in their rendering of this Hebrew phrase, they in fact had in mind disheveled or unbound hair. It is far more plausible that the LXX translators, like some later rabbis, understood the phrase רֹאשׁ פָּרוּעַ as referencing the removal of a head-covering, and selected the Greek words that best corresponded to that understanding (as Gielen rightly notes, see above). This is best illustrated by the LXX translation of רֹאשׁ פָּרוּעַ in Lev 10:6 and Lev 21:10 into ἀποκιδαρόω, which literally means "to take the priestly turban off." In this rendering of רֹאשׁ פָּרוּעַ, therefore, there is no ambiguity as to what is meant: the LXX translators clearly understood this Hebrew phrase in these verses to refer to the removal of a particular head-covering, and so it makes little sense to argue that they had a different understanding of רֹאשׁ פָּרוּעַ elsewhere.¹¹⁷ Indeed, Preston Massey has looked at the usage of the κατακαλύπτω word group in Greek sources from the Classical, Hellenistic, and Imperial periods, and concluded that in none of the available entries is this word group used to describe loosed or disheveled hair—when unbound hair is in question, other verbs or adjectives are employed.¹¹⁸ It is highly improbable, then, that the LXX translators imbued this word group with a novel meaning that would have been unfamiliar to most readers, yet somehow picked up by Paul and his addressees in Corinth.

---

[116] Massey, "The Meaning," 513.
[117] See also, Fitzmyer, *First Corinthians*, 413–14.
[118] Massey, "The Meaning," 502–23.

Furthermore, in commenting on the so-called ordeal of the bitter water (Num 5:11–28), both Philo and Josephus understand the ritual to have involved the removal of the accused woman's head-covering by a priest, but not the disheveling or loosening of her hair. In Josephus's account, for example, the priest removes the woman's outer garment from her head but there is no mention of hair (καὶ τῆς κεφαλῆς τὸ ἱμάτιον ἀφελών, *Ant.* 3.11.6 §270). Philo uses a more general term for the head-covering, commenting that the priest removes it so that the woman can be judged bareheaded, but also says nothing of the woman's hair (καὶ τοὐπίκρανον ἀφελών, ἵν' ἐπικρίνηται γεγυμνωμένη τῇ κεφαλῇ, *Spec. Laws* 3.56). Both Philo and Josephus likely worked with the Greek text of the Hebrew Scriptures (or with a tradition influenced by the Greek text), and they exhibit no awareness that the Greek of Num 5:18 speaks of hair. Thus, even though the Hebrew original of Num 5:18 may have been understood by *some* later readers as referencing the loosening of hair, it appears that the Greek translations, which rendered רֹאשׁ פָּרֻעַ with "uncover," were not thus perceived. It is therefore most likely that the phrase ἀκατακαλύπτῳ τῇ κεφαλῇ was understood by both Paul and his readers to refer to an uncovered head in a sense that it was missing some form of a head-covering.

Considering all of the above, I deem the proposal that 1 Cor 11:4–5 addresses hair lengths or hairstyles untenable. As such, any hypothesis that is built upon the assumption that hair is the only subject matter of 1 Cor 11:2–16 should be automatically disqualified as well. However, a few things may nevertheless be said here regarding the above hypotheses in their own right to further demonstrate the unworkability of the so-called hair theory in the interpretation of 1 Cor 11:2–16. For example, it seems illogical for Paul to be concerned with long hair on men and disorderly or short hair on women only during praying or prophesying, especially if such appearances are claimed to have been associated with some form of sexually inappropriate behavior.[119] If the issue were indeed sexual impropriety, we should rather expect Paul to criticize such appearances regardless of context. Furthermore, considering that earlier in 1 Cor, Paul openly rebukes a man for having sexual

---

[119] Several of the interpreters in this section use specifically the term "homosexuality" without defining what they mean by it. It seems that they work with some modern concept and expect it to apply equally to first century data. This in itself is a major hermeneutical flaw that undermines the arguments presented. Since Gillian Townsley provides a thorough critique of the above scholars' anachronistic use of "homosexuality" in their readings of 1 Cor 11:2–16 (Townsley, *Straight Mind in Corinth*, 62–79), I will not delve much deeper into this issue here. For the purposes of my argument, I will work with the assumption that by "homosexuality" the above scholars have in mind some form of sexually deviant behavior that disturbed Paul.

relations with his father's wife (i.e., with his stepmother,[120] 1 Cor 5:1–2), demands of the Corinthian Christians to shun all πόρνοι (1 Cor 5:9), and speaks at length on the topic of πορνεία[121] (1 Cor 6:12–20), it makes little sense for him to tiptoe around another problem with sexual impropriety in 1 Cor 11:2–16, using euphemisms and convoluted reasoning. Why would Paul change tack in this matter?

Finally, long hair on men and disorderly or short hair on women was by no means solely associated with sexuality in ancient sources. While sexuality is in focus in some cases, such appearances are more commonly linked to mourning rituals.[122] We cannot assume, therefore, that the problem addressed in 1 Cor 11:2–16 must have been sexual in nature solely on the basis of how the hair is claimed to have appeared on men and women. Yet, the above scholars have inexplicably ignored the more common context for disorderly hair in antiquity in their reconstructions of the Corinthian situation behind 1 Cor 11:2–16. All in all, therefore, there is no reason to think that 1 Cor 11:4–5 addresses hair lengths or hairstyles that were associated with some form of sexually deviant behavior that Paul found problematic specifically and only during praying and prophesying.

1.5 Ritual Transvestism as Paul's Enemy

While the scholars discussed in the previous section are convinced that 1 Cor 11:2–16 is concerned only with hair and not with head-coverings, not all interpreters influenced by the so-called hair theory have been willing to go so far as to say that 1 Cor 11:2–16 does not address head-coverings at all. In this section, we will analyze several hypotheses in which the foundational premise is that Paul addresses both hairstyles and head-coverings in 1 Cor 11:4–5.

---

[120] On issues surrounding the identity of the woman in this passage, see, for example, Joshua M. Reno, "Γυνὴ τοῦ Πατρός: Analytic Kin Circumlocution and the Case for Corinthian Adultery," *JBL* 135 (2016): 827–47.

[121] Translating πορνεία adequately into English has been a notoriously difficult task in biblical scholarship. Joshua Reno has recently suggested that πορνεία should be understood in Pauline literature as a broad reference to inordinate and uncontrolled sexual desire. Joshua M. Reno, "Pornographic Desire in the Pauline Corpus," *JBL* 140 (2021): 163–85. However, there is a lack of consensus on this issue and so I leave the Greek term untranslated here.

[122] E.g., Charles H. Cosgrove, "A Woman's Unbound Hair in the Greco-Roman World, with Special Reference to the Story of the 'Sinful Woman' in Luke 7:36–50," *JBL* 124 (2005): 675–86.

1.5.1 Catherine Kroeger

Catherine Kroeger argues that in certain cults at the time of Paul (but particularly in the popular Dionysiac cult), men and women practiced "sex reversal," in that among other things, men wore long hair and veils that usually women wore, while women went about with shorn hair, without a veil, and in the garments usually worn by men.[123] In 1 Cor 11:2–16, therefore, Paul addresses these "vestigial pagan practices" and demands that Christians "maintain their own identity in the clear differentiation of the sexes in garments, hairstyle and self-expression."[124]

1.5.2 Birgitte Graakjær Hjort

Birgitte Graakjær Hjort likewise suggests that the problem in the Corinthian congregation was that the Christian men and women "aspired to transvestism and the neutralization of the sexes by dressing and cutting their hair in accordance with the customs of the opposite sex."[125] Hjort believes that these men and women had picked up this behavior from certain cults—particularly from the cult of Dionysos—which they had been familiar with prior to them joining the Christian community.[126] In support of this way of reading the text, Hjort argues that since 1 Cor 11:2–16 immediately follows 1 Cor 8–10, in which Paul deals with idolatry, this passage must also be primarily concerned with "idol worship." Hjort points out, for example, that some of Paul's other concerns with the Corinthians' gatherings were drunkenness and ecstasy (or religious madness), which purportedly also accompanied the Dionysiac cult, and so in Hjort's view, ritual transvestism is the most logical subject matter of 1 Cor 11:2–16.[127] Thus, Hjort concludes that 1 Cor 11:2–16 should be read as Paul's call for the Corinthian Christians to respect the differentiation of sexes ordained at creation.[128]

1.5.3 Gillian Townsley

Like Kroeger and Hjort, Gillian Townsley also argues that the problem Paul addresses in 1 Cor 11:2–16 relates to ritual transvestism, a behavior which the

---

[123] Catherine Kroeger, "The Apostle Paul and the Greco-Roman Cults of Women," *JETS* 30 (1987): 37.
[124] Kroeger, "The Apostle Paul," 38.
[125] Birgitte Graakjær Hjort, "Gender Hierarchy or Religious Androgyny? Male-Female Interaction in the Corinthian Community—A Reading of 1 Cor. 11,2–16," *ST* 55 (2001): 68.
[126] Hjort, "Gender Hierarchy," 67, 72–74.
[127] Hjort, "Gender Hierarchy," 60–61, 63, 67, 72–74.
[128] Hjort, "Gender Hierarchy," 65–66.

congregants had adopted from their previous association with the Dionysiac cult in particular.[129] Townsley highlights that the god Dionysos, even though male, "was closely associated with feminine clothing," and thus his followers imitated such gender role reversal in how they dressed and how they attended their hair during celebrations and festivals held in his honor.[130] According to Townsley, then, Paul in 1 Cor 11:2–16 argues against this manner of ritual cross-dressing, stressing instead that women must appear as women and men as men.[131]

1.5.4 Analysis

Much of the criticism that I have leveled against other interpretations of 1 Cor 11:2–16 in the previous sections also applies to the hypothesis that this passage addresses ritual transvestism. First, as has been discussed in section 1.3.15, there is conflicting evidence regarding men's and women's behavior and appearances in the mystery cults, including in the cult of Dionysos.[132] It is thus irresponsible to base a hypothesis on selectively chosen evidence from various time periods, regarding various locations and events, while disregarding contrary evidence. When all evidence regarding men's and women's behavior in the Dionysiac cult is taken into consideration, we have little confidence to claim that the Dionysiac cross-dressing was so pervasive at the time of Paul that the majority of the Corinthian Christian men and women specifically in the 50s CE would have known no other form of worshiping. Second, as I have already discussed in section 1.4.8, it is very unlikely that Paul in 1 Cor 11:4–5 addresses men's and women's hairstyles. And third, this

---

[129] Gillian Townsley, "Gender Trouble in Corinth: Que(e)rying Constructs of Gender in 1 Corinthians 11:2–16," *The Bible and Critical Theory* 2/2 (2006): 17.6–17.7. See also, Townsley, *Straight Mind in Corinth*, 111–15.

[130] Townsley, "Gender Trouble in Corinth," 17.6–17.7.

[131] Townsley, "Gender Trouble in Corinth," 17.8–17.9.

[132] In her study on why women were drawn to the Dionysiac cult, Ross Kraemer cautions that "what we know about the worship of Dionysus must be reconstructed from a multitude of sources whose reliability is uneven, yielding a composite image which is at best an approximation. The particular rites observed, the exact geographic locations in which they were practiced, the specific mythology and interpretations which accompanied them, their extent and influence in various periods, all must be reconstructed from sources whose intention is often anything but to facilitate historical research." Ross S. Kraemer, "Ecstasy and Possession: The Attraction of Women to the Cult of Dionysus," *HTR* 72 (1979): 56–57. With this caution in mind, it is indeed possible to make certain generalizations, but it is another matter altogether to make a case concerning specific rites at a specific location at a specific time period for a specific group of people. For the latter we cannot use generalizations based on selective evidence, but would require concrete evidence related to the location, rites, and time period in question.

hypothesis fails to take seriously the specific contexts in which Paul found the Corinthians' behavior problematic—namely, during praying and prophesying. Are we to imagine that the Corinthian Christians assembled in appropriate attire and hairstyles, only to then cross-dress whenever it was time to pray or prophesy? Or are we to assume that Paul tolerated such behavior at other times but not during these two activities? Neither scenario seems plausible, and in any case, this hypothesis raises more questions regarding Paul's arguments in 1 Cor 11:2–16 than it resolves.

1.6 Roman Rites as Background to 1 Cor 11:2–16

For a long time, interpreters of 1 Cor 11:2–16 have recognized that Romans at the time of Paul covered their heads during certain devotional acts in worship. However, until the 1980s, the relevance of this ritual covering of the head for understanding 1 Cor 11:2–16 was largely dismissed in biblical scholarship for various reasons. Hermann Olshausen in the early nineteenth century, for example, thought it "thoroughly improbable that the Christians should have transplanted anything of heathen rites into ecclesiastical usage,"[133] a view shared by many other nineteenth and early twentieth-century biblical scholars.[134] It was also repeatedly pointed out that this Roman ritual gesture could not have been Paul's concern in 1 Cor 11:2–16 because: a) this gesture only accompanied Roman sacrifices, but 1 Cor 11:2–16 says nothing about sacrifices; and b) gender was not an issue for Romans during sacrificing as both men and women sacrificed with covered heads, whereas in 1 Cor 11:2–16, Paul focuses on gender distinctions.[135] Thus, biblical scholars could not work out a scenario in which this Roman rite could in any way clarify Paul's arguments in 1 Cor 11:2–16. From the 1980s onwards, however, several scholars have attempted to demonstrate that Paul's concern in 1 Cor 11:2–16 is precisely with this Roman ritual of covering the head in worship. In this section, we will analyze the hypotheses that take Roman rituals as background to 1 Cor 11:2–16.

---

[133] Olshausen, *Biblical Commentary*, 173.

[134] E.g., Hodge, *An Exposition*, 207–8; Meyer, *Critical and Exegetical Handbook*, 319.

[135] E.g., Johannes Weiss, *Der erste Korintherbrief* (Göttingen: Vandenhoeck & Ruprecht, 1910), 268–69; Hans Lietzmann, *An die Korinther I/II* (Tübingen: J. C. B. Mohr (Paul Siebeck), 1949), 53.

1.6.1 Richard Oster

Richard Oster is credited as one of the first modern scholars to challenge this long-standing reluctance in scholarly circles to take Roman rituals seriously as background to 1 Cor 11:2–16. In his first article on the issue, Oster amasses an impressive catalogue of literary descriptions and archaeological depictions of Roman men and women performing religious rites while covered of the head with a garment. Oster explains that this ritual gesture of covering the head was known as *capite velato*, and that it was practiced by emperors, religious officials (such as priests and augurs), and common people (both men and women) alike.[136] According to Oster, this "gesture consisted of pulling part of one's garment or toga over the back of the head and then forward until it approached or covered the ears."[137] Oster further argues that archaeological finds demonstrate that this way of worshiping was also practiced in the Roman colony of Corinth during the first century CE, at a time when Roman culture, religion, and administration prevailed.[138] Based on this evidence, Oster claims that in 1 Cor 11:4, Paul must be addressing the ritual gesture of *capite velato*, which certain Christians of Roman background had continued to practice in the Christian congregation.[139] Oster's hypothesis ends here, however, as he does not explain how one should understand Paul's comments about women not to pray uncovered in light of *capite velato*. Thus, even though Oster provides a compelling reading of specifically 1 Cor 11:4, he does not explain how one should read the whole of 1 Cor 11:2–16 from this perspective.

1.6.2 Cynthia L. Thompson

Cynthia L. Thompson is another early pioneer for the view that the Roman ritual of wearing a garment over the head during sacrifices is the basis for Paul's concern in 1 Cor 11:4. In her work, Thompson examines artifacts unearthed specifically at the site of ancient (Roman) Corinth which depict the heads of men and women. Thompson discusses the different hairstyles and head-coverings portrayed on the discovered coins, statues, and statuettes. Among other things, Thompson notes that two statues—one of Augustus, who is in the pose of a sacrificer, and one of Nero (of which only the head survives)—appear with the toga drawn over the

---

[136] Richard Oster, "When Men Wore Veils to Worship: The Historical Context of 1 Corinthians 11.4," *NTS* 34 (1988): 493–502.
[137] Oster, "When Men Wore Veils," 496.
[138] Oster, "When Men Wore Veils," 488–93, 496.
[139] Oster, "When Men Wore Veils," 504–5.

head.[140] Thompson then suggests that Paul's admonition in 1 Cor 11:4 for men not to pray or prophesy with covered heads "fits the context of shunning the worship of idols," of which *capite velato* was a visible symbol.[141] As far as portraits of women are concerned, Thompson observes that most women are depicted without head-coverings (such as mantles or veils), and with various hairstyles.[142] In light of this, Thompson is not entirely sure as to why Paul in 1 Cor 11:2–16 would have wanted the Corinthian Christian women to be covered of the head, given that the local archaeological finds do not indicate that it was a widespread custom at the time. Thompson speculates that Paul may have been influenced by the mores of Asia Minor (particularly Tarsus), Syria, Arabia, or Judea, which appear to have been, by some estimations, more conservative regarding women's appearances than Roman customs.[143] Like Oster, however, Thompson does not delve further into the broader implications of her hypothesis in interpreting 1 Cor 11:2–16 as a whole.

1.6.3 David W. J. Gill

In his take on 1 Cor 11:2–16, David Gill responds directly to Thompson's hypothesis regarding 1 Cor 11:4. While Gill agrees with Thompson that *capite velato* is behind 1 Cor 11:4, he disagrees with the idea that Paul's admonition for men not to pray or prophesy with covered heads is related to shunning idol worship.[144] Gill suggests instead that *capite velato* was a symbolism of the elite, and thus in 1 Cor 11:4, Paul responds to a situation in the Corinthian congregation in which "the social elite within the church ... were adopting a form of dress during worship which drew attention to their status in society."[145] Gill is less certain, however, about what Paul addresses in 1 Cor 11:5. He notes that elite Roman women also participated in Roman worship *capite velato*, so Paul in 1 Cor 11:5 must have had a

---

[140] Cynthia L. Thompson, "Hairstyles, Head-Coverings, and St. Paul: Portraits from Roman Corinth," *BA* 51 (1988): 101, 103.

[141] Thompson, "Hairstyles," 104.

[142] Thompson, "Hairstyles," 107–111.

[143] Thompson, "Hairstyles," 112–13.

[144] David W. J. Gill, "The Importance of Roman Portraiture for Head-Coverings in 1 Corinthians 11:2–16," *TynBul* 41 (1990): 251.

[145] Gill, "The Importance of Roman Portraiture," 250. Daniel Röthlisberger offers essentially the same hypothesis regarding the meaning of 1 Cor 11:4. Daniel Röthlisberger, "Die *capitis velatio* von Männern und ihre Bedeutung für 1 Cor. 11,4," *JAC* 55 (2012): 47–71. However, Röthlisberger makes no effort to interpret the rest of 1 Cor 11:2–16 in light of *capite velato* nor does he offer an explanation regarding Paul's statements concerning the behavior of the Corinthian women and so I will not discuss his work here separately.

different head-covering practice in mind for women, since it would not make much sense for Paul to ask men not to pray and prophesy *capite velato* but demand women to do so.[146] Yet, Gill struggles to explain what that head-covering for women was without which they brought shame on their husbands during praying and prophesying, and he is also unsure as to why they would have wanted to remove it in the first place.[147] Despite these uncertainties, Gill concludes with a suggestion that Paul in 1 Cor 11:2–16 most likely wished women "to continue to place a high value on marriage" and thus admonished them not to "flout social conventions in the church meeting."[148]

1.6.4 Ben Witherington III

In his treatment of 1 Cor 11:2–16, Ben Witherington III seeks to answer this most pressing question that scholars who take *capite velato* as background of 1 Cor 11:2–16 have struggled to answer: "Why does Paul want to maintain for women, but not for men, the Roman practice of covering the head when engaging in a religious act?"[149] In his own answer, Witherington suggests that the Corinthians were entangled in a complex conflict over the issue of head-coverings, as beside *capite velato* there were other influences at play such as certain Jewish customs and certain mystery cults. According to Witherington, then, Paul's goal in 1 Cor 11:2–16 was for the Corinthian Christians "to model new Christian customs, common in the assemblies of God but uncommon in the culture."[150] In other words, Witherington proposes that Paul was less concerned about what other cultures and forms of religion prescribed in terms of the appearances of the head, and more concerned that Christians be unique in their identity. Thus, the head-covering customs Paul introduced to the congregation were intended to stand out against the practices of the wider society.[151]

1.6.5 Bruce W. Winter

Bruce Winter closely follows Gill in arguing that 1 Cor 11:4 addresses men of the social elite in the Christian congregation who were covering their heads "after the

---

[146] Gill, "The Importance of Roman Portraiture," 252–53.
[147] Gill, "The Importance of Roman Portraiture," 253–56.
[148] Gill, "The Importance of Roman Portraiture," 260.
[149] Ben Witherington III, *Conflict and Community in Corinth: A Socio-Rhetorical Commentary on 1 and 2 Corinthians* (Grand Rapids: Eerdmans, 1995), 235.
[150] Witherington III, *Conflict and Community*, 235–36.
[151] Witherington III, *Conflict and Community*, 236–40.

manner of the pagan priests" whenever they prayed or prophesied, in order to draw attention to their social status.[152] In regards to the behavior of women in the Corinthian congregation, however, Winter suggests that Paul was concerned specifically with married women removing their (marriage) veils.[153] According to Winter, the married Corinthian Christian women had begun removing their veils during praying and prophesying to likewise draw attention to their social status, since disregarding marriage and its symbolism (i.e., "the veil") is what the so-called "'new' elite Roman women" were doing in the society at the time.[154] In 1 Cor 11:2–16, therefore, Paul was concerned about the dishonor this behavior brought on these women's husbands, and about the congregation's reputation in the eyes of the government which had implemented laws to curb such behavior, and whose spies frequented the Christian meetings (Winter reads "angels" in 1 Cor 11:10 as "messengers," see section 5.4.4).[155]

1.6.6 Mark Finney

Mark Finney is also of the opinion that 1 Cor 11:4 addresses the Roman ritual gesture of *capite velato*. Finney argues that at the time of Paul, it was a requirement for those Roman men taking an active and leading part in worship to cover their heads with a garment, while outside of liturgical settings, covering the head with a garment was optional.[156] Finney suggests, then, that after Paul left Corinth, some new members of Roman background joined the Christian congregation and continued to pray and prophesy there in a manner of leading men in society, which caused a conflict over social status. Thus, according to Finney, Paul's goal regarding the behavior of men in 1 Cor 11:2–16 was twofold: to discourage certain members from acting as social superiors and to dissuade them from practicing customs associated with idol worship.[157] In regards to women's head-coverings, however, Finney suggests that while the Greco-Roman women at the time were required to

---

[152] Bruce W. Winter, *After Paul Left Corinth: The Influence of Secular Ethics and Social Change* (Grand Rapids: Eerdmans, 2001), 121–23, 139–40.

[153] Winter, *After Paul Left Corinth*, 126–27.

[154] Winter, *After Paul Left Corinth*, 123–30, 140.

[155] Winter, *After Paul Left Corinth*, 133–38, 140. The above hypothesis regarding the Corinthian situation that 1 Cor 11:2–16 addresses is in its essentials reproduced in Bruce W. Winter, *Roman Wives, Roman Widows: The Appearance of New Women and the Pauline Communities* (Grand Rapids: Eerdmans, 2003), 77–96.

[156] Mark Finney, "Honour, Head-coverings and Headship: 1 Corinthians 11.2–16 in its Social Context," *JSNT* 33 (2010): 37, 41.

[157] Finney, "Honour," 45–48.

be covered of the head in social settings, they had the option to be uncovered in liturgical settings, particularly if in their own homes.¹⁵⁸ Thus, Finney proposes that the situation regarding the women of the Corinthian congregation that 1 Cor 11:2–16 addresses may have involved the new female members who, seeing that the male neophytes continued to participate in the Christian worship in a Roman manner, wished to uncover during praying and prophesying to also appear in a manner they had been used to in liturgical settings (particularly if in a home setting).¹⁵⁹ Paul, however, found such an appearance on a woman dishonorable, because in the Christian congregation she was in the presence of non-kin, thus violating the agreed-upon social norms with her uncovered head.¹⁶⁰ Finney concludes, then, that in 1 Cor 11:2–16, Paul "is attempting to establish a radical new perspective for male worshippers yet demand a traditional one for women."¹⁶¹

1.6.7 Cynthia Long Westfall

In Cynthia Long Westfall's interpretation of 1 Cor 11:2–16, *capite velato* also plays a role, though not as central as in the readings of the scholars mentioned above. Rather, the two main premises that Westfall works with are the following: a) the Middle Assyrian Laws (from around the 11th century BCE¹⁶²) required most women to cover their heads in public, but prohibited prostitutes, slaves, and freedwomen from doing so, and these laws still influenced women's behavior in first-century Corinth; and b) in most ancient and modern veiling cultures, it is men, not women, who set the rules concerning what constitutes appropriate female appearance.¹⁶³ Based on these premises, Westfall suggests two possible (not mutually exclusive) scenarios that may have prompted Paul to pen 1 Cor 11:2–16: a) Paul had earlier prohibited men from worshiping with a covered head in the Roman manner, which led these Christian men to demand that the Christian women follow the same rule; and b) influential Corinthian Christian men prevented women of lower social classes from veiling—despite these women's wishes to do so—in order to maintain social hierarchy or perhaps in order for these women to continue to

---

¹⁵⁸ Finney, "Honour," 36, 41, 45.
¹⁵⁹ Finney, "Honour," 49.
¹⁶⁰ Finney, "Honour," 50–52.
¹⁶¹ Finney, "Honour," 53.
¹⁶² For dating and contents, see, Martha T. Roth, "Women and Law," in *Women in the Ancient Near East: A Sourcebook*, ed. Mark Chavalas (New York: Routledge, 2014), 158–70.
¹⁶³ Westfall, *Paul and Gender*, 26–29.

show that they were sexually available as, according to Westfall, an uncovered head on a woman was at the time a sign of sexual availability.[164]

Westfall argues that the language of 1 Cor 11:2–16 itself demonstrates that, whatever the exact trouble in Corinth, the instigators were men, not women. She points out, for example, that the most natural meaning of the phrase ὀφείλει ἡ γυνὴ ἐξουσίαν ἔχειν ἐπὶ τῆς κεφαλῆς ("the woman ought to have authority over the head") in 1 Cor 11:10 is that a woman should have the freedom to choose herself how to display her head. Thus, this phrase would only be intelligible in the context of 1 Cor 11:2–16 if certain men were preventing women from exercising that freedom.[165] Westfall further observes that in the phrase εἰ δέ τις δοκεῖ φιλόνεικος εἶναι ("if anyone is determined to be contentious") in 1 Cor 11:16, the adjective φιλόνεικος is in the masculine form, and while this adjective could theoretically refer to a group consisting of both men and women, it would be an odd choice if Paul considered only women to be in opposition on the issue of head-coverings.[166] Westfall concludes, then, that Paul's objective in 1 Cor 11:2–16 was to equalize social relationships in the congregation by allowing all women to cover their heads, contrary to the wishes and arguments of some influential male members.[167]

1.6.8 Analysis

The scholars discussed in this section share the belief that 1 Cor 11:4 refers to the Roman practice of covering the head with a garment during certain devotional acts.[168] However, there are some differences of opinion as to why Paul would have found it problematic. Thompson suggests, for example, that Paul was concerned with idol worship, while Gill and Winter argue that the issue was rather that certain members behaved as social superiors. Finney, for his part, posits that Paul addressed both of these concerns. These differences of opinion notwithstanding, the

---

[164] Westfall, *Paul and Gender*, 31–34.
[165] Westfall, *Paul and Gender*, 34–36.
[166] Westfall, *Paul and Gender*, 36–37.
[167] Westfall, *Paul and Gender*, 43–44.
[168] Preston T. Massey has more recently argued for this position as well. However, in his work on the passage, Massey does not formulate a singular hypothesis as to what may have been going on in the Corinthian congregation that prompted Paul's response in 1 Cor 11:2–16. Instead, based on some ancient literary descriptions of Roman head-coverings, Massey lists five possible reasons why Paul may have associated a covered head on a man with shame in 1 Cor 11:4. Preston T. Massey, "Veiling among Men in Roman Corinth: 1 Corinthians 11:4 and the Potential Problem of East Meeting West," *JBL* 137 (2018): 501–17. I will engage with some of Massey's suggestions in Chapter 2.

1.6 Roman Rites as Background to 1 Cor 11:2–16

above scholars have not had to strain too hard to demonstrate linguistic and conceptual links between *capite velato* and 1 Cor 11:4. However, confusion reigns when attempts are made to connect *capite velato* with the rest of 1 Cor 11:2–16, particularly with verse 5. As several of the above scholars note, *capite velato* was also practiced by Roman women, making it difficult to envision a scenario in which Paul would demand of the Corinthian Christian men to cease praying and prophesying *capite velato* while requiring women to continue doing so. Thus, several of these scholars suggest that the problem with the Corinthian Christian women was something other than *capite velato*. As discussed, Thompson thinks that certain conservative cultural norms more familiar to Paul may have influenced his instructions concerning women; Witherington adds that certain mystery cults may have also played a role; Winter believes that in the case of women, Paul was concerned with the removal of the marriage veil; and Westfall relies on the Middle Assyrian Laws to argue that Paul addressed the cultural inequality that allowed only some women in Corinth to veil.

These suggestions regarding the behavior of women in the Corinthian Christian congregation prove unsatisfactory, however. We simply cannot rely on the Middle Assyrian Laws to inform us about the behavior and appearance of women in first-century Corinth, especially as contradictory evidence is available from a much closer time period and location (e.g., Thompson's review of the archaeological finds from Corinth). We also have no evidence that Roman matrons made use of a specific piece of clothing called a "marriage veil," as Winter would have us believe. While Roman brides indeed covered their heads during their weddings,[169] this covering was not known as a marriage veil that was then worn for the duration of the marriage.[170] We do have some evidence that certain cultures may have been more conservative regarding women's head-coverings, as Thompson notes, but

---

[169] Most infamously, the emperor Nero, according to Tacitus (ca. 56–120 CE), publicly wed a man named Pythagoras while wearing the bridal veil for the occasion, signifying his role as the bride in this relationship: "Nero himself, defiled by every natural and unnatural lust had left no abomination in reserve with which to crown his vicious existence; except that, a few days later, he became, with the full rites of legitimate marriage, the wife of one of that herd of degenerates, who bore the name of Pythagoras. The veil was drawn over the imperial head (*inditum imperatori flanimeum*), witnesses were despatched to the scene; the dowry, the couch of wedded love, the nuptial torches, were there: everything, in fine, which night enshrouds even if a woman is the bride, was left open to the view" (*Ann.* 15.37 [Jackson]). There is no indication that Nero continued to wear this veil as a sign of his marriage beyond the ceremony.

[170] For criticism of Winter's thesis as a whole see, Preston T. Massey, "Is There a Case for Elite Roman 'New Women' Causing Division at Corinth?" *RB* 118 (2011): 76–93.

this does not explain 1 Cor 11:2–16 in light of *capite velato*: for what purpose would the Christian women flout the social norms dear to Paul by *uncovering* their heads during praying and prophesying in response to the Christian men *covering* their heads at the same time because of some Roman rites? This remains unexplained.

Finney is the only scholar to recognize this shortcoming and he has attempted to provide a reading of 1 Cor 11:2–16 in which Paul's instructions to both men and women pertain to *capite velato*. As discussed above, Finney's proposed solution suggests that while it was a requirement for Roman men to cover their heads in liturgical settings, it was optional for women, especially if in their own homes. Thus, according to Finney, 1 Cor 11:2–16 addresses a situation in which the Christians of Roman background continued to behave in Christian worship as they had in Roman worship—men with covered heads and women with uncovered heads. This argument does not align with the evidence, however. Finney points to certain ancient depictions of sacrificial scenes in which some women are portrayed with covered heads and others with uncovered heads as proof that it was optional for women to be covered in liturgical settings. However, he overlooks that in these same scenes, the same is true of men as well—some are covered of the head, and some are not (see Chapter 2). Thus, we cannot claim based on these depictions alone that *capite velato* was a requirement for men but optional for women. If some men and some women are portrayed *capite velato* in these scenes, but other men and other women are not, then the dividing line cannot be gender, but must be something else.

Given the challenges that the above scholars face in trying to make *capite velato* fit with the whole of 1 Cor 11:2–16—not just with 1 Cor 11:4—many biblical scholars remain skeptical about the relevance of *capite velato* to this passage, despite the efforts of Oster and others to prove otherwise.[171] Yet, there is no denying the strong linguistic and conceptual link between *capite velato* and 1 Cor 11:4. For instance, the phrase κατὰ κεφαλῆς ἔχων is an apt description of *capite velato* and was used by ancient authors to describe this ritual gesture (see Chapter 2). Furthermore, *capite velato* only accompanied certain Roman rites such as prayer and divination, which may explain why Paul's concern with head-coverings is only in the context of praying and prophesying and not otherwise. In balance, therefore, the *capite velato* hypothesis has clear strengths that make it a more attractive option as background to 1 Cor 11:2–16 than the other suggestions discussed in this chapter. The challenge is

---

[171] E.g., Keener, *Paul, Women and Wives*, 28; Gielen, "Beten und Prophezeien," 225–26; Fitzmyer, *First Corinthians*, 412; Jerome Murphy-O'Connor, *Keys to First Corinthians: Revisiting the Major Issues* (Oxford: Oxford University Press, 2009), 171–75.

to find a solution that satisfies Paul's argument concerning both men and women in relation to *capite velato* without straining the available evidence. This is where Westfall's undeveloped hypothesis—that some Christian men (of Roman background) may have wished to remove certain head-coverings from Christian women during praying and prophesying in response to Paul's ban on *capite velato*—offers a possible way forward,[172] if it can be shown that there was a reason for Paul to ban *capite velato* in the first place and that there were certain head-coverings which the Christian women wished to keep on during praying and prophesying. These are the lines of inquiry that the remainder of this thesis will explore.

1.7 Conclusion

In the above assessment of the various hypotheses regarding the customs Paul addresses in 1 Cor 11:2–16, I have highlighted two main problems: the disregard or misrepresentation of the available evidence concerning the appearances of men's and women's heads in the relevant time period in antiquity, and the inattentiveness to or misapprehension of Paul's language and grammar in 1 Cor 11:4–5. In particular, I have argued that there is little evidence to suggest that Paul's concern in this text relates to certain Jewish customs, and I have also questioned the relevance of ancient descriptions of mystery cults to 1 Cor 11:2–16. Furthermore, I have highlighted the confusion in biblical scholarship in regards to whether, and to what extent, ancient women of any culture covered their heads. This uncertainty demonstrates that the available evidence concerning this issue is not as straightforward as some have argued it to be, whether in favor of the position that all women at the time wore head-coverings, or that women in general did not wear head-coverings. Concerning Paul's language and grammar in this passage, I have demonstrated that 1 Cor 11:4–5 cannot be read as reference to long hair, disheveled hair, or short hair. I have also challenged the dominant scholarly view that Paul's only real concern in 1 Cor 11:2–16 is with the behavior of women by pointing out that Paul's argument regarding men is as complete as that about women, and that there are no clear clues in the text itself to suggest that only women were causing a problem in relation to head-coverings in the Corinthian congregation. And finally,

---

[172] In fact, this is a suggestion I advanced in my master's thesis independently of Westfall (her book came out after my graduation). Aldar Nõmmik, "'Is It Proper for an 'Uncovered' Woman to Pray to God?' (1 Cor 11:13): A Socio-Historical and Exegetical Examination of 1 Cor 11:2–16" (MTh diss., The University of Edinburgh, 2016), 26–27. However, this question was not the main focus of my thesis and so I likewise made the suggestion in passing.

I have shown that several of the above hypotheses fail to adequately take into account the contexts in which Paul found the covering or uncovering of the head to be problematic—namely, praying and prophesying.

That being said, I have suggested that the hypothesis which takes the Roman ritual gesture of *capite velato* as background to 1 Cor 11:2–16 has the strongest evidence to support it and aligns best with Paul's language in 1 Cor 11:4–5. The literary and archaeological evidence which shows that Roman men and women throughout the empire in the first century CE covered their heads in certain liturgical settings (such as during praying) is abundant. Furthermore, in several instances in the ancient literature, this ritual pose is described with the same grammatical construct as we find in 1 Cor 11:4. However, the *capite velato* hypothesis faces several challenges, none bigger than the issue of why Paul would find this ritual gesture problematic for men but not so for women. In order to be in a better position to answer this question, we must carefully examine the literary and archaeological evidence describing and depicting *capite velato*, since at least some of the problems with the above *capite velato* hypotheses stem from a lack of familiarity with the available evidence.

2. Having a Garment Down from the Head

Ancient Descriptions and Depictions of *capite velato*

I concluded the previous chapter with a suggestion that of the various theories advanced regarding the customs that Paul addresses in 1 Cor 11:2–16, the *capite velato* hypothesis has the strongest evidence to support it and best aligns with Paul's language and grammar of 1 Cor 11:4 in particular. In this chapter I take a closer look at the available evidence for *capite velato*. In biblical scholarship, Richard Oster's 1988 study remains the most comprehensive overview of the evidence for this ritual gesture (see section 1.6.1). Yet, the primary evidence Oster presents is mainly buried in his footnotes—he quotes only two ancient descriptions of *capite velato* in the main body of his article and offers no photographic evidence for it. Other biblical scholars who have followed Oster's thesis, such as David Gill (see section 1.6.3), Bruce Winter (see section 1.6.5), and Mark Finney (see section 1.6.6), have highlighted certain conclusions of Oster and drawn attention to one or another of the ancient descriptions or depictions of *capite velato*, but have not conducted an in-depth study of the available evidence. This lack of comprehensive analysis in biblical scholarship of *capite velato* has given rise to certain misconceptions about what *capite velato* is, when and why it was practiced, and who practiced it. In the following pages, I present all the literary descriptions of *capite velato* that I have been able to find, along with a sizable collection of images depicting this ritual gesture on altars, friezes, walls, statues, and monuments, in order to provide greater clarity on *capite velato*.

I begin my presentation with some preliminary remarks about what the Latin phrase *capite velato* represents in modern scholarship. I then present and analyze the various literary references to *capite velato*, as well as a selection of depictions of it from the first two centuries following Augustus's religious reforms. The evidence I present here demonstrates that *capite velato* was widespread at the time of

Paul, both geographically and across social strata. This ritual gesture was practiced by public figures and private individuals, both men and women, mainly in the context of prayer, sacrifice, and divination, throughout the empire for several centuries. Most importantly for 1 Cor 11:2–16, *capite velato* was conspicuously present in visual form in the center of Corinth in the middle of the first century CE, and the Greek descriptions of this ritual gesture closely align with Paul's language and grammar in 1 Cor 11:4.

2.1 What Do We Mean by *capite velato*?

Capite velato basically means "with covered head" in Latin, and so the phrase can be used to describe any appearance of the head that has some form of a covering on it. Modern scholars, however, have used *capite velato* as a shorthand for a particular ritual gesture (or ritual appearance) to distinguish it from other practices and appearances related to head-coverings, even though in the ancient literary sources, this ritual gesture is also described in other ways than strictly *capite velato* (the exact phrase *capite velato* appears only a handful of times). Ignorance of this crucial point can lead to confusion about what we mean when we speak of *capite velato*. Thus, before I present the literary entries concerning this ritual gesture which modern scholarship knows as *capite velato*, some preliminary remarks are in order that help us distinguish this head-covering practice from other Roman customs related to head-coverings.

2.1.1 The Outer Garment as Head-Covering

First-century Romans, like many other ancients, had a number of different head-covering options available to them. However, some head-coverings were only allowed to be worn by certain individuals and some were restricted to only certain contexts. For example, the *flamens* (Roman priests) wore specific types of caps, and the high priest of Jupiter, *flamen Dialis*, was never allowed to appear without a white cap peculiar to his office (e.g., Aulus Gellius, *Noct. att.* 10.15; Plutarch, *Marc.* 5.4). Soldiers wore different types of crowns specific to their rank or role (e.g., Aulus Gellius, *Noct. att.* 5.6), and there is some evidence that slaves had to wear certain caps when being auctioned off (Aulus Gellius, *Noct. att.* 6.4). A freed slave, on the other hand, was presented with a head-covering known as the (Roman) *pileus* (e.g., Plutarch, *Flam.* 13.6), and Suetonius describes, for example, how upon the death of Nero, the people of Rome donned these "liberty-caps" (*pilleata*) and ran around the city with joy, thus exhibiting their newfound freedom

2.1 What Do We Mean by capite velato?

from tyranny (*Nero* 57.1).[1] It was also common for Romans to wear garlands during sacrificial ceremonies (e.g., Plutarch, *Cam.* 42.5; Suetonius, *Galb.* 18.3), while laurel wreaths were worn by victorious generals during triumphs—a practice attributed to Romulus, the mythic founder of Rome (e.g., Plutarch, *Rom.* 16.6; Ovid, *Metam.* 1.558–560).[2] The twelve members of the college of Arval Brothers, on the other hand, wore garlands composed of wheat ears and white fillets as a sign of their priesthood (e.g., Pliny the Elder, *Nat.* 18.2 [6]; Aulus Gellius, *Noct. att.* 7.7; see also section 2.6.2).

This list of different head-coverings available to certain Roman individuals or used in certain contexts could be extended further, but modern scholarly shorthand of *capite velato* refers to none of such head-covering practices—or rather, biblical scholars should not confuse any of the above listed head-covering customs with the technical sense of *capite velato*.[3] What modern scholars have in mind (or should have in mind) by using *capite velato* is a head-covering that was essentially available to everyone at nearly all times, but which took on special significance only in association with certain rituals—the outer garment. Plutarch's observation regarding the Roman customs associated with the outer garment as a head-covering is an apt illustration of this here:

> Διὰ τί τοὺς θεοὺς προσκυνοῦντες ἐπικαλύπτονται τὴν κεφαλήν, τῶν δ' ἀνθρώπων τοῖς ἀξίοις τιμῆς ἀπαντῶντες, κἂν τύχωσιν ἐπὶ τῆς κεφαλῆς ἔχοντες τὸ ἱμάτιον, ἀποκαλύπτονται;
> (*Quaest. rom.* 6 [266c])
>
> Why do they [the Romans] cover the head when they worship the gods, but when they meet those among men deserving honor and happen to have a garment upon the head, they uncover?

Plutarch, a Greek writer and philosopher who lived ca. 46–119 CE, traveled to Rome and other parts of Italy, where he received Roman citizenship and formed

---

[1] According to Isabella Benda-Weber, certain *pilleata* were also regularly worn by Roman sailors, fishermen, and craftsmen. Isabella Benda-Weber, "Non-Greek Headdresses in the Greek East," in *Tiarae, Diadems and Headdresses in the Ancient Mediterranean Cultures: Symbolism and Technology*, ed. Carmen Alfaro Giner, Jónatan Ortiz García, and María Antón Peset (Valencia: SEMA, 2014), 109.

[2] According to Suetonius, the emperor Tiberius also wore a laurel wreath during thunderstorms, believing that this head-covering would protect him from harm (Suetonius, *Tib.* 69.1), but this particular use of laurel wreaths does not seem to have been a common practice.

[3] In Daniel Röthlisberger's study on *capite velato* as background of 1 Cor 11:4, for example, this distinction between *capite velato* proper and other types of Roman head-covering customs is not maintained, which leads to considerable confusion regarding the relevance of *capite velato* for interpreting of 1 Cor 11:2–16. See, Röthlisberger, "Die *capitis velatio*," 52–62.

friendships with Romans of high status. Some of these friends even followed Plutarch back to his native land upon his return there.[4] Thus, Plutarch had an interested observer's perspective on Roman customs. As noted, one of the things that piqued Plutarch's interest was that Romans would take off the garment from the head (if they had it on) when meeting a person of honor, but would place the garment on the head when worshiping the gods. It is this latter practice—covering the head with a garment "towards the gods" (τὸ πρὸς τοὺς θεούς, Plutarch, *Quaest rom.* 6 [266c])—and only this that modern scholarship has in mind (or should have in mind) with the phrase *capite velato*.

However, before we get into examples of *capite velato* in ancient literature, a bit more needs to be said here in regards to the covering of the head with a garment outside of such contexts which Plutarch deems "worship." It is important to note, for example, that it seems that it was more common for women to cover their heads with a garment than for men to do so (e.g., Plutarch, *Quaest. rom.* 14 [267a–b]), but since we will deal with women's head-covering practices in Chapter 5, here we will focus on mainly why Roman men might have needed or wanted to cover their heads with the outer garment outside of liturgical settings. That it was fairly common for Roman men to have a garment over the head as they went about their day is suggested by Plutarch's above observation that they were expected to remove it in the presence of more honorable individuals. We find further support for this custom in the Roman historian Sallust, who reports that the only person in whose presence the Roman general Sulla uncovered his head (*caput aperire*) was Pompey (*Hist.* 5.16). Plutarch adds that this act of Sulla's—τῆς κεφαλῆς ἀπάγοντος τὸ ἱμάτιον (*Pomp.* 8.2–3); κεφαλὴν ἀποκαλύπτεσθαι (*Crass.* 6.4)—was all the more remarkable since Pompey was Sulla's junior and there were other persons of rank and honor present. In contrast, another acquaintance of Pompey, Demetrius, failed to remove his garment even for Pompey. Plutarch describes how Demetrius would not wait for anyone at the banquet thrown by Pompey, but would lie down on the couch even before the host had done so, leaving his garment hanging off his head and over his ears (ἔχων δι' ὤτων κατὰ τῆς κεφαλῆς τὸ ἱμάτιον[5]), removing it for no one (Plutarch, *Pomp.* 40.4). This expectation to uncover one's head in the presence of social superiors seems to have persisted well into the first century CE, as evidenced by Pliny the Elder's comment that the custom of uncovering the head (*capita aperiri*) in the presence of magistrates was instituted not for the sake of

---

[4] Albrecht Dihle, *Greek and Latin Literature of the Roman Empire: From Augustus to Justinian*, trans. Manfred Malzahn (New York: Routledge, 1994), 188.

[5] Notice the grammatical construct here which closely corresponds to 1 Cor 11:4.

showing respect but for the sake of health, since uncovering the head was thought to strengthen it (*Nat.* 28.17 [60]). But regardless of the rationale, the above entries demonstrate that it was not uncommon for men to have a garment over the head, even indoors, and it was only considered rude if one did not remove it upon meeting an honorable person.

It appears that the outer garment may have been especially handy as a protective head-covering against adverse weather conditions such as heat, cold, rain, or snow.[6] Those men who never covered their heads, regardless of the weather, were held in legendary status. Thus, Cicero reports with awe how a certain Masinissa, at ninety years of age, refused to cover his head even in the cold or in the rain (*nullo imbri, nullo frigore adduci ut capite operto sit, Sen.* 10 [34]). Plutarch similarly marvels at how Cato the Younger remained bareheaded even in the heat and in a snowstorm (καὶ καύματα καὶ νιφετὸν ἀκαλύπτῳ κεφαλῇ, *Cat. Min.* 5.3). And Suetonius describes how Julius Caesar would lead the army bareheaded whether in the sun or in the rain (*capite detecto, seu sol seu imber esset, Jul.* 57.1). These examples suggest that it was generally expected for men to cover their heads at least when weather conditions called for it and an uncovered head in the heat, rain, or cold seems to have been an unexpected and noteworthy sight.[7]

Another well-attested reason Roman men covered their heads particularly with the outer garment was the need to conceal one's identity from onlookers. According to Suetonius, Nero did so to escape notice when fleeing for his life (*paenulam obsoleti coloris superinduit adopertoque capite*—"he put on a cloak of faded color and covered his head," *Nero* 48.1), and Julius Caesar did so to go undetected by enemies when at war (*obvoluto capite conscendit, neque aut quis esset ante detexit*—"he boarded with a covered head, without revealing his identity," *Jul.* 58.2). In Plutarch's recounting of the deeds of Scipio the Younger, this Roman general also covered his head with a garment (κατὰ τῆς κεφαλῆς ἔχων τὸ ἱμάτιον[8]) to conceal his identity during a visit to Alexandria (*Reg. imp. apophth.* 13 [200f]). Similarly, Livy describes how a certain Appius covered his head (*capite obvoluto*) and

---

[6] See, for example, Elaine Fantham, "Covering the Head at Rome: Ritual and Gender," in *Roman Dress and the Fabrics of Roman Culture*, ed. Jonathan Edmonson and Alison Keith (Toronto: Toronto University Press, 2008), 160.

[7] This is not to say that the outer garment was the only available head-covering for protection against the elements. Suetonius reports, for example, that Augustus could not endure the sun even in the winter and thus always wore a cap (*petasatus*), whether outdoors or indoors (*Aug.* 82.1). However, it seems that the outer garment was the most common head-covering for this purpose since it was available nearly at all times.

[8] Notice again the grammatical construct here which closely resembles 1 Cor 11:4.

hid in a house near the Forum when a crowd turned against him (*Ab urbe cond.* 3.49.5), and covering the head for the purpose of concealment of identity seems also to be described in Plutarch's recounting of the adventures of Marcius Coriolanus (καὶ τὴν κεφαλὴν ἐγκαλυψάμενος, *Cor.* 23.1–2). From these and other such entries, it appears that covering the head with a garment must have been common enough sight in antiquity so that individuals who wanted to hide their identity could do so without drawing undue attention by wearing a garment over the head.

There is also evidence that the Romans covered their heads when they were about to die, a custom believed to have ancient roots. For example, Livy reports that in the seventh century BCE, a war hero by the name of Horatius killed his sister on his return from battle and was sentenced to death for his crime. He was to have his head covered (*caput obnubito*) before being tied to a tree and beaten (*Ab urbe cond.* 1.26.6). However, Horatius successfully appealed his sentence with the help of his father on the count of his heroics in battle, and was acquitted. Horatius's father was then tasked with making atonement for his son's error, and so he offered expiatory sacrifices, set up a beam across the street, and made Horatius walk under it with a covered head (*capite adoperto, Ab urbe cond.* 1.26.13). It seems that Horatius performed this ritual as a substitute for actually dying with a covered head. Livy also reports that due to a period of political and economic crisis in the middle of the fifth century BCE, many Romans lost hope and, having first covered their heads (*capitibus obvolutis*), committed suicide by jumping into the river Tiber (*Ab urbe cond.* 4.12.10–11).

The most famous scene of covering the head with a garment in the face of death, however, is the murder of Julius Caesar, which finds mention in several ancient authors. Plutarch, for example, describes how Caesar, having seen Brutus hold a dagger, covered his head with the garment (τῷ ἱματίῳ τὴν κεφαλὴν ἐγκαλυψάμενος, *Brut.* 17.3; ἐφειλκύσατο κατὰ τῆς κεφαλῆς τὸ ἱμάτιον, *Caes.* 66.6) and stopped resisting the blows, resigning himself to his fate. Suetonius similarly recounts how Caesar covered his head with his toga (*toga caput obvolvit*) when he saw that he was surrounded by daggers, but that he also arranged the rest of his toga in a way that in his eventual fall the lower part of his body would remain covered (*Jul.* 82.2). And Dio Cassius reports that Julius Caesar covered himself (συνεκαλύψατο) when he realized that he was not able to fight off his attackers nor escape them (*Hist. Rom.* 42.4.5).[9]

---

[9] This custom of covering the head with an outer garment in the face of death may not have been peculiar to the Romans. Valerius Maximus reports, for example, that a certain foreign

2.1 What Do We Mean by capite velato?

A careful reader will have noticed that in none of the above Latin entries describing the garment as a head-covering is the verb *velare* used. Instead, verbs such as *operire, obvelare, obvolvere,* and *obnubere* are employed. This raises an intriguing possibility that the Latin authors were careful to distinguish between *capite velato* proper (i.e., the practice of covering the head with the garment in worship) and other head-covering practices that involved a garment. It may be, for example, that these other verbs for "to cover" more readily convey the idea of a disorderly concealment of the whole head—whether against adverse weather, for the sake of hiding one's identity, or in the face of death.[10] As will be demonstrated below, the concealment of the whole head was not sought after in *capite velato*. In ancient depictions of this ritual gesture, the facial features are clearly visible, and the garment seems to be neatly arranged so that part of the head and hair remain visible as well. This may suggest, then, that Latin authors used the verb *velare* in association with the word "head" in a slightly different way to its synonyms, but we must proceed cautiously with this assumption, since there is contrary evidence. For example, the exact phrase *capite velato* is used in contexts that do not align with what we mean by *capite velato* in a technical sense (e.g., Quintilian, *Inst.* 2.13.13, mentions covering the whole head as a sign of grief; and Livy, *Ab urbe cond.* 1.32.6, speaks of covering the head with a fillet).[11] Besides, Greek texts do not differentiate between

---

brigand by the name of Coma was caught and brought in for interrogation, but Coma covered his head (*caput operuit*), fell on his knees, and held his breath until he died (*Memorable Doings and Sayings* 9.12e.1).

[10] We may also add to this list of reasons why Romans covered their heads with a garment outside of liturgical settings Suetonius's mocking comment about Gaius Caligula that whenever Caligula heard even the slightest sound of thunder, he would shut his eyes and cover his head (*caput obvolvere*), and if the thunder continued, he would hide under the bed (*Cal.* 51.1). An interesting entry is also found in Aulus Gellius, who reports that he was once invited to a dinner in which a dispute arose between the Roman guests and a Latin scholar in regards to poems. At one point the Latin scholar announced that he was going to cover his head with his mantle (*operire pallio caput*), like Socrates had done when making immodest remarks. The scholar then laid down on the bench with his head covered (*capite convelato*) and chanted some verses of a poem (*Noct. att.* 19.9.9–11). It is difficult to tell what the purpose of covering the head with the mantle is here. Perhaps it was done out of shame at the immodesty of one's words, although how this relates to chanting of poems remains unclear.

[11] Also, Seneca uses the verb *velare* in association with "head" to describe someone covering the head with a cloak (*ut pallio velaretur caput*) "like a runaway rich man portrayed in a mime" (*non aliter quam in mimo fugitivi divitis solent*), suggesting that in this context, the purpose of *velare* of the head is not worship but concealment (*Ep.* 114.6).

the verbs or grammatical constructs they use when describing *capite velato* proper versus other uses of the garment as a head-covering.

Be that as it may, the bottom line here is that the evidence shows that it was common for Romans to cover their heads with a garment outside of liturgical settings, and we must not confuse these uses of the garment with *capite velato* proper, even though the appearances may have been similar. We distinguish *capite velato* from other head-covering customs as the specific practice of neatly placing the outer garment over the head during certain worshipful acts.

2.1.2 The Garment of *capite velato*

Before we demonstrate the specific worshipful acts that *capite velato* accompanied, we must also clarify what we mean by "the outer garment." In discussions about *capite velato* in biblical scholarship, the toga is often highlighted, the implication being that wearing the toga over the head communicated that the person was of status in the Roman society.[12] Indeed, the toga was an outer garment that only Roman citizens were allowed to wear, distinguishing them from non-citizens and foreigners.[13] The design of the toga varied slightly based on the age and status of the wearer. The *toga virilis* or the *toga pura*, worn by freeborn adult male Roman citizens, seems to have been wholly white in color.[14] The *toga praetexta*, on the other hand, was worn by the Roman boys and girls as well as by some important officials,[15] and featured a purple band along either the bottom or top edge of the

---

[12] E.g., Oster, "When Men Wore Veils," 496; Gill, "The Importance of Roman Portraiture," 246–48; Winter, *After Paul Left Corinth*, 121–23; Massey, "Veiling among Men in Roman Corinth," 504, 512–14.

[13] In some sense, "outer garment" may be a misnomer here. While it was expected that a Roman man would wear something underneath the toga—most commonly a tunic or tunics—there is evidence that it could also be worn without any undergarment. Furthermore, other garments could be worn over the toga, particularly in cases of foul weather. See, Kelly Olson, *Masculinity and Dress in Roman Antiquity* (New York: Routledge, 2017), 16, 71. However, *ideally*, the toga was the outermost garment of a Roman man.

[14] Fanny Dolansky, "*Togam Virilem Sumere*: Coming of Age in the Roman World," in *Roman Dress and the Fabrics of Roman Culture*, ed. Jonathan Edmonson and Alison Keith (Toronto: Toronto University Press, 2008), 50. The formal assumption of the *toga virilis*, which took place between the ages of thirteen and eighteen, was accompanied by certain private and public ceremonies. Olson, *Masculinity and Dress*, 48.

[15] Kelly Olson lists tribunes, aediles, praetors, consuls, consul designates, censors, *triumviri*, *vivomagistri*, *magistri* of *collegia*, magistrates of *coloniae*, emperors, augurs, *flamines*, *epulones*, Pontifex Maximus, and *quindecemviri* as those who had the right to wear the *toga praetexta* either at all times or during certain special occasions. Olson, *Masculinity and Dress*, 44.

garment[16] and was therefore known as the purple-bordered toga.[17] The *toga picta* of purple color and with gold stars was reserved solely for victorious military commanders during the triumphs.[18] Yet, all these different togas were loose at the top, allowing this excessive material, which otherwise rested on the shoulder (and on the hand, see figure 2.1 for an example), to be drawn over the head if necessary.[19]

Figure 2.1: A funerary statue of a man wearing a toga from the first half of the first century CE. Notice that the loose upper edge of the toga hangs over the shoulder and over the hand and could thus easily be drawn over the head if necessary. This statue is housed in Antiquarium di Pompeii.

---

[16] There is some debate about where on the *toga praetexta* the purple stripe was located as the evidence is inconclusive. Olson, *Masculinity and Dress*, 44–46.

[17] Dolansky, *"Togam Virilem Sumere,"* 53.

[18] Jonathan Edmonson, "Public Dress and Social Control in Late Republican and Early Imperial Rome," in *Roman Dress and the Fabrics of Roman Culture*, ed. Jonathan Edmonson and Alison Keith (Toronto: University of Toronto Press, 2008), 23, 33–36. See also, Olson, *Masculinity and Dress*, 49–50.

[19] Olson, *Masculinity and Dress*, 31.

However, it is not entirely clear that the toga was the only type of outer garment used for *capite velato*. It is important to note, for example, that the toga was not an everyday item of clothing. People generally wore cloaks of darker hues, and the toga was reserved for special occasions—such as for religious festivals, *salutatio* (the clients greeting their patrons in the mornings), and imperial banquets—and for certain places such as the Forum, the theatre, and the law-courts.[20] According to Suetonius, Augustus was especially strict in enforcing that Roman men appear in the Forum clad only in a toga (*Aug.* 40.5). Yet, these rules of decorum may not have been as rigidly followed. For example, Aulus Gellius reports in the second century CE that his teacher, Titus Castricius, once observed a group of his students of senatorial rank wearing tunics and (short) cloaks (*tunicis et lacernis*) on a holiday and advised them that he preferred they wear togas for the occasion, but if that was too much to ask, they should at least wear girded (long) cloaks (*cinctos saltem esse et paenulatos*, *Noct. att.* 13.22.1). This suggests that while the toga may have been idealized as a garment of Roman citizenship—and thus dominates depictions of emperors in the pose of *capite velato*, as we shall see below—it was not the only outer garment of choice even during special occasions.[21] Considering that other types of cloaks, such as the above-mentioned *lacerna* and *paenula*, could also be drawn over the head,[22] we must remain open to the possibility that in the more private settings (such as in one's home), but even in some public settings, Romans covered their heads in worship with an outer garment that was not necessarily the toga. This is of course especially true for Roman matrons, who did not wear a toga

---

[20] Edmonson, "Public Dress," 23–24; Olson, *Masculinity and Dress*, 53. According to Kelly Olson, the first-century Roman rhetorician Quintilian believed the toga also to be "the most appropriate garment for orating." Olson, *Masculinity and Dress*, 42.

[21] As Kelly Olson notes, dressing in a toga in a proper manner most likely required assistance, as it was difficult to put on and uncomfortable to wear. Olson, *Masculinity and Dress*, 24, 53. Thus, some may have preferred to avoid the effort whenever possible. Furthermore, togas were expensive, so not all Roman citizens were able to afford one. Olson, *Masculinity and Dress*, 52–53.

[22] Kelly Olson categorizes Roman outer garments into three broad types: a) "mantle"—"an outer garment draped around the body with no fastening," of which *pallium*, *abolla*, and *endromis* are examples; b) "cloak," which "at its simplest was a rectangle of cloth fastened by a separate brooch almost always on the right shoulder, leaving both hands free, and could be of any length," of which *sagum*, *chlamys*, *lacerna*, and *laena* are examples; and c) "cape" which "usually had a hood, and afforded better protection from the elements than a cloak," of which *bardocucullus* and *paenula* are examples. Olson, *Masculinity and Dress*, 68.

at all but instead a stola and a *palla*.²³ It is important to keep this in mind when examining entries on *capite velato* which do not specify the type of garment used—if "the toga" is always the default option, we may not get an accurate understanding of *capite velato*.

2.2 *Capite velato* in the Roman Epics and Histories

With the above points in mind, we are now in a position to examine the literary texts in which *capite velato* finds mention. We begin by considering works that focus on the distant past of the Roman people. The desire to trace the lineage of the Romans to time immemorial became especially acute in the reign of Augustus (31 BCE–14 CE), and many of the entries that place *capite velato* in the mythological past and early history of the Romans originate precisely from this time period.

2.2.1 *Capite velato* and Aeneas

In the last ten years of his life, the Roman poet Virgil (70–19 BCE) worked on composing a Roman epic at the commission of Augustus. Virgil died before he could finish the work, and his will stipulated that the unpublished work be burned, but Augustus disregarded this request and had the work published nonetheless.²⁴ As it happened, Virgil's *Aeneid* quickly became one of the most important works in Roman culture. It was added to the curriculum, and anyone exposed to Roman education in the first century CE must have thoroughly read it.²⁵ The *Aeneid* follows the story of the Trojan hero and mythological forefather of the Romans, Aeneas, but it is presented in a way that foreshadows the inevitability of the global reach of the Roman Empire, and its creation as divine will.²⁶ As such, the hero of the epic embodies the ideal citizen of imperial Rome as Michael von Albrecht comments: "The hero of the Aeneid is the noblest example of a type of

---

²³ Edmonson, "Public Dress," 24–25; Kelly Olson, *Dress and the Roman Woman: Self-Presentation and Society* (New York: Routledge, 2008), 25. Apparently, togas were worn by Roman prostitutes, which distinguished them from respectable women, but numerous other clothing options were also available to them, so we do not know how frequently Roman prostitutes were actually clad in togas. Olson, *Dress and the Roman Woman*, 47–50.

²⁴ Michael von Albrecht, *A History of Roman Literature: From Livius Andronicus to Boethius* (Leiden: Brill, 1997), 1:669.

²⁵ Dihle, *Greek and Latin Literature*, 113.

²⁶ Dihle, *Greek and Latin Literature*, 115.

man who, in less exalted guise—as an anxiously superstitious primitive or as a pedantic ritualist—must have been frequent in Rome."[27]

One of the more significant scenes in the *Aeneid* is Aeneas's first-ever sacrifice upon reaching the land of Italy. When Aeneas is still on the way to Italy, he meets a seer by the name of Helenus, who instructs Aeneas on how he must perform this first sacrifice of his in Italy:

> "Moreover, when your ships have anchored across the sea, and you set up altars and say prayers (*positis aris iam vota*) on the shore, cover the hair with a covering of a purple garment (*purpureo velare comas adopertus amictu*), so that you may not observe any hostile face in the midst of the holy fire in worship of the gods (*in honore deorum*) and thus spoil the omens (*omina*). This you and your companions should keep as a sacred custom (*morem sacrorum*). By this religious observance (*in religione*) your descendants shall remain pure (*casti*)." (*Aen.* 3.403–409)

Upon reaching Italy, Aeneas follows Helenus's advice:

> Then we pray (*precamur*) to the divine power of armed Pallas, who first received our rejoicings. And we cover our heads before the altars in Phrygian robe (*et capita ante aras Phrygio velamur amictu*) according to the great instructions which Helenus gave. We worship the Argive Juno through sacrifices in a proper manner as has been commanded (*rite Iunoni Argivae iussos adolemus honores*). (*Aen.* 3.543–547)

A number of things stand out in Virgil's description of the original *capite velato*. First, the color purple is emphasized and we shall discuss its significance below (see section 2.2.3). Second, the outer garment is identified as the "Phrygian robe," and the gods Pallas (Athena) and Argive Juno are specifically mentioned as the recipients of the worship conducted *capite velato*, so this ritual gesture is tied to eastern origins. Third, and more importantly for our study, two worshipful acts are explicitly mentioned in connection with *capite velato*: praying (*precari*; *votum*) and sacrificing (*adolere*). But perhaps most important of all is the significance which Virgil attaches to *capite velato*: it is presented as a divinely ordered sacred custom (*morem sacrorum*) and as *religio* by which the Romans remain pure. Considering von Albrecht's assessment of the *Aeneid* above, we can be confident that many Romans in the first century CE viewed *capite velato* in precisely these terms.

Virgil's *Aeneid* was not the only version of the origins of *capite velato*, however. Virgil's contemporary, Dionysius of Halicarnassus (ca. 60–7 BCE), provides an alternative version of Aeneas's inaugural sacrifice in the land of Italy:

> They say that Aeneas, the son of Anchises and Aphrodite, when he had anchored in Italy, purposed to sacrifice (θῦσαι) to one of the gods. After the prayer (μετὰ τὴν εὐχήν)

---

[27] Von Albrecht, *A History of Roman Literature*, 1:35.

he was about to prepare the sacrificial animal to begin the sacrificial ceremonies (μέλλοντα τοῦ παρεσκευασμένου πρὸς τὴν θυσίαν ἱερείου κατάρχεσθαι) when he saw one of the Achaeans coming from afar—either Odysseus when he was about to consult the oracle by [the lake] Avernus, or Diomedes when he came to fight alongside Daunus. Being troubled by this occurrence and wishing to avert the sight of the enemy's appearance as an evil omen in the midst of sacrificing (ἐφ' ἱεροῖς), he turned and covered (ἐγκαλύψασθαί[28]). But after the departure of the enemy, he washed his hands again in holy water (χερνιψάμενον) to complete the sacrifice (τὴν θυσίαν). But when the sacrifices (τῶν ἱερῶν) turned out better than expected, he was delighted with the occurrence and kept this same custom (ἔθος) at every prayer (ἐπὶ πάσης εὐχῆς), and those born of this man observe this as one of the laws of the religious services (τῶν περὶ τὰς ἱερουργίας νομίνων). (*Ant. rom.* 12.16.1–3)

Dionysius of Halicarnassus was a Greek rhetorician who came to Rome in the beginning of Augustus's reign and who thus wrote a history of the Romans from somewhat of an outsider's perspective. This may explain the crucial differences between Dionysius's version of Aeneas's sacrifice and that of Virgil. Virgil considers *capite velato* a divinely mandated rite, but Dionysius presents it as a custom born out of an accident. One gets an impression that Dionysius considers *capite velato* a superstitious behavior—repeating an action simply because it had fortuitously and unintentionally worked in the past. Plutarch, who also wrote about the Romans from an outsider's perspective, albeit a century later, knows Dionysius's version of Aeneas's sacrifice, as he comments: "If what is said about Aeneas is true, that when Diomedes passed by, he completed the sacrifice having covered (ἐπικαλυψάμενος)..." (*Quaest. rom.* 6 [266c]). Plutarch's remark suggests that Dionysius's version had enduring popularity regarding the origins of *capite velato*, at least among the non-native Romans. It is possible, therefore, that while the pious Romans in the first century CE viewed *capite velato* as a divinely ordered practice for their purity's sake, outsiders and foreigners may have thought of it as nothing more than superstitious behavior.

These different perspectives notwithstanding, however, both Virgil and Dionysius (as well as Plutarch) trace the origins of *capite velato* to the mythological past of the Romans—a time when the earth was roamed by the sons and daughters of the gods, and when one of these sons of the gods found his way into the land of Italy to become the founder of the Latin state.[29] Thus, regardless of whether

---

[28] While Dionysius does not specify here that Aeneas covered his head, the context (along with Virgil's parallel) suggests that this is what he has in mind.

[29] It may be that Ovid (ca. 43 BCE–18 CE), in his epic poetry *Metamorphoses*, wishes to trace the origins of *capite velato* even further back in time. Ovid describes how Deucalion and Pyrrha,

Dionysius considers *capite velato* a superstitious behavior, he still acknowledges it as an ancient tradition which his contemporary Romans adhered to during their religious services (ἱερουργία), particularly during their prayers and sacrifices.

2.2.2 *Capite velato* and Mopsus

Before we leave mythology proper behind, a quick mention must be made here of Valerius Flaccus's (d. ca. 90 CE) epic poem *Argonautica*, in which the famed seer and diviner Mopsus is portrayed with a covered head. In the relevant scene, Mopsus and his companions are caught in a violent storm at sea and the apparition of a certain Sthenelus (who had been slain) appears to them: "While Mopsus marvels at the omen (*omina*), he sees the barrow far away at the limit of the strand, and veiling his head (*obnubensque caput*) pours wine and calls upon (*vocato*) the ghost" (*Argonautica* 5.95–97 [Mozley]). Here the verb *obnubere* is used instead of *velare*, yet it still appears to describe *capite velato*, since this ritual gesture is often depicted accompanying the act of pouring libation, as we shall see. Thus, this entry serves as an important reminder of the point made earlier that the rite modern scholars refer to as *capite velato* is not always described with the verb *velare* in the Latin sources.

2.2.3 *Capite velato* and Numa

Numa was the legendary second king of Rome who succeeded Romulus, the mythical founder of the city, after a short period of interregnum (in Livy's chronology, Numa's lifespan is dated to ca. 753–673 BCE). In later historical memory, Numa was regarded as the founder of Roman religion—he was credited with instituting various religious rituals and creating new and lasting priestly offices (cf. Livy, *Ab urbe cond.* 1.20.1–6; Cicero, *Nat. d.* 3.2 [5]). Thus, Numa is portrayed as a

---

the survivors of the great flood, visit the goddess Themis in their grief, fearing they are the only ones left in the world. Themis is moved by their sorrow and instructs them as follows: "Depart the temple, cover the head (*velate caput*), unfasten the girded garments, and throw the bones of your great ancestor behind you as you go" (*Metam.* 1.381–383). Deucalion and Pyrrha decide that by "the great ancestor," Themis has in mind "the earth" and not their biological mother, so they pick up stones from the ground, cover their heads (*velantque caput*), unloosen their robes, and begin throwing these stones behind them. As they do so, the stones transform into humans, and Deucalion and Pyrrha thus create a new *genus* (*Metam.* 1.384–415). This ritual creation of the Roman race with covered heads is intriguing, but it is not entirely clear that Ovid has in mind *capite velato* proper here. The image of a covered head is not used in the context of worship (as by Virgil, Dionysius, and Plutarch do), and there is an additional command to ungird, which does not appear in any other context in which *capite velato* proper is presented.

2.2 Capite velato in the Roman Epics and Histories

ruler who was especially meticulous in religious matters, even before his kingship. We are told, for example, that Numa was initially hesitant to accept the offer of kingship from the Romans and agreed only on the condition that the gods were to unmistakably demonstrate that this is what they desired. The Augustan historian Livy (59 BCE–19 CE) preserves in his *History of Rome* the subsequent account of the Romans consulting the gods about Numa's election as king of Rome in which *capite velato* also features:

> Accordingly an augur (who thereafter, as a mark of honor, was made a priest of the state in permanent charge of that function) conducted [Numa] to the citadel and caused him to sit down on a stone, facing the south. The augur seated himself on Numa's left, having his head covered (*capite velato*), and holding in his right hand a crooked staff without a knot which they called a *lituus*. Then, looking out over the City and the country beyond, he prayed to the gods (*deos precatus*), and marked off the heavens by a line from east to west, designating as 'right' the regions to the south, as 'left' those to the north, and fixing in his mind a landmark opposite to him and as far away as the eye could reach; next shifting the crook to his left hand and, laying his right hand on Numa's head, he uttered the following prayer (*precatus*): "Father Jupiter, if it is Heaven's will that this man Numa Pompilius, whose head I am touching, be king in Rome, do thou exhibit to us unmistakable signs within those limits which I have set." Then he specified the auspices which he desired should be sent, and upon their appearance Numa was declared king, and so descended from the augural station. (*Ab urbe cond*. 1.18.6–10 [Foster])

Plutarch follows a similar storyline in his description of this episode, but there is ambiguity in his Greek concerning whether it was the augur who covered his head or Numa. The relevant lines read as follows:

> ἐνταῦθα τῶν μάντεων ὁ πρωτεύων τὸν μὲν εἰς μεσημβρίαν τρέψας ἐγκεκαλυμμένον[30], αὐτὸς δὲ παραστὰς ἐξόπισθεν καὶ τῇ δεξιᾷ τῆς κεφαλῆς ἐφαπτόμενος αὐτοῦ κατεύξατο. (*Num.* 7.2)

> Then the chief of the diviners turned the enwrapped [head] towards the south but he himself, having stood behind and having laid his right [hand] on his [Numa's] head, prayed.

It is not entirely clear whether the enwrapped head here belongs to Numa or the augur. The LCL translation opts for Numa, and there are good reasons for this

---

[30] Notice that just like in Dionysius's version of Aeneas's sacrifice (see section 2.2.1), the verb ἐγκαλύπτω appears on its own and the object of the verb is not specified. Considering, however, that the Latin parallels in both cases specifically mention the head, we have no reason to believe that Dionysius and Plutarch had any other object for the verb "enwrap" in mind. The reader is expected to infer from the context that ἐγκαλύπτω refers to the covering of the head, which suggests that *capite velato* was so widespread that specifying the object of covering in every instance was not necessary.

choice as the adversative conjunction δὲ appears in the second clause that begins with "he himself" in reference to the augur, suggesting perhaps a change in subject (i.e., *but* the augur himself). However, considering the parallel in Livy, in which it is unmistakably the augur who covers his head, we may read Plutarch here as saying that the augur turned his covered head towards the south, but positioned his own self behind the seated Numa. But we also cannot discount the possibility that the ambiguity here is purposeful for whatever reason. In any case, what is important for our study here is that in both Livy's and Plutarch's accounts of Numa's election, *capite velato* accompanies prayer and the process of divination known as augury (we shall say more about augurs and augury in section 2.2.4 and in Chapter 3).

In Ovid's calendrical poem *Fasti*, however, there is a clear reference to Numa himself performing the ritual gesture of *capite velato*. In the relevant scene, Numa has tricked Jupiter to meet him face to face to discuss the problem of lightning which scares the Romans. In their meeting, Jupiter promises to provide Numa with the "sure pledges of empire" the following day. Ovid then describes the events of the next day as follows:

> Scarcely had Phoebus shown a rim above the horizon: their anxious minds with hope and fear did quake. The king [Numa] took his stand, and, his head veiled in a snow-white hood (*atque caput niveo velatus amictu*), lifted up his hands, hands which the gods already knew so well. And thus he spoke: "The time has come to receive the promised boon; fulfil thy promise, Jupiter." Even while he spoke, the sun had already lifted his full orb above the horizon, and a loud crash rang out from heaven's vault. Thrice did the god thunder from a cloudless sky, thrice did he hurl his bolts. Take my word for it: what I say is wonderful but true. At the zenith the sky began to yawn; the multitude and their leader lifted up their eyes. Lo, swaying gently in the light breeze, a shield fell down. The people sent up a shout that reached the stars. The king lifted from the ground the gift, but not till he had sacrificed a heifer, which had never submitted her neck to the burden of the yoke. (*Fast.* 3.361–376 [Frazer])

It is interesting that Ovid mentions here that the color of the garment with which Numa covered his head was white, whereas in Virgil's description of Aeneas's inaugural sacrifice *capite velato*, the color purple is emphasized (see section 2.2.1). White and purple were the main colors of the togas as we have seen (see section 2.1.2), though other types of garments could also be fashioned in these colors. It seems that the wearing of purple (whether on togas or on other cloaks) was an indicator of one's economic wealth or of one's social status (even if limited and local),[31] and so some rulers of Rome sought to curb the excessive display of purple. Thus, according to Suetonius, for example, Julius Caesar only allowed purple to be worn by persons of certain positions and of certain ages, and even then, only on certain days (*Jul.* 43.1). Suetonius further reports that the later emperor Nero prohibited the dyeing of garments in specifically the Tyrian purple and once, when he noticed a certain woman wearing this color in the audience during one of his recitals, he had her stripped of the garment as well as of her property (*Nero* 32.3). However, it is unclear whether this sensitivity around the color purple that certain rulers exhibited plays any role in Virgil's or Ovid's decision to emphasize one or the other color in the context of *capite velato*. In any case, what is more important for our study here is that in Ovid's poem about Numa, *capite velato* accompanies a prayer (which is also performed with raised hands) and perhaps also a sacrifice (if Ovid envisions *capite velato* to have lasted the whole scene).

In all, given that Numa was regarded by later Romans as the founder of Roman religion, the mention of *capite velato* in the context of his election as king and in the context of his duties as king gains additional importance. While he may not have been thought of as the originator of this ritual gesture, his reputed adherence to it no doubt imbued *capite velato* with extra significance.

2.2.4 *Capite velato* and Attus Navius

Attus Navius is described in our sources as a legendary augur from the days of king Tarquinius Priscus (who by Livy's chronology reigned ca. 616–579 BCE). An augur was a priest in charge of a form of divination that involved observing and interpreting the flight and behavior of birds for knowledge of the will of the gods (cf. Plutarch, *Aem.* 3.1–2). According to Dionysius of Halicarnassus, Attus Navius (also known as Nevius Attus), was "the most notable of the augurs" (ὁ τῶν οἰωνοσκόπων ἐπιφανέστατος) and "considered to be of all those who had perfected the craft the most beloved of the gods and to have gained on account of it a great name, having displayed some incredible, unbelievable [feats] through the science of augury" (ὃς ἁπάντων θεοφιλέστατος ὁμολογεῖται γενέσθαι τῶν ἀκριβούντων τὴν τέχνην καὶ μεγίστου τυχεῖν δι' αὐτὴν ὀνόματος ἀπίστους τινὰς ὑπερβολὰς τῆς οἰωνοματικῆς ἐπιστήμης ἐπιδειξάμενος, *Ant. rom.* 3.70.1).

---

[31] Based on this, Preston Massey suggests that the problem addressed in 1 Cor 11:2–16 may have involved the wearing of purple garments (particularly on the head), which caused conflicts over social status. Massey, "Veiling among Men in Roman Corinth," 504, 512–14. There is no reason to think, however, that purple was the only color associated with *capite velato* (as also Ovid's entry demonstrates).

The most famous exhibition of Navius's skills reportedly occurred when king Tarquinius attempted to prove through trickery that Attus Navius was in fact a false diviner (ψευδόμαντις). In this story, which is also reported in Livy (*Ab urbe cond.* 1.36.3–5), the king informs Navius that he wishes to undertake a great project and asks Navius to seek auspices in order to determine whether the project is feasible. When Navius returns with a report of favorable omens, the king reveals amid general laughter that he had in fact wanted to know whether he could strike a whetstone in half with a razor. The king then proclaims Navius a mere impostor on the evidence that cutting a whetstone in half would be an impossible feat for anyone. However, Navius remains unfazed and tells the king to strike the displayed whetstone with the razor—in Livy's version, Navius strikes the whetstone himself—and to the amazement of all gathered, the whetstone is halved. The king is so taken aback by this display of Navius's skills that he begins to seek ways to regain the augur's goodwill. Most memorably, the king sets up a statue of Attus Navius in the Forum, and Dionysius at the time of Augustus comments that this statue, "smaller in size than an average man and having a garment down from the head, stood in front of the Senate next to the sacred fig tree until my time" (ἣ καὶ εἰς ἐμὲ ἦν ἔτι πρὸ τοῦ βουλευτηρίου κεθμένη πλησίον τῆς ἱερᾶς συκῆς ἐλάττων ἀνδρὸς μετρίου τὴν περιβολὴν ἔχουσα κατὰ τῆς κεφαλῆς, *Ant. rom.* 3.71.5).

Livy confirms that the statue of Attus Navius stood in the Forum "with a covered head" (*capite velato*), and specifies that it stood on the exact spot where the miracle of the whetstone had taken place (*Ab urbe cond.* 1.36.5). Livy also adds that as a result of Navius's miraculous demonstration of his augural skills,

> auguries and the augural priesthood so increased in honor that nothing was afterwards done, in the field or at home, unless the auspices had first been taken: popular assemblies, musterings of the army, acts of supreme importance—all were put off when the birds refused their consent. (*Ab urbe cond.* 1.36.6 [Foster]).

Considering, then, that this statue of one of the most famous of augurs may have stood with a covered head in a prominent spot in the Forum in Rome for centuries, it is likely that all subsequent augurs would have been eager to imitate Navius by practicing their skills likewise *capite velato*.

It is also important to make a more careful note here of the language that Livy and Dionysius use in describing Navius's statue, as both authors had presumably seen it with their own eyes. Livy uses the exact phrase *capite velato* without specifying the nature of the covering, so he expects his readers to understand the phrase on its own as a reference to a garment over the head. Dionysius, on the other hand, uses language strikingly similar to 1 Cor 11:4: both texts have the participial ἔχω accompanying κατὰ κεφαλῆς, and while 1 Cor 11:4 does not specify the direct object of the verb (see discussion in section 1.4.8), in 1 Cor 11:15 mention is made of τό περιβόλαιον, the neuter form of ἡ περιβολή ("covering"), which Dionysius uses as the direct object of ἔχω in his description of the statue. Such strong parallels between 1 Cor 11:4 and certain Greek descriptions of *capite velato* should not be ignored in any interpretation of 1 Cor 11:2–16.

2.2.5 *Capite velato* and Camillus

In section 2.2.1, Dionysius of Halicarnassus's version of the origins of *capite velato* was discussed, which, as we noted, ends with Dionysius's remark that Aeneas's descendants continued to observe this ritual gesture as one of the laws of their religious services. In Dionysius's *Roman Antiquities*, however, this comment is immediately followed by another story in which *capite velato* features, but from a time period much later than Aeneas:

> Camillus [ca. 446–365 BCE], following then the ancestral customs (τοῖς πατρικοῖς νόμοις), when he made the prayer and drew the garment over the head (τὴν εὐχὴν ἐποιήσατο καὶ κατὰ τῆς κεφαλῆς εἵλκυσε τὸ ἱμάτιον), wished to turn but the step gave way underneath him. He was not able to catch himself [and] fell flat on his back. (*Ant. rom.* 12.16.5)

Dionysius then notes that it must have been clear even to ordinary people that this accident did not bode well for Camillus, but Camillus ignored the mishap and did nothing to avert the apparent danger. Rather, Camillus interpreted the incident in favorable terms and believed that his prayers had been heard (*Ant. rom.* 12.16.5).

Dionysius's remark here is interesting, considering that in Livy's version of Camillus's slip and fall (in which *capite velato* is not mentioned), the verdict is that this accident not only forecasted Camillus's own condemnation, but also the capture of Rome that took place a few years later (*Ab urbe cond.* 5.21.16). Nothing is said of Camillus's own take on the matter. These differences of emphasis in Dionysius and Livy may perhaps again underline Dionysius's conviction that *capite velato* was nothing more than a Roman superstition (see also section 2.2.1). That is, Dionysius may want to demonstrate here that just like Aeneas interpreted an accidental coincidence as a necessity for religious services on a whim, so Camillus interpreted his accident when *capite velato* as favorable to him on a whim. Whether or not that is actually the case here, there must be some good reason why Dionysius wishes to connect these two stories separated by a long time-span through the shared motif of *capite velato*. And considering that in contrast to Livy, who takes the consequences of Camillus's fall seriously for the history of Rome, Dionysius downplays the impact of the accident on Camillus's conduct, there may be a sentiment of condescension here regarding Roman religion, especially as it concerns *capite velato*.

2.2.6 *Capite velato* and the College of *Fetials*

According to Dionysius of Halicarnassus, the priestly college of the *fetials* (εἰρηνοδίκαι in Greek) was instituted by Numa. The *fetials* were made responsible for ensuring that peace treaties were followed (on both sides) and that Rome would not enter into an unjust war. Their duty was also to investigate the conduct of army generals and to negotiate with any opposing government in case of conflicts or political tensions (*Ant. rom.* 2.72.1–9). According to Livy, Numa's grandson Ancus Marcius (ca. 677–617 BCE in Livy's chronology) additionally tasked the *fetials* with delivering the formal declarations of war. In Livy's description of this Roman rite of declaring war, the *fetial* goes to the borders of the land of the enemy, covers his head with a woolen fillet (*capite velato filo—lanae velamen est*), and then makes the announcement using certain prescribed formulas before hurling a spear into the enemy territory in the presence of at least three grown men as witnesses (*Ab urbe cond.* 1.32.5–14).

Dionysius of Halicarnassus provides a specific historical example of a *fetial* declaring war in his account of the First Samnite War (343–341 BCE). In Dionysius's report, after one of the *fetials* at that time makes the declaration of war against the Samnites, "when he is about to leave, he draws the garment down from the head and lifting the hands towards the heaven as is the custom, he makes (imprecatory) prayers to the gods" (μέλλων δ' ἀπιένται τήν τε περιβολὴν κατὰ κεφαλῆς εἴλκυσε καὶ τὰς χεῖρας ἀνασχὼν εἰς τὸν οὐρανόν, ὡς ἔθος ἐστίν, ἀρὰς ἐποιήσατο τοῖς θεοῖς, *Ant. rom.* 15.9.1–2). In the case of the *fetials*, then, we see two head-covering practices in conjunction: the custom of covering the head with a woolen fillet when declaring war, and the custom of covering the head with a garment when uttering a prayer. As will be shown below, it was not uncommon to depict *capite velato* in Roman art performed over another head-covering, such as a wreath. It is important to note here, however, that while Livy describes both these head-covering customs with the phrase *capite velato*, it is only the practice of covering the head with a garment during devotion that modern scholarship should reserve for the technical sense of *capite velato*.

2.2.7 *Capite velato* and the Decii

Livy tells us that in the Battle of Vesuvius in 340 BCE, the Roman co-consuls Decius and Manlius were leading the Roman troops against the Latins when Decius's side fell back, unable to withstand the pressure from the enemy. In response, Decius devised the following plan to turn the tide back in favor of the Romans:

> In the confusion of this movement [of his side falling back,] Decius the consul called out to Marcus Valerius in a loud voice: "We have need of Heaven's help, Marcus Valerius. Come therefore, state pontiff (*pontifex*) of the Roman People, dictate the words, that I may devote (*devoveam*) myself to save the legions." The pontiff bade him don the purple-bordered toga (*togam praetextam*), and with veiled head (*velato capite*) and one hand thrust out from the toga and touching his chin, stand upon a spear that was laid under his feet, and say as follows: "Janus, Jupiter, Father Mars, Quirinus, Bellona, Lares, divine Novensiles, divine Indigites, ye gods in whose power are both we and our enemies, and you, divine Manes,—I invoke (*precor*) you and worship (*veneror*) you, I beseech and crave your favor, that you prosper the might and the victory of the Roman People of the Quirites, and visit the foes of the Roman people of the Quirites with fear, shuddering, and death. As I have pronounced the words, even so in behalf of the republic of the Roman People of the Quirites, and of the army, the legions, the auxiliaries of the Roman People of the Quirites, do I devote (*devoveo*) the legions and auxiliaries of the enemy, together with myself, to the divine Manes and to Earth." (*Ab urbe cond.* 8.9.4–8 [Foster])

After this prayer, Decius rode into the midst of the enemy and despite dying under a barrage of missiles, his bravery and devotion galvanized the entire Roman army so that they ended up defeating the Latins (*Ab urbe cond.* 8.9.9–8.10.9).

Decius's courageous gallop into certain death to save the Roman army from defeat was later emulated by his son in the Battle of Sentinum in 295 BCE. This devotion of the two Decii received legendary status and became a subject of reflection for numerous Roman writers, although its meaning was differently interpreted. Some, for example, viewed this act of the Decii as a sacrifice to the gods. One of the interlocutors in Cicero's *On the Nature of the Gods* says, for example, that "among our ancestors religion was so powerful that some commanders actually offered themselves as victims to the immortal gods on behalf of the state, veiling their heads and formally vowing themselves to death" (*dis inmortalibus capite velato verbis certis pro re publica devoverent, Nat. d.* 2.3 [10] [Rackham]). Seneca seems to share this view, commenting that the younger Decius's ride into certain death was a sacrifice intended to gain favorable omens (*litare, Ep.* 67.9). However, others viewed it in less religious terms, as expressed by another interlocutor in Cicero's *On the Nature of the Gods*, for example:

> Again, you think that the gods were actually propitiated by the *devotio* of the Decii. But how can the gods have been so unjust that their wrath against the Roman people could only be appeased by the death of heroes like the Decii? No, the *devotio* was a device of generalship, or *stratēgēma* as it is termed in Greek, though a device for generals who were ready to give their lives in their country's service; their notion was that if a commander rode full gallop against the foe his troops would follow him, and so it proved. (*Nat. d.* 3.6 [15] [Rackham], with modifications)

Our understanding of *capite velato* here depends, therefore, on one's interpretation of the *devotio* of the Decii. If it is viewed as a sacrifice, *capite velato* assumes deeper significance as component of a formal vow to die a sacrificial death on behalf of the people (cf. *Nat. d.* 2.3 [10]). However, if this rite of *devotio* is merely interpreted as a military strategy to galvanize the troops, *capite velato* need not be imbued with such a weighty role, but may be seen merely as a customary gesture accompanying the prayer that Decius utters (cf. *Ab urbe cond.* 8.9.4–8). That is, irrespective of the other ritual elements present in this scene, *capite velato* may only be referenced in regards to its most common use—as a traditional gesture associated with Roman prayers. Whatever the case may be, however, it is worth noting here that in Livy's account of the *devotio* of Decius senior, the purple-bordered toga is specifically mentioned as the garment which Decius is ordered to wear and which then covers his head during prayer.

This image of Decius senior's *devotio* was invoked by his son prior to his own emulation of it in his campaign for the plebeians to be eligible for election as pontiffs and augurs. Up until this point, these posts had been the prerogative of only the patricians. Decius junior argued, however, that the *devotio* of his father (a plebeian) would have been equal in purity in the sight of the gods to the *devotio* of Decius senior's co-consul Manlius (a patrician), had the latter done the same (Livy, *Ab urbe cond*. 10.7.4–5). Based on this, Decius junior did not see a reason to deny the plebeians the opportunity to be elected as pontiffs and augurs. In his speech, as formulated by Livy, Decius junior argued further that victorious plebeian generals were awarded the same triumph as victorious patrician generals, so to refuse them the offices of pontiffs and augurs was insensible:

> What god or man can deem it inappropriate that those heroes whom you have honored with curule chairs, with the purple-bordered robe (*toga praetexta*), with the tunic adorned with palms, and with the embroidered toga (*toga picta*), the triumphal crown and the laurel wreath, whose houses you have made conspicuous amongst the rest with the spoils of your enemies which you have fastened to their walls, — who, I say, can object if such men add thereto the insignia of the pontiffs and the augurs? May the man who, decked with the robes (*ornatu decorates*) of Jupiter Optimus Maximus, has been borne through the City in a gilded chariot and has mounted the Capitol—may that man not be seen with chalice and crook, when, covering his head (*capite velato*), he offers up

the victim (*victimam caedat*), or receives an augury from the Citadel (*auguriumve ex arce capiet*)? (Livy, *Ab urbe cond.* 10.7.9–10 [Foster])

In this speech of Decius junior, then, we see that *capite velato* is referred to in the context of offering sacrifices and in the context of receiving auguries.

Excursus: A Covered Head and the Murder of Tiberius Gracchus

The ancient Roman historians tell us that in 133 BCE, the tribune Tiberius Gracchus (along with a number of his supporters) was bludgeoned to death by an angry mob of senators and their attendants on the Capitoline Hill when he was bidding to be re-elected. In their recounting of this story, both Plutarch and Appian mention a curious detail regarding the behavior of pontifex maximus Publius Cornelius Scipio Nasica—a leading figure in the unfolding of this massacre—that has led some scholars to form an opinion that Nasica performed the ritual gesture of *capite velato* in connection to the killing of Tiberius Gracchus. As this interpretation of Nasica's behavior is contested, I will consider the literary descriptions of this incident separately here in an excursus.

According to Plutarch's report, when Nasica stormed to the Capitol because he had heard some unsavory rumors about Tiberius's conduct, he "covered his head with the (bottom) edge of his outer garment" (τὸ κράσπεδον τοῦ ἱματίου θέμενος ἐπὶ τῆς κεφαλῆς, *Ti. C. Gracch.* 19.4). Appian (ca. 95–165 CE), who, like Plutarch, was of Greek origin but had obtained Roman citizenship, pauses in his retelling of this story to ponder the significance of this gesture:

> And he [Nasica] dragged the (bottom) edge of the garment onto the head (καὶ τὸ κράσπεδον τοῦ ἱματίου ἐς τὴν κεφαλὴν περιεσύρατο), either to draw more [people] to come together through this singular appearance, or to fashion a helmet of war as a symbol for the observers, or to cover before the gods because of what he was about to accomplish (εἴτε θεοὺς ἐγκαλυπτόμενος ὧν ἔμελλε δράσειν). (*Bell. civ.* 1.2.16)

In his overview of the history of interpretation of the above references, Jerzy Linderski credits D. C. Earl (1963) as being the first to clearly articulate what earlier scholars had only intimated: Nasica's covering of the head signaled his intention to sacrifice Tiberius Gracchus, and this gesture must therefore be interpreted as *capite velato*.[32] Linderski concurs with Earl's assessment that Plutarch and Appian describe *capite velato* in this scene, but suggests that Nasica intended to perform a specific rite known as *consecratio* (not to be confused with *devotio*), in which "the

---

[32] Jerzy Linderski, "The Pontiff and the Tribune: The Death of Tiberius Gracchus," *Athenaeum* 90 (2002): 345.

miscreant was abandoned to the gods to be destroyed by their wrath."[33] In support of this reading, Linderski refers to a passage in Cicero's *De Domo Sua*, where *capite velato* and *consecratio* are mentioned together. In Linderski's estimation, this passage demonstrates that it was a Roman ritual to consecrate humans for destruction with a garment over the head.

There is a major issue with Linderski's interpretation of the evidence, however. The referenced passage in Cicero does not, in fact, support Linderski's reading of Nasica's behavior. In this text, Cicero is delivering a speech concerning restitution of his property after his exile, and one of the issues discussed is the correct procedure for consecrating *property*.[34] In this context, then, Cicero mentions how one of his opponents, a pontiff, had consecrated a property of a friend of his: "You yourself [pontiff]; I say, with your head veiled (*capite velato*), having summoned an assembly, having placed a brazier on the spot, consecrated (*consecrasti*) the property of your dear friend Gabinius" (*Dom.* 124). It is a considerable leap to argue, on the basis of this entry, that Nasica performed a *consecratio* of Tiberius (a human) *capite velato*. We do not have any corroborating evidence in the ancient Roman sources indicating that humans were consecrated for destruction *capite velato*. Thus, it is highly unlikely that it is the rite of *consecratio* that Plutarch and Appian describe in regards to Nasica's behavior.

While Nasica is indeed described as covering his head before the murder of Tiberius Gracchus, it is unlikely that he is presented by Plutarch and Appian as performing the ritual gesture of *capite velato* for several reasons. First, Plutarch's and Appian's description of Nasica's behavior is unusual for *capite velato*. Both authors specifically mention that Nasica covered his head with the κράσπεδον of the outer garment. The κράσπεδον was especially associated with the bottom edge of the garment (as Linderski himself argues at length[35]), and in no other ancient text featuring *capite velato* is there mention of κράσπεδον. Available evidence indicates that *capite velato* was not typically performed with the *bottom* edge of the garment. Second, considering that Appian spent a significant portion of his life in Rome, it is reasonable to assume that he would have been well-acquainted with Roman customs and should not have struggled to explain the symbolism of Nasica covering his head if it had indeed been *capite velato*. While Appian's third suggestion—that Nasica "covered before the gods because of what he was about to accomplish"—

---

[33] Linderski, "The Pontiff and the Tribune," 355.

[34] For a concise overview of the speech, see Anders Lisdorf, "The Conflict over Cicero's House: An Analysis of the Ritual Element in *De Domo Sua*," *Numen* 52 (2005): 445–64.

[35] Linderski, "The Pontiff and the Tribune," 355–64.

may be read as a reference to *capite velato* if "to accomplish" is taken to mean "to sacrifice," the sentence can also be read as suggesting that Nasica covered before the gods out of shame or fear because of his intent to kill another man. The latter is the more likely explanation here. And finally, in the accounts of Velleius Paterculus and Valerius Maximus of this episode, Nasica wraps the hem of his garment around his left hand and not around his head. This gesture had its own symbolism, as Anna Clark explains, and was not associated with *capite velato*.[36] Taking the above into consideration, it may be that Plutarch (and by extension, Appian) was either simply mistaken about what Nasica did with his κράσπεδον or that he had one or the other of Appian's explanations in mind, but it is unlikely that Plutarch thought of *capite velato* proper in his report of Nasica's behavior, particularly since in all of his other references to *capite velato*, Plutarch uses different language to describe it.

2.2.8 *Capite velato* and Lucius Vitellius

Suetonius informs us that Lucius Vitellius, father of emperor Vitellius (who briefly reigned in 69 CE), began performing *capite velato* in the presence of emperor Gaius Caligula (reigned 37–41 CE), as if he were in the presence of a god:

> He [Lucius Vitellius] had also a wonderful gift for flattery and was the first to begin to worship (*adorare*) Gaius Caesar as a god; for on his return from Syria he did not presume to approach the emperor except with veiled head (*capite velato*), turning himself about and then prostrating himself (*circumvertensque se, deinde procumbens*). (*Vit.* 2.5 [Rolfe])

It is important to note here that the covered head by itself did not signal that one was offering worship. As discussed in section 2.1.1, to be covered of the head in the presence of an honorable person was considered rude. Vitellius's gesture of covering the head was only interpreted as *capite velato* proper because in the presence of Caligula, he first spun himself around (*circumvertere*)[37] and then fell to the ground (*procumbere*).

2.2.9 *Capite velato* and Vespasian and Titus

Although this section is concerned with Roman histories, we find a mention of *capite velato* also in that part of Josephus's *Jewish War* which deals with the Romans at Rome. Josephus reports that when Vespasian and Titus returned

---

[36] Anna F. Clark, "Nasica and *Fides*," *ClQ* 57 (2007): 125–31.

[37] Spinning around in the vicinity of sacred objects was a common ritual gesture of the Romans. See, Anthony Corbeill, *Nature Embodied: Gesture in Ancient Rome* (Princeton: Princeton University Press, 2004), 28–29.

victoriously from Judea, they were honored with a triumph. In Josephus's description, Vespasian and Titus were first given purple robes to wear and laurel wreaths to cover their heads with, after which they were led in a procession to be seated on ivory seats atop an erected platform. Once Vespasian and Titus had taken their seats, the soldiers let out a roar of approval (*J. W.* 7.5.4 §§123–127). It is in this context, then, that we have a mention of *capite velato*:

> But having received their praise, Vespasian, wishing to speak, made the sign for silence. And after all became quiet, he rose and having covered a part of the head with the garment, he performed the customary prayers (καὶ τῷ περιβλήματι τὸ πλέον τῆς κεφαλῆς μέρος ἐπικαλυψάμενος εὐχὰς ἐποιήσατο τὰς νενομισμένας). And Titus also prayed likewise (ὁμοίως δὲ καὶ Τίτος ηὔξατο). (*J. W.* 7.5.4 §128)

It is noteworthy that Josephus specifies here that Vespasian covered only part of his head with the garment while praying. As was discussed in section 2.1.1, it is possible that this distinguished *capite velato* from other appearances in which the garment was used as a head-covering. However, such differences may not have been readily apparent unless the context was known. And in this case, the context of Vespasian covering his head with his garment (which seems to have been the *toga picta*) was prayer.

2.2.10 *Capite velato* and Hadrian

In the *Historia Augusta*, a collection of stories about the emperors of the second and third centuries CE, likely compiled in the fourth or fifth century CE,[38] we find a mention of *capite velato* in connection to emperor Hadrian (reigned 117–138 CE):

> The premonitions of [Hadrian's] death were as follows: On his last birthday, when he was commending (*commendaret*) Antoninus to the gods, his bordered toga fell down without apparent cause and bared his head (*praetexta sponte delapsa caput ei aperuit*). (*Hist. Aug. Hadrian.* 26.6–7 [Magie])

We see here that *capite velato* accompanies a special type of prayer for divine protection (*commendare*), and that a mishap in relation to *capite velato* was considered an evil omen.[39]

---

[38] The dating of *Historia Augusta* is a contested issue. For a short overview see, for example, Von Albrecht, *A History of Roman Literature*, 2:1388–89.

[39] Valerius Maximus reports that a certain priest by the name of Quintus Sulpicius lost his priestly office because his *apex* (special headgear reserved for the *flamens*) fell off his head when he was sacrificing (*Memorable Doings and Sayings*, 1.1.5). This further shows that Romans considered proper covering of the head during rituals an important matter.

2.3 *Capite velato* in Plays, Satires, and Other Works

We find references to *capite velato* also in other types of Roman literature besides the epics and histories. We must keep in mind here that in some of these other genres such as satire or comedy, exaggerations abound, and the characters and scenes are purposefully presented in a manner to provoke the audience into laughter, anger, disgust, or any other strong reaction. However, as long as we are aware of the purposes of these genres, we may often gain a more realistic portrayal of everyday life from these sources than from the oft-idealized histories or epics, for example. Thus, the below entries on *capite velato* are just as important (if not more so) in contributing to our understanding of this ritual gesture.

2.3.1 *Capite velato* in Plautus

Plautus (ca. 254–184 BCE) was a famous Roman playwright. It appears that in his tragicomedy *Amphytrion*, a mention is made of *capite velato*, which would make it the earliest surviving literary reference to this ritual gesture. The plot of *Amphytrion* is as follows: the character Amphytrion has to leave for military duty for a longer period of time. In his absence, the god Jupiter takes on the form of Amphytrion and has sexual relations with Amphytrion's wife, Alcmena. As a result, Alcmena becomes pregnant and in due time gives birth to twins, after which the real Amphytrion returns and all manner of confusion arises. It is in the context of a maidservant's report about the birth of the twins to the real Amphytrion upon his return that a reference to *capite velato* occurs:

> "Then today your wife began to go in labor when pain suddenly sprang forth in the womb as usually happens to women in labor. She called upon the immortal gods (*invocat deos immortales*) that they would come to her aid—[she did so] with clean hands and a covered head (*capite operto*)." (*Amph.* 1092–1095)

It seems that in this scene the maidservant wants to assure Amphytrion that Alcmena prayed to the gods in a customary manner, because everything that followed Alcmena's prayer (which the maidservant is about to report to Amphytrion) was far from ordinary. First, terrible thunder immediately followed, so that the house shook violently and shone like gold. Then, no sound, not even a groan, was heard from Alcmena, even though she was giving birth to twin boys. Then, one of the boys appeared so big and strong that no one could wrap him in swaddling clothes (to which Amphytrion interjects that this must mean that his wife received divine aid like she had prayed for). In the maidservant's continuation of the story, two enormous snakes then showed up and tried to attack the twins, but one of the newborns jumped out of the crib and killed both snakes, at which point Jupiter called out to Alcmena to reveal that he was in fact the father of the twins (*Amph.* 1095–1126).

The purpose of this scene is to elicit laughter at the expense of Amphytrion, who becomes increasingly more bewildered as the details of his wife giving birth become more incredible with every line of the maidservant's report. The humor here is heightened by the fact that the report begins as innocuously as presumably any report of childbirth would have begun: a woman begins to experience labor pains and prays for divine assistance. Thus, while most of the details in this scene are purposefully so incredible as to be far removed from ordinary life, the reference to *capite velato* appears in the context in which normalcy is in focus. Thus, even though Plautus does not use the verb *velare* here but *operire*, he nevertheless seems to refer to *capite velato*, a customary ritual gesture during Roman prayers. If so, *capite velato* must have been well established already in the early second century BCE.

2.3.2 *Capite velato* in Lucretius

Lucretius (ca. 99–55 BCE) was an Epicurean philosopher who lived during the turbulent times of civil unrest at Rome in the first half of the first century BCE. In his fifth book of the poem *On the Nature of Things*, Lucretius argues that the world cannot be divine and must be devoid of the gods because it is full of defects.[40] As such, Lucretius laments the fact that his forefathers had created all manner of religious rites out of their fear of nature and their misguided assumption that the gods were behind it all. It is in this context, then, that we have a reference to *capite velato*:

> O unhappy race of mankind, to ascribe such doings [e.g., lightning] to the gods and to attribute to them bitter wrath as well! What groans did [our ancestors] then create for themselves, what wounds for us, what tears for generations to come! It is no piety to show oneself often with covered head,[41] turning towards a stone and approaching every altar (*nec pietas ullast velatum saepe videri vertier ad lapidem atque omnis accedere ad aras*), none to fall prostrate upon the ground and to spread open the palms before shrines of the gods, none to sprinkle altars with the blood of beasts in showers and to link vow to vow; but rather to be able to survey all things with tranquil mind. (*De rerum natura* 5.1194–1203 [Rouse])

---

[40] The first part of the book as summarized in Von Albrecht, *A History of Roman Literature*, 1:286.

[41] Notice that the Latin text only includes the verb *velare* and does not include the noun "head" but it is clear that *capite velato* is in view here, and so the addition of "head" in LCL translation is appropriate.

While Lucretius does not explicitly state here that he has in mind the *velare* of the "head," the context strongly suggests that this is what he means. If so, his assertion that approaching altars and (sacred) stones *capite velato* was actually no piety at all implies that this sight must have been frequent and widespread enough in his day for the statement to carry any weight.

2.3.3 *Capite velato* in Varro

Varro (116–27 BCE) was a prolific Roman writer, but unfortunately only a fraction of his literary output survives to modern day. In his *On the Latin Language*, of which the books that remain deal mostly with the etymology of Latin words, we find a somewhat incidental reference to *capite velato*: "Likewise *rica* ("veil") is derived from *ritus* ("rite"), because it is according to the Roman *ritus* that women cover their heads when they make sacrifices" (*Sic rica ab ritu, quod Romano ritu sacrificium feminae cum faciunt, capite velant, Ling.* 5.29.130). Varro's etymology here is suspect to say the least, as there is no reason for us to believe that *rica* derives from *ritus* because of *capite velato*. What is of interest to us, however, is the identity of *rica* and Varro's remark about *capite velato* in relation to *rica*. It seems that *rica* was a special veil of purple color that the *flaminicae* (certain female priests) wore during sacrifices.[42] Varro then connects this special veil with the word *ritus* because, according to him, Roman women customarily sacrificed with covered heads as was the Roman *ritus*. It is unlikely that Varro here thinks that all women who sacrificed wore specifically the *rica*, but his point seems to be that since it was a common rite for Roman women to sacrifice with covered heads, then the name that was given to this special veil that the *flaminicae* came to don during *their* sacrifices must have been derived from this commonplace *ritus*. Whatever the exact thought process of Varro here, however—and this remains unclear—he does seem to suggest that in his day, Roman women of all social ranks, and not only the *flaminicae*, sacrificed with covered heads.

2.3.4 *Capite velato* in Plutarch

We began this chapter with Plutarch's observation that Romans covered their heads during worship but uncovered them in the presence of social superiors to demonstrate that while it seems to have been common practice for Romans to cover their heads with outer garments, this appearance only assumed special significance in liturgical settings (see section 2.1.1). In the context of this observation

---

[42] Meghan J. DiLuzio, *A Place at the Altar: Priestesses in Republican Rome* (Princeton: Princeton University Press), 39–40.

of his, however, Plutarch has more to say about *capite velato* that interests us here. For example, Plutarch lists several reasons why he thinks the Romans wished to worship with a covered head:

> Τοὺς δὲ θεοὺς οὕτω προσεκύνουν ἢ ταπεινοῦντες ἑαυτοὺς τῇ ἐπικρύψει τῆς κεφαλῆς, ἢ μᾶλλον εὐλαβούμενοί τινα φωνὴν προσπεσεῖν αὐτοῖς ἔξωθεν εὐχομένοις ἀπαίσιον καὶ δύσφημον ἄχρι τῶν ὤτων ἀνελάμβανον τὸ ἱμάτιον· ὅτι γὰρ ἰσχυρῶς ἐφυλάττοντο ταῦτα, δῆλόν ἐστι τῷ προσιόντας ἐπὶ μαντείαν χαλκωμάτων πατάγῳ περιψοφεῖσθαι. ἢ ὡς Κάστωρ λέγει τὰ ʽΡωμαϊκὰ τοῖς Πυθαγορικοῖς συνοικειῶν, τὸν ἐν ἡμῖν δαίμονα δεῖσθαι τῶν ἐκτὸς θεῶν καὶ ἱκετεύειν, τῇ τῆς κεφαλῆς ἐπικαλύψει τὴν τῆς ψυχῆς αἰνιττόμενος ὑπὸ τοῦ σώματος ἐγκάλυψιν καὶ ἀπόκρυψιν. (*Quaest. rom.* 10 [266d–e])

> But they were worshiping the gods in this manner either to humble themselves through the concealment of the head, or rather to ensure that having taken up the garment over the ears, no ill-omened or evil sound should reach them from without—that they kept strong guard against these [sounds] is shown in that whenever they went for divination, they clattered bronze objects all around—or as Castor says when he connects the things of the Romans to Pythagoreanism: the divine power within us entreats and beseeches the gods without; through the covering of the head, the concealment and hiddenness of the soul by the body is intimated.

The Castor referred to here seems to be a certain Castor of Rhodes, a contemporary of Cicero. Since Castor's work has not survived, we must take Plutarch at his word that Castor wrote a treatise in which he attempted to trace connections between Roman customs and Pythagorean philosophy. If then Plutarch's above citation of Castor is true to the original, we would possess a philosophical rumination from the mid-first century BCE about the symbolism of *capite velato*. Such a deeply symbolic take would be unique in the collection of available entries on this ritual gesture. Plutarch himself, for example, proffers more practical reasons for *capite velato*—that it was a sign of humility or that it protected from ill-omened sounds. In any case, Plutarch's choice of conversation partners here may be significant—instead of engaging with his contemporary Romans, he has tried to come up with reasons for *capite velato* on his own, while his only outside help is a non-Roman source from more than a century prior. It may indicate that there was no lively debate about the purpose of *capite velato* among the first-century CE Romans.[43] It is possible that Roman attitudes at the time were shaped by Virgil's

---

[43] It has also been argued that the way in which Plutarch deals with Roman customs in *Moralia* may evidence that he considers Roman culture at large "strange and difficult to explain." Kathy Ehrensperger, *Paul at the Crossroads of Cultures: Theologizing in the Space Between*, LNTS 456 (New York: Bloomsbury T&T Clark, 2013), 80. For example, when Plutarch poses questions about Greek customs, he usually provides a singular answer, but when he asks questions about

portrayal of *capite velato* as divinely mandated ancient tradition (see section 2.2.1), leaving little need for further explanation. We shall explore this possibility more closely in Chapter 4.

Plutarch also informs us that not all of the gods were worshiped with a covered head by the Romans. According to Plutarch, the Romans worshiped Saturn and Honor with uncovered heads (ἀπαρακαλύπτῳ τῇ κεφαλῇ). Plutarch offers several possible reasons for this. Regarding Saturn, for example, he suggests that either the Romans worshiped him with uncovered heads because the worship of Saturn predated Aeneas, or because Saturn was a deity of the underworld and the other gods were heavenly, or because truth was not to be covered, and Saturn was the father of truth (*Quaest. rom.* 11–12 [266e-f]). And regards to Honor, Plutarch proposes that its worship with uncovered heads may have been related to the custom of Romans uncovering in the presence of honored persons (*Quaest. rom.* 13 [266f-267a]). Regardless of the true reasons for these anomalies in Roman worship, however, the fact that Plutarch only identifies two deities whom the Romans worshiped with uncovered heads demonstrates that if all the other Roman gods and goddesses were worshiped *capite velato*, this ritual gesture must have been conspicuous indeed.

2.3.5 *Capite velato* in Juvenal

In his sixth satire, the famous Roman satirist Juvenal (ca. 55–127 CE) castigates Roman women about a number of things that he finds fault with. In one of such rebukes, *capite velato* features:

> A certain lady of the lineage of the Lamiae and the Appii inquired (*rogabat*) of Janus and Vesta, with offerings of cake and wine, whether Pollio could hope for the Capitoline oak-chaplet and promise victory to his lyre. What more could she have done had her husband been ill, or if the doctors had been shaking their heads over her dear little son? There she stood before the altar, thinking it no shame to veil her head (*velare caput*) on behalf of a harper; she repeated, in due form, all the words prescribed to her; her cheek blanched when the lamb was opened. Tell me now, I pray, O father Janus, thou most ancient of the Gods, dost thou answer such as she? You have much time on your hands in heaven; so far as I can see, there is nothing for you Gods to do. One lady consults you about a comedian, another wishes to commend to you a tragic actor; the soothsayer (*haruspex*) will soon be troubled with varicose veins. (*Sat.* 6.385-397 [Ramsay])

Here Juvenal satirizes women for treating the winning chances of their favorite comedians, tragic actors, or musicians as though it were a matter of life and death.

Roman customs, he provides several suggestions but without a definite conclusion of his own (as here in regards to *capite velato*). Ehrensperger, *Paul at the Crossroads of Cultures*, 80.

In this particular scene, then, *capite velato* is not in focus, but features as an accompaniment to the process of divination. The woman in question is portrayed as standing in front of the altar *capite velato*, repeating the words of the *haruspex* as she observes the lamb being cut open to find out the divine answer to her concern. Juvenal does not poke fun at this woman for being *capite velato* during divination, but for troubling the gods with trivial matters unworthy of their attention.

2.4 Summary of the Literary References to *capite velato*

In the above overview of literary references to *capite velato*, a few things stand out that are worth highlighting here. First, while some entries (such as Plutarch's observation discussed in section 2.1.1) describe *capite velato* as accompanying Roman worship in general, three acts of worship are most frequently associated with *capite velato*: prayer, sacrifice, and divination. Second, both men and women are described in the pose of *capite velato*, and there seem to be no gender-based differences in regards to how this ritual gesture was performed. Third, references to *capite velato* appear in Roman writings from the early second century BCE to as late as the fourth or fifth century CE, with the Augustan period claiming the highest concentration of these descriptions (e.g., Livy, Dionysius of Halicarnassus, Virgil, Ovid). Fourth, while most of the references to *capite velato* (particularly in the histories) are concerned with prominent figures—generals, consuls, emperors, augurs, priests, and so on—several entries suggest that *capite velato* was a customary ritual gesture for Romans at large, not exclusively reserved for the social elite or religious specialists. And fifth, while some, or perhaps even most, of the Romans may have viewed *capite velato* with reverence due to the influence of the *Aeneid*, comments by Lucretius and Dionysius of Halicarnassus suggest that some non-Romans as well as Romans could have seen nothing more than superstitious behavior and thus viewed it with derision.

2.5 *Capite velato* as a Symbol of Augustan Propaganda

We will now examine several depictions of *capite velato* on mainly Roman altars and statues dating from the time of Augustus to the late second century CE. These chronological limitations are necessary here because of the nature of the evidence. For example, unlike literary sources, which have been largely organized into searchable databases, much of the archaeological evidence regarding *capite velato* remains unsorted and even unknown.[44] Thus, an exhaustive overview of the archaeological evidence regarding *capite velato* would first require years of work to document all possible depictions of *capite velato*, an undertaking beyond the scope of this project. What really matters here is evidence contemporaneous with 1 Cor 11:2–16, so it makes the most sense to start with Augustus because with him Rome entered a new epoch in terms of politics as well as of religion.[45] And as we shall see, *capite velato* appears to have been adopted by Augustus as a key symbol of his religious revival that the subsequent emperors then also employed in their efforts to emulate Augustus. In the following pages, therefore, we will analyze the surviving depictions of *capite velato* from the relevant time period for which scholars have been able to establish provenance with a reasonable degree of confidence.

2.5.1 Ara Pacis Augustae

When victorious Augustus returned from Gaul in 13 BCE after a three-year absence from Rome, the Senate commissioned the construction of an altar in celebration of him. This massive altar, standing over six meters tall and approximately eleven meters long on each side, was dedicated to *Pax Romana* on the birthday of Augustus's wife Livia in 9 BCE. The symbolism on this altar is rich, and *capite velato* heavily features. For example, before one enters the steps leading to the altar of sacrifice itself, one is greeted by two large scenes on the top two quadrants of either side of the opening. On the right side, Aeneas's inaugural sacrifice in the land of Italy is depicted and Aeneas has his head covered with his garment as he pours libation over the altar (figures 2.2 and 2.3). The adjacent side wall to this illustration of Aeneas's sacrifice portrays a procession of dignitaries making their way towards the altar of sacrifice. The first dignitary in this procession to catch one's attention is Augustus himself, his head covered with his garment and his face turned towards Aeneas (figures 2.4 and 2.5). This creates a deliberate and symbolic connection

---

[44] For example, during my trip to Greece and Italy in October and November 2023 to document *capite velato* in various museums and archaeological sites, I encountered many depictions of what appeared to be *capite velato* that I had been unaware of through secondary literature and which have not yet been documented.

[45] Both Livy and Suetonius inform us, for example, that Augustus repaired many temples and renewed the services within them, reinstalled priestly offices that had been neglected, revived certain festivals and ceremonies, and in general made religious observance more conspicuous on the streets and in the homes of Rome and beyond (Livy, *Ab urbe cond.* 4.20.7; Suetonius, *Aug.* 31.3–4). According to Suetonius, Augustus even changed his name from Octavian to Augustus because he wanted his name to be tied to augury, the divinatory rite by which Rome had reportedly been founded (*Aug.* 7.2).

between Aeneas, the first to sacrifice in the land of Italy, and Augustus, the first to sacrifice on the Ara Pacis.[46] Considering that Virgil's *Aeneid*—which Augustus had saved from destruction only a decade prior to the dedication of the Ara Pacis—was beginning to enter national consciousness, we may take the portrayal of Augustus here to symbolize Augustus's belief that he was overseeing the rebirth of the Roman state by divine mandate, just as Aeneas had founded it in the *Aeneid* through divine guidance and protection (see section 2.2.1). But regardless of the exact message conveyed by this portrayed connection between Aeneas and Augustus, what is crucial for us to note is that *capite velato* serves as a conspicuous visual link between Augustus and Aeneas.[47]

Augustus is not the only one portrayed *capite velato* in this procession, however. Further back, the *flaminius lictor*, Agrippa, Livia (Augustus's wife), and Antonia Maior (grandmother of Nero) also have their heads covered with their garments, while most others (including Antonia Minor, mother of emperor Claudius) are bareheaded or wear only garlands but not garments on their heads (figures 2.6 and 2.7). In the procession depicted on the opposite wall (to the left of the front entrance to the altar), three priestly colleges are portrayed: the *quindecemviri*, who were responsible for consulting the Sibylline books; the *augurs*, who were responsible for divination based on the behavior of birds (see section 2.2.4); and the *septemviri*, who were in charge of certain festivals and celebrations in honor of the gods.[48] Interestingly, only one member from each of these priestly colleges is

---

[46] See discussion concerning the connecting details in Richard Gordon, "The Veil of Power: Emperors, Sacrificers and Benefactors," in *Pagan Priests: Religion and Power in the Ancient World*, ed. Mary Beard and John North (Ithaca, NY: Cornell University Press, 1990), 209–10; John Elsner, "Cult and Sculpture: Sacrifice in the Ara Pacis Augustae," *JRS* 81 (1991): 54; John R. Clarke, *Art in the Lives of Ordinary Romans: Visual Representation and Non-Elite Viewers in Italy, 100 B.C.–A.D. 315* (Berkeley: University of California Press, 2003), 24–26; Kathleen S. Lamp, *A City of Marble: The Rhetoric of Augustan Rome* (Columbia, SC: University of South Carolina Press, 2013), 121–22; James B. Rives, "Roman Empire and Roman Emperor: Animal Sacrifice as an Instrument of Religious Convergence," in *Religious Convergence in the Ancient Mediterranean*, ed. Sandra Blakely and Billie Jean Collins (Atlanta: Lockwood Press, 2019), 529.

[47] It seems that Julius Caesar was the first ruler of Rome to advertise an individual descent from Aeneas (up to this point, the descent of Romans from Aeneas was spoken of in general terms). Augustus appropriated his great-uncle's strategy and likewise advertised his direct personal lineage from Aeneas. See, Michael Kochenash, "You Can't Hear 'Aeneas' without Thinking of Rome," *JBL* 136 (2017): 674–75.

[48] These Roman priestly colleges are so described in John Scheid, "The Priest," in *The Romans*, ed. Andrea Giardina, trans. Lydia G. Cochrane (Chicago: University of Chicago Press, 1993), 57, 60.

depicted with his head covered by a garment, while the other priests only have wreaths on their heads (figures 2.8 and 2.9). It may be that those portrayed *capite velato* had an active role in the inaugural sacrifice on Ara Pacis or some future role in the upkeep of this altar—Augustus himself declared, for example, that all the priestly colleges as well as the magistrates were to perform an annual sacrifice on Ara Pacis (*Res Gestae Divi Augusti* 12). However, the specific reason for this distinction remains unclear. Whatever the case, it is important to note here that this distinction on Ara Pacis is not based on gender (as some women and some men are covered while others are not) nor on social status (as some priests are covered while others are not).

Figure 2.2: The top right-hand quadrant above the front entrance to the Ara Pacis altar depicts Aeneas's inaugural sacrifice in the land of Italy. Aeneas has his head covered with his garment. Interestingly, Aeneas is portrayed without an undergarment in this scene.

Figure 2.3: The museum of Ara Pacis has tried to imagine what the frieze of Aeneas's inaugural sacrifice may have looked like in color. Based on Virgil's description, Aeneas is depicted with a purple robe. Here we can also see more clearly Aeneas holding a libation dish over the altar and we can also more clearly make out that Aeneas is wearing a wreath over which the garment is drawn.

2.5.2 Statues of Augustus in Rome, Corinth, and Beyond

The Ara Pacis is not the only place where we find Augustus *capite velato*. There are a number of statues in various locations around the former empire which portray Augustus covered of the head with the toga in the pose of a sacrificer. It is difficult to estimate the original number of such statues, since those made from more precious metals were destroyed long ago, but of the approximately 230 surviving statues of Augustus, about 20 portray him *capite velato*.[49] If we apply this ratio to the premise that thousands of statues of Augustus were erected throughout the empire, it is possible that the original number of statues which portray Augustus *capite velato* reached to several hundreds.[50] Yet, whatever the exact number of the originals, the significant proportion of surviving *capite velato* statues of

---

[49] These numbers are provided by Gordon, "Veil of Power," 211–12.
[50] Gordon, "Veil of Power," 211.

Augustus, especially when compared to those of his predecessors and successors, demonstrates the importance of *capite velato* for Augustus. As Paul Zanker exclaims: "It is astonishing how many portraits of Augustus made during his lifetime, both on coins and as honorific statues, show him veiled in a toga."[51]

Figure 2.4 (left): Augustus is in the middle of this frame, his head turned towards the viewer's left, towards the depiction of Aeneas and the front entrance to the altar. Most of those surrounding Augustus in this frame look in different directions which puts Augustus's gaze towards what is important into focus. This part of the frieze has extensive damage and so one can make out capite velato here only with much difficulty

Figure 2.5 (right): Reconstructed frame of Ara Pacis featuring Augustus. Augustus is imagined to have been originally portrayed as wearing an all-purple toga (like Aeneas). Most men in this frame wear garlands (with one exception), but only Augustus has his head covered with the garment as he gazes towards Aeneas's inaugural sacrifice and towards the front entrance to the altar.

---

[51] Paul Zanker, *The Power of Images in the Age of Augustus*, trans. Alan Shapiro (Ann Arbor, MI: The University of Michigan Press, 1988), 127.

118 2. Having a Garment Down from the Head

Figure 2.6: A frame of the procession a bit further back from Augustus. From the left here, flaminius lictor has his head covered with his garment as he carries an axe and faces towards the sacrificial altar. In the middle of the frame is Agrippa with his head covered, and on the right is Livia, Augustus's wife, her head also covered. They all face towards Aeneas, while some others in this frame gaze in different directions.

Figure 2.7: On the left of this frame of the procession we have Antonia Minor (mother of emperor Claudius) facing away from Aeneas while her head is uncovered. In the middle of the frame is Antonia Maior (grandmother of emperor Nero) facing towards Aeneas while her head is covered. It is unclear why one woman is portrayed with a head-covering on and the other is not.

2.5 Capite velato as a Symbol of Augustan Propaganda

Figure 2.8: This is a frame from the procession depicted on the wall that is to the left of the front entrance to the altar. On the left side of this frame are some members of the quindecemviri. One of them (the one seemingly in possession of a box) is covered of the head. On the right side of this frame are four augurs, but only one of them is portrayed capite velato.

Figure 2.9: In this frame of the procession, the college of the septemviri is depicted. Only one member has his head covered with a garment.

Figure 2.10: Statue of Augustus capite velato, which stood in the center of Corinth in the middle of the first century CE. The hands have been broken off, but the position of the remaining portion of the arms suggests that Augustus was originally depicted as holding a libation dish (patera) as is common in capite velato statues (see below). Archaeological Museum of Ancient Corinth, inv. S-1116.

What is most important for us here is that one of the statues of Augustus *capite velato* stood in (or in an adjacent building of) the Forum—the hub of commercial, social, political, and judicial activity—in the city of Corinth at the time of Paul (figures 2.10, 2.11, and 2.12).[52] The statue in Corinth is similar in size (approx. 2 meters tall) to the one discovered near Via Labicana in Rome, which is preserved in a better condition and thus provides a clearer idea of what the Corinthian statue may have looked like during the first century CE (figures 2.13 and 2.14). These statues of Augustus *capite velato* in Rome, Corinth, and elsewhere communicated

---

[52] The statue was discovered between 1914–1915 during an archaeological dig at a building site known as Julian Basilica, which is located on the east side of the Forum (figure 2.12). See Franklin P. Johnson, "Sculpture: 1896–1923," *Corinth* 9 (1931): 70–72.

Augustus's role either as the chief priest of Roman religion or as the *paterfamilias* of Roman people, but most importantly, such an appearance highlighted the virtue of *pietas*.[53] *Pietas* encompassed loyalty to one's family and to Rome; regard for the gods, dead ancestors, and social norms; and concern for ritual purity. Thus, some modern scholars consider *pietas* to have been the most important virtue for the Romans.[54] If so, Augustus's statue which stood *capite velato* in the center of activity in Corinth at the time of Paul would have served as a potent reminder to Roman citizens and colonial viewers of what was important to the Romans.

Figure 2.11: Close-up of the head of Augustus on the statue from Corinth. Notice that the garment covers only part of the head. Augustus's ears as well as much of the hair remain visible.

---

[53] Zanker, *The Power of Images*, 127; Gordon, "Veil of Power," 211; Clarke, *Art in the Lives of Ordinary Romans*, 82; Laura Gawlinski, "Dress and Ornaments," in *A Companion to the Archaeology of Religion in the Ancient World*, ed. Rubina Raja and Jörg Rüpke (Chichester, UK: John Wiley & Sons, 2015), 101–2.

[54] See, for example, Von Albrecht, *A History of Roman Literature*, 1:36; Ehrensperger, *Paul at the Crossroads of Cultures*, 181–82; Margaret Y. MacDonald, *The Power of Children: The Construction of Christian Families in the Greco-Roman World* (Waco, TX: Baylor University Press, 2014), 9; Jonathan Schwiebert, "Honoring the Divine," in *Early Christian Ritual Life*, ed. Richard E. DeMaris, Jason T. Lamoreaux, and Steven C. Muir (New York: Routledge, 2018), 22.

Figure 2.12: The Archaeological Museum of Ancient Corinth has provided a map of the ancient city based on archaeological remains and Pausanias's description from the second century CE. The leftmost area in this photograph depicts the ancient Forum of the city. The larger building at the bottom of the Forum is the Julian Basilica where the capite velato statues of Augustus and Nero were found.

Figure 2.13: Statue of Augustus capite velato dated to the last decade of the first century BCE that stood along Via Labicana in Rome. The position of the arms here is similar to the Corinthian statue. Museo Nazionale Romano, Palazzo Massimo, inv. 56230.

Figure 2.14: Close-up of the head of Augustus on the Via Labicana statue. Notice that in this depiction, the toga covers the ears (although they still remain visible), but similarly to the Corinthian statue much of the hair is not covered by the garment.

2.5.3 *Capite velato* and Livia

Augustus was not the only member of his family to be portrayed *capite velato*. We have already noted that Augustus's wife Livia is depicted *capite velato* on the Ara Pacis, but there are also other contexts in which Livia is shown with a covered head. However, we must proceed with caution here, since, as we shall see in Chapter 5, there were other virtues besides *pietas* that some Roman women communicated through being covered of the head with a garment on portraits, and it is not always clear from the depictions themselves what is indicated. Thus, here we will limit ourselves to portrayals where it is evident that the head-covering is associated with the worship of the gods (especially praying, sacrificing, or divination), or with *pietas*. For example, a large bronze statue of Livia found in the theatre of Herculaneum (a town near Pompeii which was likewise destroyed and buried by the volcanic eruption of Mount Vesuvius in 79 CE) depicts her praying with hands raised while covered of the head with a garment (figures 2.15 and 2.16). Another, smaller bronze statue found in Herculaneum appears to portray Livia in the posture of an offerer—the palm of her outstretched left hand faces upwards, while she wears a diadem which is partly covered by her garment drawn over the head (figure 2.17). And interestingly, even though emperor Tiberius, Livia's son, issued several coin types depicting Livia, it is only on the coin type portraying her as *Pietas* (issued in 22/23 CE) that she is shown with her head covered by a garment (in addition to the diadem).[55] These images of Livia with a covered head stand out because on the majority of her portrayals, she is not shown with a garment over the head.[56] Thus, the choice to depict Livia with a garment over the head in the context of worship or *pietas* seems deliberate.

Figure 2.15: A large statue from the first half of the first century CE that stood in the theatre in Herculaneum depicts Livia praying with her hands raised and with a covered head. Museo Archeologico Nazionale di Napoli, inv. 5589.

---

[55] Margarete Bieber, "The Development of Portraiture on Roman Republican Coins," *ANRW* 1 (1974): 897–98.

[56] For a comprehensive list of depictions of Livia with illustrations see, Elizabeth Bartman, *Portraits of Livia: Imaging the Imperial Woman in Augustan Rome* (New York: Cambridge University Press, 1999). A comprehensive analysis but without illustrations can also be found in Susan E. Wood, *Imperial Women: A Study in Public Images, 40 BC – AD 68* (Boston: Brill, 1999), 75–141.

2.5 Capite velato as a Symbol of Augustan Propaganda

Figure 2.16 (left): Close-up of the head of Livia on the Herculaneum statue. Notice that Livia's ears and much of her hair remain visible.

Figure 2.17 (right): A bronze statue of Livia from the second quarter of the first century CE discovered in Herculaneum depicts Livia as an offerer. Livia has her head covered, but her crown and part of her hairdo remain visible. Museo Archeologico Nazionale di Napoli, inv. 5013.

2.5.4 The Altars of the *vicomagistri*

In 7 BCE, Augustus re-organized the city of Rome into 265 *vici*. A *vicus* was an area organized around a crossroad (where two or more roads met), and four freedmen were set in charge of each *vicus*.[57] These officials known as *vicomagistri* were responsible for dealing with local crime, traffic, and fires, but most importantly, they were in charge of public worship of Roman tutelary deities known as the

---

[57] Zanker, *Power of Images*, 129–30.

Lares and of the *genius*[58] of Augustus in their *vici*.[59] Starting with 7 BCE, therefore, new altars were erected at street corners by the *vicomagistri*, depicting "neighborhood freedmen and slaves engaged in sacrifice to the *Lares* and the *genius*, surrounded by Augustan family symbols and, in some cases, portraits of the imperial family itself."[60] Most importantly for our study, *capite velato* features prominently on the surviving altars of the *vicomagistri*, and we will discuss several examples of these altars here.

We have, for example, an altar of the *vicomagistri* from the very first year of Augustus's re-organization of Rome (7 BCE), as the inscription on it specifies that the altar was dedicated by "the first officers who entered office."[61] The front of the altar shows two Lares, next to whom a figure (perhaps *genius*) pours libation *capite velato*. The side panels, on the other hand, depict the four *vicomagistri* (two per panel), each also covered of the head with a garment, as they pour libation over an altar.[62] Another altar from the same period (7 BCE), which also most likely stood

---

[58] We do not have a precise one-word equivalent in English for *genius* that fully captures the meaning of the original Latin term, and the concept itself is variously understood. Michael Peppard, for example, describes *genius* as "unseen spiritual power," James Rives as "divine alter ego," Duncan Fishwick as one's "spiritual companion," and Kathy Ehrensperger as "the guardian spirit of the head of the household." See, Michael Peppard, *The Son of God in the Roman World: Divine Sonship in Its Social and Political Context* (New York: Oxford University Press, 2011), 113; Rives, "Roman Empire and Roman Emperor," 535; Duncan Fishwick, *The Imperial Cult in the Latin West: Studies in the Ruler Cult of the Western Provinces of the Roman Empire* (New York: Brill, 1991), 2.1:382–83; Kathy Ehrensperger, "Between Polis, Oikos, and Ekklesia: The Challenge of Negotiating the Spirit World (1 Cor 12:1–11)," in *The First Urban Churches 2: Roman Corinth*, ed. James R. Harrison and L. L. Welborn, WGRWSup 8 (Atlanta: SBL Press, 2016), 115. Pedar Foss, however, argues that *genius* "represented the procreative force of the family, particularly the *paterfamilias*." Pedar W. Foss, "Watchful *Lares*: Romand Household Organization and the Rituals of Cooking and Eating," in *Domestic Space in the Roman World: Pompeii and Beyond*, ed. Ray Laurence and Andrew Wallace-Hadrill (Portsmouth, RI: *JRA*, 1997), 199. Given the range of interpretations, I will avoid providing a singular English definition and will retain the Latin term *genius* throughout.

[59] Clarke, *Art in the Lives of Ordinary Romans*, 81.

[60] Peppard, *The Son of God*, 64. See also, J. Bert Lott, *The Neighborhoods of Augustan Rome* (New York: Cambridge University Press, 2004), 136–37.

[61] Lott, *The Neighborhoods*, 140.

[62] For identification of the figures and for pictures of the altar see, Lott, *Neighborhoods*, 140–42; Harriet I. Flower, *The Dancing Lares and the Serpent in the Garden: Religion at the Roman Street Corner* (Princeton: Princeton University Press, 2017), 304–6; Amy Russell, "The Altars of the Lares Augusti," in *The Social Dynamics of Roman Imperial Imagery*, ed. Amy Russell and Monica Hellström (New York: Cambridge University Press, 2020), 42.

at a street corner of a *vicus*, depicts two Lares on the front, but on both side panels of this altar, a woman is portrayed pouring libation—a rarity in Roman art—*capite velato*.[63] Harriet Flower and Meghan DiLuzio argue that this altar was dedicated by certain brides or by their relatives who were serving or had served as *vicomagistri* on the occasion of a wedding, since the Roman brides traditionally visited the local crossroad shrines on their wedding day.[64] Whatever the exact circumstances of the dedication of this altar, however, what matters to us is that covered heads are conspicuously visible in an act of worship.

Another altar of the *vicomagistri*, known as the Altar of the Vicus Sandaliarius and dedicated in the year 2 BCE, depicts three figures on its front panel, all of whom are covered of the head with their garments. The central figure holds a *lituus*, a curved staff used by the augurs (cf. Plutarch, *Cam.* 32.5), and is generally identified as Augustus. To Augustus's left stands a woman holding a libation dish and an incense box, believed to be Livia (or an unidentified priestess), while on his right stands a man thought to be Augustus's adopted son, Gaius Caesar. The front panel also depicts a pecking bird between the figures of Gaius and Augustus, which has led interpreters to suggest that the altar portrays Augustus and Livia (or a priestess) in an act of divination as they send Gaius off on a military campaign to the east.[65] Then there is the Altar of Vicus Aesculeti, dated to 2 CE, which shows on its front panel all four *vicomagistri* pouring libation over an altar *capite velato*. The scene also includes a musician and attendants leading the sacrificial animals—a pig for the Lares and a bull for the *genius* of Augustus—but these figures are not depicted wearing garments over the head.[66]

If these surviving altars of the *vicomagistri* are representative of the rest of the altars of the *vicomagistri* now destroyed, we can say that *capite velato* was publicly and conspicuously present on street corners throughout Rome within a decade of the city's re-organization. At least the surviving altars demonstrate that the *vicomagistri* of the freedmen class were keen to emulate their emperor, as he was

---

[63] A thorough analysis of the altar with pictures can be found in Harriet I. Flower and Meghan J. DiLuzio, "The Women and the Lares: A Reconsideration of an Augustan Altar from the Capitoline in Rome," *AJA* 123 (2019): 213–36.

[64] Flower and DiLuzio, "The Women and the Lares," 232.

[65] These figures are so identified in Lott, *Neighborhoods*, 144; Peppard, *The Son of God*, 77; Lamp, *A City of Marble*, 120. An alternative interpretation can be found in Russell, "The Altars," 41. For a photograph of the altar and additional discussion of its symbolism, see also Flower and DiLuzio, "The Women and the Lares," 220–21.

[66] For images and discussion see, Lott, *Neighborhoods*, 142–44; Clarke, *Art in the Lives of Ordinary Romans*, 81–85; Russell, "The Altars," 29–30.

portrayed on the Ara Pacis and on prominent statues. And it is very likely that the actual worship at these altars—sacrifice, prayer, divination—was conducted by the *vicomagistri* or by the local citizens on important personal or public occasions in the same manner as portrayed on the altars—*capite velato*.

2.5.5 Augustus Honored in Pompeii and Corinth

Pompeii offers us a relatively well-preserved view into how Augustus was honored outside of Rome, even decades after his death. For example, on the east side of the Forum in Pompeii there is a small temple dedicated to Augustus. Within the precincts of this temple stands a well-preserved altar, the erection of which is generally dated to the reign of Augustus.[67] The front panel of the altar shows a sacrificial scene: a slave with an axe leads a bull to be sacrificed (for the emperor), a musician plays the double flute, and some other attendants are positioned around the altar as well, but the central figure is the one pouring libation over the altar, his head (and only his) covered with the garment (figures 2.18 and 2.19). Adjacent to this temple of Augustus is a large building dedicated to Augustan *Pietas* and *Concordia*. The sponsor of this structure was a local wealthy priestess by the name of Eumachia, and this portico may have been constructed in the lifetime of Augustus or shortly after his death.[68] There are many references to Augustus, his family, and his values in the decoration of the building, and a statue of Aeneas stood at the entrance. However, most notably for our purposes, within this building dedicated to Augustan *Pietas*, a statue of Eumachia herself stood, and she is portrayed *capite velato* (figure 2.20).[69]

The above evidence from Pompeii suggests that the buildings and altars set up outside of Rome in honor of Augustus stood in use well into the first century CE, and that *capite velato* was a prominent symbol associated with them. If Pompeii is representative of other first-century CE towns in the land of Italy, as well as in Roman colonies outside of Italy, it is possible that the Forum in Corinth originally contained many more depictions of *capite velato* associated with Augustus than the one statue of him in the pose of *capite velato* that survives (see section 2.5.2). For example, in the middle of the Forum in Corinth (slightly towards the Julian Basilica) a large base (over two meters tall) remains of a now-lost statue dedicated by the *Augustales*—the "municipal organizers of the imperial cult" made up of

---

[67] Alison E. Cooley and M. G. L. Cooley, *Pompeii and Herculaneum: A Sourcebook*, 2nd ed. (New York: Routledge, 2014), 136–37.

[68] Cooley and Cooley, *Pompeii and Herculaneum*, 140.

[69] Cooley and Cooley, *Pompeii and Herculaneum*, 140–43.

freeborn and freedmen—to *divus* Augustus.[70] The statue was most likely set up between the end of Augustus's reign and the end of Tiberius's reign. Margaret Laird argues that the statue, which itself may have stood up to three meters tall based on the markings left on the base, likely portrayed Augustus himself.[71] Laird further suggests that this tall statue may have been purposefully positioned so that the deified Augustus faced Temple E, which some scholars believe served as the "town's imperial cult center."[72] Unfortunately, the statue itself has not survived, nor has Temple E unearthed much beyond the rudiments of a structure, so we do not know what symbolism accompanied the prominent statue of *divus* Augustus nor how Temple E was decorated, but if we take Pompeii as a model, it may be that *capite velato* featured in some capacity.

Figure 2.18: A well-preserved altar, located at the site of a temple dedicated to Augustus on the east side of the Forum in Pompeii, depicts a sacrificial scene on its front panel.

---

[70] Margaret L. Laird, "The Emperor in a Roman Town: The Base of the *Augustales* in the Forum at Corinth," in *Corinth in Context: Comparative Studies on Religion and Society*, ed. Steven J. Friesen, Daniel N. Schowalter, and James C. Walters (Boston: Brill, 2010), 72, 74, 76.

[71] Laird, "The Emperor in a Roman Town," 73, 84–85, 88–91.

[72] Laird, "The Emperor in a Roman Town," 93.

Figure 2.19: A close-up of the front panel of the altar from Pompeii that faces the Forum. The figure who pours libation over the altar has his head covered with a garment. He is the only one capite velato in this scene.

Figure 2.20: A statue of Eumachia, a local Pompeiian priestess from the first half of the first century CE, stood in a building sponsored by her, which was dedicated to Augustan Pietas and Concordia. This building was adjacent to the temple of Augustus. Eumachia's head is covered with a garment but much of her hair remains visible. Museo Archeologico Nazionale di Napoli, inv. 6232.

2.6 *Capite velato* and Augustus's Successors

As has already been noted, *capite velato* seems to have been more important for Augustus as a symbol of piety than for his predecessors or successors (see section 2.5.2). We do not possess nearly as much material on *capite velato* in association with the later emperors as we do in the case of Augustus. Nevertheless, *capite velato* still features in imperial art well into the fourth century CE,[73] and in this section, we will examine several examples of it from the first and second centuries.

2.6.1 *Capite velato* and the Julio-Claudian Dynasty

Augustus's struggles to secure a suitable heir to succeed him are well documented. His only biological child was his daughter Julia, and so throughout his career, Augustus adopted several male relatives as his legal sons and potential heirs to the throne. One of the first male relatives whom Augustus groomed for this purpose was Marcellus, Augustus's nephew, to whom Augustus gave Julia in marriage. However, Marcellus died of illness at the tender age of 19 (23 BCE), and the plan did not materialize. Despite dying at such a young age, Marcellus seems to have made quite an impression on his contemporaries, and his fame spread outside of Rome. Thus, we find that a statue in honor of Marcellus had been set up in Pompeii in a prominent location (of which only the base with inscription survives).[74] But what interests us here is a bust of Marcellus *capite velato*, discovered beneath one of the buildings in Pompeii that belonged to a wealthy family, and interestingly, it seems to have been commissioned several decades after Marcellus's death (figure 2.21). While this statue seems to have been discarded by the time of the eruption of Vesuvius, it must have held some significance for the owners of the property at some earlier time period, perhaps during the reign of Augustus. It is important to note here that even though we only possess the head of Marcellus and so we do not have any indicators of what the original context may have been—whether sacrifice, prayer, or divination—it is safe to assume that in the case of depictions of prominent Roman men in the first two centuries CE, *capite velato* is in view when a garment covers the head. Unlike Roman women, who may have communicated other symbols besides *capite velato* through covering the head with the garment (see Chapter 5), Roman men of status at that time period seemed to have used this gesture in art primarily to signify *capite velato*.

---

[73] Rives, "Roman Empire and Roman Emperor," 529, 531.
[74] Cooley and Cooley, *Pompeii and Herculaneum*, 205.

Figure 2.21: Head of Marcellus capite velato found in a dump under the House of Championnet in Pompeii. The bust is dated to the first half of the first century CE, so some decades after Marcellus's death. It is now housed in Antiquarium di Pompeii.

Augustus was eventually succeeded by Tiberius, Livia's son from a previous relationship, whom Augustus adopted as his own. Just like his adopted father, Tiberius is also portrayed *capite velato* in certain ritual settings. Thus, a large bronze statue of Tiberius in the pose of an offerer stood at the theatre in Herculaneum and may have been set up there immediately following Tiberius's death (figure 2.22). Another large statue of Tiberius *capite velato* in the pose of a sacrificer has been unearthed in modern-day Nin in western Croatia, a city known in Roman times as Aenona.[75] Tiberius was succeeded by Caligula, his brother's grandson. Even though Caligula only ruled for less than four years (37–41 CE), a larger-than-life statue of him *capite velato* was set up all the way in Gortyn, Crete.[76] A statue of

---

[75] For discussion and an image see, Marija Buzov, "The Imperial Cult in Dalmatia," *Classica et Christiana* 10 (2015): 72, 85, 89. See also, J. J. Wilkes, *Dalmatia* (London: Routledge and Kegan Paul, 1969), 203–5.

[76] For discussion and an image see, Jan Stubbe Østergaard, "Reflections on the Typology and Context of the Richmond Caligula," in *New Studies on the Portraits of Caligula in the Virginia Museum of Fine Arts*, ed. Peter J. M. Schertz and Bernard Frischer (Boston: Brill, 2020), 52–53.

Caligula *capite velato* apparently also stood in a northern Italian town called Velleia, but this statue was later reworked to represent Caligula's uncle and successor, Claudius.[77] Of Claudius (reigned 41–54 CE), we additionally have a *capite velato* bust from Sparta (figure 2.23).

Figure 2.22: A large bronze statue from the mid-first century CE depicting emperor Tiberius in the pose of an offerer stood in the theatre of Herculaneum. Tiberius's head is covered by his garment. Museo Archeologico Nazionale di Napoli, inv. 5615.

---

[77] Østergaard, "Reflections on the Typology," 51.

Figure 2.23: A portrait of emperor Claudius from the first century CE that stood in Sparta, mainland Greece. Claudius's head is partially covered with a garment, his ears fully visible. Arcaheological Museum of Sparti, inv. 10812.

In 49 CE, Claudius married Julia Agrippina, a great-granddaughter of Augustus from her mother's side. Agrippina had a son from a previous relationship, Nero, whom Claudius adopted as his own, and who then succeeded him (reigned 54–68 CE). It appears that early in his reign, Nero had a statue made of himself *capite velato* which stood in a prominent place in the center of ancient Rome. However, since Nero (and with him the Julio-Claudian dynasty) was overthrown with vengeance, many statues of him were removed, destroyed, or re-worked to represent other figures. Thus, of the *capite velato* statue that had stood in prominence in Rome at the time of Nero, only the head has been found buried under the temple of Apollo (figure 2.24).[78] Another statue of Nero that stood *capite velato* in Aquileia, an Italian town close to the border of modern-day Slovenia, was reworked into depicting Augustus.[79] Some scholars have argued that a *capite velato* bust found in Corinth, in the vicinity where the *capite velato* statue of Augustus was

---

[78] Eric R. Varner, *Mutilation and Transformation: Damnatio Memoriae and Roman Imperial Portraiture* (Boston: Brill, 2004), 67–68.

[79] Varner, *Mutilation and Transformation*, 61.

unearthed (see section 2.5.2), may depict emperor Nero (figure 2.25). However, it has also been suggested that it may instead portray Nero Julius Caesar (6–31 CE), a grandson of emperor Tiberius's brother, whom Tiberius had adopted as heir.[80] If the latter is the case, this statue would have stood alongside that of Augustus in the Forum of Corinth at the time of Paul's communication with the Corinthians. But in either case, we can say that in the middle of the first century CE, at least two statues of prominent Julio-Claudians *capite velato* lined the Forum in Corinth.

Figure 2.24 (left): The head of a statue of emperor Nero that was made early in his reign and that stood capite velato in a prominent place in the center of Rome (possibly by the temple of Apollo). The statue was discarded after the overthrow of Nero. Museo Nazionale Romano, Palazzo Massimo, inv. 616.

Figure 2.25 (right): A capite velato head found in the vicinity of Julian Basilica in Corinth. There is debate around whether this depicts emperor Nero or an earlier figure who also went by the name of Nero (and who was likewise a prominent Julio-Claudian). Archaeological Museum of Ancient Corinth, inv. S-1088.

---

[80] See the debate, for example, in Johnson, "Sculpture," 76–77; Brunilde Sismondo Ridgway, "Sculpture from Corinth," *Hesperia* 50 (1981): 433.

2.6.2 *Capite velato* and the Nerva-Antonine Dynasty

I have not found readily available evidence depicting the emperors of the Flavian dynasty in the pose of *capite velato*. This may be an accident of history or a deliberate choice of the Flavians. For example, it may be that the Flavians wished to emphasize other values through art than *pietas*, an apparent favorite of Augustus. In any case, the lack of material evidence for *capite velato* in connection to the Flavian dynasty does not mean that they did not worship in this manner. We have discussed, for example, how Josephus describes both Vespasian and Titus performing the ritual gesture of *capite velato*, which Josephus himself may have witnessed in person (see section 2.2.9). In any case, with the assassination of Domitian in 96 CE, the Nerva-Antonine dynasty came to rule Rome for the next century, and we do find *capite velato* depicted in association with the emperors of this dynasty. Thus, for example, in several sacrificial scenes on Trajan's Column (completed in 113 CE), which depicts Trajan's military victories over the Dacians, Trajan himself (reigned 98–117) is depicted pouring libations *capite velato*.[81] However, it is noteworthy that in several other sacrificial scenes on this monument, Trajan is portrayed in the act of pouring libation with an uncovered head.[82] Roger Ulrich describes Trajan in these latter scenes as wearing traveling garbs, whereas in the *capite velato* scenes, he is dressed in the toga.[83] But does this show that the choice of garment affected how sacrifice was conducted? Or were the Romans not expected to sacrifice *capite velato* when traveling through a foreign (non-conquered) territory on a military campaign? This remains unclear.

Trajan was succeeded by Hadrian (reigned 117–138 CE), who had a larger-than-life statue set up of himself *capite velato* in the center of Rome (figure 2.26). Lillian Joyce has shown that Hadrian was especially fond of the memory of Augustus and that he sought to emphasize his connection to the Augustan legacy in numerous ways.[84] The *capite velato* statue in the center of Rome may have served such a function for Hadrian. We also have a roundel of Hadrian sacrificing *capite velato* to the

---

[81] Roger B. Ulrich, professor in the Department of Classics at Dartmouth, has dedicated a website for photographic evidence of all the scenes on Trajan's Column at https://www.trajans-column.org/. For sacrificial scenes involving Trajan see, Roger B. Ulrich, "Trajan Conducting Sacrifice," https://www.trajans-column.org/?page_id=1041. For the images of Trajan in the pose of *capite velato* see plates VIII, LIII, and CIII on this link.

[82] See plates LXXXVI, XCI, and XCIX on the above website.

[83] https://www.trajans-column.org/?page_id=1041.

[84] Lilian Joyce, "In the Footsteps of Augustus: Hadrian and the Imperial Cult," in *Emperors in Images, Architecture, and Ritual: Augustus to Fausta*, ed. Francesco de Angelis (Boston: Archaeological Institute of America, 2020), 79–94.

goddess Diana, which had first been carved on a monument in Rome in the 130s CE (thus in the reign of Hadrian), but which was later incorporated into the Arch of Constantine.[85] Another fascinating example of *capite velato* in association with the emperors of the Nerva-Antonine dynasty is the Great Antonine Altar, discovered in Ephesus. It depicts both Hadrian and his immediate successor Antoninus Pius (reigned 138–161 CE) *capite velato*, while a youthful Marcus Aurelius stands on the side (his head is uncovered), and Lucius Verus (co-emperor with Marcus Aurelius from 161–169 CE) is presented as a child (also uncovered of the head) standing between Hadrian and Antoninus Pius.[86] The date of the altar is debated (the range of late 130s to 169 is usually suggested[87]), but the portrayal of three generations of emperors in unity, with the two elder statesmen *capite velato* in the pose of sacrificers, may suggest that Hadrian together with Antoninus Pius are depicted here as seeking divine favors for the continued prosperity of the empire.

A particularly well-preserved example of *capite velato* in association with the Nerva-Antonine dynasty is a relief depicting a sacrificial scene, likely originally displayed on a triumphal arch in Rome dedicated to Marcus Aurelius.[88] The scene includes a sacrificial animal, attendants (including musicians), a *flamen* wearing an *apex*, an altar, and Marcus Aurelius pouring libation over the altar *capite velato* (figures 2.27 and 2.28). Dietrich Boschung suggests that the sacrifice conducted here relates to "*lustratio execritus*, a ritual sacrifice of purification of the army, executed by the emperor according to his responsibilities."[89] Whatever the exact purpose of the sacrifice, however, the scene itself is similar to other depictions of Roman sacrifices that we have already encountered from the first and second centuries CE.

---

[85] For discussion and an image see, Jaś Elsner, *Imperial Rome and Christian Triumph: The Art of the Roman Empire AD 100–450* (New York: Oxford University Press, 1998), 16–17.

[86] Elsner, *Imperial Rome and Christian Triumph*, 123–24.

[87] Cornelius C. Vermeule, *Roman Imperial Art in Greece and Asia Minor* (Cambridge, MA: Harvard University Press, 1968), 96–97.

[88] Dietrich Boschung, "The Reliefs: Representation of Marcus Aurelius' Deeds," in *A Companion to Marcus Aurelius*, ed. Marcel van Ackeren (Chichester, UK: Wiley-Blackwell, 2012), 308.

[89] Boschung, "The Reliefs," 310.

Figure 2.26: A larger-than-life statue of Hadrian, portrayed as pontifex maximus, was set up during his reign in the center of Rome. Hadrian holds a libation dish in his right hand and has his head covered with his garment. Musei Capitolini, inv. S 54.

Figure 2.27: A well-preserved relief that may have originally decorated a triumphal arch in Rome dedicated to Marcus Aurelius. In the center of the frame stands Marcus Aurelius capite velato, pouring libation over the altar. Behind him, and next to the sacrificial bull, stands a flamen who wears an apex, a special headdress reserved for these priests (see also section 2.1.1). The flautist also has some type of a head-covering on, but only Marcus Aurelius has a garment over the head. Musei Capitolini, inv. S 807.

We will conclude this section with a discussion of two very similar busts of Lucius Verus and Marcus Aurelius (reigned 161–180), who were co-emperors from 161 until the premature death of Lucius Verus in 169 CE. Both busts are of the same size and portray the emperors wearing a wreath of corn, over which the outer garment is drawn. Such similarities suggest that these busts belonged together in a collection.[90] The wreath of corn was an insignia of the Arval Brothers (see also section 2.1.1), and these busts therefore present Marcus Aurelius and Lucius Verus as

---

[90] Jane Fejfer, *Roman Portraits in Context* (New York: Walter de Gruyter, 2008), 87–89. These pages also include images of both busts.

members of this college of priests. Originally, the Arval Brothers were solely responsible for the worship of Dea Dia, a fertility goddess, but after Augustus revived this priestly office, their duty was also to sacrifice for the well-being of the emperor, including on the Ara Pacis.[91] The Arval Brothers kept a detailed record of their cultic activities on marble at the site where worship to Dea Dia was conducted, and thus we have extensive knowledge of the various rituals they performed.[92] For example, one inscription dated to 91 CE describes how sacrifice to Dea Dia was performed on a particular date:

> In the same consulship, on January 7, in the vestibule of the Temple of Concord, the Arval Brethren, under the mastership (for the second time) of Lucius Veratius Quadratus, proclaimed a sacrifice to Dea Dia. In the vestibule of the Temple of Concord Lucius Veratius Quadratus, master of the Arval Brethren, having washed his hands and veiled his head, under the sacred roof and facing east, proclaimed together with his colleagues a sacrifice to Dea Dia: "May it be good, auspicious, propitious, fortunate, and salutary for the Emperor Caesar Domitian Augustus Germanicus, *pontifex maximus*, and for his wife Domitia Augusta, and for their whole house, and for the Roman people, the Quirities, and for the Arval Brethren, and for me! There will be a sacrifice to Dea Dia this year on May 17 at my home, on May 19 at the grove and at my home, and on May 20 at my home."[93]

We see here that sacrifice to Dea Dia was accompanied by prayers for the well-being of the current emperor, his family, the Roman people, the Arval Brothers, and the petitioner himself. This ritual was performed with the garment placed over the head, which already bore the wreath of corn. Thus, the above discussed busts of Lucius Verus and Marcus Aurelius appear to depict them as priests of the college of Arval Brothers in the pose of sacrificers.

---

[91] Zanker, *The Power of Images*, 119–20; Fejfer, *Roman Portraits*, 86; Rives, "Roman Empire and Roman Emperor," 533.

[92] Greg Woolf, "Posterity in the Arval *Acta*," in *The Future of Rome: Roman, Greek, Jewish and Christian Visions*, ed. Jonathan J. Price and Katell Berthelot (New York: Cambridge University Press, 2020), 64.

[93] Naphtali Lewis and Meyer Reinhold, eds. *Roman Civilization, Sourcebook II: The Empire* (New York: Harper & Row, 1966), 557.

Figure 2.28: A close-up of Marcus Auerlius pouring libation over the altar. Notice that he holds the libation dish in his right hand while his left hand tightly holds the hem of his garment, perhaps to ensure that the garment does not fall off the head during the ritual. As discussed in section 2.2.10, some believed that emperor Hadrian's impending death had been signaled through the garment falling off his head during prayer. This mishap may have been of concern to the succeeding Nerva-Antonine emperors.

2.7 *Capite velato* and Domestic Religion

Thus far, we have observed mainly the social elites—imperial families, priests, magistrates—performing the ritual gesture of *capite velato*. It is no surprise that material evidence for *capite velato* is dominated by depictions of dignitaries, since evidence associated with important people, events, or places in history has generally a higher chance of survival. Fortunately for historians, however, the sudden burial of Pompeii under mounts of ashes in 79 CE has preserved for posterity also unexceptional neighborhoods and structures, together with their decorations and artifacts from the first century CE, that might otherwise have been razed, pillaged, re-built, or re-used and therefore lost forever. Thus, Pompeii's sad fate has allowed us glimpses into the everyday life of non-elite citizens, revealing that *capite velato* was also a regular feature in domestic religion.

The Roman household worship typically centered around a shrine known as *lararia*, named after the *Lares*, the tutelary deities of the Romans. A common *lararia* was a wall-niche, which held statuettes of the *Lares* or other gods, and which often depicted in a painted scene the *genius* of the household pouring libation while flanked by the *Lares*.[94] We have several examples of such scenes from the houses in Pompeii, in which the *genius* is portrayed *capite velato* as he holds the libation dish. For example, such a scene can be found on the *lararia* of a building in Pompeii that also functioned as a tavern, providing drinks and hot food for the locals (figure 2.29). A similar scene also decorates the *lararia* of one of the richest households in town, the House of the Vettii, owned by a wealthy family of merchants (figures 2.30 and 2.31). Similar motifs appear also on the wall of a more modest house, the ownership of which remains unknown (figure 2.32). And a painting in the House of the Red Walls depicts a *genius* wearing a white toga as he pours libation over an altar with his right hand and holds a cornucopia in his left hand, with two *Lares* standing on either side of him.[95]

Figure 2.29: A wall-painting that decorated the lararia of the house and thermopolium (tavern) of a certain Vetutius Placidus in Pompeii. In the center of the scene, the household genius pours libation over the altar with his right hand while his left hand holds a cornucopia (a symbol of abundance). The genius has his head covered with the garment and he is flanked by two Lares. The scene also includes depictions of the gods Mercury and Dionysos.

---

[94] Fanny Dolansky, "Household and Family," in *The Oxford Handbook of Early Christian Ritual*, ed. Risto Uro, et al. (Oxford: Oxford University Press, 2019), 174.

[95] For discussion and an image see, Flower, *The Dancing Lares*, 50–51.

2.7 Capite velato and Domestic Religion

Figure 2.30: A wall-painting that decorated the lararia of the wealthy House of Vettii in Pompeii. The genius in the middle holds a libation dish in his right hand (no altar is depicted) and an incense box in his left hand. He is flanked by two Lares.

Figure 2.31: A close-up of the genius depicted on the lararia of the House of Vettii. Notice that the head of the genius is covered with the purple stripe of the toga. Part of the genius's head remains visible, but in this depiction of capite velato, the ears are covered.

Figure 2.32: A wall-painting from one of the houses in region VII of Pompeii dated to the middle of the first century CE (now displayed in the National Archaeological Museum of Naples). The genius with a garment over his head holds a libation dish in his right hand and a cornucopia in his left hand. The Lares stand on the sides, while three attendants are also depicted, one of whom leads the sacrificial animal and one of whom plays an instrument. However, they are quite miniscule in stature to accentuate the importance of the genius and the Lares. Museo Archeologico Nazionale di Napoli, inv. 8905.

An interesting drawing is also found on the wall of a tiny kitchen of a relatively modest dwelling in Pompeii, known as the House of Sutoria Primigenia, which portrays the *paterfamilias* of the household (not the *genius* in this case) and his wife both standing *capite velato* next to an altar.[96] The *Lares* in this scene wear *pilleata* ("liberty-caps," see section 2.1.1), which is uncommon in Roman depictions of the *Lares* and may thus suggest something about the status of the dwellers in this household (i.e., that they were freedmen).[97] The *paterfamilias* and his wife are also portrayed as being of the same height (smaller than the *Lares* but taller than the attendants), which may suggest that the wife played an equally integral role in

---

[96] For discussion and an image see, Clarke, *Art in the Lives of Ordinary Romans*, 75–78.
[97] See, Flower, *The Dancing Lares*, 58.

the household's domestic worship.[98] This modest drawing, hidden from public view, demonstrates that the symbol of *capite velato* had penetrated deep into the layers of society by the middle of the first century CE.

Finally, the statuettes that typically complemented the household *lararia* were of gods and goddesses, but we also find *capite velato* statuettes of the *genius* which may have been used for that purpose. The two examples I will present here are small figurines from the first century CE, originating either from Pompeii or Herculaneum. They depict the *genius* holding a *patera* (libation dish) in the right hand and cornucopia in the left, while the head is covered by a garment (figures 2.33 and 2.34). This image of the *genius* therefore corresponds to the paintings found on the *lararia* and shows that *capite velato* on statues was not only found in city squares and other highly visible spaces but also in miniature form in the privacy of homes. If Pompeii is then representative of other towns and villages in the Roman Empire, we can say that it must have been quite common to encounter an image of *capite velato* when frequenting the Roman households in the first century CE. And it is likely that the actual worship at the *lararia* in Roman homes was conducted in a manner depicted on these shrines—*capite velato*.

2.8 Summary of the Selected Archaeological Evidence

The above overview of the archaeological evidence for *capite velato* is by no means exhaustive, as I am sure many more depictions can be found in the vast territory that once constituted the Roman Empire. Furthermore, some accessible depictions of *capite velato* lack context, and while they are interesting to look at, they offer no information that could be useful here. For instance, one of my favorite examples of this is a statue of a woman in the act of offering grain and incense over a candelabrum, now housed in the Uffizi Gallery in Florence (figures 2.35 and 2.36). It is a finely crafted and well-preserved piece, which the museum has dated to the middle of the second century CE, yet its provenance remains unknown. We do not know where the statue originally stood, who is portrayed, to whom it belonged, or what purpose it served, but it is a fine presentation of the ritual gesture of *capite velato*.

---

[98] Flower, *The Dancing Lares*, 58. See also, DiLuzio, *A Place at the Altar*, 46.

Figure 2.33 (left): A statuette of a genius that complemented a lararia in either Pompeii or Herculaneum in the first century CE. The head of the genius is covered with the garment as he holds a libation dish in his right hand and a cornucopia in his left hand. Museo Archeologico Nazionale di Napoli, inv. 133334.

Figure 2.34 (right): A statuette of a genius possibly from Pompeii. He has his head covered with a garment as he holds a libation dish in his right hand and a cornucopia in his left hand. Museo Archeologico Nazionale di Napoli.

Nevertheless, the above selection of depictions of *capite velato* from the first two centuries after Augustus's religious reforms should suffice to demonstrate what is most important here—that this ritual gesture was prevalent during the specified time period. We have examples of *capite velato* in art form from all across Italy, as well as from modern-day Croatia, Turkey, mainland Greece, Crete, and other regions. Most crucially for us, *capite velato* was conspicuously present in the center of Corinth at the time of Paul's communication with the Christian congregation there. Furthermore, we see that this ritual gesture not only decorated imperial monuments, but also street corners and private dwellings. We find emperors, imperial family members, priests and priestesses, magistrates, and private individuals (both men and women) strike this ritual pose on statues, monuments, altars, and paintings. Thus, *capite velato* seems to have been a widespread custom of the Romans at the time of Paul.

Figure 2.35: A statue of an unknown female in the act of offering grain and incense over a candelabrum. She holds a libation dish in her left hand while her head is covered with her garment. The statue is provisionally dated to the middle of the second century CE, but we lack information of the statue's provenance. Le Gallerie degli Uffizi, inv. 1914 no. 131.

Figure 2.36: A close-up of the head of an unknown woman in the act of offering. The sculptor has carefully crafted the folds of the garment on the woman's head, but one can clearly behold the woman's face, ears, and even her hairstyle.

A few additional points are worth noting in summary. First, in material depictions of *capite velato*, this ritual gesture most often appears in the context of sacrificial scenes, particularly as accompanying the pouring of libation, whereas in the literary references, praying seems to be the most oft-mentioned context. This discrepancy may be related to the fact that it was much more difficult to portray Roman praying postures in art form. As Frances Hahn notes, material evidence of praying in Roman art is generally scarce,[99] so a small number of archaeological finds depicting *capite velato* in relation to prayer should not surprise us. However, we need to keep in mind that all Roman sacrifices were accompanied by prayers (and at times by divination), meaning that prayer is implied in the background of all sacrificial scenes.[100] Second, in some scenes, only a single figure is portrayed *capite velato*, while others (if present) may wear different head-coverings or none at all, but we also have scenes in which multiple individuals are shown with a garment over the head. And finally, it is worth keeping in mind that most portraits from the relevant time period in antiquity portray both men and women without any head-

---

[99] Frances Hickson Hahn, "Performing the Sacred: Prayers and Hymns," in *A Companion to Roman Religion*, ed. Jörg Rüpke (Malden, MA: Blackwell, 2007), 235.

[100] Ehrensperger, *Paul at the Crossroads of Cultures*, 183.

coverings, so the choice to carve or paint the garment to cover the head must have been a deliberate one to communicate something about the person, event, or place involved. As discussed, *capite velato* was especially associated with *pietas*, a virtue highly esteemed by the Romans, and so when a garment covers the head in ritual contexts in Roman art, we must be cognizant of the possibility that *pietas* is emphasized.

2.9 Conclusion

The above overview of the descriptions and depictions of *capite velato* demonstrates that this ritual gesture was important for the Romans and accompanied Roman prayers, sacrifices, and divination for centuries. We find evidence for *capite velato* in multiple locations throughout the vast territory of the Roman Empire, including in Corinth, and we also encounter *capite velato* in diverse literary contexts. Importantly for us, the Greek references to *capite velato* are often similar in grammar and language to 1 Cor 11:4, and considering, then, that *capite velato* would have been publicly visible to the Christian congregants in Corinth at the time of Paul, it is unlikely that 1 Cor 11:4 could have been understood by these Christ-followers as a reference to anything else but *capite velato*. This much confirms, therefore, what Richard Oster and others following him have suggested—that *capite velato* is a concern for Paul in 1 Cor 11:2–16.

However, as has been discussed in section 1.6.8, biblical scholars who have embraced the *capite velato* hypothesis have struggled to explain the relevance of this ritual gesture to Paul's overall argument in 1 Cor 11:2–16. This difficulty is partly due to lack of familiarity with the literary and material evidence for *capite velato*. The above overview has thus also helped clear up some of the misconceptions about *capite velato* in biblical scholarship. For example, there is no evidence to suggest that this ritual gesture was only performed by the social elites, as several biblical scholars have argued (see section 1.6). Rather, the practice seems to have permeated all layers of Roman society. Also, there is no evidence to suggest that there were any major differences in how men and women performed *capite velato*. Both men and women are described and depicted with an outer garment drawn over (part of) the head in contexts of worship, and the gesture was not mandatory for only men but voluntary for women (contrary to what Finney has argued, see section 1.6.6). The dividing line between who needed to be covered and who did not appears to have been based on whether one was actively engaged in a worshipful act, such as praying, sacrificing, or seeking or performing divination, not on gender.

In all, based on the above presented evidence, it is highly likely that *capite velato* had been (or still was) a customary ritual gesture for at least some members of the Corinthian Christian congregation with whom Paul was in contact (as will be argued more carefully in Chapter 4). It is plausible that some of these individuals had performed this gesture many times during private and public sacrifices, prayers, and acts of divination. In light of this, Paul's concern with head-coverings solely in the context of "praying or prophesying" requires a deeper investigation. In the next chapter, therefore, we will conduct a thorough examination of Paul's "praying or prophesying" in light of *capite velato*.

3. Whoever Prays or Prophesies

The Acts of Worship at the Heart of Paul's Concern with the Corinthians' Heads

In the previous chapter I demonstrated the prevalence of *capite velato* at the time of Paul. The literary and archaeological evidence strongly suggests that the Corinthian Christians (both men and women) with whom Paul was in contact were, at the very least, familiar with this ritual gesture, and that those of Roman background had likely practiced it themselves in private and public settings. The previous chapter also showed that *capite velato* most often accompanied the activities of praying, sacrificing, and divination. That we find this ritual gesture in the context of particular acts of worship ties with 1 Cor 11:4–5, in which Paul is concerned with head-coverings only in relation to particular activities—praying and prophesying. As noted in Chapter 1, however, most biblical scholars who have tackled 1 Cor 11:2–16 have ignored the literal reading of Paul's phrase "praying or prophesying" and have opted to interpret this phrase as a reference to Christian worship more broadly. Gordon Fee, for example, speaks for many when he argues that the terms praying and prophesying in this passage "are neither exhaustive nor exclusive but representative: they point to the two foci of Christian worship—God and the gathered believers."[1] This broader interpretation of "praying or prophesying" has allowed for readings in which the practices or appearances associated with head-coverings (or hairstyles) are thought to have been problematic for Paul over extended periods of time (e.g., for the duration of Christian gatherings). In this chapter, however, I work with the premise that Paul's phrase "praying or prophesying" should be taken literally, in that it should be taken to refer to two specific acts of worship—praying and prophesying—during which head-coverings were an issue for Paul. What speaks in favor of such a position is that Paul uses the coordinating conjunction "or" rather than "and" in this phrase, which suggests that two specific

---

[1] Fee, *First Corinthians: Revised*, 558. Similarly, Payne, *Man and Woman*, 149–50.

activities are in view, rather than "worship" in general. In this chapter, therefore, I will explore why Paul mentions specifically "praying or prophesying" in relation to head-coverings in light of what we have learned about *capite velato*.

In the first half of the chapter, I discuss Paul's understanding of prayer in comparison to Roman conceptions of prayer. I show that while the Romans were very much concerned with correct formularies in regards to prayer (such as correct wording, word order, and posture), Paul exhibits remarkably little concern for any of such things. The only clear exception is 1 Cor 11:2–16, which I argue demonstrates that Paul in this passage has to deal with an understanding of the efficacy of prayer that is foreign to his way of thinking, but which aligns more closely with the Roman worldview. In the second half of the chapter, I demonstrate that the term "prophesying" in Paul's writings has often been misunderstood in traditional biblical scholarship. "Prophesying" is usually taken as a reference to an inspired speech-act, but a careful examination of Paul's entries on "prophesying" demonstrates that it had a broader meaning for Paul than that. I contend that in light of how Paul's near-contemporaries Philo and Josephus make use of the "prophecy" terminology, "prophesying" in Paul's letters should be understood in a sense of "accessing of divine (fore)knowledge," which could take various forms. In that sense, "prophesying" for Paul covers some of what the ancient Greeks and Romans considered "divination," during which head-coverings were a feature for the Romans. 1 Cor 11:2–16 seems to address a situation, then, that had something to do with the Roman conviction that covering the head with a garment was an indispensable component of the performances of prayer and of accessing divine (fore)knowledge.

3.1 Head-Coverings in the Context of Prayer

In the previous chapter, we encountered *capite velato* in the context of various Latin and Greek terms for prayer, such as *votum* ("vow"), *precari* ("to pray"), *commendare* ("to commend"), *vocare* or *invocare* ("to call upon"), *rogare* ("to ask"), εὐχή ("prayer"), εὔχομαι ("to pray"), κατεύχομαι ("to pray over"), ἀρά ("prayer," especially imprecatory prayer), as well as in the context of the most common Roman prayer posture of raised hands. Given then that *capite velato* is found in the context of the most common words for prayer in Latin and Greek, and the most common prayer posture of the Romans, it appears that this ritual gesture was not reserved solely for certain special prayers but accompanied praying in general. We see also that in the context of head-coverings in 1 Cor 11:2–16, Paul uses the Greek verb προσεύχομαι, which is the most common term for prayer in the NT. Thus, the context for Paul's instructions regarding head-coverings is likewise praying in general. In this section, therefore, we will look at the concept of praying in Roman worship in comparison to Paul's understanding of prayer in his letters to trace any similarities or differences that would allow us to clarify Paul's instructions in 1 Cor 11:2–16.

3.1.1 Roman Prayers

Scholars of Roman religion are in general agreement that, among the ancients, the Romans were particularly meticulous about precise formularies in their prayers.[2] Aulus Gellius informs us that Roman priests possessed books of prayers (*Noct. att.* 13.23.1), which seem to have contained set prayers for various circumstances (e.g., military, agricultural). Given that the Romans believed that specific words had to be uttered in the correct order for maximum efficacy, a religious specialist, such as a priest, was often required to dictate the prayer to the praying individual (or to a group or even a crowd), especially if the language was arcane or archaic.[3] In the previous chapter, for example, we observed that Decius senior required the help of *pontifex maximus* to utter the prayer for his *devotio* (see section 2.2.7), and the lady whom Juvenal satirizes for inquiring of the gods concerning the winning chances of her favorite musician repeats the words that the *haruspex* dictates (see section 2.3.5). A prompter would ensure that no errors occurred in prayer for the ritual to be effective. Roman literature contains examples of several prayers that were considered "false," and therefore ineffective or even harmful to the one praying, because of errors in the performance of prayer (whether in words or gestures, such as *capite velato*).[4] Thus, even though there may have been more leeway for personalized language and structure in private prayer, the prayers performed in public (especially if they accompanied sacrifices) were treated with utmost seriousness to

---

[2] E.g., Frances V. Hickson, *Roman Prayer Language: Livy and the Aneid* [sic] *of Vergil* (Stuttgart: Teubner, 1993), 1, 7; Mary Beard, John North, and Simon Price, *Religions of Rome: A History* (New York: Cambridge University Press, 1998), 32; Hahn, "Performing the Sacred," 236; David E. Aune, "Prayer," in *The Oxford Handbook of Early Christian Ritual*, ed. Risto Uro, et al. (Oxford: Oxford University Press, 2019), 257.

[3] Beard, North, and Price, *Roman Religions*, 29; Matthias Klinghardt, "Prayer Formularies for Public Recitation: Their Use and Function in Ancient Religion," *Numen* 46 (1999): 4; Valerie M. Warrior, *Roman Religion* (Cambridge: Cambridge University Press, 2006), 18–20; Hahn, "Performing the Sacred," 236.

[4] Klinghardt, "Prayer Formularies for Public Recitation," 14–18. Recall that emperor Hadrian's impending death was thought to have been signaled by the incident of his garment falling from his head when in prayer (see section 2.2.10).

avoid any mistakes that could compromise the desired outcome.[5] Also, the Romans appear to have been suspicious of silent prayers, and so praying was expected to be an audible activity.[6]

From the available evidence, it appears that the most common Roman prayer was the petitionary prayer—a request of the gods—under which vows and oaths should also be categorized.[7] A vow was a form of petitionary prayer in which something was promised to a deity in return of a fulfilled request, while an oath was a form of petitionary prayer in which a deity was called to witness a statement or an action, or to punish an infringement.[8] Thanksgiving prayers, in which thanks was given for divine blessings, are also attested, but we do not possess many extant copies of such prayers.[9] And even rarer are prayers of lamentation and confession.[10] Of the prayers performed *capite velato* that we encountered in the previous chapter, of which the content is reported, petitions indeed dominate. For example, in Livy's retelling of Numa's election as king, the augur prays for divine signs of confirmation (see section 2.2.3); the fetial who declares war on the Samnites in Dionysius's version of this event prays for the gods to grant success to the Romans if they are in the right (see section 2.2.6); Decius senior prays for the destruction of Rome's enemies, according to Livy (see section 2.2.7); Alcmena prays for divine help in childbirth in Plautus's *Amphytrion* (see section 2.3.1); and the unnamed lady in Juvenal's satire asks of the gods regarding the winning chances of her favorite musician (see section 2.3.5). We have no entry in which *capite velato* accompanies thanksgiving, lamentation, or confession. It appears, therefore, that *capite velato* especially accompanied prayers in which a request was made of the gods.

3.1.2 Prayer in the Letters of Paul

Contrary to Roman prayers, in which thanksgiving is not as pronounced, prayers of thanksgiving occupy a place of prominence in Paul's letters. This is most evident in the so-called thanksgiving sections, in which it was customary for Paul to remind his readers that he "constantly" gave thanks to God for them in his prayers

---

[5] Hahn, "Performing the Sacred," 237.
[6] Klinghardt, "Prayer Formularies for Public Recitation," 17.
[7] Hahn, "Performing the Sacred," 239; Hickson, *Roman Prayer Language*, 3.
[8] Hahn, "Performing the Sacred," 240–42; Hickson, *Roman Prayer Language*, 4.
[9] Hahn, "Performing the Sacred," 242–43.
[10] Warrior, *Roman Religion*, 18; Thomas Kazen and Rikard Roitto, *Revenge, Compensation, and Forgiveness in the Ancient World*, WUNT 515 (Tübingen: Mohr Siebeck, 2024), 378.

(cf. 1 Thess 1:2–3; 2:13; 1 Cor 1:4; Phil 1:3–4; Phlm 4–5).[11] Paul's thanksgivings also stand out in relation to contemporary Hellenistic letters, in which gratitude is at times expressed for health and safety, but which rarely (if ever) do so in such an abundant and complex manner as Paul does for spiritual blessings.[12]

In showing high regard for thanksgiving, Paul seems to follow his traditions, since prayers of thanksgiving were a prominent feature in Second Temple Judaism.[13] This is especially evident in the writings associated with the Qumran community. According to Eileen Schuller, for example, the prayers of the Qumran community "were predominantly psalms and hymns of praise that confessed and acknowledged the sovereignty and power of the God who has determined all things in his wisdom."[14] Schuller connects the prominence of thanksgiving prayers at Qumran to the deterministic theology of the Qumran sectarians: they believed in a god who had determined all things from the beginning, and so the most appropriate response to and address of god was one of thanksgiving, and not so much one of petition.[15] In fact, Schuller argues that most of the petitionary prayers in the

---

[11] This feature is prominent also in the letters bearing Paul's name, but which most likely were not authored by him directly (cf. Eph 1:16–17; Col 1:3; 2 Thess 1:3; 2:13; 2 Tim 1:3).

[12] A common assumption in biblical scholarship has been that Paul modeled his thanksgiving sections after Hellenistic letters. This view has been challenged recently, as evidence shows that Paul's thanksgiving sections are unique in comparison to Hellenistic letters. See, for example, Robert E. van Voorst, "Why Is There No Thanksgiving Period in Galatians? An Assessment of an Exegetical Commonplace," *JBL* 129 (2010): 160–66; David W. Pao, "Gospel within the Constraints of an Epistolary Form: Pauline Introductory Thanksgivings and Paul's Theology of Thanksgiving," in *Paul and the Ancient Letter Form*, ed. Stanley E. Porter and Sean A. Adams (Boston: Brill, 2010), 103–13. However, Jeffrey Weima maintains that the *"form* of the thanksgiving sections [in Paul's letters] is largely Hellenistic, but its *content* is influenced mainly by Judaism. In other words, although to a large extent the Pauline thanksgiving owes its existence and structure to the standard epistolary form in Hellenistic letter writing, its contents are influenced by OT and Jewish thought." Jeffrey A. D. Weima, *1–2 Thessalonians*, BECNT (Grand Rapids: Baker Academic, 2014), 74 (italics original).

[13] Paul F. Bradshaw, *Daily Prayer in the Early Church: A Study of the Origin and Early Development of the Divine Office* (repr., Eugene, OR: Wipf and Stock, 2008), 12–16.

[14] Eileen Schuller, "Petitionary Prayer and the Religion of Qumran," in *Religion in the Dead Sea Scrolls*, ed. John J. Collins and Robert A. Kugler (Grand Rapids: Eerdmans, 2000), 45.

[15] Schuller, "Petitionary Prayer," 41. John Barclay is also of the opinion that the thanksgiving hymns of the Qumran sectarians are imbued with a theology of predeterminism. According to Barclay, "the articulation of this theology [of predeterminism] in the form of thanksgiving prayers is peculiarly appropriate: a theology composed from this perspective is best articulated in such a form." See, John M. G. Barclay, *Paul and the Gift* (Grand Rapids: Eerdmans, 2015), 251–65, here 263–64.

Qumran literature are non-sectarian, which to Schuller suggests that the Qumranites themselves did not value petitionary prayers as much as thanksgivings, even though they preserved petitionary prayers in their library of writings.[16] Russell Arnold agrees with this assessment of Qumran prayers, and adds that the sectarians only prayed the petitionary prayers "as an act of obedience and holiness" in response to "divine commandment," even though due to their deterministic theology, such prayers were "considered fruitless."[17]

Whether this evaluation of the Qumran sectarians' attitude towards prayer is right is up for debate, but what is important for us here is that, even though thanksgiving is also prominent in Paul's letters, he does not therefore devalue petitionary prayer. On the contrary, Paul seems to place high value on petitionary prayer. For example, Paul charges the Christians in Rome to pray with him and for him with specific requests:

> I beseech you through our Lord Jesus Christ and through the love of the Spirit to wrestle together with me in the prayers to God for me (συναγωνίσασθαί μοι ἐν ταῖς προσευχαῖς ὑπὲρ ἐμοῦ πρὸς τὸν θεόν), so that I may be rescued from the unbelievers in Judea and that my service for Jerusalem may be acceptable to the saints, so that when I come to you in joy, I may be refreshed together with you. (Rom 15:30–32)

This imagery of wrestling in prayer here suggests that Paul regarded petitionary prayer as a real means by which change could be affected, even though it required dedication and perseverance (cf. also Rom 12:12, τῇ προσευχῇ προσκαρτεροῦντες). Paul also informs the Roman Christians that he always petitioned in his prayers (πάντοτε ἐπὶ τῶν προσευχῶν μου δεόμενος) for a prosperous journey to visit them (Rom 1:10). Furthermore, in his letter to Philemon, Paul expresses his hope to be restored to Philemon and the *ekklēsia* at his house through their prayers (διὰ τῶν προσευχῶν ὑμῶν, Phlm 22), and in his letter to the Philippians, Paul encourages his addressees that his imprisonment will be turned into his "deliverance" through their prayer (εἰς σωτηρίαν διὰ τῆς ὑμῶν δεήσεως,[18] Phil 1:19). And Paul is grateful to

---

[16] Schuller, "Petitionary Prayer," 38, 41–42, 44–45. Israel Knohl had earlier argued in a similar fashion, suggesting that the "doctrine of predestination, which was dominant in the Qumran sect, does not allow for petitional prayer in the usual sense of the word." Israel Knohl, "Between Voice and Silence: The Relationship between Prayer and Temple Cult," *JBL* 115 (1996): 29.

[17] Russell C. D. Arnold, "Qumran Prayer as an Act of Righteousness," *JQR* 95 (2005): 523–25.

[18] It is suggested that in the LXX in particular, the noun ἡ δέησις has the specific meaning of "petition" or "supplication." See, for example, Shively, T. J. Smith, *Strangers to Family: Diaspora and 1 Peter's Invention of God's Household* (Waco, TX: Baylor University Press, 2016), 107.

3.1 Head-Coverings in the Context of Prayer

the Corinthians for their help in praying for him and for his co-workers (συνυπουργούντων καὶ ὑμῶν ὑπὲρ ἡμῶν τῇ δεήσει), which had resulted in God's deliverance of Paul and others from death (2 Cor 1:10–11). These entries suggest that Paul believed petitionary prayers to have real efficacy, and thus considered them absolutely essential for a believer's devotion.[19]

Yet, even petitionary prayers were not complete for Paul without a thanksgiving component. Thus, for example, Paul encourages the Philippians not to worry, but rather "in everything make your requests be known to God through prayer and supplication with thanksgiving" (ἐν παντὶ τῇ προσευχῇ καὶ τῇ δεήσει μετὰ εὐχαριστίας τὰ αἰτήματα ὑμῶν γνωριζέσθω πρὸς τὸν θεόν, Phil 4:6).[20] Here Paul specifically reminds the addressees that their requests to God should be made with thanksgiving. The importance of thanksgiving in petitionary prayers is also expressed in 1 Thess 3:9–10:

> For what thanksgiving (τίνα γὰρ εὐχαριστίαν) are we able to repay to God concerning you for all the joy in which we rejoice on account of you before our God by praying

---

However, it does not seem that Paul is too careful to distinguish between ἡ δέησις and ἡ προσευχή in his references to prayer. It appears that for Paul both words can stand for "prayer" in general and for "petition" in particular. See, for example, Moisés Silva, *Philippians*, BECNT, 2nd ed. (Grand Rapids: Baker Academic, 2005), 55.

[19] In the discussion of Roman prayers, it was suggested that vows and oaths should also fall under the category of petitionary prayers (see section 3.1.1). While there are no clear examples of vows addressed to the deity in Paul's letters, Paul does use the language of oaths. For example, in 2 Cor 1:23 Paul exclaims: "But I call God as a witness against my soul..." (Ἐγὼ δὲ μάρτυρα τὸν θεὸν ἐπικαλοῦμαι ἐπὶ τὴν ἐμὴν ψυχήν...). According to Murray Harris, such language indicates that Paul utters here a "formal oath." Murray J. Harris, *The Second Epistle to the Corinthians*, NIGCT (Grand Rapids: Eerdmans, 2005), 212. Considering that Paul also refers to God as a witness in Rom 1:9, Phil 1:8, and 1 Thess 2:5, 10, it may be that oaths were a habitual part of Paul's devotion. However, Matthew Novenson has argued that "the Pauline phrase 'God is witness' is not a self-imprecatory oath at all, but rather a figure of speech" in which "God is not testifying against Paul in case Paul should default on a promise; rather God is testifying for Paul that Paul's character can be trusted." Matthew V. Novenson, "'God is Witness': A Classical Rhetorical Idiom in Its Pauline Usage," *NovT* 52 (2010): 356. Considering the importance of oaths in ancient devotion, I think Novenson dismisses the relevance of Paul's language here rather too lightly.

[20] A similar emphasis on thanksgiving in petitionary prayer is also found in Col 4:2–4: "Persist in prayer, keeping watch in it with thanksgiving (Τῇ προσευχῇ προσκαρτερεῖτε, γρηγοροῦντες ἐν αὐτῇ ἐν εὐχαριστίᾳ), praying (προσευχόμενοι) at the same time for us, in order that God may open for us a door to speak the mystery of the word of Christ on account of which also I am bound, so that I may make it manifest as it is necessary for me to speak." Even though Paul is unlikely to be the author of this passage, it nevertheless shows how influential such a way of thinking about prayer was in the Christian circles speaking in Paul's name.

(δεόμενοι) exceedingly night and day to see your face and to equip your faith with that which is lacking?[21]

Here we see that thanksgiving and petition are almost inseparable—Paul rejoices in his petition to see the Thessalonian Christians. Later in the same letter, Paul urges the Thessalonians to "pray unceasingly, give thanks in everything" (ἀδιαλείπτως προσεύχεσθε, ἐν παντὶ εὐχαριστεῖτε, 1 Thess 5:17–18), once again emphasizing the importance of thanksgiving in prayer.

It even appears that for Paul, increasing thanksgivings addressed to God is a mission in its own right. To the Corinthians Paul writes, for example, that as grace abounds (πλεονάζω), so too will thanksgivings addressed to God (2 Cor 4:15), and Paul also encourages the Corinthians to give generously so that even more thanksgivings will be offered to God (2 Cor 9:11–12). It is interesting here that Paul uses the potential increase in thanksgivings addressed to God as a goal in itself to motivate the Corinthians into action. And it seems that Paul also considered thanksgiving prayers an important part of food consumption (e.g., Rom 14:6; 1 Cor 10:30; 11:23–24; cf. also 1 Tim 4:4–5).[22] This emphasis on thanksgiving in devotion is in stark contrast to the Roman attitude towards prayer as we have seen.

Another contrast to Roman prayers in Paul's letters is that Paul does not seem to care too much for correct formularies or postures in regards to praying (leaving 1 Cor 11:2–16 aside for the moment). Paul even admits that "we do not know what is necessary that we should pray" (τὸ γὰρ τί προσευξώμεθα καθὸ δεῖ οὐκ οἴδαμεν, Rom 8:26). This is not a problem for Paul, however, since Paul believes that the saints have an intercessor in God's *pneuma*, who searches the hearts of the believers and then intercedes for them according to the will of God (Rom 8:26–27). Thus,

---

[21] Translators have not agreed on how 1 Thess 3:9 and 1 Thess 3:10 should relate to one another. Some translations break the two verses into two separate sentences, so that verse 9 consists solely a question regarding thanksgiving and verse 10 consists solely a statement regarding petitionary prayer (e.g., AMP, CEB, ISV, NIV, NRSV). However, the first verb in verse 10, δεόμενοι, is in the participial form, which suggests that the two verses should be treated as one continuous sentence. In my translation, therefore, I have followed Jeffrey Weima's explanation of how the clauses in this passage relate to one another: "The pattern of Paul's ... thanksgivings ... is to follow a verb of thanksgiving with a participle that expresses the manner of giving thanks, namely, by praying, and this is the likely function of the participle [δεόμενοι] here ("we rejoice because of you before our God *by* pleading ...")." Weima, *1–2 Thessalonians*, 227.

[22] It is suggested that giving thanks at mealtimes was a Jewish practice that predated Paul. E.g., Douglas J. Moo, *The Epistle to the Romans*, NICNT (Grand Rapids: Eerdmans, 1996), 843 n. 79. However, Vojtěch Kaše has recently argued that the evidence for such a position is inconclusive. See, Vojtěch Kaše, "Meal Practices," in *The Oxford Handbook of Early Christian Ritual*, ed. Risto Uro et al. (Oxford: Oxford University Press, 2019), 415.

3.1 Head-Coverings in the Context of Prayer

there is no need for a religious specialist to ensure correct words or word order for maximum efficacy of the said prayers. On the contrary, the Spirit's intercession allows even an unintelligible utterance to become an efficacious prayer. Thus, while "praying in a tongue" might not be useful in building up another person, as it is unintelligible to onlookers, it can still be a well-executed prayer:

> If you then bless (εὐλογῇς[23]) in spirit, how can the one in a position of an uninitiated (τοῦ ἰδιώτου) say "Amen" in response to your thanksgiving (ἐπὶ τῇ σῇ εὐχαριστίᾳ) as he does not know what you are saying? For you may indeed give thanks well (καλῶς εὐχαριστεῖς), but the other is not built up. (1 Cor 14:16–17)

Paul's point here is that in God's sight, an otherwise unintelligible utterance is as good of a prayer as any (notice again the emphasis on thanksgiving). The potential problems with prayers unintelligible to onlookers lie elsewhere.

However, given that Paul in the above passage mentions the word "Amen" as a response to thanksgiving, it may be that Paul knows this Aramaic word as a customary ending to prayers (cf. also 2 Cor 1:20). Furthermore, Paul's reference to "Abba! Father!" in the context of prayer may also suggest that he knows this exclamation as a customary opening of prayers (Rom 8:15; Gal 4:6).[24] Thus, we may speak of "Amen" and "Abba! Father!" as prayer formulas that Paul knows and uses. Yet, at no point does Paul attach any such significance to these formulas that would imply that Paul considered his and his congregations' prayers ineffective without the use of these words. And nowhere does Paul instruct his readers on how they should open or close their prayers, even if he employed certain formulas himself for this purpose.

With the exception of 1 Cor 11:2–16, which will be discussed below, the undisputed letters of Paul also provide no instructions regarding any praying postures.

---

[23] Paul Bradshaw has argued that the benediction (*berakah*), in which God is blessed, was in the Hebrew Scriptures a separate form of prayer to the thanksgiving (*hodayah*), in which God is thanked. However, Bradshaw also shows that in Hellenistic Judaism, the *hodayoh* prayers gained ascendancy at the expense of the *berakah* prayers, and that the elements of the two mingled to the point that separating them was not as clear-cut, which pertains to the NT as well. At the same time, Bradshaw maintains that we must not treat these terms as synonyms. Bradshaw, *Daily Prayer in the Early Church*, 12–16, 32–33. In the context of the passage discussed here, however, "blessing" and "thanksgiving" appear near-synonyms for Paul.

[24] Krister Stendahl, "Paul at Prayer," *Int* 34 (1980): 245; David A. DeSilva, *The Letter to the Galatians*, NICNT (Grand Rapids: Eerdmans, 2018), 356–58. Based mainly on the fact that "Abba" is an Aramaic term, James Dunn suggests that it may have already been "a characteristic feature of Jesus' own prayer." Dunn, *The Theology of Paul the Apostle*, 193. While this is a possibility, it is by no means certain.

We do, however, find praying postures mentioned in the deutero-Pauline letters. In Eph 3:14, for example, "I bend my knees" (κάμπτω τὰ γόνατά μου) is used as a synonym for "I pray,"[25] and 1 Tim 2:8 calls on all men in every place to pray (προσεύχεσθαι) with raised hands (ἐπαίροντας ὁσίους χεῖρας), a common praying posture of the Romans (as well as the Jews and the Greeks[26]), as we have seen (although, by the time of Tertullian, Christians distinguished how they raised their hands in prayer from how the Romans did so, see section 6.7). There is also evidence that certain early Christians prayed facing toward Jerusalem.[27] It is entirely possible that Paul also adopted a particular posture whenever in prayer, and that the above entries in the deutero-Pauline letters reflect that, but as far as the undisputed letters go, there is no indication that Paul considered praying in a certain posture a necessity for the sake of efficaciousness.

Finally, it is also noteworthy that Paul has left no instructions on any set prayers, such as the Shema, which Jews prayed twice a day at the time,[28] or the Lord's prayer, which in Matthew and Luke is presented as a prayer taught by Jesus himself and which the Didache commands to be prayed three times a day (Did. 8:2–3). There may have been other set prayers that Jews and early Christians regularly recited, perhaps even at specific times in a day or a week.[29] However, their precise nature is more difficult to identify, since much depends on how we apply the later

---

[25] E.g., Harold W. Hoehner, *Ephesians: An Exegetical Commentary* (Grand Rapids: Baker Academic, 2002), 473.

[26] Reidar Hvalvik, "Praying with Outstretched Hands: Nonverbal Aspects of Early Christian Prayer and the Question of Identity," in *Early Christian Prayer and Identity Formation*, ed. Reidar Hvalvik and Karl Olav Sandnes, WUNT 336 (Tübingen: Mohr Siebeck, 2014), 82–83.

[27] F. Stanley Jones, "The Pseudo-Clementines," in *Jewish Christianity Reconsidered: Rethinking Ancient Groups and Texts*, ed. Matt Jackson-McCabe (Minneapolis: Fortress Press, 2007), 298–99; Hvalvik, "Praying with Outstretched Hands," 64–65.

[28] E.g., Josephus, *Ant.* 4.8.13 §212. See discussion also in Daniel K. Falk, "Qumran Prayer Texts and the Temple," in *Sapiential, Liturgical and Poetical Texts from Qumran: Proceedings of the Third Meeting of the International Organization for Qumran Studies, Published in Memory of Maurice Baillet*, ed. Daniel K. Falk, F. García Martínez, and Eileen M. Schuller (Leiden: Brill, 2000), 122; Erik Waaler, *The Shema and the First Commandment in First Corinthians: An Intertextual Approach to Paul's Re-Reading of Deuteronomy* (Tübingen: Mohr Siebeck, 2008), 128.

[29] Bradshaw, *Daily Prayer in the Early Church*, 28–29; Hvalvik, "Praying with Outstretched Hands," 72–74.

rabbinic and early Christian sources to the time period in question[30] and how we interpret the "liturgical texts" of the NT.[31] In any case, nowhere does Paul appear to concern himself with instructions regarding set prayers or set times for prayers. This does not mean of course that Paul did not engage in saying any set or traditional prayers, only that in his writings, Paul's focus is rather on *ad hoc* and personalized thanksgivings and petitions than on fixed formulas. That being said, Paul's lack of instructions regarding set prayers is nevertheless curious, considering the importance of such prayers in Roman religion, Second Temple Judaism, and later rabbinic and early Christian writings. It may show that Paul did not find as much value in set prayers as his contemporaries did, but we cannot be sure, since Paul says nothing about it in the collection of letters that we possess of him.

However, I find two passages in Paul's letters that may challenge the view held here that Paul was not overly concerned with any set times or formulas for prayers. First, there is the curious instruction to married couples in 1 Cor 7:5: "Do not withdraw from one another, except perhaps by agreement for a certain time (πρὸς καιρόν) so that you may devote yourselves to prayer (ἵνα σχολάσητε τῇ προσευχῇ)." That husbands and wives should separate for agreed-upon times for the purpose of prayer seems at odds with the concept of unceasing prayer, which otherwise dominates Paul's thinking on the matter. It may seem as if Paul encourages here praying at certain times and doing so individually. However, the Greek εἰ μήτι ἂν ("except perhaps") here shows that Paul is rather hesitant in his suggestion that husbands and wives should even separate for prayer.[32] Paul's hesitancy may demonstrate that he is only willing to make concessions for the Corinthian Christians in response to particular needs expressed by the community. Some scholars

---

[30] Some have argued, for example, that the later Christian practice of praying in the third, the sixth, and the ninth hours of the day (Terce, Sext, None) can be traced to apostolic origins. E.g., L. Edward Phillips, "Early Christian Prayer," in *The Oxford Handbook of Early Christian Ritual*, ed. Risto Uro et al. (Oxford: Oxford University Press, 2019), 580. Even if this is so, we possess no evidence that shows that it was specifically Paul's concern that his congregants should pray on specific hours in a day.

[31] Bradshaw rightly warns of "panliturgism," which is the tendency to see liturgical texts on every page of the NT. Bradshaw, *Daily Prayer in the Early Church*, 29.

[32] Paul D. Gardner, *1 Corinthians* (Grand Rapids: Zondervan, 2018), 301. An interesting parallel is found in T. Naph. 8:8, which may be roughly contemporary with 1 Cor 7:5: καιρὸς γὰρ συνουσίας γυναικὸς αὐτοῦ καὶ καιρὸς ἐγκρατείας εἰς προσευχὴν αὐτοῦ ("For there is a time for intercourse with his wife, and a time for self-control for his prayer"). Greek text from M. De Jonge, ed., *The Testaments of the Twelve Patriarchs: A Critical Edition of the Greek Text* (Leiden: Brill, 1978), 123. It shows that there were certainly some who thought that men should separate from women for the time of prayer, which puts Paul's hesitancy on the matter into perspective.

propose, for example, that Paul reacts here to a situation in Corinth in which some spouses had abstained from sexual relations in order to focus more fully on spiritual matters.[33] If so, Paul's response here may be an attempt to balance this trend. That is, Paul may be arguing that "not withdrawing from one another" is more conducive for one's spirituality than abstaining from sexual relations altogether, but that if his addressees do not experience spirituality in this way, the spouses may separate for prayer but only by mutual agreement. Yet, regardless of what we think of the situation addressed in 1 Cor 7:5, there is no indication here that Paul proposes this segregated prayer to be conducted at a set time, with set words, or in a particular posture.

Secondly, Paul also tells the Corinthian Christians that he had beseeched (παρακαλέω) the Lord three times for the "thorn in the flesh" to be removed (2 Cor 12:7–9). That Paul would count the exact number of times he petitioned for something is again at odds with Paul's general tenor on the topic of prayer. However, it is important to note that in this passage, Paul does not employ the verbs he normally uses in the context of prayer, such as δέομαι or προσεύχομαι, but rather uses a more general παρακαλέω. Furthermore, the addressee of Paul's requests here is "the Lord" (κύριος), generally identified as Jesus,[34] but, as Pamela Eisenbaum points out, in Paul's letters "words of prayer and worship are exclusively directed to God."[35] Thus, this passage does not line up with Paul's other references to prayer and may therefore be a description of something other than prayer in its most common sense. Matthew Sharp has recently argued, for example, that 2 Cor 12:7–10 is a description of a "healing oracle," a ritual of some kind (e.g., sleeping in the temple

---

[33] E.g., Antoinette Clark Wire, *The Corinthian Women Prophets: A Reconstruction through Paul's Rhetoric* (Minneapolis: Fortress Press, 1990), 83; Thiselton, *The First Epistle to the Corinthians*, 506–7. This traditional take has been recently challenged by Barry Danylak, who offers that Paul's concern in 1 Cor 7:1–7 is not asceticism but rather that the Corinthian Christian men and women were not having sexual relations with their married partners, but were doing so with prostitutes and slaves (essentially for reasons of birth control when enough children had been born in marriage). See, Barry N. Danylak, *Paul and Secular Singleness in 1 Corinthians 7*, SNTSMS 184 (New York: Cambridge University Press, 2024), 214–24. Regardless of the exact *Sitz im Leben*, however, there is agreement that Paul responds here to a specific situation that had arisen in the Corinthian congregation.

[34] E.g., Harris, *Second Corinthians*, 860.

[35] Pamela Eisenbaum, *Paul Was not a Christian: The Original Message of a Misunderstood Apostle* (New York: HarperCollins, 2009), 180. See also, Dunn, *The Theology of Paul the Apostle*, 258–59.

of a god) through which healing was sought in antiquity.[36] If so, Paul's focus here may be on some kind of ritual of which petitionary prayers may have been a constitutive part, but which was not thought of as prayer in the whole.

If my assessment of the above two passages is correct, then my argument that Paul, in his letters, is not overly concerned with set times, formulas, or postures in relation to prayer remains intact. In this regard, then, 1 Cor 11:2–16 sticks out as the only passage in which the main focus of Paul in the context of prayer is with such things.

3.1.3 Prayer in 1 Cor 11:2–16

If we were to ask Paul what makes petitionary prayer efficacious, then based on the above discussion, he would probably consider the intercession of the Spirit, thanksgiving, and perseverance as the most important in this regard. He would be unlikely to argue for the necessity of set words, correct word order, or a particular posture—elements that a first-century Roman might find paramount for the maximum efficacy of prayer. This is why 1 Cor 11:2–16 stands out as an atypical reference to prayer in the corpus of Paul's undisputed letters—the concern here with posture and garments, especially as it is tied to one's sex, is unlike anything else we encounter in Paul's references to prayer. This suggests to me, therefore, that the issue addressed in 1 Cor 11:2–16 does not originate with Paul but that he is here forced to respond to a particular understanding or ideology of prayer that is foreign to his way of thinking. Given that Romans at the time of Paul considered covering their heads with garments an important component of petitionary prayers, it is plausible that some Christ-believing neophytes of Roman background continued to think about prayer in those terms, which could have then elicited a reaction from Paul, because such an approach clashed with *his* understanding of prayer. We shall say much more about the potential *Sitz im Leben* of the Corinthian congregation that prompted Paul to pen 1 Cor 11:2–16 in Chapter 4 and Chapter 5. Here it suffices to note that considering Paul's overall understanding of prayer and what makes it efficacious, 1 Cor 11:2–16 appears to address a competing view about prayer and about its efficacy. *Capite velato* fits the bill as the subject matter of such a competing view, given that it was a widespread and influential head-covering practice that accompanied prayers at the time of Paul, and that it was associated with the efficacy and correctness of prayers.

---

[36] Matthew T. Sharp, *Divination and Philosophy in the Letters of Paul* (Edinburgh: Edinburgh University Press, 2023), 94–95.

3.2 Head-Coverings in the Context of Prophesying

In 1 Cor 11:4–5, Paul uses the verb προφητεύω in the context of head-coverings, but in our overview of the available literary references to *capite velato* in Chapter 2, προφητεύω does not feature as a context of this ritual gesture. This raises serious questions regarding the applicability of *capite velato* as the subject matter of 1 Cor 11:4–5. In this section I will argue, however, that Paul uses the term "prophesying" in 1 Cor 11:4–5 as a general reference to acts that encompass what the Romans called "divination," and as we have seen, *capite velato* certainly featured in Roman divination.

3.2.1 "Prophesying" in the Letters of Paul

Unlike references to prayer, which can be found in more or less equal measure in almost all of the undisputed letters of Paul (with Galatians as the most underrepresented in this regard), the term προφητεύω and its cognates are used by Paul mainly in 1 Corinthians 11–14. Of the 29 times that Paul employs the terms "to prophesy" (προφητεύω), "prophet" (ὁ προφήτης), "prophecy" (ἡ προφητεία), or "prophetic" (προφητικός) in the undisputed letters, 22 occurrences (roughly three quarters) appear across only these four chapters. Furthermore, references to "prophesying" and its cognates outside of 1 Cor 12–14 (leaving 1 Cor 11:2–16 aside for a moment) have generally proved unhelpful for scholars in determining Paul's understanding of the phenomenon of prophesying, as these are too brief or too general: three times reference is made to "prophets" as a general category of people from Israel's past, but without any qualifying remarks concerning who a "prophet" is (1 Thess 2:14–15; Rom 1:2; 11:3); two times reference is made to Hebrew Scriptures ("law and the prophets" in Rom 3:21; "prophetic writings" in Rom 16:26[37]); once the term ἡ προφητεία appears in a list of charismata in Rom 12:6 with the qualifier κατὰ τὴν ἀναλογίαν τῆς πίστεως ("according to the proportion of faith"), which, however, does not explain what is meant by ἡ προφητεία; and in 1 Thess 5:20, Paul tells his readers not to despise "prophecies" without any further explanation as to what a "prophecy" is.

---

[37] It may very well be that Rom 16:25–27 was not part of the original letter that Paul addressed to the Roman Christians, in which case this entry on "prophesying" does not count as authored by Paul. An overview of the text-critical issues associated with the ending of Romans can be found in D. C. Parker, *An Introduction to the New Testament Manuscripts and Their Texts* (New York: Cambridge University Press, 2008), 270–74.

Thus, scholars who come across προφητεύω and its cognates in Paul's undisputed letters outside of 1 Cor 12–14 often suggest that a definition for this term in Paul's writings must be gleaned from 1 Cor 12–14 (particularly chapter 14), where this phenomenon is discussed more extensively.[38] While this seems like a sensible strategy, given that 1 Cor 12–14 is Paul's most extensive treatment of the phenomenon of prophesying, a significant issue arises: Paul's many references to "prophesying" and its cognates in 1 Cor 12–14 do not form a harmonious collection. A careful examination of each mention of προφητεύω and its cognates in 1 Cor 12–14 will demonstrate this.

1 Cor 12:8–10

This unit is a list of *charismata* akin to Rom 12:6–8. However, here προφητεία appears without any qualifiers, making 1 Cor 12:8–10 unhelpful in determining the meaning of προφητεύω and its cognates in Paul.

1 Cor 12:28–29

This unit is another list, but this time concerning whom and what God has "appointed" (ἔθετο) in the church: "first apostles, second prophets (προφήτας), third teachers, then miracles (δυνάμεις), then gifts of healing, helpful deeds (ἀντιλήμψεις),[39] forms of leadership (κυβερνήσεις),[40] various kinds of tongues." While προφήτης appears here again without qualifiers, its inclusion in this particular list has raised several questions regarding Paul's understanding of who a prophet is. The most vexing problem has been that "prophet" seems to be distinguished from "teacher," but scholars have struggled to figure out where exactly the differences lie, given that 1 Cor 14 indicates that "prophesying" is didactic in

---

[38] E.g., Weima, *1–2 Thessalonians*, 406–7; Moo, *Romans*, 765. David Aune even deems 1 Cor 12–14 "the single most important source for our knowledge of first-century Christian prophecy." David E. Aune, *Prophecy in Early Christianity and the Ancient Mediterranean World* (Grand Rapids: Eerdmans, 1983), 220.

[39] This is how James Dunn translates the Greek here (*The Theology of Paul the Apostle*, 556). Anthony Thiselton, on the other hand, suggests that the Greek ἀντίλημψις has a more specific meaning here: "kind of administrative support." Thiselton, *The First Epistle to the Corinthians*, 1019–21.

[40] This is how NRSV translates the Greek here. Again, Thiselton would like to be more specific and offers that the Greek κυβέρνησις here stands for "ability to formulate strategies." Thiselton, *The First Epistle to the Corinthians*, 1021–22.

nature.⁴¹ Furthermore, Paul's separation of προφήτης here from other offices and gifts into a separate entity seems to contradict 1 Cor 14, in which Paul calls *all* of his addressees to show eagerness for prophesying. Should then the *office* of a prophet be considered a separate matter from the *gift* of prophecy, which is available to all, whereas the former is a privilege of a select few? If, however, Paul does not intend to separate offices and gifts here, what is the purpose of listing these *charismata* with ordinal numbers (e.g., first, second, third)? These and other such questions pose a challenge to biblical scholars attempting to understand the phenomenon of prophesying in Paul's writings, and this passage, on its own, is of little help in clarifying the issue.

1 Cor 13:2

In his famous ode to love, Paul ponders the futility of προφητεία without love in the following manner: "And if I have prophecy and I understand all mysteries and all knowledge (καὶ ἐὰν ἔχω προφητείαν καὶ εἰδῶ τὰ μυστήρια πάντα καὶ πᾶσαν τὴν γνῶσιν) and if I have faith so as to remove mountains, but I do not have love, I am nothing." It is not entirely clear whether Paul discusses here three (or even four) separate ideas—e.g., possessing prophecy, understanding mysteries and knowledge (or even, understanding mysteries *and* understanding knowledge), and possessing faith—or two separate ideas: possessing prophecy and possessing faith.⁴² The latter seems to me the most probable here, in which case the qualifier "understanding all mysteries and all knowledge" should help explain what Paul means by προφητεία. However, a number of issues make the definition here a complicated matter.

First, the terms "mystery" and "knowledge" have been highly contested in Pauline studies. Part of the problem is that they do not appear with any great frequency in Paul's undisputed letters. "Mystery," for example, occurs eight (or perhaps even seven⁴³) times but only in Romans (two times) and 1 Corinthians (five

---

⁴¹ For example, in his attempt to trace the differences between "teaching" and "prophesying" in Paul's theology, James Dunn admits that "the line between teaching and prophecy would often be thin." Dunn, *The Theology of Paul the Apostle*, 583. Anthony Thiselton likewise attempts to draw a distinction between "teacher" and "prophet" in Paul's literary output, but confesses that "prophecy ... does not necessarily exclude teaching and doctrine." Thiselton, *The First Epistle to the Corinthians*, 963, 1016–18.

⁴² See, Gardner, *1 Corinthians*, 563.

⁴³ The count here depends on how one interprets the manuscript evidence for 1 Cor 2:1. In regards to the earliest and most influential manuscripts, μυστήριον appears in ℵ* (the original

3.2 Head-Coverings in the Context of Prophesying

or six times). Recent scholarship proposes that μυστήριον in Paul should be understood in a sense of divine revelation of eschatological wisdom or events,[44] and while this is a reasonable suggestion, confusion remains as to how it all relates to the definition of "prophecy" in 1 Cor 13:2 in light of how "prophecy" and "mystery" are treated in 1 Cor 14 (see below). And while "knowledge" appears with greater frequency in Paul's undisputed letters (nineteen times), the majority occurrences are found in the Corinthian correspondence (fifteen times), which has led biblical scholars to believe that "knowledge" was in fact a "Corinthian catchword."[45] Our understanding of γνῶσις, therefore, depends on what we think of the social standing and theology of Paul's addressees (or opponents) in Corinth. But since we do not possess any literature from them, this issue is hotly debated in biblical scholarship.

Despite the difficulty in defining "mystery" and "knowledge" in Paul's letters, however, the use of εἴδω ("I understand") in 1 Cor 13:2 suggests that the focus here is on one's internal mental processes—that is, on individual perception or illumination of whatever the content of "mystery" and "knowledge" is. If so, we should be able to define προφητεία in the context of individual εἴδω, but this conflicts with 1 Cor 14, in which "prophesying" is presented as a speech-act aimed at encouraging, consoling, and upbuilding *others* (see below). Furthermore, in 1 Cor 14:2, "speaking in mysteries" (λαλεῖ μυστήρια) is associated with "speaking in a tongue" (λαλῶν γλώσσῃ), which is set in antithesis to "prophesying" because speaking mysteries in a tongue only builds up the speaking person, whereas prophesying builds up the entire congregation. And in 1 Cor 14:6, Paul distinguishes between speaking "in knowledge" (ἐν γνώσει) and speaking "in prophecy" (ἐν προφητείᾳ), which raises yet further questions regarding the precise relationship between "prophecy" and "knowledge" in Paul's thinking. As we shall see, these are not the only inconsistencies in Paul's treatment of "prophesying" in 1 Cor 12–14.

---

layer), A, C, and possibly P46 (although that is not certain), while in ℵ², B, D, and many later manuscripts, μαρτυριον appears instead.

[44] E.g., Benjamin L. Gladd, *Revealing the Mysterion: The Use of Mystery in Daniel and Second Temple Judaism with Its Bearing on First Corinthians* (New York: Walter de Gruyter, 2008), 108, 194–98; Birger A. Pearson, "Mystery and Secrecy in Paul," in *Mystery and Secrecy in the Nag Hammadi Collection and Other Ancient Literature: Ideas and Practices; Studies for Einar Thomassen at Sixty*, ed. Christian H. Bull, Liv Ingeborg Lied, and John D. Turner (Boston: Brill, 2012), 293.

[45] Thiselton, *The First Epistle to the Corinthians*, 1040.

1 Cor 13:8–9

A few lines later in this ode to love, Paul revisits the phenomenon of "prophesying," this time highlighting its inadequacy in comparison to love: prophecies cease (προφητεῖαι, καταργηθήσονται) whereas love does not, and prophesying only happens "in part" (ἐκ μέρους). While we learn from this entry that Paul does not value prophecies and prophesying as much as love, and that prophecy will cease to exist at a certain unidentified point in the future, it does not otherwise help us determine Paul's understanding of this phenomenon, since there are no explanatory qualifiers.

1 Cor 14:1–5

This unit serves as an introduction to Paul's fairly lengthy comparison of the activities of "prophesying" and "speaking in a tongue." Paul begins by urging the Corinthian Christians to pursue spiritual things (τὰ πνευματικά), but especially prophesying (μᾶλλον δὲ ἵνα προφητεύητε). Paul claims that the one who prophesies is greater (μείζων) than the one who speaks in a tongue, because prophesying builds up the entire congregation, whereas those who speak in a tongue only build up themselves. In contrast to 1 Cor 13:2, where Paul focuses on the internal aspect of προφητεία (see above), here Paul highlights the external nature of prophesying: it involves speaking to other people (λαλεῖ ἀνθρώποις) in a way that provides upbuilding (οἰκοδομήν), consolation (παράκλησις), and encouragement (παραμυθία). In contrast, speaking in a tongue is not as valuable precisely because it does not address other people but only God.

While we learn from this reference that Paul values prophesying more highly than speaking in a tongue, and what Paul thinks prophesying is capable of *achieving*—it builds up, encourages and consoles other people—there is not much here to tell us what exactly "prophesying" *is*. How does it differ, for example, from other Christian speech-acts such as proclamation, teaching, or the reading of Scriptures, which by all means could also build up, encourage, and console? And how would a Corinthian Christian have known when his or her or a fellow congregant's speech-act was a prophecy—was it recognizable in the moment of the speech-act or was it recognized as such only retrospectively based on whether it achieved the set goals of upbuilding, consolation, and encouragement? None of such questions are addressed in this section. Thus, all we can say here is that *in this context*, Paul treats "prophesying" as a speech-act, although we have seen in relation to 1 Cor 13:2 that in Paul's thinking, προφητεία seems not to have been limited to a speech-act only.

3.2 Head-Coverings in the Context of Prophesying

1 Cor 14:6

With 1 Cor 14:6, Paul begins a new section of his argument that zooms in on the problem of uninterpreted tongues. Paul suggests to the Corinthians that if he came to them speaking in tongues, he would be of no benefit to them; he can only be of value if he came speaking "in revelation, in knowledge, in prophecy, or in teaching" (τί ὑμᾶς ὠφελήσω ἐὰν μὴ ὑμῖν λαλήσω ἢ ἐν ἀποκαλύψει ἢ ἐν γνώσει ἢ ἐν προφητείᾳ ἢ ἐν διδαχῇ;). While in the preceding section, Paul pitted prophesying solely against speaking in a tongue, here some more speech-acts are brought into the equation: speaking in revelation, speaking in knowledge, and speaking in teaching. This expanded list, however, has created several problems for modern interpreters of Paul. Most crucially, determining the nature of these speech-acts and how they differ from one another has proved elusive.[46] We have already discussed the problems of distinguishing prophesying from teaching and knowledge in Paul (see discussion on 1 Cor 12:28–29 and 1 Cor 13:2), but here we can pose yet another question: why is speaking in revelation presented in 1 Cor 14:6 as a separate speech-act to speaking in prophecy, if in 1 Cor 14:29–31, revelation appears integral to prophetic activity (see further below)? Paul offers no clarification here, and thus once again, we do not know exactly what Paul has in mind by προφητεύω and its cognates. There are no clues in the context of 1 Cor 14:6 that would allow us to determine what distinguishes speaking in prophecy from speaking in revelation, speaking in knowledge, or speaking in teaching.

1 Cor 14:21–25

Having discussed the problem of uninterpreted tongues in greater depth, Paul returns to the comparative analysis of speaking in a tongue versus prophesying. He begins with a partial and modified quotation of LXX Isaiah 28:11–12, in which Yhwh (in Paul's rendering of these verses) predicts that he will speak to "this people" (τῷ λαῷ τούτῳ) in "foreign tongues" (ἐν ἑτερογλώσσοις), but that they will not listen.[47] Paul then claims that this text shows that "tongues, therefore, are for a sign

---

[46] See discussion in, for example, Gardner, *1 Corinthians*, 602–3; Fee, *First Corinthians: Revised*, 733–35.

[47] There are a number of curious differences between LXX Isaiah 28:11–12 and Paul's quotation of these verses in 1 Cor 14:21, which has led Christopher Stanley to claim that "determining the precise relationship between the wording of 1 Cor 14.21 and the text of the LXX is one of the greatest challenges in the entire corpus of Pauline citations." Christopher D. Stanley, *Paul and the Language of Scripture: Citation Technique in the Pauline Epistles and Contemporary*

(εἰς σημεῖον) not to the ones who believe, but to the unbelievers (τοῖς ἀπίστοις), whereas prophecy is [for a sign] not to the unbelievers, but to the ones who believe." This is a rather perplexing application of this quote from Isaiah to the situation that Paul is dealing with, especially in light of Paul's follow-up argument:

> If then the whole congregation came together in one place and everyone spoke in tongues, would not the uninitiated (ἰδιῶται) or the unbelievers who enter say that you are mad (μαίνεσθε)? But if all prophesy and an unbeliever or uninitiated happens to enter, he will be put to shame by all (ἐλέγχεται ὑπὸ πάντων), he will be examined by all (ἀνακρίνεται ὑπὸ πάντων), the secrets of his heart will become manifest, and thus, falling upon the face he will worship God, reporting that God is really among you.

How is speaking in a tongue, then, a sign for the "unbelievers"[48] if they associate it with "madness"? And why is prophesying not a sign for the "unbelievers" if it leads them to worship God? And what has Paul's belief that Isaiah predicted God to

---

Literature (New York: Cambridge University Press, 1992), 198. The differences that should be noted here for our purposes are: a) the LXX has λαλήσουσιν ("they will speak"), in reference to the drunk priest and prophet speaking in a foreign tongue, where Paul has λαλήσω ("I will speak"), in reference to Yhwh speaking in first person (the MT has the relevant verb in third person singular, "he speaks"); and b) the LXX has "foreign tongue" in the singular (διὰ γλώσσης ἑτέρας), whereas Paul envisions that Yhwh promised to speak in several foreign tongues. See, Stanley, *Paul and the Language of Scripture*, 198–202. John Paul Heil has suggested that Paul modified LXX Isa 28:11–12 through LXX Deut 28:49 and Jer 5:15, which address God's communication with his people through foreigners, and that Paul's recourse to these texts counts for the discrepancies. See, John Paul Heil, *The Rhetorical Role of Scripture in 1 Corinthians* (Atlanta: Society of Biblical Literature, 2005), 192–94.

[48] There is some debate about how the label ἄπιστοι should be understood (and translated) in the Corinthian correspondence. Recently, T. J. Lang has argued that "the designation ἄπιστοι was a technical term in the [Corinthian Christian] community's sociolect for a group of individuals who maintained intimate social ties with the believers and were even counted as 'insiders' in certain senses." T. J. Lang, "Trouble with Insiders: The Social Profile of the ἄπιστοι in Paul's Corinthian Correspondence." *JBL* 137 (2018): 983. Lang's point is that the term ἄπιστος has less to do with lack of belief and more to do with disloyalty, disobedience, and unreliability, and so the ἄπιστοι should not be thought of as demarcated "outsiders," but should rather be viewed as "deviant insiders": "These individuals are in significant ways internal to the community's life, yet they resist exclusive loyalty to Christ-devotion, even if they may perhaps be attracted to it. The social profile of the ἄπιστοι in Corinth is thus one of deviant insiders who sustain thick social bonds with the community but, because they fail to extract themselves from pagan ritual life, remain outside the 'temple of God' (1 Cor 3:16–17, 2 Cor 6:16). Although they are still welcome in worship, they are not counted as siblings in the ecclesial family." Lang, "Trouble with Insiders," 986. Even though Lang may have a point here, I will retain the term "unbelievers" for the sake of convenience throughout, but I will do so with quotation marks to indicate that the term should not be read literally (in a modern sense).

speak in foreign tongues to the people of Israel anything to do with it? These are just some of the questions that biblical scholars have struggled to answer. In fact, some commentators believe this passage to be the most difficult to understand in the whole of the epistle,[49] which gives us an idea of the level of complexity these verses present, as there are a number of other exegetical conundrums in 1 Cor.

Many attempts have been made to clarify Paul's thought processes in this passage. Proposed solutions commonly focus on the meaning of "sign" or on certain grammatical nuances, such as how the datives of τοῖς ἀπίστοις and τοῖς πιστεύουσιν should be read.[50] I will not pursue these interpretations in full here, since the many variables in this passage and their convoluted interpretations by modern scholars require a study in its own right. What interests us here is whether Paul says anything of such nature that would allow us to define what he means by the term "prophesying." And while we learn more about what Paul believes prophesying can accomplish—it puts "unbelievers" and "uninitiated"[51] to shame, examines them, and reveals the secrets of their hearts so much so that they begin to worship God—this passage fails to clarify what prophesying *is*. What exactly are Paul and the Corinthian Christians engaging in that is called "prophesying" and that up-builds, consoles, encourages, puts to shame, examines, and reveals secrets? This remains unexplained, and Paul's qualifier in this passage that prophecy serves as a

---

[49] E.g., Thiselton, *The First Epistle to the Corinthians*, 1122.

[50] See, for example, Krister Stendahl, *Paul among Jews and Gentiles and Other Essays* (Philadelphia: Fortress Press, 1976), 115–16; Karl Olav Sandnes, "Prophecy—A Sign for Believers (1 Cor 14,20–25)," *Bib* 77 (1996): 1–15; Thiselton, *The First Epistle to the Corinthians*, 1122–26; Garland, *1 Corinthians*, 645–54; Heil, *The Rhetorical Role of Scripture*, 200–202; Stephen J. Chester, "Divine Madness? Speaking in Tongues in 1 Corinthians 14.23," *JSNT* 27 (2005): 417–46; Fitzmyer, *First Corinthians*, 519–22; Fee, *First Corinthians: Revised*, 750–62; Gardner, *1 Corinthians*, 611–17; Sharp, *Divination and Philosophy*, 171–75.

[51] T. J. Lang suggests that "uninitiated" here should be taken in a sense of "generic class of outsiders." Lang, "Trouble with Insiders," 993. Richard Last has more recently argued, however, that the phrase ἰδιῶται ἢ ἄπιστοι in 1 Cor 14:23 should be read as referencing one and the same group of people—"private citizens who are untrustworthy" (because they do not accept Christ), but who live in the same neighborhood as the *ekklēsia*, and who thus have close social ties with the believers. Richard Last, "Christ Worship in the Neighbourhood: Corinth's *ekklēsia* and its Vicinity (1 Cor 14.22–5)," *NTS* 68 (2022): 319–25. I am not entirely convinced by Last's arguments here, but I will reserve my judgment until his position has garnered more scholarly feedback. In any case, Lang's and Last's recent articles add an additional layer of difficulty to the interpretation of this passage, since they demonstrate that even the precise identity of "visitors" that Paul is concerned about in relation to the Corinthians' tongue-speaking and prophesying is far from clear.

sign to the ones who believe has proved to be an unhelpful note for modern interpreters—confusing rather than clarifying.

1 Cor 14:29–32

Having explained why prophesying should be considered superior to speaking in tongues, Paul proceeds to give the Corinthian Christians practical guidance on how they should conduct their meetings in light of this information. Concerning prophesying during the gatherings, Paul suggests the following:

> But let two or three prophets speak and let the others evaluate (διακρινέτωσαν). But if to another who sits a revelation is given (ἀποκαλυφθῇ), the first must be quiet. For you are all able to prophesy one by one, so that all may learn and all may be consoled. And the spirits of the prophets are made subject to the prophets (καὶ πνεύματα προφητῶν προφήταις ὑποτάσσεται).

While it appears that in this context, prophesying is again treated as a speech-act, a number of questions arise concerning what exactly is the nature of this speech-act. First, we again encounter the uneasy tension between the designation of "prophet" and Paul's idea that all should prophesy: is "prophet" anyone who prophesies in a given moment or are there also designated prophets as certain office-holders (cf. also 1 Cor 12:28–29)?

Second, Paul introduces here the idea of "evaluation"[52] as belonging with the prophetic activity, but what exactly are "the others" supposed to evaluate? So far in his letter, Paul has only explained what prophesying should achieve—upbuilding, consolation, encouragement, feelings of shame, examination of "unbelievers," revelation of secrets—so are the congregants supposed to assess whether such goals have been met? If, however, the evaluation here concerns the *content* of what is spoken, by what criteria is it to be done?[53] Or should we rather understand διακρίνω here in the sense of "to interpret," as the term is so used, for example, by

---

[52] This is how διακρίνω has traditionally been understood by biblical scholars. E.g., Thiselton, *The First Epistle to the Corinthians*, 1140; Garland, *1 Corinthians*, 662; Fitzmyer, *First Corinthians*, 526; Fee, *First Corinthians: Revised*, 768; Gardner, *1 Corinthians*, 626–27.

[53] James Dunn suggests that it was a standard practice of the early church to evaluate prophecies, because it was not automatically assumed that the prophetic utterances had been inspired by the "Spirit of Jesus." Dunn calls this "hermeneutic of suspicion," but he does not explain how the Christian congregants would have gone about determining whether what was uttered during gatherings was inspired by the "Spirit of Jesus." James D. G. Dunn, *Jesus Remembered* (Grand Rapids: Eerdmans, 2003), 189–90. David Garland, on the other hand, generously lists seven criteria by which he thinks the Christian prophecies were gauged in Paul's congregations, even though he admits that "Paul does not list any criteria." Garland, *1 Corinthians*, 664.

3.2 Head-Coverings in the Context of Prophesying

Philo in the context of dream interpretation.[54] If so, how should we understand the speech-act of prophecy that requires interpretation? Where the Corinthian prophets receiving and relaying visionary (or apocalyptic) images that needed decoding?[55]

Third, what exactly is the role of the verb ἀποκαλύπτω here? Paul's language in this context seems to suggest that he considers the receiving of a revelation an integral part of prophetic activity, but in 1 Cor 14:6, as we have seen, "speaking in revelation" is treated as a separate speech-act to "speaking in prophecy." This discrepancy has led some biblical scholars to argue that "prophecy" and "revelation" should be treated as separate speech-acts also in the context of 1 Cor 14:29–32— that is, prophets prophesy while some others speak in revelations.[56] However, this reading does not align well with Paul's language here. Paul specifies that if a revelation is given "to another," "the first" must be quiet, but the most probable antecedents for "another" and "the first" are the "two or three prophets," which suggests that these same "prophets" are also the ones who Paul envisions receiving and relaying revelations. Furthermore, Paul justifies his instruction that the "first" must be quiet when "another" receives a revelation with a remark that "for you are all able to prophesy one by one," which seems like a clear indication that Paul considers the receiving of a revelation an integral part of prophetic activity here.[57] We

---

[54] In his *On the Life of Joseph*, for example, Philo uses the verb διακρίνω, as well as the noun διάκρισις, on several occasions to describe the phenomenon of dream interpretation: ὀνείρους ... τοῦ διακρινοῦντος (17.90); τῆς τῶν ὀνείρων διακρίσεως (18.98); ὀνείρατα ... διέκρινεν (19.104); ὀνείρων διάκρισιν (21.116); φαντασιῶν διάκρισιν (22.125); ἐνύπνια καὶ φάσματα ... διακρίνειν (24.143); τὰ ὀνείρατα διέκρινεν (41.248); τῶν ὀνειράτων διάκρισις (44.269).

[55] This is the position taken by Gerhard Dautzenberg, for example, who argues that διακρίνω here should be understood as "interpretation of Spirit revelations" ("Deutung von Geistesoffenbarungen"). Gerhard Dautzenberg, *Urchristliche Prophetie: Ihre Erforschung, ihre Voraussetzungen im Judentum und ihre Struktur im ersten Korintherbrief*, BWA(N)T (Stuttgart: Kohlhammer, 1975), 146–48. Thiselton rejects this reading in favor of the traditional understanding of διακρίνω on the basis that Dautzenberg's "speculative explanation is more complex and difficult" than the traditional reading (*The First Epistle to the Corinthians*, 1141). However, Matthew Sharp has more recently upheld Dautzenberg's conclusion that διακρίνω as "to interpret" fits the context of 1 Cor 14:29 (*Divination and Philosophy*, 104 n. 31). The rest of this chapter will demonstrate that there is merit in Dautzenberg's suggestion.

[56] Joseph Fitzmyer, for example, argues that "revelation" in Paul's understanding is different and also more important "gift" than prophesying and so what Paul means in the context of 1 Cor 14:29–32 is that if anyone in the congregation receives a revelation, the one prophesying needs to stop to allow for the revelation to be heard. Fitzmyer, *First Corinthians*, 526.

[57] See also, Garland, *1 Corinthians*, 662; Fee, *First Corinthians: Revised*, 770.

must, therefore, accept the possibility that Paul is simply inconsistent in his presentation of the relationship between "prophecy" and "revelation."

Fourth, in the context of 1 Cor 14:29–32, Paul's juxtaposition of "revelation" and "prophesying" seems to highlight the spontaneous nature of prophetic activity—that is, prophecy is subject to revelations that may appear suddenly. But if this is the case, how should we understand Paul's follow-up statement that "the spirits of the prophets are made subject to the prophets"? If a prophet is in control of what to say and when to say it, why is Paul then concerned that a new revelation should immediately quiet the one who is in the midst of prophesying? It seems as if Paul has conflicting thoughts about prophesying—on the one hand, Paul wishes to limit engagement in prophesying to two or three persons during any given gathering of the congregation, and that they do so one by one,[58] but on the other hand, Paul acknowledges that all are capable of prophesying (he even encourages it) and that prophesying is an activity that is subject to spontaneous revelations, the timing of which cannot be predicted.

Finally, it should also be noted that Paul adds here another *function* of prophesying—that all may learn (μανθάνωσιν). Thus, throughout 1 Cor 12–14, Paul mentions altogether nine functions that prophesying should accomplish: understanding of mysteries, understanding of knowledge, upbuilding, consolation, encouragement, putting "unbelievers" and uninitiated to shame, examination of "unbelievers" and uninitiated, revelation of secrets, and learning. Yet, despite this extensive list, Paul provides little explanation as to what the nature of this activity of prophesying is that achieves all that. This unit of 1 Cor 14:29–32, which presents prophesying as a speech-act that is subject to sudden revelations and which needs to be evaluated or interpreted, perhaps comes closest to providing some clarification, but as we have discussed, questions remain about how this view of prophesying aligns with the rest of Paul's entries on the subject.

---

[58] István Czachesz has argued that Paul's remarks about prophesying one by one in 1 Cor 14:31 "suggests that people were lacking conscious control when they were prophesizing, which in terms of neurological correlates [*sic*] means the deactivation of executive areas in the frontal lobes. Participation in prophecy as a collective ritual probably involved an involuntary synchronization of behavior by means of 'emotion sharing' or 'emotional contagion'." István Czachesz, *Cognitive Science and the New Testament: A New Approach to Early Christian Research* (Oxford: Oxford University Press, 2017), 152. Risto Uro interprets 1 Cor 14:31 in a similar manner. See, Risto Uro, *Ritual and Christian Beginnings: A Socio-Cognitive Analysis* (Oxford: Oxford University Press, 2016), 150. While in principle, it is possible that people in antiquity lacked conscious control when they engaged in "prophesying," I think the evidence in Paul's letters does not allow us to say that this was the *only* way prophesying was performed (see below).

1 Cor 14:37–39

Paul concludes his discussion on speaking in tongues and prophesying with a warning that "if anyone thinks to be a prophet or a spiritual (πνευματικός), let such a one recognize (ἐπιγινωσκέτω) the things which I write to you as the commandment of the Lord." We are again unsure whether Paul is addressing certain designated (or self-proclaimed) prophets or whether his warning applies to all, as *all* are encouraged to prophesy. It is also not certain whether "prophet" and "spiritual" should be taken here as more or less synonymous terms or whether Paul has in mind distinctive categories.[59] In any case, Paul's warning demonstrates that, even though he values prophesying for all the positives it can achieve and encourages the Corinthians to pursue it earnestly (ζηλοῦτε τὸ προφητεύειν, 1 Cor 14:39), he nevertheless considers the prophecies of his addressees subordinate to his own apostolic authority. Thus, Paul appears to present himself as a more perfect conduit of God's communication—whether or not he considers himself a prophet—than the prophesying Corinthian Christians could ever be.

Summary

The above presentation of Paul's entries on προφητεύω and its cognates demonstrates that 1 Cor 12–14 does not provide a readily available definition of "prophesying" that we can seamlessly plug into Paul's discussion about head-coverings in 1 Cor 11:2–16. While we do learn what προφητεύω is supposed to achieve, there is little information regarding what prophesying is, and even that is conflicting. For example, 1 Cor 13:2 implies that prophesying is introspective in nature, whereas 1 Cor 14 presents it as an outward-oriented speech-act. And 1 Cor 14:29–32 describes prophesying in terms of sudden revelations that require evaluation or interpretation, but that description does not align easily with some other entries on προφητεύω by Paul, as we have seen. Thus, Dennis Smith's conclusion that "it is not clear what kind of phenomenon is being referred to with this terminology [of προφητεύω and its cognates], other than to say that ... in chapter 14 its function is primarily hortatory in nature" appears a fair assessment of Paul's entries on prophesying that we have discussed.[60] However, most biblical scholars are not so willing to concede that Paul's several references to προφητεύω and its cognates in 1 Cor 12–

---

[59] On the ambiguity of πνευματικός in Paul's letters, see, for example, John M. G. Barclay, "Πνευματικός in the Social Dialect of Pauline Christianity," in *Pauline Churches and Diaspora Jews*, by John M. G. Barclay, WUNT 275 (Tübingen: Mohr Siebeck, 2011), 214–15.

[60] Dennis E. Smith, *From Symposium to Eucharist: The Banquet in the Early Christian World* (Minneapolis: Fortress Press, 2005), 205.

14 fail to offer a readily available and coherent definition of "prophesying" in the letters of Paul. We will examine the claims of some of such scholars next.

3.2.2 1 Cor 12–14 and the Definition of "Prophesying"

As was discussed in the preceding section, some modern biblical scholars believe that Paul's entries on "prophesying" in 1 Cor 12–14 allow us to define this term in his letters. I will examine some of such claims here. This is by no means an exhaustive overview, as the many scholarly works in which Paul's references to προφητεύω and its cognates in 1 Cor 12–14 are analyzed calls for a study in its own right. I will only present a representative selection of scholarly works in which a definition for "prophesying" in Paul's letters is provided in the context of 1 Cor 12–14, and which are considered to represent more or less the traditional view on this matter in biblical scholarship.

Christopher Forbes

In his book on prophecy in early Christianity, published in 1995, Christopher Forbes expresses his delight that his contemporary biblical scholars had reached a near-consensus on how "prophesying" should be understood in the letters of Paul: that it was the receiving and proclaiming of divinely inspired and spontaneous revelations.[61] This definition is clearly dependent on 1 Cor 14:29–32, but as we have discussed, this text does not align well with some other entries of Paul on prophesying. And indeed, as Forbes attempts to unpack this concise definition of prophesying that he provides, things become much more complicated. Forbes admits, for example, that Paul's letters provide no example of "prophetic speech explicitly so called," rendering the exact nature of this revelatory proclamation difficult to ascertain.[62] Forbes ultimately concedes that any number of speech-acts can actually belong to prophetic activity, such as prognostication of future; "unsolicited guidance, exhortation, or remonstration"; some form of gospel proclamation; and even "inspired interpretation" of Hebrew Scriptures.[63] Thus, despite the assertion that a clear definition for prophesying is readily available in 1 Cor 12–14, Forbes's

---

[61] Christopher Forbes, *Prophecy and Inspired Speech in Early Christianity and its Hellenistic Environment*, WUNT (Tübingen: J. C. B. Mohr (Paul Siebeck), 1995), 219, 229. Forbes discusses "prophesying" in Paul together with "prophesying" in Luke, in a sense of "prophesying" in the earliest layers of Christianity. Here I will only deal with those arguments of Forbes that are explicitly concerned with Paul's understanding of the phenomenon of prophesying.

[62] Forbes, *Prophecy and Inspired Speech*, 222.

[63] Forbes, *Prophecy and Inspired Speech*, 223, 229, 234, 236.

analysis allows us to be no more specific than to conclude that "prophesying" in Paul's use of the term must have been a reference to some form of "inspired speech." However, as we have seen, it is not at all certain that Paul associates prophecy only with an act of speech.

Anthony Thiselton

In his colossal commentary on 1 Corinthians, Anthony Thiselton discusses Paul's use of προφητεύω and its cognates on several occasions. In dealing with 1 Cor 12:28, for example, Thiselton cautions that "it is difficult to be more specific than ... identifying [prophecy] as *the proclamation of revealed truth in relation to a pastoral situation*."[64] In other places, however, Thiselton appears dissatisfied with such a broad characterization and ventures to add clarifications, modifications, additions, and specifications, demonstrating in the process that a clear idea of what Paul means by "prophesying" has eluded him too. Thus, for example, in the context of 1 Cor 14:1–5, Thiselton proposes that "here prophecy amounts to healthy preaching, proclamation, or teaching which is pastorally applied for the appropriation of gospel truth and gospel promise, in their own context of situation, to help others."[65] In relation to the whole of 1 Cor 14, on the other hand, Thiselton suggests that "prophesying ... is the performing of intelligible, articulate, communicative speech-acts, the operative currency of which depends on the active agency of the Holy Spirit mediated through human minds and lives ... in the context of interpersonal relations."[66] In yet another place, Thiselton submits that prophecy "combines pastoral insight into the needs of persons, communities, and situations with the ability to address these with a God-given utterance or longer discourse (whether unprompted or prepared)."[67] However, in the context of Paul's discussion on head-coverings and prophesying in 1 Cor 11:2–16, Thiselton is unwilling to allow Christian prophecy to stand for "spontaneous mini-messages" (seemingly out of fear that it comes dangerously close to "pagan" practices), insisting instead that "prophecy" is first and foremost associated with "theological teaching, encouragement, and exhortation," and is therefore "serious, sustained, and reflective."[68] Such varied interpretations reveal significant inconsistencies in Thiselton's attempts to define Paul's notion of prophecy.

---

[64] Thiselton, *The First Epistle to the Corinthians*, 1016. Italics original.
[65] Thiselton, *The First Epistle to the Corinthians*, 1084.
[66] Thiselton, *The First Epistle to the Corinthians*, 1094.
[67] Thiselton, *The First Epistle to the Corinthians*, 964.
[68] Thiselton, *The First Epistle to the Corinthians*, 826.

David Garland

In his commentary on 1 Cor, David Garland also offers several slightly different definitions for προφητεύω and its cognates without clarifying how such definitions relate to one another and to Paul's collection of entries on prophesying as a whole. In commenting on 1 Cor 12:10, for example, Garland states that he understands "prophesying" to be the "declaration of God's will to the people."[69] However, in commenting on 1 Cor 12:28–29, 1 Cor 13:2, and 1 Cor 13:8–9, Garland fails to analyze how such a definition applies in these contexts. And once Garland reaches 1 Cor 14:1–5, the definition has slightly changed—"prophesying" is now understood in a sense of "to proclaim divine revelation ... in rational, intelligible language."[70] Then, in commenting on 1 Cor 14:24–25, Garland suggests that in this context prophesying "must be gospel proclamation."[71] And in commenting on Paul's discussion about head-covering and prophesying in 1 Cor 11:4–5, Garland offers that "prophecy is pastoral preaching that offers guidance and instruction."[72]

Joseph Fitzmyer

Unlike the above scholars, Joseph Fitzmyer is remarkably consistent in his definition of "prophesying" in 1 Cor 11–14. In almost every encounter with "prophesying" in 1 Cor, Fitzmyer insists that it should be understood as "Spirit-inspired preaching."[73] Fitzmyer's commitment to a uniform understanding of "prophesying" across 1 Cor 11–14 even brings him to interpret 1 Cor 14:29–32 in a way that divorces prophesying from the idea of spontaneous revelation, even though in Paul's text they seem to be closely associated (see above).[74] Fitzmyer fails to explain, however, how his definition of "prophecy" as "Spirit-inspired preaching" fits with 1 Cor 13:2, in which prophecy is something one possesses that allows for insight into mysteries and knowledge.

---

[69] Garland, *1 Corinthians*, 582.
[70] Garland, *1 Corinthians*, 632.
[71] Garland, *1 Corinthians*, 652.
[72] Garland, *1 Corinthians*, 516.
[73] Fitzmyer, *First Corinthians*, 412, 467, 482, 493. The one exception to this general trend can be found in Fitzmyer's treatment of 1 Cor 13:8–9, in which "prophecies" are taken to mean "prophetic talents" without further comment as to what those talents are. Fitzmyer, *First Corinthians*, 497.
[74] Fitzmyer, *First Corinthians*, 526.

Gordon Fee

When Gordon Fee first attempts to define "prophesying" in the context of 1 Cor 12 in his revised commentary on 1 Cor, he claims that given Paul's extended discussion of prophesying in 1 Cor 14, "we have a fairly good idea as to how Paul himself understood this phenomenon."[75] Fee then offers the following definition of prophecy: "it consisted of spontaneous, Spirit-inspired, intelligible messages, orally delivered in the gathered assembly, intended for the edification or encouragement of the people."[76] However, once Fee reaches 1 Cor 14 itself, his confidence has eroded, and as he tries to determine how "revelation," "teaching," "prophecy," and "knowledge" should all be understood in relation to one another, Fee admits that "there is a general lack of precision in Paul."[77]

Summary Analysis

The above overview of works deemed to represent traditional biblical scholarship on the definition of "prophesying" in 1 Cor 12–14 demonstrates that, despite the proclaimed confidence in the ability to define "prophesying" in Paul's letters based on Paul's own comments, remarkably little of substance has been said. While all of the above scholars would agree that prophesying should be taken as some form of inspired speech, this is where the agreements end. Some take prophesying to be spontaneous, others do not; some are willing to entertain the idea that prophesying is predictive, others reject this association; some consider prophesying dependent on revelation, others are wary of connecting the two; some take prophecy to be akin to a sermon, others think more in terms of short utterances. In some cases, these conflicting perspectives even coexist within a single work. This demonstrates that Paul's entries on prophesying do not form a harmonious collection that leads to a straightforward definition, despite claims to the contrary. And as I have repeatedly pointed out, even the basic assumption that prophesying must be some form of inspired speech is questionable, given that 1 Cor 13:2 demonstrates that Paul does not think of "prophecy" only in terms of a speech-act.

Furthermore, the above scholars have to a large degree confused the *function* of prophesying with the *nature* of prophesying. Since Paul emphasizes that prophesying should achieve a number of things, such as upbuilding and consolation, modern scholars seem to think that this demonstrates what prophesying *is*. And while to a certain degree a given function of a phenomenon indeed limits what the

---

[75] Fee, *First Corinthians: Revised*, 660.
[76] Fee, *First Corinthians: Revised*, 660.
[77] Fee, *First Corinthians: Revised*, 734.

nature of that phenomenon can be, it does not yet demonstrate what it is. Thus, to say that something builds up, consoles, encourages, reveals secrets, puts "unbelievers" to shame, and aids in the understanding of mysteries does not yet say that this something must be "Spirit-inspired preaching" (to use Fitzmyer's definition), even though this activity may indeed achieve the given goals to a certain degree (at least in the mind of a modern biblical scholar). The key problem here is that any proposed definition for "prophesying" in Pauline literature should, in principle, apply across all contexts where this phenomenon is mentioned, but as the above overview demonstrates, traditional definitions do not fit this bill. Thus, as much as we wish for a definition of "prophesying" to be available in 1 Cor 12–14, a different strategy is needed to understand what Paul may mean by the term. We now turn to Paul's contemporaries.

3.2.3 "Prophesying" in Philo and Josephus

Philo, a wealthy and influential Alexandrian Jew, was a slightly older contemporary of Paul (ca. 20 BCE–50 CE), while Josephus, who served as a military leader in the First Jewish-Roman War and later obtained Roman citizenship, was a slightly younger contemporary of Paul (ca. 37–100 CE). Both Philo and Josephus engaged extensively with the Hebrew Scriptures in non-Judean settings in response to certain major developments in society. Philo, for example, attempted to explain the Hebrew Scriptures in light of some influential developments in philosophy, while he also served as a negotiator on behalf of the Alexandrian Jewish community during a period of major conflict with the city's Greek communities. Josephus, on the other hand, ended up residing in Rome after his capture by the Roman army, where he wrote extensively on the history of his native people in light of the dramatic and damaging defeat at the hands of the Romans that had left the city of Jerusalem as well as the temple in ruins. As such, the literary output of both of these men is an important interlocutor with Paul, who also engaged with the Hebrew Scriptures mostly outside of Judea, as he attempted to make sense of what he considered the cosmos-altering event of the ages—the death and resurrection of Jesus the Messiah. Given, therefore, that both Philo and Josephus mention "prophesying" many more times than Paul in his letters, examining their treatment of προφητεύω and its cognates may offer valuable clues concerning how "prophesying" should be interpreted in Paul's letters, particularly in 1 Cor 11:2–16.

3.2 Head-Coverings in the Context of Prophesying

In Josephus's retelling of the history of his people, προφητεύω and its cognates are mostly associated with the prognostication of future.[78] It seems that Josephus places high value on the phenomenon of prophesying precisely for its ability to illuminate what lies ahead. Concerning the Hasmonean ruler John Hyrcanus (ca. 164–104 BCE), for example, Josephus writes the following:

> τρία γοῦν τὰ κρατιστεύοντα μόνος εἶχεν, τήν τε ἀρχὴν τοῦ ἔθνους καὶ τὴν ἀρχιερωσύνην καὶ προφητείαν· ὡμίλει γὰρ αὐτῷ τὸ δαιμόνιον ὡς μηδὲν τῶν μελλόντων ἀγνοεῖν, ὅς γε καὶ περὶ δύο τῶν πρεσβυτέρων υἱῶν ὅτι μὴ διαμενοῦσι κύριοι τῶν πραγμάτων προεῖδέν τε καὶ προεφήτευσεν.[79] (J.W. 1.2.8 §§68–69)

> He was the only one who possessed the three most excellent things: the rulership of the people, the high priesthood, and prophecy—for the divine spirit was close to him so he was not ignorant of anything that was about to happen; he foresaw and prophesied that the two eldest sons would not remain overseers of affairs.

Here Josephus ranks "prophecy" among the three most excellent things and intimately ties it with divinely inspired foresight. Likewise, in a context of his discussion on ancient prophets, Josephus exclaims that "nothing is more profitable than prophecy and the foreknowledge that is provided through such things from God, so as [to know] what is necessary to guard against" (ὅτι προφητείας καὶ τῆς διὰ τῶν τοιούτων προγνώσεως οὐδέν ἐστι συμφορώτερον παρέχοντος οὕτω τοῦ θεοῦ τί δεῖ φυλάξασθαι, Ant. 8.15.6 §418).

---

[78] See, for example, Ant. 6.6.3 §115 (προφητεύειν αὐτῷ περὶ τῶν μελλόντων); Ant. 6.12.4 §254 (προφητεύω, τὰ μέλλοντα); Ant. 6.14.2 §334—Saul justifies his visit to the "ventriloquist" of Endor by lamenting that he had not received a prediction (πρόρρησις) through prophets (διὰ προφητῶν); Ant. 7.4.1 §§72–73 (προφητεία, περὶ τῶν ἐσομένων, προφητεύω, προλέγω); Ant. 8.4.2 §109–110 (προφητεία, προεῖπον, περὶ τῶν μελλόντων, δηλώσειε); Ant. 8.9.1 §§232–234—prophet Iddo possesses divine foreknowledge (θείαν ἔχοντα πρόγνωσιν) and foretells (προερέω) a sign (σημεῖον); Ant. 8.11.1 §§266–267—a certain prophet Achaias is described as "a man with a wonderful power of foretelling the future" (εἶναι γὰρ θαυμαστὸν ἄνδρα περὶ τῶν μελλόντων περιειπεῖν); Ant. 9.6.6 §139 (προφήτης, προεῖπον); Ant. 9.8.3 §168 (προφήτης, προλέγω); Ant. 9.11.3 §242 (προφήτης, προφητεύω, προερέω); Ant. 10.1.3 §§13–14 (προφήτης, προλέγω); Ant. 10.2.2 §35 (προφήτης, προφητεύω, προφητεία, τέλος); Ant. 10.4.2 §60–61 (προφήτης, προλέγω); Ant. 10.5.1 §79 (προφήτης, προκηρύσσω, τὰ μέλλοντα, προθεσπίζω); Ant. 10.7.2 §106 (προφητεύω, τὰς μελλούσας, προφητεία); Ant. 10.9.6 §§177–180 (προφήτης, προλέγω, προεῖπον); Ant. 10.11.7 §§267–269—Daniel stands out among the prophets because his prophecies include a fixed time of fulfillment (προφήτης, προφητεύω, προφητεία, προλέγω, τὰ μέλλοντα); Ant. 11.4.5 §96 (προφήτης, προλέγω); Ant. 13.3.1 §64 (προφήτης, προεῖπον); J.W. 4.6.3 §§386–388 (προφήτης, προθεσπίζω, προφητεία).

[79] Compare with Ant. 13.10.7 §299–300: τριῶν τῶν μεγίστων ἄξιος ὑπὸ τοῦ θεοῦ κριθείς, ἀρχῆς τοῦ ἔθνους καὶ τῆς ἀρχιερατικῆς τιμῆς καὶ προφητείας· συνῆν γὰρ αὐτῷ τὸ θεῖον καὶ τὴν τῶν μελλόντων πρόγνωσιν παρεῖχεν αὐτῷ τε εἰδέναι καὶ προλέγειν οὕτως, ὥστε καὶ περὶ τῶν δύο τῶν πρεσβυτέρων παίδων ὅτι μὴ μενοῦσιν τῶν πραγμάτων κύριοι προεῖπεν.

However, even though the above indicates that Josephus values prophecy highly as an instrument of acquiring foreknowledge, there is a curiosity in Josephus's treatment of the matter: the closer Josephus gets to his own time, the less likely he is to refer to the prognostication of future as "prophecy." This is most evident in how Josephus treats the prognostication abilities of the Essenes, a Jewish group still active in Josephus's own time. In one of his descriptions of the Essenes, for example, Josephus says the following:

> And there are among them those who profess to foreknow the things to come (τὰ μέλλοντα προγινώσκειν), having been educated in the holy books, and in the various purities, and in the apothegms of the prophets, and they rarely miss the mark in the predictions (ἐν ταῖς προαγορεύσεσιν). (*J.W.* 2.8.12 §159, notice the present tense)

Elsewhere, Josephus even deems the Essenes worthy (ἀξιοῦνται) of this ability to foreknow the future (*Ant.* 15.10.5 §379). Yet, despite thinking highly of the Essenes and believing their ability to predict the future to be divinely inspired, in none of the entries in which Josephus discusses the particular instances of Essene prognostication does he use the term προφητεύω or its cognates. Rather, in addition to all the words of prognostication that he normally employs in association with prophesying (foreknowledge, foreseeing, foretelling, etc.), Josephus uses the words ὁ μάντις ("diviner") and τὸ μάντευμα ("divination"; e.g., *Ant.* 13.11.2 §§311–313; 17.13.3 §§345–346). What is interesting about the use of the μαντεύοαμι word group by Josephus is that such an activity had been specifically prohibited by LXX Deut 18 (as we shall see below).

Steve Mason has argued that the reason why "Josephus allows hardly any extrabiblical applications of prophet terminology" seems to lie in Josephus's wish to guard prophecy as an ancient phenomenon, one that could not be replicated in his present time.[80] This belief that prophecy proper had ceased seems to have been shared by certain other Second Temple and later Jews. Thus, Joseph Blenkinsopp has argued, for example, that for the author(s) of Chronicles, "prophecy is no longer a presence that makes claims of a peremptory nature in the religious sphere. It is essentially a thing of the past."[81] It has also been argued that 1 Maccabees evidences that Hasmonean Jews believed that "'the spirit of prophecy' ... was no

---

[80] Steve Mason, "Josephus and His Twenty-Two Book Canon," in *The Canon Debate*, eds. Lee Martin McDonald and James A. Sanders (Peabody, MA: Hendrickson, 2002), 117–19.

[81] Joseph Blenkinsopp, "The Formation of the Hebrew Bible Canon: Isaiah as a Test Case," in *The Canon Debate*, eds. Lee Martin McDonald and James A. Sanders (Peabody, MA: Hendrickson, 2002), 56.

longer present in their nation."⁸² And this conviction that prophecy had ceased with the deaths of the prophets Haggai, Zechariah, and Malachi seems evident also in later rabbinic tradition.⁸³ This understanding of prophecy as an antiquated phenomenon thus appears to have been quite influential in certain segments of Second Temple Judaism, which would explain Josephus's reticence in employing the προφητεύω terminology in his discussions of more contemporary times. However, this view of προφητεία was clearly not shared by Paul, who takes it for granted that his congregants engaged in certain activities which could be described with the προφητεύω word group. In this regard, Paul's view of prophecy is more aligned with Philo's, who likewise does not deem προφητεία only a thing of the past.

In Philo's several extended treatments of the phenomenon, prophesying is associated more generally with gaining access to divine knowledge, of which prognostication is an important, although not necessarily the defining, feature. Concerning Moses, for example, Philo comments that he "also necessarily gained prophecy (προφητείας ἔτυχεν), so that those things which he was unable to comprehend with reason, he found in the foreknowledge of God, for prophecy reaches towards those things that the mind fails with" (ἵν' ὅσα μὴ λογισμῷ δύναται καταλαμβάνειν, ταῦτα προνοίᾳ θεοῦ εὕροι· ὧν γὰρ ὁ νοῦς ἀπολείπεται, πρὸς ταῦθ' ἡ προφητεία φθάνει, *Moses* 2.6). A "prophet" in Philo's terms, therefore, is someone who "prophesies through prophecy the things not comprehended by reason" (διὰ δὲ τῆς προφητείας ὅσα μὴ λογισμῷ καταλαμβάνεται θεσπίζῃ, *Moses* 2.187).⁸⁴ We see, then, that in Philo's understanding, prophecy includes both an introspective element—a prophet comes to comprehend otherwise incomprehensible things—and an outward speech-act, as the prophet declares (in oracles) the divine (fore)knowledge he has gained access to.

Philo also ponders more deeply about the possible methods by which a prophet gains access to this divine (fore)knowledge. In his discussion of Moses's divinely inspired prophetic utterances, recorded for posterity's sake, Philo provides the following argument:

> I am then indeed not ignorant [of the fact] that all the things recorded in the holy books are oracles declared through him (χρησμοί ... χρησθέντες δι' αὐτοῦ), but I will speak

---

⁸² Lee Martin McDonald, *The Formation of the Biblical Canon* (New York: Bloomsbury T&T Clark, 2017), 1:176.

⁸³ McDonald, *The Formation of the Biblical Canon*, 1:183.

⁸⁴ Philo seems to use the synonymous verbs θεσπίζω and προφητεύω interchangeably and without discernible distinction. This interchange appears to be purely for stylistic reasons, as I am yet to detect a usage of these terms where they are clearly distinguished.

concerning those that are his own (τὰ ἰδιαίτερα) with the following preliminary remark: of the oracles some are spoken personally by God through the divine interpreter, the prophet (τῶν λογίων τὰ μὲν ἐκ προσώπου τοῦ θεοῦ λέγεται δι' ἑρμηνέως τοῦ θείου προφήτου); some are prophesied through question and answer (τὰ δ' ἐκ πεύσεως καὶ ἀποκρίσεως ἐθεσπίσθη); and some by Moses personally when divinely possessed and seized from himself (ἐπιθειάσαντος καὶ ἐξ αὑτοῦ κατασχεθέντος). The first [type of oracles] are then on the whole signs (δείγματα) of divine prosperity, and graciousness, and beneficence through which He instigates men—but especially the people that serve him—towards good conduct, through which he opens up a way that leads towards true happiness. And the second [category of oracles] includes communion and fellowship—the prophet inquires concerning the things which he seeks [to know] and God answers and teaches. And the third [kind] are attributed to the lawgiver—God shares with him the power of prognostication (τῆς προγνωστικῆς δυνάμεως) by which he prophesies concerning the things to come (θεσπιεῖ τὰ μέλλοντα). The first [kind], then, must be left aside for they are too great to be praised by any human—they can scarcely be worthily praised by heaven and cosmos and the whole nature. And another thing, they are spoken through an interpreter as it were, but interpretation and prophecy differ from one another (ἑρμηνεία δὲ καὶ προφητεία διαφέρουσι). I will now attempt to demonstrate the second [type of oracles], intermingling with them the third type in which the one who speaks appears possessed (ἐνθουσιωδες)—it is especially and chiefly according to this that a prophet is acknowledged as such (καθ' ὃ μάλιστα καὶ κυρίως νενόμισται προφήτης). (*Moses* 2.188–191)

While Philo outlines several ways of accessing divine (fore)knowledge, he highlights that only when a prophet is divinely possessed and taken from himself is he most readily recognized as a prophet. Indeed, it is this "divine possession" that Philo often accentuates in his discussion on what true prophecy is. In *Heir* 265–266, for example, Philo puts it this way:

> This is what usually happens to the prophetic kind (τῷ προφητικῷ γένει), for indeed the mind is removed upon the arrival of the spirit of God in us and returned again upon its migration (μετανάστασιν). On account of this, the setting of reason and the darkness surrounding it give birth to ecstasy and divinely possessed madness (ἔκστασιν καὶ θεοφόρητον μανίαν ἐγέννησε).... For when the prophet (ὁ προφήτης) appears to speak, he is in fact silent. But another makes full use of his speech organs—mouth and tongue—to provide knowledge concerning whatever he wishes.

Thus, whereas Josephus distinguishes "prophesying" from all other similar phenomena by relegating it to the past, Philo's strategy of demarcating "prophesying" is to argue that in true prophecy, a prophet is completely overtaken by the deity.

Philo acknowledges, for example, that there are many other practices which are touted as being capable of achieving access to divine (fore)knowledge. However, inspired by LXX Deut 18:9–22, Philo deems these practices and their practitioners—such as haruspices (θύτης), purifiers (καθαρτής), augurs (οἰωνοσκόπος), interpreters of unusual phenomena (τερασκόπος), enchanters (ἐπαείδω), and those who rely on ominous sounds (κληδόσιν ἐπανέχοντας)—unreliable and illegitimate (*Spec. Laws* 1.60–63). In Philo's understanding, none of the practitioners of such arts can claim to "prophesy" proper. Only when the true God completely possesses a person can prophesying occur:

> But since in all men a desire for knowledge of the things to come (ἔρως τῆς τῶν μελλόντων ἐπιστήμης) is established, and it is on account of this desire that they turn towards haruspication (ἐπὶ θυτικήν) and other forms of divination (μαντικῆς), wishing to find clarity through such things, even though these things are full of much uncertainty and they are always refuted in themselves—indeed, he very strongly forbids to pursue such things—still, he says that if they were to live in unswerving piety, they would not be left without a share in the knowledge of things to come (τῆς τῶν μελλόντων ἐπιγνώσεως), but that a certain divinely possessed prophet (προφήτης θεοφόρητος), who appears suddenly, will foretell and prophesy (θεσπιεῖ καὶ προφητεύσει).[85] Indeed, nothing he says is his own—for he is unable to comprehend what he says, having been laid hold of and having been divinely possessed (ἐνθουσιῶν). Whatever passes through and comes out of his mouth is dictated by another. For the prophets are interpreters of God (ἑρμηνεῖς γάρ εἰσιν οἱ προφῆται θεοῦ), who makes full use of their organs for whatever purpose he wishes. (*Spec. Laws* 1.64–65)

And again:

> And such ones [who deceive] are interpreters of unusual phenomena, and augurs, and haruspices and others who practice fraudulent divination (μαντικὴν ... κακοτεχνίαν) with cunning, pursuing what is in fact counterfeit of the true divinely inspired possession (παράκομμα τῆς ἐνθέου κατοκωχῆς). For indeed, a prophet (προφήτης) declares absolutely nothing of his own, but he is an interpreter who presents everything that is dictated by another. At that time, he becomes possessed without his knowing (ἐνθουσιᾷ ... ἐν ἀγνοίᾳ)—indeed, the reasoning faculty is removed and the citadel of the soul makes way, while the spirit of God enters and inhabits [the person] and strikes every organ of sound and whatever he foretells (προθεσπίζει), he transforms into understandable speech. (*Spec. Laws* 4.48–49)

We see, then, that Philo does not deny that there are other competing methods whereby divine (fore)knowledge is sought. However, in comparison to those, "prophesying" proper stands out in that the (true) prophet has absolutely no control over what he (fore)tells. All others who claim to access and present divine (fore)knowledge are, according to Philo, ψευδοπροφῆται precisely because they rely on their own abilities (*Spec. Laws* 4.50–51).

However, when Philo attempts to apply the above principle to the story of Balaam, a curios conundrum emerges. Philo first introduces Balaam as follows:

---

[85] I have translated θεσπίζω here as "foretell" for stylistic reasons, but as I have already explained above, Philo appears to use θεσπίζω and προφητεύω interchangeably and without much distinction.

> There was at that time a man from Mesopotamia who was famous for divination (ἐπὶ μαντείᾳ περιβόητος)—indeed, he had been instructed in all forms of divination (τὰ μαντικῆς εἴδη), but among them he was especially admired for his great ability in (bird) augury (οἰωνοσκοπίαν). Many times and to many people did he display unbelievable and wonderful feats. For to some, he foretold (προεῖπε) heavy rains in the middle of summer; and to others, drought and also burning heat in the midst of winter; and to others, lack of produce during a good season, and the reverse, produce during famine; and to some, flooded and dried out rivers; and cures from pestilential diseases; and myriad other things. Each of these things that he foretold (προθεσπίζειν) made him more and more famous as the report [of him] spread everywhere. (*Moses* 1.264–265)

In this introduction, Balaam is presented as a successful μάντις, capable of achieving incredible feats through methods Philo otherwise considers unreliable and deceitful, as we have seen. Yet here, the legitimacy of Balaam's success is left unchallenged. But as the story progresses, Balaam's otherwise successful enterprise is cast in a negative light and when the time calls for it, a more correct form of θεσπίζω (in Philo's perspective) is imposed upon the μάντις. Thus, in Philo's rendering of the story, God informs Balaam that his tongue will be used to utter a prophetic oracle (τὸν λόγον θεσπίζων) without the consent of his mind (*Moses* 1.274). And when Balaam then engages in seeking auspicious omens through augury (ἐπ' οἰωνοὺς καὶ φήμας αἰσίους), he suddenly becomes divinely possessed (ἐξαίφνης θεοφορεῖται), his reasoning faculty is removed (μετανισταμένου τοῦ λογισμοῦ), and he prophesies (προφητεύων) favorably concerning the Israelites (*Moses* 1.282–284). This happens several times, and Philo comments that when Balaam was overtaken by the prophetic spirit (προφητικοῦ πνεύματος), his skill of divination (ἔντεχνον μαντικήν) was driven out of his soul (*Moses* 1.277).

On the one hand, then, Balaam is presented as an incredibly successful μάντις, whose achievements are truly remarkable. However, Philo cannot allow that Balaam's success in favorably predicting the future of the Israelite people had anything to do with the methods he normally employed in prognostication. Thus, in order for Balaam's prognostication concerning the Israelites to be "prophecy" in its purest sense (and therefore legitimate), Philo asserts that, even though Balaam engaged in ornithomancy—the method of divination that he was most skilled in— he was in fact in that moment emptied of his skill as well as of his reasoning faculty, and taken over by the prophetic spirit, thus becoming a conduit of divine messages without his consent and without any input of his own. Philo does not explain, however, how an onlooker would have been able to tell the difference whether Balaam prognosticated concerning the Israelites based on his observance of birds or whether he did so as a non-consenting conduit emptied of his skill and of his reasoning faculty. Philo's insistence that in those moments of favorable predictions

3.2 Head-Coverings in the Context of Prophesying

concerning the Israelites, Balaam must have been divinely possessed seems to find its inspiration in the belief that this is how Israelite prophesying worked, and since Balaam's predictions were deemed accurate and praiseworthy in hindsight, Balaam could not have gained access to such knowledge by any other means. However, a neutral observer would have seen nothing more than a successful μάντις declaring through ornithomancy predictions that were favorable to one party and disadvantageous to another.

This demonstrates, then, that even though Philo would like to guard "prophesying" from all other practices with similar aims by narrowly defining it as a complete possession of the divine that replaces the reasoning faculty, maintaining such clear boundaries proves challenging. And indeed, when Philo operates outside of the strict framework of LXX Deut 18:9–22, he is much laxer about how "prophesying" operates. Consider the following argument of Philo's:

> The nature of the liver is such that it is high up [in the body] and very smooth. It is on account of this smoothness that it functions as a bright mirror, so that whenever the mind goes over the cares of the day—once the body is relaxed in sleep and none of the senses stand in the way—it [the mind] begins to revolve and to consider clearly its thoughts. It gazes at the liver as if at the mirror, contemplating each of the thoughts and observing the images in a circular manner, [to see] whether there is anything shameful so that it may be put to flight and that the opposite to such things may be chosen. And by all the well-pleasing images (φαντασίαις), it prophesies through dreams the things to come (προφητεύῃ διὰ τῶν ὀνείρων τὰ μέλλοντα).[86] (*Spec. Laws* 1.219)

It is quite incredible that the same Philo, who in certain contexts is adamant that the only legitimate and reliable prognostication is through a divinely possessed prophet, would also argue that the mind itself prognosticates concerning the future with the aid of the liver—an organ commonly used in extispicy, a method of divination that seeks divine knowledge through the examination of the entrails of sacrificial animals. If indeed each mind (and body) possesses such a power of prognostication, we are left disoriented as to the need of an emptied and possessed prophet. Further complicating matters, Philo elsewhere even argues that "every soul is highly divinatory (μαντικώτατον), particularly in difficulties," which allows people to sense what is about to happen (*Flaccus* 186). But if all bodies prophesy

---

[86] A similar idea is presented in a speech that Josephus puts in the mouth of Eleazar ben Simon, one of the leaders in the First Jewish-Roman War. In this speech, Eleazar is encouraging his companions to fight to the death and asks them to contemplate on the nature of the soul which he claims can prophesy during sleep concerning what is to come (τῶν ἐσομένων προθεσπίζουσι, *J.W.* 7.8.7 §349). There is no mention of the liver here, however.

and all souls are highly divinatory, where exactly can we draw a line between what is prophecy and what is divination?

3.2.4 The Relationship between Prophesying and Divination

It was a common and widespread belief in antiquity that divine beings communicated their will to humans in a variety of observable, experiential, and traceable ways, such as through involuntary bodily movements (e.g., a sneeze); through the physical features of humans; through dreams and visions; through the entrails of sacrificial animals; through oracles, whether written or oral; through the behavior of birds, animals, snakes, insects, and other living creatures; through birth defects, whether among humans or animals; through rare or unusual terrestrial, celestial, or other natural phenomena (e.g., lightnings, earthquakes, eclipses); through anything that was considered abnormal behavior, sight, sound, or experience; through manipulation of certain material artefacts (e.g., casting of lots); through the dead ancestors; and the list can go on.[87] When an effort was made to seek divine knowledge through any of the above means (e.g., observation of bird behavior for knowledge of what one should do in a particular situation), or to decode what was perceived as unprompted divine communication (e.g., an earthquake), this was understood as engagement in divination. In simplistic and general terms, then, "divination is the name given to ritual practices intended to access knowledge from the god(s)."[88] In Greek, the phenomenon was known by the μαντεία word group, and in Latin by the *divinatio* word group (cf. Cicero, *Nat. d.* 1.20 [55] and *Div.* 1.1 [1], in which these Greek and Latin terms are treated as equivalents).

In Greek sources outside of the LXX, NT, Philo, and Josephus, the προφητεύω word group is often associated with oracles, of whom the Delphic oracle is the most famous example.[89] Oracles were believed to be inspired or possessed by

---

[87] Herodotus's *Historiae*, Livy's *History of Rome*, Plutarch's *Lives*, and Suetonius's biographies of the emperors are just a few examples of such ancient writings, which abound with examples of how this belief concerning divine communication was put into practice in the listed ways. See also, Jennifer Eyl, *Signs, Wonders, and Gifts: Divination in the Letters of Paul* (New York: Oxford University Press, 2019), 48, 60–69.

[88] Ritva H. Williams, "Accessing Divine Knowledge," in *Early Christian Ritual Life*, ed. Richard E. DeMaris, Jason T. Lamoreaux, and Steven C. Muir (New York: Routledge, 2018), 55. See also, James B. Rives, *Religion in the Roman Empire* (Malden, MA: Blackwell, 2007), 25; Martti Nissinen, "Divination," in *The Oxford Handbook of Early Christian Ritual*, ed. Risto Uro, et al. (Oxford: Oxford University Press, 2019), 320–22; Eyl, *Signs, Wonders, and Gifts*, 49.

[89] E.g., Herodotus, *Hist.* 7.111; 8.135; 9.93; Plutarch, *Pel.* 16.3; *Alex.* 27.3–5; Pausanias, *Descr.* 8.37.11; Lucian, *Astr.* 23.

3.2 Head-Coverings in the Context of Prophesying

deities, as they responded to inquirers in utterances that often required interpretation and, on occasion, even translation.[90] These oracular utterances were sometimes recorded in written form and then treated by later readers as "prophecies" that had relevance in their own time period. The Sibylline books, for example, were deemed a collection of prophetic utterances that Romans consulted whenever the circumstances called for it (e.g., Cicero, *Div.* 1.2 [4]; Aulus Gellius, *Noct. att.* 1.19).[91] But Greek sources do not deem this manner of προφητεύω separate from μαντεία, but treat it as a *type* of μαντεία. And in Latin sources, oracular activity is likewise considered a form of *divinatio* and not separate from it (e.g., Cicero, *Nat. d.* 1.20 [55]; 2.65 [162–163]; *Div.* 1.2 [4]). Thus, προφητεύω seems not to have been treated as qualitatively different from other divinatory practices through which divine knowledge was sought, such as augury or extispicy.[92] Even though certain individuals or groups seem to have preferred oracular προφητεύω above other forms of divination or thought it more necessary in certain circumstances, this phenomenon is in Greek sources generally viewed as just another form of μαντεία.[93]

---

[90] The nature of this divine possession in oracular activity has been variously understood in both ancient and modern literature. See discussion in Martti Nissinen, *Ancient Prophecy: Near Eastern, Biblical, and Greek Perspectives* (Oxford: Oxford University Press, 2017), 171–200. In Philo's view, as we have seen, the ideal form of prophesying occurs when the deity completely possesses a person, removes his or her thinking faculty, and assumes control of speech organs (which then results in divine ecstasy or madness). This understanding of divinely possessed prophetic activity was not universally shared, however. Plutarch, for example, considers it entirely silly and childish (εὔηθες γάρ ἐστι καὶ παιδικὸν κομιδῇ) to think that the deity would act as a ventriloquist (ἐγγαστρίμυθος), entering into prophets (τὰ σώματα τῶν προφητῶν) and controlling their speech organs (*Def. orac.* 9 [414e]).

[91] See also, Williams, "Accessing Divine Knowledge," 62. According to Suetonius, Augustus collected together lots of books that were claimed to contain prophetic utterances and had them burned, preserving only the Sibylline books for the purpose of accessing divine knowledge, and even these he had edited and trimmed (*Aug.* 31.1).

[92] Somewhat problematically, Laura Nasrallah, in her study on divine communication in antiquity, has deemed it appropriate to refer to "the phenomenon that encompasses divination, prophecy, dreams, visions, and ecstasy" as "prophetic experience(s)." Laura Nasrallah, *An Ecstasy of Folly: Prophecy and Authority in Early Christianity* (Cambridge, MA: Harvard University Press, 2003), 2. Given the connotations that the term "prophecy" has accrued in Christian history, I suggest it is more appropriate to refer to this phenomenon as "divinatory experiences" or as "accessing of divine (fore)knowledge" (see below).

[93] Cicero discusses, for example, how the Assyrians preferred observing the movement of stars in accessing divine (fore)knowledge; the Chaldeans and Egyptians, constellations; Cilicians and their neighboring areas, songs and flights of birds; and Greeks, the various oracles (*Div.* 1.2

The problem of applying this framework on biblical and related sources, however, is that LXX Deut 18:9–22 not only forbids certain *forms* of divination but divination *in general* (μαντευόμενος μαντείαν), clearly setting προφητεύω in antithesis to divination as a separate and also as a truer phenomenon. We have seen how this way of thinking influences Philo in certain contexts, and modern biblical scholars have for this reason also traditionally shown disdain for divination as a "pagan" or idolatrous practice that should find no place in anything associated with the God of the Hebrew Scriptures. In this line of thinking, "prophesying" is something that the one true God uses to communicate with his people, whereas all other practices that claim to achieve the same are deemed false, unreliable, counterfeit, or even outright diabolic. Yet, evidence suggests that despite the rhetoric of LXX Deut 18:9–22, the ancients for whom the LXX Torah was authoritative did not in fact maintain a clear demarcating line around μαντεία as something incompatible with προφητεύω that should not be found among God's people.

We have already seen, for example, that both Philo and Josephus use the μαντεία word group in certain contexts with positive connotations, indicating that the idea of "divination" was not as repulsive to these authors outside of direct engagement with LXX Deut 18:9–22 as reading this passage itself would suggest. And if we take a closer look at the specific types of μαντεία that LXX Deut 18:9–22 prohibits, we see that these also often receive positive evaluations rather than outright rejection. For example, LXX Deut 18:10–11 specifically prohibits accessing divine knowledge through the interpretation of unusual phenomena (τερατοσκόπος) and omens (κληδονίζω). However, Josephus's historical writings are filled with instances in which unusual or unexpected phenomena serve—either in the subject's or in Josephus's interpretation of them—as signs of divine approval or disapproval and as tokens of what is to come: divine will may be revealed through a sudden collapse of a building (*J.W.* 1.17.4 §§331–332), a sudden caving in of a roof (*Ant.*

[2–3]). For heuristic purposes, modern scholars generally divide ancient Greek and Roman divination into two broad categories: inductive and non-inductive divination. Inductive divination, in the words of Martti Nissinen, involves "systematization of signs and omens by observing physical objects (extispicy, astrology, bird divination, etc.)," and is therefore "cognitive" and "technical," whereas non-inductive divination is more "intuitive" and "non-technical" and reliant on inspiration or possession. Greco-Roman oracular prophesying is therefore categorized under non-inductive divination. Martti Nissinen, "Prophecy and Omen Divination: Two Sides of the Same Coin," in *Divination and Interpretation of Signs in the Ancient World*, ed. Amar Annus (Chicago: The University of Chicago, 2010), 341–42. However, it does not appear that the ancients themselves categorized their methods of seeking divine knowledge neatly into either "technical" or "intuitive."

3.2 Head-Coverings in the Context of Prophesying

14.15.11 §455), thunder and lightning and hailstorm (*Ant.* 5.1.17 §60; 6.5.6 §92), unexpected showers of rain (*Ant.* 18.8.6 §§285–288), getting spattered by blood from a sacrificial animal (*Ant.* 19.1.13 §87), an earthquake and strong wind (*J.W.* 4.4.5 §§286–287), and other such things.[94]

Josephus's high regard for unusual phenomena as divine communication is especially evident in his retelling of the events that were claimed to have preceded the fall of Jerusalem in 70 CE. Josephus laments that the Judeans had paid more attention to the many "false prophets" who had promised "signs of deliverance" (τὰ σημεῖα τῆς σωτερίας) rather than to the "prominent and foreboding marvels" (ἐναργέσι καὶ προσημαίνουσι ... τέρασιν), which God was actually sending as warning signs of the coming destruction (*J.W.* 6.5.2–3 §§285–288). Josephus claims, for example, that a sword-shaped star that stood over Jerusalem served as one of such foreboding marvels, as well as a comet that could be seen for a year (*J.W.* 6.5.3 §289). Then one night, such brilliant light shone around the altar and the temple for half an hour that it felt like it was daytime, which, according to Josephus, was interpreted as a positive sign by the "inexperienced" (τοῖς ἀπείροις), but which was correctly understood by the sacred scribes (τοῖς ἱερογραμματεῦσι) to signify what actually came to pass (*J.W.* 6.5.3 §§290–291). During that same festival, a cow brought to be sacrificed gave birth to a lamb in the temple court,[95] and in the

---

[94] While for the most part, certain unexpected natural and unnatural phenomena serve as acceptable and necessary modes of divine communication for Josephus, he does put in the mouth of Herod the Great a speech that can be taken as criticism of reading too much into such phenomena. According to Josephus, this speech was given by Herod during his conflict with the Arabs, after a devastating earthquake had demoralized his troops. In an effort to raise the morale of his fighting men, Herod argued among other things as follows: "Do not let the convulsions of inanimate nature disturb you or imagine that the earthquake is a portent (τέρας) of a further disaster. These accidents to which the elements are subject have physical causes, and beyond the immediate injury inflicted bring no further consequences to mankind. A pestilence, a famine, subterranean commotions may possibly be preceded by some slighter premonition, but these catastrophes themselves are limited by their very magnitude to their instant effects" (*J.W.* 1.19.4 §377 [Thackeray]). It may be that Josephus crafted this speech in order to show what a skillful orator Herod was in motivating his troops to keep fighting despite demoralizing setbacks. It is unlikely to represent Josephus's own views, since Josephus himself deems this same earthquake "an act of God," and also because he otherwise accepts such occurrences as divine communication. But it is nevertheless interesting to note that Josephus includes in his works such a criticism of interpreting unexpected natural phenomena as signs of things to come.

[95] Strange animal births are interpreted as omens of impending misfortune also in Herodotus (e.g., *Hist.* 7.57), and Pliny the Elder discusses the portentous nature of unusual human births (*Nat.* 7.3 [33–35]).

middle of the night, the massive eastern gate of the temple court, that had been well secured and which usually took at least twenty men to open, swung open on its own accord (*J. W.* 6.5.3 §§292–294). Josephus again notes that to the "uninitiated" (τοῖς ἰδιώταις), this unaided opening of the gate appeared as "the best of marvels" (κάλλιστον ἐδόκει τέρας), because they thought it signified God's blessings, but that "the learned" (οἱ λόγιοι) correctly recognized it as a "sign of desolation" (ἐρημίας ... τὸ σημεῖον, *J. W.* 6.5.3 §295).

Josephus then recounts a "marvel" that he admits seems almost impossible to believe, were it not for the many eyewitnesses that had reported it: one evening just before sunset, armies were seen in the sky surrounding the cities all over the country (*J. W.* 6.5.3 §§296–298).[96] And then one night, the priests heard a multitudinous voice within the temple, announcing departure from the temple (*J. W.* 6.5.3 §299). But the most awe-inspiring (φοβερώτερον) of all the marvels for Josephus was the appearance of a certain commoner from the country-side, named Jesus (son of Ananias), who spent seven years announcing woe upon Jerusalem, undeterred by beatings or floggings until he was ultimately killed by a Roman missile in the final stages of the war (*J. W.* 6.5.3 §§300–309). It is interesting here that Josephus counts this appearance of Jesus under the various τέρατα, even though this activity, in its essence, must not have been too much different from what those whom Josephus deems "false prophets" were doing in Jerusalem prior to its fall. In any case, Josephus ends his report of these unusual phenomena with a reflection that God cares for his people, and therefore provides them with all manner of premonitory signs (παντοίως προσημαίνοντα) for the sake of their salvation (*J. W.* 6.5.4 §310). Thus, even though LXX Deut 18:10–11 specifically prohibits accessing divine knowledge through interpretation of unusual phenomena, Josephus not only uncritically recounts the various τέρατα that were claimed to have preceded the fall of Jerusalem but also hails those who correctly interpreted them, even implying that the τέρατα were a much better and more accurate way to understand divine will than listening to the (self-proclaimed) prophets.[97]

LXX Deut 18:10 also prohibits accessing divine knowledge through bird augury (οἰωνίζομαι), and a similar prohibition is also found in LXX Lev 19:26 (οὐκ

---

[96] Compare with Pliny the Elder, *Nat.* 2.58 (148), in which similar phenomena are described.

[97] When fear-inducing strange phenomena were observed by the contemporary Greeks or Romans, certain rites were generally performed to appease the gods (e.g., Plutarch, *Marc.* 28.1–3). Perhaps Josephus expected his people to do the same for Yhwh in response to reports of such unusual phenomena, in order to avert the coming destruction.

3.2 Head-Coverings in the Context of Prophesying

οἰωνιεῖσθε οὐδὲ ὀρνιθοσκοπήσεσθε).[98] Bird augury, or ornithomancy, appears to have been one of the preferred forms of divination among Romans (e.g., Livy, *Ab urbe cond.* 1.7.1; 1.36.6; Suetonius, *Aug.* 95.1–97.3; Valerius Maximus, *Memorable Doings and Sayings*, 1.4.1–7).[99] In his apologetic work *Against Apion*, however, Josephus dares to mock ornithomancy as he approvingly recounts an anecdote about a certain Mosollamus of Judean heritage who, having observed a diviner engaged in ornithomancy (μάντεώς τινος ὀρνιθευομένου), shot out an arrow and killed the bird being observed. When confronted, Mosollamus retorted that the bird could not have possibly provided any useful information, since if it had any ability of foreknowledge (εἰ γὰρ ἠδύνατο προγιγνώσκειν τὸ μέλλον), it would not have come to the spot where it was to be killed (*Ag. Ap.* 1.22 §§202–205). Yet, more often than not, Josephus does not deny that observation of bird behavior can provide divine (fore)knowledge. Josephus claims, for example, that the Nabatean king Aretas IV Philopatris (ca. 9 BCE–40 CE) used ornithomancy (οἰωνοσκοπέω) with success in his conflicts with Judea and Rome (*Ant.* 18.5.3 §125), and that an unnamed German prisoner correctly foretold the "prediction of the gods" (τὴν προαγόρευσιν τῶν θεῶν) to Agrippa—that he will become a king and the timing of his death—based on his observation of the movements of a bird (*Ant.* 18.6.7 §§195–202; 19.8.2 §346).

Josephus also does not deny that ventriloquism, prohibited in LXX Deut 18:11, achieves the desired result of accessing divine (fore)knowledge. In his retelling of the story of the ventriloquist (ἐγγαστρίμυθος) of Endor, for example, Josephus lauds the woman as an exemplar of kindness who accurately predicted the future to Saul through an act of divination which posed great danger to herself (τῆς

---

[98] It should be pointed out here that neither text in the original Hebrew specifically prohibits bird augury. The verbs נחש and ענן, that the LXX translates as terms related to bird augury, are more general terms for divination. While bird augury may constitute one aspect of these Hebrew terms, it does not cover the whole meaning in either case. On the meaning of the above Hebrew verbs see, for example, Jacob Milgrom, *Leviticus 17-22: A New Translation with Introduction and Commentary*, AB (New York: Doubleday, 2000), 1686–89. That being said, however, the Greek term οἰωνίζομαι can also be used as a reference to divination more generally. Even though ὁ οἰωνός means "large bird" or "bird of prey," it seems that this word came to be identified so intimately with the act of divination that it also took on a meaning of "omen" in a more general sense. LSJ, s.v. "οἰωνός." Thus, even though οἰωνίζομαι in its most literal sense refers specifically to bird augury, the word can also be used to describe omen observation more generally. LSJ, s.v. "οἰωνίζομαι"; *GELS*, s.v. "οἰωνίζομαι." The Greek ὀρνιθοσκοπέομαι, however, is much more limited in its meaning and should be taken as a specific reference to bird augury. *GELS*, s.v. "ὀρνιθοσκοπέομαι."

[99] See also, Eyl, *Signs, Wonders, and Gifts*, 60; Peppard, *The Son of God*, 115–18.

παραβόλου μαντείας, *Ant.* 6.14.2–4 §§327–342). Thus, despite the warnings of LXX Deut 18 to shun divination in favor of paying heed to a divinely inspired prophet, Josephus seems to believe on the whole that these forbidden methods of accessing divine (fore)knowledge effectively yield accurate results. And in the case of interpreting unnatural phenomena, Josephus even deems it preferable to listening to (self-proclaimed) prophets—after all, it is much easier to interpret the meaning of a "marvel" if one believes God to be behind it than to figure out which one of the many proclaimers is a divinely possessed prophet.

And then there is a whole list of practices that ancient Greeks and Romans would have classified as μαντεία and which the ancient Jews purportedly made use of or which they thought could reveal divine foreknowledge, but which LXX Deut 18 does not explicitly forbid. For example, LXX Gen 44:5–15 appears to describe either hydromancy or oleomancy—interpreting patterns of either water or oil in a cup—in connection to Joseph (κόνδυ ... οἰωνισμῷ οἰωνίζεται);[100] the Qumranites appear to have made use of horoscopes and brontologia ("a technique for predicting the future by reading omens of thunder in connection with the moon's path through the zodiac");[101] and casting of lots seems to have been widely practiced over a lengthy period of time (e.g., Lev 16:8; Josh 18:10; 1 Chr 24:5; Jonah 1:7; Prov 18:18; Acts 1:26; Josephus, *Ant.* 6.6.5 §125; *J. W.* 3.7.25 §§258–259; 3.8.7 §§387–391).[102] Furthermore, according to Josephus, God foreshowed (προμηνύω) to the Israelites victory in battle through the twelve stones on the high priest's breastplate—an object Philo claims was modeled after the zodiac (*Spec. Laws* 1.87)—leading reverent Greeks to refer to this breastplate of the high priest as "oracle" (λόγιον, *Ant.* 3.8.9 §§216–218, cf. also LXX Exod 28:22). Also, Philo argues that celestial bodies function as signs of things to come (σημεῖα μελλόντων), enabling humans to anticipate what lies ahead (*Creation* 19.58). And both Philo and Josephus regard dreams and visions as highly important and accurate means of accessing divine knowledge (e.g., Josephus, *J. W.* 2.7.3–4 §§111–118; *Ant.* 2.2.2–3 §§11–15; 6.14.2 §334; 10.10.2 §194; 11.8.4 §§327–328; 12.2.14 §§112–113; 13.12.1 §322; 14.15.11 §451; 17.13.3 §§345–346; *Life* 42 §§208–211; Philo, *Dreams* 1.1–2). Notably, Philo explicitly states

---

[100] See, Milgrom, *Leviticus 17–22*, 1687.

[101] Williams, "Accessing Divine Knowledge," 67.

[102] Philo, however, is quite critical of casting lots, particularly in the context of choosing leaders, since he considers it to be about "luck" (εὐτυχία) more than anything else (*Spec. Laws* 4.151). Josephus also debates at times whether the results gained by casting of lots are down to pure luck (εἴτε ὑπὸ τύχης) or whether they stem from the foreknowledge of God (εἴτε ὑπὸ θεοῦ προνοίας, *J. W.* 3.8.7 §391). However, in general, he seems to view this activity as a useful means by which the future can be planned.

that those who interpret dreams (ὀνείρων κριταῖς) engage in prophesying (προφητεύουσι, *Joseph* 18.95), and Josephus presents himself as a skilled interpreter of dreams (ἦν δὲ καὶ περὶ κρίσεις ὀνείρων ἱκανὸς), an ability which he interestingly ties to his knowledge of the prophecies of the sacred scriptures (τῶν γε μὴν ἱερῶν βίβλων οὐκ ἠγνόει τὰς προφητείας, *J. W.* 3.8.3 §352).

And even though both Philo and Josephus are critical of (certain forms of) μαντεία in some contexts, as we have seen, they generally do not deny that the divinatory practices of non-Jews succeed in achieving their aims. Philo, for example, describes the god Apollo as a good diviner (μάντις ἀγαθός), whose oracles declare the things to come (χρησμοῖς προλέγων τὰ μέλλοντα) for the benefit of humanity (*Embassy* 14.109). Josephus claims that the Egyptians at the time of Moses learned of God's counsel (συμβουλεύσαντος τοῦ θεοῦ) from their various oracles and divinations (χρησμοὺς καὶ μαντείας, *Ant.* 2.10.1 §241). And Josephus also claims that emperor Tiberius, who was reliant on all forms of divination (τὰ πάντα μαντειῶν) in governing the empire, was especially skilled in astrology (γενεθλιαλογίᾳ) and gained better results from it than anyone else (*Ant.* 18.6.9 §216–217). These are just a few examples to demonstrate how the success of non-Jews in their affairs was often attributed to their ability to gain divine (fore)knowledge through various forms of divination.

In the idealized vision of LXX Deut 18:9–22, then, μαντεία is not a legitimate method of accessing God's foreknowledge, which is reserved exclusively to individuals known as prophets specifically chosen for this task. In the real world of first-century Roman Empire, however, μαντεία was very much alive, and the various forms of divination not only provided access to divine foreknowledge for non-Jews but also for Second Temple Jews. This dichotomy is especially acute in Philo, who would like to imagine that the ideal of LXX Deut 18:9–22 is possible to maintain, as we have seen, but who, outside of the strict confines of LXX Deut 18:9–22, also allows the προφητεύω terminology to overlap with the practices of μαντεία. Thus, this narrow idea of προφητεύω as an activity in which a human becomes completely possessed or inspired by the deity to speak (the truth) only works as an ideal that hardly meets the real. In the complex reality of first-century CE engagement with the divine, the προφητεύω word group appears to encompass various methods of accessing divine (fore)knowledge, including dream and vision interpretation as well as omen and marvel interpretation. In this sense, the προφητεύω word group covers much of what the μαντεία word group does, and vice versa.¹⁰³

This does not mean, however, that all forms of μαντεία were therefore considered equally valid or immune from criticism, ridicule, or rejection. When context calls for it, μαντεία or its various manifestations, including the ecstatic oracular performance most readily associated with προφητεύω, are condemned or dismissed as false or ineffective.¹⁰⁴ But the dividing line is not between "prophesying" as correct and holy and "divination" as incorrect and profane, but between what works and what does not in any given situation. Thus, Josephus, as we have seen, deems the "prophets" who declared signs of salvation in Judea's struggle with Rome false and deceitful, but hails those who correctly interpreted marvels (including Josephus himself)—an otherwise forbidden activity—as learned and accurate. Thus, in this particular case, "prophesying" in its strictest sense fails to yield access to divine (fore)knowledge and is therefore deemed "false," whereas another form of μαντεία succeeds and is therefore praised. The question remains, however, whether Paul also could have understood προφητεύω in this broader sense of "accessing divine (fore)knowledge" rather than in a more limited sense of "delivering inspired speech," as traditional biblical scholarship has maintained (see section 3.2.2).

3.2.5 Divination in the Letters of Paul

In traditional biblical scholarship, Paul has been especially guarded from all hints of any association with divination. However, recent studies have demonstrated that Paul, like other ancients, embraced certain practices that can be deemed "divinatory." Thus, Jennifer Eyl argues that "Paul engaged in numerous forms of divination"¹⁰⁵ and Matthew Sharp finds that "Paul's various means of communication with the divine are best situated within the context of ancient divination."¹⁰⁶ Both authors point out, for example, that Paul's engagement with the LXX in his

---

¹⁰³ Compare, for example, Philo's definition of "prophecy" as something that "reaches towards those things that the mind fails with" or that are not comprehended by reason (*Moses* 2.6) with Lucian's definition of "divination" as something through which (fore)knowledge is gained of the unknown (τὰ ἄδηλα ... προγιγνώσκειν, *Hesiod* 8). The broad aim of προφητεύω in Philo is very similar to the broad aim of μαντεία in Lucian.

¹⁰⁴ Criticism, ridicule, or rejection of (various forms of) divination in certain contexts was common in antiquity. E.g., Cicero, *Nat. d.* 1.20 (55–56); Juvenal, *Sat.* 6.548–591; Lucian, *Hesiod* 8.

¹⁰⁵ Eyl, *Signs, Wonders, and Gifts*, 1.
¹⁰⁶ Sharp, *Divination and Philosophy*, 2.

3.2 Head-Coverings in the Context of Prophesying 197

letters can be described as "oracular"—treating a certain collection of ancient writings as divine utterances in need of interpretation in light of current events or for the sake of prognostication.[107] Paul does indeed designate the Hebrew Scriptures as "oracles of God" (τὰ λόγια[108] τοῦ θεοῦ, Rom 3:2), and his frequent allegorical and recontextualized use of the LXX may demonstrate that he "provides oracular readings to his followers."[109] We know that Romans used the Sibylline books in an oracular way whenever the circumstances called for it—such as when diseases broke out on a large scale, a famine hit, or unusual phenomena were observed (e.g., Livy, *Ab urbe cond*. 3.10.7; 5.13.5)—and there are certainly similarities here with how Paul uses the LXX in trying to make sense of the Christ-event and the subsequent experiences in his own life as well as in those of his contemporaries.

And not only does Paul receive divine oracles through sacred texts, but it appears that there were also other ways by which Paul came into possession of divine oracles. Paul informs the Corinthians, for example, that after he had beseeched the Lord three times about the "thorn in the flesh," he received the following reply: "My grace is sufficient for you, for the power is perfected in weakness" (2 Cor 12:9). Paul does not elaborate on how he came into possession of this oracle, but since we do not have a LXX equivalent of this statement, Paul may have learned of this oracular guidance through other means. Furthermore, in the words of Ritva

---

[107] Eyl, *Signs, Wonders, and Gifts*, 54; Sharp, *Divination and Philosophy*, 133–62.

[108] The term τό λόγιον ("oracle") should not be confused with the term ὁ λόγος ("word"). τό λόγιον most readily refers to a pithy oral or written utterance that is thought to be of divine origin and relevant (with interpretation) to a particular contemporary or future situation (e.g., Josephus, *J.W.* 6.5.4 §313–315; Philo, *Spec. Laws*, 4.48–52).

[109] Eyl, *Signs, Wonders, and Gifts*, 104, 112. Eyl even wonders whether Paul and other early Christians could have engaged in bibliomancy—a mode of divination in which a randomly opened text in a scroll or a book serves (with interpretation) as a guide in response to an inquiry. Eyl, *Signs, Wonders, and Gifts*, 103–4. There is evidence in some biblical manuscripts from the third to eighth centuries CE (such as certain scribbles at the bottom of the pages) that these manuscripts were used as tools of prognostication: "it is evident that some Christians ascribed special powers to the manuscripts of scripture themselves: they could be used not only for purposes of apotropaic magic (the amulets) but also to influence, or at least predict, one's future." Bart D. Ehrman, "The Text as Window: New Testament Manuscripts and the Social History of Early Christianity," in *The Text of the New Testament in Contemporary Research: Essays on the Status Quaestionis*, ed. Bart D. Ehrman and Michael W. Holmes, 2nd ed. (Boston: Brill, 2013), 818. It is impossible to tell how early this practice started among Christ-followers, since our manuscript evidence for Christian writings before the third century CE is very slim. But it is not beyond the realm of possibility that already Paul's congregants used certain scriptural manuscripts as tools of prognostication.

Williams, "Paul introduces innovative teaching as oracular pronouncements with phrases such as 'through the Lord Jesus' (1 Thess 4:2–6), 'by the word of the Lord' (1 Thess 4:15–17), or as 'mystery' (1 Cor 15:51–52; Rom 11:25–26)."[110] In these instances, Paul does not inform his readers how exactly he had received the content of his (innovative) teachings "through the Lord" or as "mystery," but it is possible that Paul accessed this knowledge through methods that his contemporaries would have categorized under divination.

Visions, revelations, and their interpretations also play a crucial role in Paul's engagement with the world. Paul informs the Galatians, for example, that God's son was "revealed" (ἀποκαλύψαι) in him, an experience about which he did not "consult" (προσανεθέμην) anyone (not even the apostles in Jerusalem), but departed for Arabia instead (Gal 1:16–17). Matthew Sharp has shown that the verb προσανατίθημι (which in the NT appears only here and in Gal 2:6) was used in contemporaneous literature in contexts of dream interpretation.[111] Thus, Paul seems not to have trusted anyone else but himself in interpreting his dreams and visions. Paul also informs the Galatians that his eventual decision to visit Jerusalem after fourteen years was likewise made in response to a revelation (κατὰ ἀποκάλυψιν, Gal 2:2). It was common for the ancients to make decisions based on (the interpretation of) dreams and visions, as it was held that the divine sphere communicated with humans through such phenomena. Thus, Paul's decision-making in response to revelatory experiences does not stand out in the Greco-Roman milieu, although Greeks and Romans at the time would have classified such activity under divination. However, Paul's confidence in his own ability to interpret dreams and visions is noteworthy.

But not only does Paul regard visions and revelations an important part of his life and ministry, he also considers his revelations superior in quality to those of others who value such means of divine communication. Paul informs the Corinthian congregation, for example, that the extraordinary nature of his visions and revelations should demonstrate to them that he stands above his rivals, whom he sarcastically dubs "the super-apostles" (ὑπερλίαν τῶν ἀποστόλων, 2 Cor 11:5; 12:1–7). As proof, and perhaps to challenge his rivals, Paul recounts an experience in which "a person I know in Christ"—likely Paul himself[112]—was transferred to

---

[110] Williams, "Accessing Divine Knowledge," 63.

[111] Sharp, *Divination and Philosophy*, 83.

[112] Some have tried to argue that Paul is relating here an experience of someone other than himself (e.g., Michael Goulder, "Vision and Knowledge," *JSNT* 17 [1995]: 53–71). This is a

3.2 Head-Coverings in the Context of Prophesying

"paradise" (εἰς παράδεισον), where he heard "unspeakable words" (ἄρρητα ῥήματα, 2 Cor 12:4). Paul speculates that this may have even been a bodily (ἐν σώματι) experience (2 Cor 12:3).[113] Thus, whatever divine communications others had received or were receiving in their dreams and visions, Paul does not think these can rival his own experiences. Paul believes that his revelatory experiences set him apart from all others (including the Jerusalem apostles), enabling him a direct access to divine knowledge without reliance on anyone else.

In his letters, Paul also engages in the interpretation of unusual phenomena to discern divine will. He tells the Corinthian congregation, for example, that the illnesses, weaknesses, and deaths among them were a demonstration of God's judgment on them for participating in the *deipnon* of the Lord "unworthily" (ἀναξίως, 1 Cor 11:27–30). Paul interprets the Corinthians' unusual health problems, then, as a divine message that needs to be decoded by him for their benefit.[114] As we have seen, it was common in antiquity to read unusual or unfortunate events as bad omens or as signs of divine judgment, and so Paul's rhetoric here participates in this belief that access to divine (fore)knowledge was possible through the observation and interpretation of unusual phenomena. But not only does Paul *interpret* unusual phenomena, he also participates in the *performance* of "signs and marvels and miracles" (σημείοις τε καὶ τέρασιν καὶ δυνάμεσιν), which the Corinthians, for example, were supposed to take as evidence that Paul was authentically an apostle (2 Cor 12:12). It is not clear what these signs, marvels, and miracles encompassed,

---

minority view, however, and seems to stem from an effort to divest Paul of all "strange" experiences according to modern standards. For further discussion see, for example, Colleen Shantz, *Paul in Ecstasy: The Neurobiology of the Apostle's Life and Thought* (New York: Cambridge University Press, 2009), 41–42.

[113] Colleen Shantz has argued that Paul's "confusion about his bodily status and his assertion of unutterable auditions" here is typical of an ASC (Altered State of Consciousness) experience. Shantz, *Paul in Ecstasy*, 108. While Paul's experience may be deemed ASC from modern neurological perspective, ancient Greeks and Romans would have understood Paul's experience within the framework of divination.

[114] Traditionally, biblical scholars have argued for a direct cause-and-effect relationship between what the Corinthians were doing during their meals and the illnesses and deaths in their midst. E.g., David J. Downs, "Physical Weakness, Illness and Death in 1 Corinthians 11.30: Deprivation and Overconsumption in Pauline and Early Christianity," *NTS* 65 (2019): 572–88. I would be cautious with this line of argument, however, as it is just as likely (if not more so) that the sufferings of the Corinthians were unrelated to their common meals, and that Paul only makes the connection for rhetorical effect.

but whatever phenomena may have been counted as such,[115] Christ-followers in Corinth and elsewhere were encouraged to interpret them as indicators of divine approval of Paul's ministry and his claim to apostleship.[116]

There are also indicators that Paul engaged in prognostication of future. For example, Paul reminds the Thessalonians that he had foretold (προλέγω) them of his impending persecution, and that they should know it had come to pass as predicted (καθὼς ἐγένετο, 1 Thess 3:4). While it is possible that Paul learned of the approaching abuse through means other than divination or prophecy (e.g., an informant), it is equally plausible that Paul came to possess this knowledge through a dream or a revelation, oracular reading of scriptures, or through any other such means. It is the overall belief of Paul that God reveals (ἀποκαλύπτω) to the "spirituals" hitherto unseen, unheard of, and inconceivable things (1 Cor 2:9–10), and Paul does not limit how this process of accessing divine knowledge is possible. While Paul likely rejected certain forms of divination, such as bird augury or extispicy, he seems to have believed in the whole that divine communication could take place in any number of ways, including through the appearance of unusual phenomena, through dreams and visions, and through oracles. In other words, what Paul imagines as engagement in spiritual discernment (cf. 1 Cor 2:15), his contemporary Greeks and Romans would have perceived as engagement in divination.[117]

What emerges, then, is overlap between Paul's presentation of "prophesying" in 1 Cor 12–14 and his broader use of divinatory language. Revelatory experiences,

---

[115] We have seen what sort of occurrences Josephus counts under "signs" and "marvels," so there is a wide range of phenomena that Paul could be referencing here. Some ancients even considered a timely sneeze during a speech a sign of divine approval of what was said (e.g., Xenophon, *Anab.* 3.2.8–9). Thus, something as commonplace as a sneeze may have been interpreted as a sign, a marvel, or a miracle in certain contexts. Colleen Shantz, on the other hand, has suggested that "the demonstration of apostolic power of which Paul speaks may have been the ability to kindle ecstatic experiences in the communities he visited," and this is also a plausible option. Shantz, *Paul in Ecstasy*, 180.

[116] It is worth noting here that in Josephus's retelling of the history of his people, the performance of signs, marvels, and miraculous feats is intimately tied with prophetic activity (e.g., *Ant.* 9.8.6 §§180–182; 10.2.1 §§28–29). And on the flip side, in his retelling of the fall of Jerusalem, Josephus deems those who promised signs, marvels, and miraculous feats "false prophets" (e.g., *Ant.* 20.5.1 §97; 20.8.6 §§168–169). Yet, despite the designation of such activity as "false," it is nevertheless spoken of in the context of "prophesying."

[117] In the words of Jennifer Eyl: "Paul's contemporaries ... would have understood his practices as types of *mantikē, teratoskopia, goēteia*, or even *mageia*, but Paul innovatively repackages them as *charismata pneumatika*." Eyl, *Signs, Wonders, and Gifts*, 7.

manifestations of secrets, and understanding of mysteries, for example, are not exclusive to Paul's discussion about prophesying but feature in Paul's overall understanding of how divine communication operates. Thus, "prophesying" in the letters of Paul appears to be a much broader term than strictly a reference to an inspired speech-act. If we take Philo's definition of prophecy as that which accesses what the mind cannot comprehend (i.e., divine knowledge) as a model, then Paul's multifarious use of the προφητεύω word group in 1 Cor 12–14 fits well within that definition. It explains why in some contexts Paul emphasizes the introspective element of prophecy, but in other contexts, the emphasis is on a speech-act; why in some contexts prophesying is connected to the idea of revelation, but in others, these concepts are treated separately; and why there are no clear demarcating lines around prophesying in relation to other activities, such as teaching or speaking in knowledge. I propose, therefore, that προφητεύω and its cognates should be understood in Paul's letters in a broad sense of "accessing of divine (fore)knowledge," and that Paul therefore does not limit "prophesying" to a singular activity (such as "inspired preaching"). Instead, depending on the context, "prophesying" in the Pauline corpus may refer to a number of activities, including vision or marvel interpretation and oracular reading of scriptures. And in some instances, Paul may refer to προφητεύω in its strictest sense (as Philo does within the confines of Deut 18)—as a speech-act which emanates from divine possession. But on the whole, what Paul means by "prophesying" seems to cover some of what other ancients mean by "divination," although these concepts should not be treated as equivalents in Paul's thinking.

3.2.6 "Prophesying" in 1 Cor 11:4–5

If "prophesying" in the letters of Paul is taken as a more general term for accessing divine (fore)knowledge, then we are much more dependent on each context of Paul's reference to this phenomenon to determine whether Paul uses προφητεύω or its cognates in a more general sense or whether he has in mind specific activities through which divine (fore)knowledge was accessed. The context of 1 Cor 11:4–5, for example, is the issue of head-coverings, and Chapter 2 demonstrated that Romans covered their heads with their garments when they accessed divine (fore)knowledge. As discussed, Livy describes how the victorious generals covered their heads when they received auguries on the Capitol (*Ab urbe cond*. 10.7.10); Valerius Flaccus describes how the seer Mopsus covered his head when he observed an omen (*Argonautica* 5.95–97); both Plutarch and Livy describe covered heads when bird auguries were taken to determine whether Numa had the divine blessing to become Rome's next king (Livy, *Ab urbe cond.* 1.18.6–10; Plutarch, *Num.* 7.2); both Livy and Dionysius of Halicarnassus report that a *capite velato* statue had been set up of the augur Attus Navius in a prominent place in Rome in celebration of his feats (Dionysius of Halicarnassus, *Ant. rom.* 3.71.5; Livy, *Ab urbe cond.* 1.36.3–5); Juvenal describes an unnamed lady with a covered head during haruspicy (*Sat.* 6.385–397); one of the keepers and interpreters of the Sibylline books on the Ara Pacis is depicted with a covered head; and the *vicomagistrii* had set up an altar in 2 BCE depicting Augustus with a covered head holding a *lituus* in the pose of an augur as he observes a pecking bird for divine knowledge (see Chapter 2 for all of the above references).

We see, then, that covered heads did not accompany only one type of divinatory activity but feature in Roman divination more generally. It is thus entirely feasible that the Corinthian Christian congregants of Roman background had been used to accessing divine (fore)knowledge with covered heads. It is thus also plausible that this manner of accessing divine (fore)knowledge continued to feature in some way in private and public devotion of these Christian neophytes. This does not necessarily mean that the Christians in Corinth continued to observe birds for divine knowledge, for example—although the Didache does prohibit (bird) augury (μὴ γίνου οἰωνοσκόπος, Did. 3:4), which suggests that it may have been practiced in some early Christian communities. Rather, covering the head with a garment may have still been an instinctive reaction to the perception that one was engaged in accessing divine (fore)knowledge, regardless of the specific form. For example, these neophytes may have felt compelled to cover their heads when "revelations" were relayed and interpreted during Christian meetings (cf. 1 Cor 14:29–32), when the LXX was read in an oracular manner, when lots were cast (cf. Acts 1:26), when unusual phenomena were observed or interpreted, when celestial bodies were observed and their movements and appearances interpreted (cf. Matt 24:7, 29; Mark 13:24; Luke 21:25–28), when they experienced divine possession and uttered oracles, or in any other context of accessing divine (fore)knowledge that the Christian community (including Paul) approved of.[118]

The problem for Paul in all of this is not that the Corinthian Christians accessed divine (fore)knowledge (or "prophesied") in any of the above ways (although Paul considers himself superior to them in this regard), but he is troubled by the use (and absence) of head-coverings in association with it. However, this is a rather odd concern, given that, just like in regards to prayer, Paul elsewhere shows

---

[118] See also, Williams, "Accessing Divine Knowledge," 65–66.

little concern for postures, appearances, or behaviors in connection to accessing divine (fore)knowledge—although he does instruct the Corinthians to prophesy in an orderly fashion, one by one (cf. 1 Cor 14:29–32). This demonstrates once again that 1 Cor 11:2–16 appears to preserve a competing perspective about how communication with the divine should be conducted—a perspective not shared by Paul. Considering the importance of *capite velato* in Roman divination, this ritual gesture is likely at the heart of these competing views that Paul in this passage addresses. But why does Paul, then, discourage only Christian men from praying and accessing divine knowledge with a covered head, but expects the opposite from Christian women? We will attempt to answer this question in the next two chapters.

3.3 Conclusion

In this chapter, I have worked with the premise that Paul's phrase "praying or prophesying" in 1 Cor 11:4–5 should be taken literally, as referring to two particular activities—praying and prophesying—during which head-coverings were an issue for Paul. I have also argued that "prophesying" in Paul's letters should be understood in a broad sense of "accessing divine (fore)knowledge." Considering, then, that Romans prayed and accessed divine knowledge with covered heads, there is a clear parallel here with 1 Cor 11:2–16, in which the issue with head-coverings has arisen precisely in these contexts. Furthermore, this chapter has demonstrated that 1 Cor 11:2–16 is an anomalous passage in the corpus of Paul's authentic letters, because nowhere else is Paul concerned to that degree with individual postures, appearances, or behaviors during praying or prophesying. On the contrary, Paul is generally quite lax about these matters, especially in comparison to Roman attitudes regarding devotion. Thus, 1 Cor 11:2–16 appears to address a way of thinking about the efficacy of prayer and accessing of divine (fore)knowledge that clashes with how Paul envisions human communication with the divine and divine communication with humans to function. And *capite velato*, which the Romans considered an important ritual gesture during prayer and divination, appears to be at the center of this clash of values. It remains to be seen, however, why Paul only discourages Christian men from praying and prophesying *capite velato* but not women. Before probing this question fully, however, we will first turn to cognitive science of religion for insights on ritual behavior in relation to individual cognition and group dynamics.

4. *Capite velato*, Human Cognition, and Group Dynamics

What Cognitive Science of Religion Hypothesizes about Ritualized Behavior and Its Relevance for 1 Cor 11:2–16

So far, we have established that *capite velato* was a prominent and widespread ritual gesture among Romans at the time of Paul, regarded as an essential component of praying and of accessing divine (fore)knowledge. We have also argued that there are strong conceptual and linguistic links between descriptions and depictions of *capite velato* and 1 Cor 11:2–16, which suggests that *capite velato* is a concern for Paul in this passage. We now turn to possible explanations for why *capite velato* came to feature in Paul's correspondence with the Corinthians. First, we want to know how the performances and non-performances of *capite velato* could have been experienced or perceived by Romans and non-Romans particularly in colonial settings, such as in first-century CE Corinth. For this, I will subject the data we have about *capite velato* to various theories about rituals that cognitive scientists of religion have advanced. These theories hypothesize that *capite velato* would have been an excellent transmitter of doctrines and complex religious teachings; that it would have functioned as an important cultural signal, enabling Romans to trust and cooperate with one other; and that it would have been difficult for Romans not to perform *capite velato*, due to this ritual's close association with the brain's hazard-precaution system.

Based on these findings, I then discuss in the second part of the chapter how *capite velato* could have featured in first-century Corinth and in the Christian congregation there. I argue that first-century Corinth had a strong Roman presence, and that in this multicultural city, *capite velato* may have been particularly important for some Romans as identity marker of Roman-ness. I also demonstrate that the Corinthian Christian assembly appears to have included certain influential members with Roman affiliations, some of whom had reasons to perform *capite velato* in the various venues they frequented in fulfillment of their social obligations. I suggest, then, that Paul's statement that praying with a head-covering is shameful for men must have been a cause for concern for such Romans, as acting upon this directive risked severing important social ties that were crucial for one's access to social and material resources. Thus, Paul's argument concerning men in 1 Cor 11:2–16 had ramifications beyond the simple request to pray differently; it called for a re-evaluation of one's social relationships, lifestyle, and worldview.

4.1 *Capite velato* and Cognitive Science of Religion

In order to be in a better position to offer a possible *Sitz im Leben* for 1 Cor 11:2–16, we need to discuss how *capite velato* could have been experienced in first-century Corinth. Here we turn to insights on ritual behavior from the burgeoning discipline known as Cognitive Science of Religion (CSR). CSR scholars study the cognitive processes that underlie religious thought and behavior, aiming to explain and predict, among other things, what happens in the mind of a person that observes or engages in ritual acts.[1] Since cognitive scientists are in general agreement that our basic cognitive structures have remained largely unchanged in the last several thousand years,[2] we expect the findings of CSR to then offer valuable insight into how ancient Romans and non-Romans in Corinth could have experienced *capite velato*. This, in turn, should allow us to clarify how Paul's instructions in 1 Cor 11:2–16 could have been heard by those who regularly prayed or accessed divine (fore)knowledge with a covered head, and by those who had never done so.

It must be noted here, however, that CSR is not a unified theory pinpointing specific cognitive processes that underlie or correspond to particular religious thoughts and behaviors. Rather, CSR is an interdisciplinary field of study that incorporates a number of various theories and hypotheses about religion and cognition. Thus, CSR is not a magic wand that permits straightforward access into the mind of a believer; the various theories (sometimes competing) offer us only glimpses into human cognition and do so from various points of interest. Here we will examine a selection of theories specifically related to (religious) ritual behavior, exploring their applicability on the data we possess on *capite velato*. Thus, the aim

---

[1] For a reader-friendly introduction to CSR see, Claire White, *An Introduction to the Cognitive Science of Religion: Connecting Evolution, Brain, Cognition, and Culture* (New York: Routledge, 2021), esp. 1–23. See also, Risto Uro, "Cognitive Science in the Study of Early Christianity: Why It Is Helpful—and How?" *NTS* 63 (2017): 517.

[2] E.g., Czachesz, *Cognitive Science*, 31–32; Uro, "Cognitive Science," 524.

here is not to prove beyond doubt what Romans or Corinthian Christians thought about *capite velato*, but only to demonstrate that engagement in ritual behavior has certain effects on human cognition (and vice versa). Awareness of what such effects may be allows us then to imagine the possible scenarios that could have prompted 1 Cor 11:2–16 in a more restricted and scientific way.[3]

4.1.1 What Do We Mean by "Ritual"?

So far, I have referred to *capite velato* as a "ritual gesture" without any explanation as to what I mean by the term "ritual." It is now time to point out (perhaps the obvious) that the term "ritual" is not self-explanatory. Thus, before we can apply the various theories from CSR on the available data regarding *capite velato*, an explanation of what we mean by "ritual" is in order. The term "ritual" has been notoriously difficult to define—while it is used in common parlance without much hesitation, it seems to lose its potential for an agreeable definition in the minds of theorists.[4] Although a number of scholars have suggested that "ritual" should be recognized by the element of repetitiveness,[5] even this very basic idea is contentious—can an act that is never repeated or an act that has no repetitive behavior not be called a ritual?

Another problem with defining "ritual" is that it has a long history of use in Western thought (both within and beyond academia), so the term comes to us with certain entrenched connotations that are hard to shake off. Thus, Catherine Bell, for example, has much preferred the term "ritualization" (or more fully "ritualization of activity"[6]) over "ritual," as she believes that the latter term has over time accrued the unnecessary "implications of universality, naturalness, and an intrinsic structure" to which "ritualization" as understood by her should provide a corrective.[7] Bell defines "ritualization" as follows:

---

[3] As Risto Uro notes, "the field [of CSR] has rightly been defined as being about 'sciencing up' the academic study of religion." Uro, "Cognitive Science," 520.

[4] See discussion in, for example, Richard E. DeMaris, "Introduction: With Respect to Ritual," in *Early Christian Ritual Life*, ed. Richard E. DeMaris, Jason T. Lamoreaux, and Steven C. Muir (New York: Routledge, 2018), 1–6; Erin K. Vearncombe, "Rituals for Communal Maintenance," in *Early Christian Ritual Life*, ed. Richard E. DeMaris, Jason T. Lamoreaux, and Steven C. Muir (New York: Routledge, 2018), 100–101; and Uro, *Ritual and Christian Beginnings*, 28–30, 64.

[5] See, Czachesz, *Cognitive Science*, 89.

[6] Catherine Bell, *Ritual Theory, Ritual Practice* (Oxford: Oxford University Press, 2009), 219.

[7] Bell, *Ritual Theory*, 222–23.

In a very preliminary sense, ritualization is a way of acting that is designed and orchestrated to distinguish and privilege what is being done in comparison to other, usually more quotidian, activities. As such, ritualization is a matter of various culturally specific strategies for setting some activities off from others, for creating and privileging a qualitative distinction between the 'sacred' and the 'profane,' and for ascribing such distinctions to realities thought to transcend the powers of human actors.[8]

While Bell's emphasis on "ritualization" over "ritual" may solve some issues regarding definition, fundamental problems remain with distinguishing ritualized activity from non-ritualized activity. For example, what are the "various culturally specific strategies" that set some activities off from others? Where do we draw the line between "sacred" and "profane"? And what counts as a "reality" that is thought to "transcend the powers of human actors"? Although Bell does attempt to address some of these issues in her work, the deeper we get into these questions, the more we end up facing the same problems that we encounter in defining "ritual"—that is, just as it is very difficult to draw a dividing line between "ritual" and "non-ritual," so it is with separating "more quotidian activity" from "ritualization." Thus, updating terminology does not yet solve the underlying issue of why some activities should be categorized differently in the first place.

More recently, Ronald Grimes has argued that defining "ritual" remains a worthwhile scholarly pursuit. Grimes himself provides the following "classroom definition" as a heuristic tool, while acknowledging its tentativeness: "Ritual is embodied, condensed, and prescribed enactment."[9] This definition is concise and memorable, and can indeed serve as a useful heuristic tool. However, all of the used words in this definition nevertheless require further explanation: what do we mean by "embodied," "condensed," "prescribed," or "enactment"? The problem we have, then, is that the term "ritual" (or "ritualization") itself is somehow more easily grasped by those who use it than any of the definitions provided for it.[10] We seem to be intuitively aware that some activities are different to such a degree that

---

[8] Bell, *Ritual Theory*, 74.

[9] Roland L. Grimes, *The Craft of Ritual Studies*, (Oxford: Oxford University Press, 2013), 195.

[10] A classic example of this is a definition of ritual provided by cultural anthropologist Stanley Jeyaraja Tambiah from 1979: "Ritual is a culturally constructed system of symbolic communication. It is constituted of patterned and ordered sequences of words and acts, often expressed in multiple media, whose content and arrangement are characterized in varying degree by formality (conventionality), stereotypy (rigidity), condensation (fusion), and redundancy (repetition)." S. J. Tambiah, "A Performative Approach to Ritual," *Proceedings of the British Academy* 65 (1981): 119. This definition has been well regarded in scholarship but it requires a whole lot of "unpacking" to have any meaningful relevance in the conversations about "ritual."

they should be categorized as "rituals," yet articulating the basis for this distinction remains challenging.

Perhaps, then, providing a definition for "ritual" which neatly categorizes all activities into rituals and non-rituals is an unachievable goal.[11] Perhaps it is wiser to discuss the idea of "ritual" on a case-by-case basis. That is, our task here should not be to define what "ritual" is in a universal sense, but to understand why a particular activity should be categorized differently from other similar activities. And *capite velato* provides an interesting case study in this regard. As was discussed in Chapter 2, *capite velato* is essentially an act of covering the head with the outer garment, which is distinguished from other acts of covering the head with the outer garment. So why do we distinguish the act of covering the head with the outer garment during prayer from the act of covering the head with the outer garment when it starts to rain, if there is no difference in terms of motor activity? Here we can think of three main reasons why one act should be considered "ritualized" and the other not.

First, covering the head in prayer for ancient Romans is accompanied by or responds to specific rules, such as that the outer garment should not slip off the head during the duration of prayer (see section 2.2.10). However, we are not aware of any explicit or implicit rules that were in place for covering the head with the outer garment in case of rainfall or in case of a wish to conceal one's identity. Some modern theorists suggest that the presence of specific rules differentiates rituals from ordinary actions. Pascal Boyer explains, for example, that the "most obvious feature that distinguishes a ritual from an ordinary action is that specific rules organize the performance."[12] Yet, even though this may be true in most cases, I would

---

[11] Pascal Boyer and Pierre Liénard would concur, explaining the impossibility of the task as follows: "'Ritual,' like 'marriage' or 'religion,' is not a proper analytical category; instead it is more of what Rodney Needham (1975) described as a 'polythetic' category, in which, typically, ritual types A and B may share features [*m, n, p*], types Y and Z may share [*p, q, r*], Z and W share [*q, r, s*]. And although A and W apparently do not share any major feature, they are both called 'rituals.' That is why it is certainly futile to collect many instances of what are commonly called 'rituals' and to tabulate their common features. This too often results in very vague formulations that would potentially apply to any social institution." Pascal Boyer and Pierre Liénard, "Whence Collective Rituals? A Cultural Selection Model of Ritualized Behavior," *American Anthropologist* 108 (2006): 814–15.

[12] Pascal Boyer, *Religion Explained: The Evolutionary Origins of Religious Thought* (New York: Basic Books, 2001), 231. This view is shared by Gerd Theissen who suggests that "rites are actions which become an end in themselves through the strict observance of rules." Gerd Theissen, *The Religion of the Earliest Churches: Creating a Symbolic World* (Minneapolis: Fortress Press, 1999), 121.

not go so far as to say that this dictum then governs *all* cases—there is no good reason to hold that a particular activity, which is not governed by clearly expressed rule(s), could not be considered a ritual in certain context(s). Nevertheless, in case of *capite velato*, the associated rules clearly distinguish this act from other similar acts, and for this reason, *capite velato* should be categorized differently.

Second, the purpose of *capite velato* is not primarily tied to the realm of our physical environment, but the primary purpose of *capite velato* is associated with the unseen and the imaginary realm. When a Roman covers his or her head with a garment in case of rainfall, the expectation is that this act provides immediate comfort in the physical world. However, when a Roman covers the head with a garment during prayer (or divination or sacrifice), the expectation is that this act somehow affects how gods operate, the process of which is not observable. Thus, the performer has to *trust* that his or her act is effective without any visible or material proof of how the act achieves what it is supposed to achieve. Some scholars have highlighted that such untraceable causality is one of the key features of rituals. Cristine Legare and André Souza, for example, discuss the intended effects of rituals and argue that "rituals intended to have particular effects are not expected to do so by causal mechanisms that are transparent or even in principle knowable" and we see that this is true in the case of *capite velato*.[13]

Third, the act of prayer (or divination or sacrifice) itself does not demand that the head must be covered. For example, unlike the blazing sun in midday heat which may cause one to cover his or her head for comfort, speaking—as in prayer—does not naturally prompt the need for a head-covering; there is no inherent cause-and-effect relationship here. Harvey Whitehouse explains that one of the features distinguishing rituals from other activities is the "incorporation of elements that are superfluous to any practical aim,"[14] and this is certainly the case with *capite velato*—covering the head with a garment does not make the basic movement of pouring liquid (i.e., libation) any more possible than when the head is uncovered. And Pascal Boyer and Pierre Liénard add that "many rituals include actions for which there could not possibly be any clear empirical goals," which fits

---

[13] Cristine H. Legare and André L. Souza, "Evaluating Ritual Efficacy: Evidence from the Supernatural," *Cognition* 124 (2012): 2. Ritual participants of course do detect causality—that is, they do generally believe that what they do has a cause-and-effect relationship with the end goal. However, these connections cannot be objectively traced. See also, Veronika Rybanska, *The Impact of Ritual on Child Cognition* (New York: Bloomsbury Academic, 2020), 19.

[14] Harvey Whitehouse, *Modes of Religiosity: A Cognitive Theory of Religious Transmission* (Walnut Creek, CA: Altamira Press, 2004), 3.

with *capite velato* as well.[15] Thus, elements associated with practicability also set *capite velato* apart, but again, this does not mean that *all* rituals should be defined by this metric.

In all, therefore, I suggest that covering the head with an outer garment during prayer, sacrifice, or divination is a *ritualized* activity, while covering the head with an outer garment in case of adverse weather conditions, for concealment of facial features, or for the sake of comfort is *not* a ritualized activity, because the former is distinguished from the latter by rules that govern its performance, by its placement in the opposite end of the practicability spectrum, and by the different realms of causality (other-worldly versus this-worldly). I must stress that I am not offering a universal definition of "ritual" here; I am merely suggesting that in the case of *capite velato*, the above features that various theorists have associated with the concept of "ritual" allow us to distinguish *capite velato* from other similar activities and categorize it as a ritual gesture or a ritual posture or more generally, as a ritualized activity. Thus, *capite velato* comes to participate in the scholarly conversations about activities marked off as "rituals," whether by the above metrics or by some other reasons. In the remainder of this section, then, we are interested specifically in the academic theorizing regarding the relationship between rituals, cognition, and group dynamics, and what these insights might tell us about *capite velato*.

4.1.2 Modes of Religiosity Theory: Overview

Based mainly on his fieldwork in Papua New Guinea, British anthropologist Harvey Whitehouse has offered a theoretical framework known as Modes of Religiosity Theory (MRT) for understanding religion and rituals in relation to cognition. In basic terms, MRT envisions two modes of religion: the imagistic mode, characterized by infrequent, emotionally arousing rituals associated with episodic memory, and the doctrinal mode, characterized by frequent, emotionally non-arousing rituals associated with semantic memory.[16] In Whitehouse's explanation, episodic memory is linked with "specific events in our life experience," while semantic memory is associated with "general knowledge about the world," the acquirement of which we cannot easily recall (if at all).[17] The key concern of MRT is

---

[15] Pascal Boyer and Pierre Liénard, "Why Ritualized Behavior? Precaution Systems and Action Parsing in Developmental, Pathological, and Cultural Rituals," *Behavioral and Brain Sciences* 29 (2006): 3.

[16] Whitehouse, *Modes of Religiosity*, 63–118. See also, Czachesz, *Cognitive Science*, 108.

[17] Whitehouse, *Modes of Religiosity*, 65. See also, Uro, *Ritual and Christian Beginnings*, 35–36.

to then explain how these two modes of religion "facilitate the transmission of religious traditions" based on the effects they have on human cognition (particularly on memory).[18]

In case of the doctrinal mode of religiosity, "ritual action tends to be highly routinized, facilitating the storage of elaborate and conceptually complex religious teachings in semantic memory, but also activating implicit memory in the performance of most ritual procedures."[19] For this reason, the doctrinal mode is deemed an effective vehicle for transmitting (religious) traditions and "complex religious concepts."[20] As Jutta Jokiranta explains, the frequent repetition of rituals "reduces the possibility that people rely on personal theories of rituals and increases the possibility that people accept the religious authorities' explanations of rituals (what is told often enough becomes a fact)."[21] Highly routinized activities require minimal conscious effort as they become part of "automatic behavior," and so, according to MRT, the participants' need to question the relevance of the performed ritual or the traditions or teachings associated with it diminishes.[22] However, even though routinization is often comforting and assuring, it can also lead to "tedium effect"—that is, participants come to deem the rituals boring because everything is familiar and predictable—which in turn may foster ritual reform or lead to the abandonment of that which is thought of as tedious.[23]

---

[18] As aptly summarized in Uro, *Ritual and Christian Beginnings*, 68.

[19] Whitehouse, *Modes of Religiosity*, 65–66.

[20] Whitehouse, *Modes of Religiosity*, 8. In his explanations of the doctrinal mode, Whitehouse also speaks of the transmission of "complex theology and doctrine" (*Modes of Religiosity*, 63), "complex religious knowledge" (*Modes of Religiosity*, 82), "complex exegesis" (*Modes of Religiosity*, 97), "verbally codified religious knowledge" (*Modes of Religiosity*, 97), and "doctrinal knowledge" (*Modes of Religiosity*, 98). However, Whitehouse nowhere explains whether he uses the terms such as "concept," "knowledge," "teaching," "doctrine," "theology," and "exegesis" synonymously. This is where Whitehouse may be criticized for lack of precision, as it is not clear what should be counted under these various categories (i.e., "religious knowledge" seems a much broader term than "doctrine" or "teaching" even). Besides, it is not clear what should count under *complex* knowledge or teaching—is it possible to determine what religious concept is "complex" and what is not?

[21] Jutta Jokiranta, "Ritual System in the Qumran Movement: Frequency, Boredom, and Balance," in *Mind, Morality and Magic: Cognitive Science Approaches in Biblical Studies*, ed. István Czachesz and Risto Uro (New York: Routledge, 2014), 146.

[22] Jokiranta, "Ritual System," 152.

[23] Whitehouse, *Modes of Religiosity*, 98, 103. See also, Jokiranta, "Ritual System," 148, 152; Kimmo Ketola, "A Cognitive Approach to Ritual Systems in First-Century Judaism," in *Explaining Christian Origins and Early Judaism: Contributions from Cognitive and Social Science*, ed. Petri Luomanen, Ilkka Pyysiäinen, and Risto Uro (Boston: Brill, 2007), 105.

In contrast, rituals performed with low frequency tend to be emotionally highly arousing. Whitehouse lists as examples of such rituals "traumatic and violent initiation rituals, ecstatic practices of various cults, experiences of collective possession and altered states of consciousness, and extreme rituals involving homicide or cannibalism."[24] The rarity of participation in such rituals calls forth "spontaneous exegetical reflection (SER)—often experienced as personal inspiration or revelation."[25] Participants tend to reflect on and seek meaning for their experiences in a deeply personal way. MRT also predicts that such experiences tend "to produce emotional bonds between participants," which the doctrinal mode is not so apt at accomplishing.[26] The key difference between the two modes of religiosity, therefore, is that while the doctrinal mode is ideal for providing traditional meaning for religious experiences, in the imagistic mode, meaning is generated through personal reflection or spontaneous interpretation and is thus less controlled by official narratives.

4.1.3 *Capite velato* and Modes of Religiosity Theory

Luther H. Martin has analyzed the religious environment of first-century Rome from the perspective of MRT, and suggests that Roman religion during that time period conforms in broad strokes to the doctrinal mode of religiosity for the following reasons:

> Roman religion was concerned with 'the meaning of Roman life and history,' and the values of this 'Romanness' were transmitted and codified through countless iterations and reiterations of sacrificial practices that resulted in a set of officially sanctioned ritual scripts. By the time of the Empire, these scripts were maintained and transmitted by a hierarchy of religio-political authorities: domestically by the *paterfamilias*, by the *magister* of the *collegia*, and at the state level by the public priests or, upon occasion, by action of the Roman Senate itself. From 12 B.C.E., all of the 'fixed and formal' practices of Roman religion became subject to prescribed and precise regulations.[27]

Martin sets this doctrinal mode of religiosity as expressed in Roman religion in contrast with the contemporaneous Hellenistic mystery cults that gained in popularity in the Roman Empire, particularly in the first and second centuries CE. Martin suggests that the infrequent rituals of these cults which "were held in

---

[24] Whitehouse, *Modes of Religiosity*, 70.
[25] Whitehouse, *Modes of Religiosity*, 72, 113–14.
[26] Whitehouse, *Modes of Religiosity*, 73.
[27] Luther H. Martin, "The Promise of Cognitive Science for the Study of Early Christianity," in *Explaining Christian Origins and Early Judaism: Contributions from Cognitive and Social Science*, ed. Petri Luomanen, Ilkka Pyysiäinen, and Risto Uro (Boston: Brill, 2007), 45.

darkness and involved exposure to life-threatening ordeals ... and employed such dramatic effects as light shows, displays of bizarre imagery, the use of masks and costumes, and sounds of evocative rhythms produced by exotic instruments and chanting" are characteristics of an imagistic mode of religiosity.[28]

Martin may be criticized for painting a much too simplistic picture here, but if Roman state religion and Hellenistic mystery cults can indeed be broadly characterized in this way, then Martin's application of MRT predicts that *capite velato* was performed without much conscious reflection, while it served as an effective conduit of (religious) traditions or teachings, given that it accompanied the most frequently performed Roman religious activities (sacrifice, prayer, divination). According to MRT, the highly repetitive nature of *capite velato* should also have kept participants from questioning its relevance. It is indeed interesting to note that the "official" Roman narrative around *capite velato*—that it was a *religio* instituted to keep the Romans "pure" (as preserved in Virgil's epic the *Aeneid*, see section 2.2.1)—was not subjected to any meaningful reflection in other *Roman* sources; reflections on the meaning of *capite velato* are, however, found in the writings of Plutarch, who was not a Roman by birth (see section 2.3.4). Yet, as we saw in Chapter 2, Plutarch struggled to come up with a singular reason for why the Romans covered their heads during worshipful acts, and Plutarch also did not engage with any Roman authors on this question, but chose as his conversation partner a Greek author from a century prior. This may suggest that a lively discussion on this question among the Romans themselves was absent, which would align with the predictions that MRT makes about the doctrinal mode of religiosity—that participants do not question the relevance of a frequently performed ritual nor the relevance of the "religious knowledge" passed along with it.

However, while meaningful reflections on *capite velato* may have been sparse, the ritual gesture itself was nevertheless visible everywhere—in homes, on street corners, on state-sponsored art, in palaces, and in temples—as evidenced by archaeological finds and by ancient literary sources. Thus, it is not the reflective analysis of this ritual gesture, but the reflexive performance of it that communicated something about Rome, its history, its values, and its people without the need for too many explanatory words. For example, as explored in Chapter 2, *capite velato* was especially associated with *pietas*, a core Roman virtue (see section 2.5.2). However, *pietas* was not something that could be easily explained in words, but was much more easily demonstrated in state-approved ritual acts such as *capite velato*.[29]

---

[28] Martin, "The Promise of Cognitive Science," 45–46.

[29] E.g., Ehrensperger, *Paul at the Crossroads of Cultures*, 178.

MRT predicts that highly repetitive rituals are good conduits of even complex religious teachings (also across generations), and so from this perspective, *capite velato* must have been particularly useful in the transference and establishment of religious concepts (including *pietas*) in participants.

MRT has been criticized for categorizing religion as either-or phenomena—either religiosity is imagistic or doctrinal—whereas most religions seem to be a mixture of the two modes and therefore do not easily conform to such categorization.[30] For example, how should we understand early Christianity from the perspective of MRT? The Corinthian correspondence in particular suggests that (some) early Christians may have engaged in emotionally highly arousing rituals (e.g., altered states of consciousness).[31] But some early Christian rituals must have become routinized fairly quickly. Thus, while for some adherents of Roman state religion, Christian rituals may have provided an exciting adventure away from the boredom of the familiar and repetitive rituals, for other Christian neophytes, these same rituals may have become a routine. Thus, where do we draw the line between the doctrinal mode of religiosity and the imagistic mode? On the level of individual experience? This is not entirely clear. Despite these issues, however, MRT can serve as a useful heuristic tool in discussions about rituals. As Risto Uro points out, MRT helps direct scholarly attention "to the capacity of ritual to function as an instrument of religious teaching and doctrinal consolidation."[32] And in the case of *capite velato*, MRT predictions seem to fit the available evidence: the frequent performance of *capite velato* seems to have diminished the participants' interest to question or ponder its relevance, while it simultaneously appears to have served as an important vehicle in transmitting and establishing state-approved traditions and religious concepts, such as *pietas*, across social strata and generations.

---

[30] E.g., Petri Luomanen, "How Religions Remember: Memory Theories in Biblical Studies and in the Cognitive Study of Religion," in *Mind, Morality and Magic: Cognitive Science Approaches in Biblical Studies*, ed. István Czachesz and Risto Uro (New York: Routledge, 2014), 36. This is a problem with MRT that Whitehouse himself acknowledges. See, for example, Robert N. McCauley and E. Thomas Lawson, *Bringing Ritual to Mind: Psychological Foundations of Cultural Forms* (New York: Cambridge University Press, 2003), 109.

[31] Colleen Shantz, for example, has argued that "glossolalia is manifestly an altered state of consciousness." Shantz, *Paul in Ecstasy*, 158. Shantz has furthermore found in Paul's letters references to other ecstatic states and activities (e.g., ecstatic prayer) that Paul and the early Christians seem to have practiced. Shantz, *Paul in Ecstasy*, 68, 126, 131, 195.

[32] Risto Uro, "The Interface of Ritual and Writing in the Transmission of Early Christian Traditions," in *Mind, Morality and Magic: Cognitive Science Approaches in Biblical Studies*, ed. István Czachesz and Risto Uro (New York: Routledge, 2014), 73.

4.1.4 Ritual Form Theory: Overview

In MRT, as we have seen, frequency is the key variable that determines the level of emotional arousal in rituals and whether episodic or semantic memory is engaged. CSR scholars Robert McCauley and Thomas Lawson, however, have provided an alternative hypothesis as to why some rituals tend to be emotionally more arousing than others. According to McCauley and Lawson's Ritual Form Theory (RFT), "it is participants' mostly tacit knowledge of ritual forms that is the critical cognitive variable that largely determines not only rituals' performance frequencies but also such things as how much emotional firepower a religious ritual possesses."[33] In very basic terms, RFT argues that rituals should be viewed as activities in which a subject performs an action on a patient (i.e., an object) with the aid of an instrument. Based on this premise, RFT envisions three forms of ritual, depending on where in the above "action representation system" the culturally postulated superhuman (CPS) agent (e.g., a god) is located: if the CPS agent is associated with the subject of an action, we come to speak of "special-agent ritual" (SAR); if with the instrument of an action, then of "special-instrument ritual" (SIR); and in the case of patient, of "special-patient ritual" (SPR). The key prediction of RFT is that SARs are more exciting, less frequent, involve more "sensory pageantry" (sounds, tastes, smells, kinesthetic sensations, and so on), and are more memorable, while SIRs and SPRs are more frequent, less imposing, have fewer permanent effects, and involve less sensory pageantry.[34]

4.1.5 *Capite velato* and Ritual Form Theory

Under SARs, McCauley and Lawson list such rituals as circumcision, wedding, funeral, and baptism; most divinatory rituals are listed under SIRs; and sacrifice, penance, and Holy Communion are given as examples of SPRs.[35] Thus, we see that *capite velato* would belong with rituals that RFT places in the category of SIRs and SPRs, meaning that RFT would predict *capite velato* not to have been particularly memorable nor imposing on participants. However, McCauley and Lawson would not consider *capite velato* itself a ritual in the technical sense of the term.

---

[33] McCauley and Lawson, *Bringing Ritual to Mind*, 100.

[34] McCauley and Lawson, *Bringing Ritual to Mind*, 44, 123. For helpful summaries of RFT see also, for example, Justin L. Barrett, *Cognitive Science, Religion, and Theology: From Human Minds to Divine Minds* (West Conshohocken, PA: Templeton Press, 2011), 120–22; Jokiranta, "Ritual System," 149; Ketola, "Cognitive Approach," 99, 102; Czachesz, *Cognitive Science*, 16, 114–16;

[35] McCauley and Lawson, *Bringing Ritual to Mind*, 26, 28.

They argue that activities such as praying or chanting or standing at specific times during religious services do not meet the criteria of the action representation system (i.e., a subject performs an action on a patient with an aid of an instrument) and these therefore classify as "religious acts" but not as religious *rituals*.[36] This limiting definition of "ritual" in RFT has often been criticized in subsequent scholarship, since most (biblical) scholars would deem praying, for example, a ritual for a number of reasons.[37] And as was discussed in section 4.1.1, *capite velato* should also be categorized with rituals based on certain elements that distinguish it from other similar activities, yet the narrow frame of RFT precludes such a categorization. Nevertheless, despite the reluctance of RFT to categorize *capite velato* under the umbrella of "ritual," it is important to note here that the predictions of RFT seem to be in agreement with the predictions of MRT as far as *capite velato* is concerned, in that this "religious act" is predicted not to have been emotionally arousing nor memorable for the performers due to the form of the rituals (SIRs and SPRs) that it accompanied.

4.1.6 Rituals and the Hazard-Precaution System

Pascal Boyer and Pierre Liénard have argued that engagement in ritualized behavior is by-product of the normal operations of the brain's so-called hazard-precaution system, which processes potential dangers to one's fitness. In Boyer and Liénard's description, the "hazard-precaution system seems to be specifically focused on such recurrent threats as predation, intrusion by strangers, contamination, contagion, social offence, and harm to offspring."[38] Humans tend to get intrusive thoughts about potential threats to their (and their offspring's) fitness in their environment, and as a result generate "action-plans" or take precautionary measures to avoid these dangers.[39] At the extreme, such anxieties can lead to obsessive-compulsive disorder (OCD).[40] According to Boyer and Liénard, the performance of scripted ritualized activities helps relieve such anxieties because now the working memory is "swamped"—individuals have to think about what they are doing and

---

[36] McCauley and Lawson, *Bringing Ritual to Mind*, 13–14.
[37] E.g., Tamás Biró, "Is Judaism Boring? On the Lack of Counterintuitive Agents in Jewish Rituals," in *Mind, Morality and Magic: Cognitive Science Approaches in Biblical Studies*, ed. István Czachesz and Risto Uro (New York: Routledge, 2014), 120–43 (esp. 141); Czachesz, *Cognitive Science*, 118; Uro, *Ritual and Christian Beginnings*, 63. See also, Whitehouse, *Modes of Religiosity*, 142–54.
[38] Boyer and Liénard, "Whence Collective Rituals?" 820.
[39] Boyer and Liénard, "Why Ritualized Behavior?" 12.
[40] Boyer and Liénard, "Why Ritualized Behavior?" 2.

thus a particular anxiety is no longer at the forefront of their thoughts.[41] Boyer and Liénard propose, then, that since collective and individual rituals seem to be centered around the above mentioned threats—such as avoidance of contamination, contagion, and social offence, and protection from strangers, predators, and harm to offspring—rituals in general must have developed in the first place to relieve anxieties associated with potential dangers.[42] And over time, the *non-performance* of particularly collective rituals becomes a cause for anxiety in itself as "most people develop the intuition that it would be really wrong and certainly dangerous not to perform a ritual without specific thoughts about what the risk is."[43]

4.1.7 *Capite velato* and the Hazard-Precaution System

As we shall see in the next section, a number of CSR scholars disagree with the position taken by Boyer and Liénard that ritualized behavior should be viewed as a *by-product* of normal cognitive operations in the evolution of humankind, favoring instead the idea that rituals were *adapted* by humans for specific purposes. Despite opposition to this claim of Boyer and Liénard, however, it is nevertheless worth analyzing the data we possess on *capite velato* in relation to the brain's hazard-precaution system that Boyer and Liénard argue to be responsible for

---

[41] Boyer and Liénard, "Whence Collective Rituals?" 823; Boyer and Liénard, "Why Ritualized Behavior?" 12. In this regard, Boyer and Liénard specifically argue that ritualization should be viewed quite differently to routinization. That is, even though a particular ritualized behavior may be performed routinely, it does not mean that it therefore becomes part of automatic behavior (contra Whitehouse, see above). They point out that rituals tend to involve demands, rules, or specifications that still require conscious engagement, no matter how many times they have been performed. For example, walking from point A to point B is automatic behavior, but "walking" in rituals tends to involve specifications, such as the precise number or style of steps to be taken, which requires conscious engagement every time, even though there is certainly a difference whether one performs a ritual for the first time or for the hundredth time ("Whence Collective Rituals?" 824).

[42] Boyer and Liénard, "Whence Collective Rituals?" 819–20; Boyer and Liénard, "Why Ritualized Behavior?" 14. While Boyer and Liénard emphasize rituals as by-products of the brain's hazard-precaution system, other cognitive scientists have suggested that ritualized behavior might instead represent an adapted response to the "hyperactive anxiety subsystem." Martin Lang and Radim Chvaja, "Hazard Precaution: Examining the Possible Adaptive Value of Ritualized Behavior," in *The Routledge Handbook of Evolutionary Approaches to Religion*, ed. Yair Lior and Justin Lane (New York: Routledge, 2023), 164–84, here 173. This is an example of the perennial adaptionist-byproduct debate within evolutionary sciences that will receive some more attention below but which cannot be solved here.

[43] Boyer and Liénard, "Whence Collective Rituals?" 822; Boyer and Liénard, "Why Ritualized Behavior?" 16. See also, Boyer, *Religion Explained*, 240.

ritualized behavior, as there are interesting connections here. For example, Dionysius of Halicarnassus links the origins of *capite velato* to avoidance of danger: Aeneas covers his head because he observes an enemy in the vicinity, whom he deems a potential threat to the desired outcome of what he is attempting to accomplish (see section 2.2.1). Virgil also connects the origins of *capite velato* to the avoidance of danger: Aeneas and his companions are instructed by Helenus to be covered of the head during sacrifices to avoid observing "hostile faces" (see section 2.2.1). And Virgil also connects the continued observance of *capite velato* to the purity of Romans (see section 2.2.1), while Plutarch ponders whether Romans of his day practiced *capite velato* in order to avoid harmful or ominous sounds during their ritual performances (see section 2.3.4). We see, then, that in the traditions surrounding *capite velato*, anxiety about contamination and about predators (whether human or divine) or strangers is most certainly evoked. It is likely, therefore, that anxiety about the *non-performance* of *capite velato* was especially heightened among Romans, as traditions surrounding this ritual gesture fed into unconscious fears that something terrible might happen if *capite velato* was not properly performed. This would provide a possible reason for why (some of) those Romans who attached themselves to the emerging association of Christ-followers in Corinth may have wished to continue to pray and seek divine (fore)knowledge with a covered head—relief from anxiety about potential dangers may only have been achieved by that which was collectively familiar and habitual.

4.1.8 Costly Signaling Theory: Overview

As mentioned above, a number of scholars disagree with Boyer and Liénard's view on the evolutionary nature of rituals. These scholars argue that religious rituals are not by-products of the evolvement of cognition but rather were *adapted* by humans for the purpose of enhancing group solidarity and co-operation.[44] This is, for example, the foundational argument of Costly Signaling Theory (CST). The main conundrum that CST attempts to solve is why humans engage in behaviors that are costly and even detrimental to individual fitness and thus counterproductive (e.g., painful, expensive, or time-consuming rites that do not serve any practical aims nor self-interests). CST hypothesizes that religion in general, and religious rituals in particular, function as hard-to-fake honest signals which communicate

---

[44] For a concise overview of the debate in which the adaptionist position is defended, see Richard Sosis, "The Adaptionist-Byproduct Debate on the Evolution of Religion: Five Misunderstandings of the Adaptionist Program," *Journal of Cognition and Culture* 9 (2009): 315–32.

to other group members that the individual can be trusted.[45] Religious rituals are hard to fake precisely because they are costly to the individual who performs them—whether in terms of physiology (e.g., painful), psychology, finances, time, or other resources. Thus, the performance of these otherwise unnecessary or impractical rituals displays that an individual is serious about his or her commitments to a particular group that adheres to these rites, and there appears to be a correlation between the costliness of a ritual performance and the honesty of a signal—the costlier the performance, the more honest the signal appears to others.[46] Costly rituals, therefore, allow groups to effectively deal with "free riders" or cheaters—the ones who only deplete the group's limited resources without contributing anything of their own—because the costliness of belonging to a group will deter those who are not willing to fully commit.[47] Thus, costly religious rituals help strengthen bonds between group members and enhance mutual trust, which allows for more effective cooperation, which in turn helps groups to survive and to thrive. For example, some studies have shown that there appears to be a correlation between the costliness of a group's rituals and the longevity of a group's existence—the groups with costly membership requirements are predicted to survive longer.[48]

---

[45] William Irons, "Religion as Hard-to-Fake Sign of Commitment," in *Evolution and the Capacity for Commitment*, ed. Randolph M. Nesse (New York: Russell Sage Foundation, 2001), 294–95; Joseph Bulbulia and Richard Sosis, "Signalling Theory and the Evolution of Religious Cooperation," *Religion* 41 (2011): 365–66. Religious rituals do not only serve as signals to *others*, but "private religious practices are [also] particularly effective at signaling to oneself, and convincing oneself, of one's religious beliefs and commitments." Richard Sosis, "Costly Signaling: The ABCs of Signaling Theory and Religion," in *The Routledge Handbook of Evolutionary Approaches to Religion*, ed. Yair Lior and Justin Lane (New York: Routledge, 2023), 212.

[46] Irons, "Religion as Hard-to-Fake Sign," 298; Bulbulia and Sosis, "Signalling Theory," 366; Francis T. McAndrew, "Costly Signaling Theory," in *Encyclopedia of Evolutionary Psychological Science*, ed. Todd K. Shackelford and Viviana A. Weekes-Shackelford (Cham, Switzerland: Springer, 2021), 1526, 1530. Signals that are impossible or nearly impossible to fake are known as "indexical signals." Sosis, "Costly Signaling," 214.

[47] Richard Sosis, "Religious Behaviors, Badges, and Bans: Signaling Theory and the Evolution of Religion," in *Evolution, Genes, and the Religious Brain*, vol. 1 of *Where God and Science Meet: How Brain and Evolutionary Studies Alter Our Understanding of Religion*, ed. Patrick McNamara (Westport, CT: Praeger, 2006), 67; Joseph Bulbulia, "Charismatic Signalling," *JSRNC* 3 (2009): 526.

[48] Irons, "Religion as Hard-to-Fake Sign," 299; Richard Sosis, "The Adaptive Value of Religious Ritual," *American Scientist* 92 (2004): 170; John Teehan, *In the Name of God: The Evolutionary Origins of Religious Ethics and Violence* (Chichester, UK: Wiley-Blackwell, 2010), 69;

However, costly signaling is primarily effective in definable groups in which close observation of other members—or more importantly, of those vying for membership—is possible. In societies at large, close observation of everyone else is impossible, but people still need to cooperate with one another, and this requires mutual trust between even those who do not know each other personally. Joseph Bulbulia explains that what makes such broader cooperation and trust possible is "charismatic signaling." "Charismatic signals" are symbols and traditions widely shared in a society at large (e.g., a flag, a holiday, etc.).[49] Here we come to speak of "culture," which is essentially a cumulation of learned behaviors and symbols that have been transmitted from one generation to the next within a particular geographical area, language group, or kin.[50] These learned behaviors may be complex but typically embraced willingly because it is tacitly believed that "genetic fitness accrues to those best able to master socially acquired repertoires."[51] While these cultural behaviors or charismatic signals are not typically "costly,"[52] they do facilitate cooperation between strangers for a particular transaction, or more basically, they allow unacquainted individuals to go about their business without a constant worry about threats to safety and life.

4.1.9 *Capite velato* and Costly Signaling Theory

Capite velato itself does not qualify as a costly signal—even though it accompanies rituals that may be deemed "costly," such as sacrifice—because all that is required for the performance of *capite velato* is an outer garment, and the gesture of placing the outer garment on the head is not physiologically nor psychologically taxing,

---

Bulbulia and Sosis, "Signalling Theory," 368, 376; Czachesz, *Cognitive Science*, 101; McAndrew, "Costly Signaling Theory," 1530; Sosis, "Costly Signaling," 219–20.

[49] Bulbulia, "Charismatic Signalling," 532–33, 538–89.

[50] On such a definition of "culture" see, for example, Harland, *Dynamics of Identity*, 12; Hugh Turpin and Jonathan A. Lanman, "Credibility Enhancing Displays (CREDs): When They Work and When They Don't," in *The Routledge Handbook of Evolutionary Approaches to Religion*, ed. Yair Lior and Justin Lane (New York: Routledge, 2023), 229.

[51] Turpin and Lanman, "Credibility Enhancing Displays," 229.

[52] "Costliness" of behavior is in some sense subjective. For example, if one truly believes that killing a lamb and burning it over a built structure affects how gods operate and that it brings about the desired outcome, then this act does not appear "costly" to the sacrificer himself or herself. However, for the one who does not share this premise about sacrifice, this behavior appears extremely "costly." Turpin and Lanman, "Credibility Enhancing Displays," 230–31. Thus, costliness is contextual—what is costly for a member of one group may not be (as) costly to a member of another group. But in general, learned behaviors within a particular culture that are widely shared (i.e., charismatic signals) do not appear prohibitively costly in the context of that culture.

nor is it time-consuming. Thus, CST would predict *capite velato* on its own not to be very effective in dealing with the "free-rider problem," because it is not hard to fake and thus it would not be effective in enhancing trust and cooperation within the confines of a social group. However, *capite velato* can be deemed a "charismatic signal" due to its high visibility on statues, altars, paintings, and through performances in important public places, on street corners, and in homes of Rome and other Romanized cities of the empire. Thus, even though *capite velato* may not have served as a useful trust-enhancing ritual gesture for any particular social group within the empire, because it was in principle easy to fake, it nonetheless appears to have served the function of allowing citizens that were otherwise strangers to one another to cooperate. In other words, *capite velato* was an integral part of Roman culture.

Conversely, however, the *non-performance* of *capite velato* would indeed have been costly for a Roman. Richard Sosis explains, for example, how bans work as costly signals just like rituals.[53] If a particular social group bans something that is commonplace in society, then adherence to such a ban stands out and draws attention. A person who refuses to behave in an expected manner may become an object of scorn and social ostracism. Thus, following a ban may come at a great personal cost. Yet, while society at large may ostracize a follower of a ban, the bonds between members of a particular social group which adheres to such a ban conversely strengthen, because members can observe that each is willing to commit to the group at a great personal cost.[54] We can count Paul's statement that praying with a head-covering is shameful for men as a ban of an expected behavior in Roman society. If so, we must say more about the possible implications of this for interpreting 1 Cor 11:2–16.

4.2 CSR Theories and 1 Cor 11:2–16

As we have seen, CSR is not a unified theory about rituals. There are disagreements among CSR scholars about whether rituals are a by-product of normal cognitive functions or whether they were adapted for particular purposes; what makes rituals emotionally more or less arousing; the level of automaticity in rituals; and even what counts as ritual. Yet, these different CSR hypotheses about rituals have

---

[53] Sosis, "Religious Behaviors, Badges, and Bans," 70.
[54] "When a member of an in-group is threatened, commitment to shared in-group beliefs and values escalates, a finding demonstrated across both social and evolutionary psychology as well as anthropology." Turpin and Lanman, "Credibility Enhancing Displays," 233.

allowed us to discuss *capite velato* in relation to cognition from a variety of angles, and to make some observations about the potential effects of *capite velato* on participants and on observers. For example, the lack of thoughtful reflections on the meaning of *capite velato* among Romans may be attributed to the frequency of its performance (see sections 4.1.1 and 4.1.2) and to the forms of rituals that it accompanies (see sections 4.1.4 and 4.1.5); the mention of *capite velato* in the context of threats to one's fitness may be explained by the close association that rituals have with the brain's hazard-precaution system (see section 4.1.6); and the prevalence and durability of *capite velato* may be explained by its usefulness as a charismatic signal in Roman society (see section 4.1.8). In this section, we will discuss the possible implications of these and other such observations on the study of 1 Cor 11:2–16, in which Paul suggests that praying and accessing of divine (fore)knowledge with a covered head is shameful for men.

4.2.1 The Make-Up of First-Century Corinth

In order to better understand how Paul's instructions in 1 Cor 11:2–16 may have been received in Corinth, it is essential to consider the composition of the society and the Christ-following social group to whom Paul's instructions were addressed. What we know about Corinth, for example, is that it had been left in ruins after its destruction in 146 BCE for more than a century until the Romans began to rebuild it in 44 BCE. Thus, the architecture and infrastructure of this city that was once an important Greek hub now began to exhibit Roman influence.[55] Furthermore, during the rebuilding process, the Romans repopulated the city with freedmen from Rome who brought with them the culture of Rome.[56] At the same time, the city had not been left completely devoid of Greek culture, and the influence of Hellenism seems to have grown as the first century CE wore on.[57] This no doubt

---

[55] See, for example, Wayne A. Meeks, *The First Urban Christians: The Social World of the Apostle Paul* (New Haven: Yale University Press, 1983), 47; C. K. Williams II, "The Refounding of Corinth: Some Roman Religious Attitudes," in *Roman Architecture in the Greek World*, ed. Sarah Macready and F. H. Thompson (London: The Society of Antiquaries of London, 1987), 31–32; Winter, *After Paul Left Corinth*, 8–11, 19; Shantz, *Paul in Ecstasy*, 157; Ehrensperger, *Paul at the Crossroads of Cultures*, 180–81.

[56] Meeks, *The First Urban Christians*, 48.

[57] See, for example, Nancy Bookidis, "Religion in Corinth: 146 B.C.E. to 100 C.E.," in *Urban Religion in Roman Corinth*, ed. Daniel N. Schowalter and Steven J. Friesen (Cambridge, MA: Harvard University Press, 2005), 141–64; Anthony J. Blasi, *Social Science and the Christian Scriptures: Sociological Introductions and New Translation*, vol. 1 (Eugene, OR: Wipf & Stock, 2017), 48–49.

created some interesting social dynamics in first-century Corinth, as the boundaries between who or what was Greek and who or what was Roman may not have been as straightforward as in some other places.[58]

However, it has also been pointed out that "it is particularly at boundaries between groups that symbols become charged with importance," and that people "are most aware of their culture when they interact with those of a different culture."[59] For example, the wearing of the toga—a symbol of Roman citizenship—was of much more significance in Roman provinces, where most people were not permitted to wear it, than in Rome.[60] Additionally, the "lure of Roman-ness" appears to have been especially strong in colonized territories. Colleen Shantz presents the ancient city of Aphrodisias as an example of this: the building projects and decorations evidence that the Greek-speaking people there sought the favorable attention of the empire and began to celebrate their oppressors "at a cost of their own ethnic identities."[61] And it is also argued that emperor worship was stronger in the East than in the West for various reasons.[62] Albrecht Dihle claims, for example, that "the Greek East celebrated Augustus as world redeemer and world ruler" with much enthusiasm in acts of worship, in construction of temples, and in celebrations in his honor.[63]

---

[58] See, Ray Pickett, "Conflicts at Corinth," in *Christian Origins*, ed. Richard A. Horsley (Minneapolis: Fortress Press, 2010), 120. Specific examples of hybridity in relation to identity in Corinth can be found in Cavan W. Concannon, *'When You Were Gentiles': Specters of Ethnicity in Roman Corinth and Paul's Corinthian Correspondence* (New Haven: Yale University Press, 2014), 47–74.

[59] Claudia Setzer, *Resurrection of the Body in Early Judaism and Early Christianity: Doctrine, Community, and Self-Definition* (Leiden: Brill, 2004), 4, 47. In biblical scholarship, the term "Greco-Roman" is often used in reference to the dominant cultural trends at the time of Paul, but Kathy Ehrensperger reminds us that "Greeks and Romans would not confuse their respective cultural peculiarities, whether they mutually appreciated these and acknowledged their values, or whether they more antagonistically mocked or denigrated each other." Ehrensperger, *Paul at the Crossroads of Culture*, 77. Given that my subject matter here is *capite velato*, a ritual gesture peculiar to the Romans, I am careful to distinguish between Greeks and Romans, although I understand that "Greco-Roman" is an appropriate term in many contexts of NT scholarship.

[60] E.g., Olson, *Masculinity and Dress*, 52.

[61] Colleen Shantz, "Emotion, Cognition, and Social Change: A Consideration of Galatians 3:28," in *Mind, Morality and Magic: Cognitive Science Approaches in Biblical Studies*, ed. István Czachesz and Risto Uro (New York: Routledge, 2014), 258–59.

[62] Raja, "Ancient Sanctuaries," 145–46.

[63] Dihle, *Greek and Latin Literature*, 2.

Taking all of the above into consideration, it is reasonable to suggest that in the cultural hodgepodge of first-century Corinth, there were bound to be those who, for one reason or another, wished to emphasize their Roman-ness—citizenship, ancestry, allegiance—and *capite velato* was an easily observable symbol for this purpose. Praying or sacrificing in a public place with a garment over the head, for example, left observers in no doubt about the cultural belonging of the performer. Consequently, if any of such persons who wished to appear "good Romans" in their environment became attached to the association of Christians in Corinth, they may not have thought it necessary nor reasonable to disassociate themselves from the (cultic) practices that displayed their Roman-ness.[64] Being an exemplary Roman and being an exemplary Christ-follower seem not to have been thought of as mutually exclusive concepts at first.[65] As time went on, "Christian-ness" indeed became more defined and guarded and its peculiarities [66] more

---

[64] In the words of Gerd Theissen: "The first Christians wanted to live up to many norms of their pagan environment in an exemplary way." Theissen, *The Religion of the Earliest Churches*, 63. See also, Czachesz, *Cognitive Science*, 102–3. Paul's Corinthian correspondence suggests that this was especially true of the Corinthian Christians at the time of Paul. See, Richard A. Wright, "Crisis Management and Boundary Maintenance: Gentile Christ-Followers, Multiple Identities, and Sacrificial Practices in Corinth," in *The Social Worlds of Ancient Jews and Christians: Essays in Honor of L. Michael White*, ed. Jaimie Gunderson, Tony Keddie, and Douglas Boin, NovTSup 189 (Boston: Brill, 2023), 50–54.

[65] According to Rikard Roitto, "many gentiles who joined the Christ-believing *ekklesia* perceived it as one out of many *collegia* with a patron deity. The typical *collegium* did not demand exclusive worship of the patron god of the *collegium*, as opposed to the Jewish faith where monotheism was a given.... Apparently, some first century Christ-believers did not perceive any need to distance themselves from their previous cultic engagements." Rikard Roitto, "Using Behavioral Sciences to Understand Early Christian Experiences of Conversion," in *Religious and Philosophical Conversion in the Ancient Mediterranean Traditions*, ed. Athanasios Despotis and Hermut Löhr (Leiden: Brill, 2022), 47. T. J. Lang suggests that 1 Cor 10:27–29 may evidence that some of such persons for whom "Christ was simply ... another deity to be incorporated into something like the household lares or penates" had attached themselves to the Corinthian Christian congregation. Lang, "Trouble with Insiders," 991.

[66] James Dunn explains the oddity of early Christianity as follows: "Paul evidently saw the new Christian assemblies as an extension of the assembly of Yahweh, but now without any of the cultic features so characteristic of Israel's temple cult, and without any category of priest as a function different in kind from the priestly ministry of all who served the gospel. This must have marked out the house churches of Paul as very unusual, not to say odd, within the cities of the Roman Empire. They shared a common meal (the Lord's Supper) and met regularly for worship. But they looked to no cult centre or temple; they had no priests, no sacrifices. In legal status they

pronounced, so that by the early second century, some Christians came to speak of themselves as belonging to a different race or *ethnos* altogether,[67] but this is far removed from the mindset of the earliest followers of Christ or Paul.[68] It is reasonable to suppose, therefore, that the earliest Christians in Corinth still identified themselves to a large degree by their cultural belonging (Roman, Greek, Jew), and did not consider their involvement with the Christ association to nullify their duty to one's *ethnos* or culture.

4.2.2 The Make-Up of the Corinthian Christian Congregation

It appears that a fairly sizable section of the Corinthian congregation at the time of Paul's correspondence was made up of Romans or those with Roman affiliations. For example, two of the three members of the delegation that reached Paul from Corinth bear Latin names—Fortunatus and Achaicus (1 Cor 16:17)— which to Anthony Thiselton suggests that "they may well have been freedmen, or of

---

were probably regarded as equivalent to the clubs or *collegia* of the time, or regarded as extensions of the Jewish synagogue. But unlike such gatherings, they did not meet in a temple dedicated to their God or acknowledge their dependence on their cult centre by sending an annual offering. Their meetings neither singled out any priest nor called on such to perform a priestly act like the ritual libation. For most of their contemporaries a religious association without cult centre, without priests, without sacrifices, must have seemed a plain contradiction in terms, even an absurdity." Dunn, *Theology of Paul the Apostle*, 547–48. However, at first such "absurdity" must not have been as pronounced because, as discussed above, the first Christians attempted to also be exemplary citizens and thus continued to engage in the cultic and cultural practices of society at large. Additionally, there were other *collegia* in the Roman Empire with odd beliefs, requirements, or practices. As long as these peculiarities did not cause disruption to the day-to-day affairs of society, they were left be.

[67] See, for example, Karen L. King, *What is Gnosticism?* (Cambridge, MA: Harvard University Press, 2003), 39; Harland, *Dynamics of Identity*, 17–18.

[68] Some scholars suggest that rudiments of second-century ideas about "Christian race" may already be found in Paul's discussions about ethnic identity, particularly as presented in his letter to the Romans. E.g., Dennis C. Duling, "Ethnicity and Paul's Letter to the Romans," in *Understanding the Social World of the New Testament*, ed. Dietmar Neufeld and Richard E. DeMaris (New York: Routledge: 2010), esp. 87–88. Others disagree. Jörg Frey asserts, for example, that the second-century idea of Christianity as a new *genos* "is a different story and is not Paul's concern." Jörg Frey, "The Relativization of Ethnicity and Circumcision in Paul and His Communities," in *Paul within Judaism: Perspectives on Paul and Jewish Identity*, ed. Michael Bird, et al., WUNT 507 (Tübingen: Mohr Siebeck, 2023), 62.

freedmen's stock from the Roman colonists."⁶⁹ Furthermore, the only two persons beside the household of Stephanas whom Paul baptized in Corinth according to his own testimony, likewise bear Latin names: Crispus and Gaius (1 Cor 1:14).⁷⁰ Crispus is mentioned in Acts 18:8 as a synagogue leader (ἀρχισυνάγωγος) in Corinth who "believed" in response to Paul's preaching and was then baptized with his household. It is not clear, however, whether the Crispus of Acts and the Crispus of 1 Cor should be considered one and the same person—Paul in 1 Cor does not mention Crispus's background, and as John Kloppenborg points out, the name itself does not indicate that the person was a Jew.⁷¹ Thus, it may be, for example, that Acts fabricates a lofty background to a famous name associated with the Corinthian Christian congregation for the purposes of its narrative about Paul. However, if the Crispus of 1 Cor had indeed been the ἀρχισυνάγωγος as Acts suggests, then the congregation of Corinth included in it a prominent and wealthy member who had been a leader in the Jewish community of the city but who bore a latinized name.⁷²

The name Gaius also finds further mention but in Paul's letter to the Romans, where Paul describes Gaius as "the ξένος of me and of the whole assembly" (Rom 16:23). It is believed that Paul most likely penned his letter to the Romans from Corinth⁷³ and so the Gaius of 1 Cor and the Gaius of Rom appear to be one and

---

⁶⁹ Thiselton, *The First Epistle to the Corinthians*, 139–40. See also, Meeks, *The First Urban Christians*, 56–57; Picket, "Conflicts at Corinth," 124; Garland, *1 Corinthians*, 770–71. Gordon Fee adds that the name Fortunatus "appears to have been common especially among slaves and freedmen" (Fee, *First Corinthians: Revised*, 919), and so John Kloppenborg is fairly confident that "Fortunatus was almost certainly a slave or a freedman." See, John S. Kloppenborg, *Christ's Associations: Connecting and Belonging in the Ancient City* (New Haven: Yale University Press, 2019), 84.

⁷⁰ Thiselton, *The First Epistle to the Corinthians*, 140–41.

⁷¹ Kloppenborg, *Christ's Associations*, 84–85.

⁷² A number of biblical scholars believe Acts to contain an accurate description of Crispus's social standing. See discussion in L. L. Welborn, "Inequality in Roman Corinth: Evidence from Diverse Sources Evaluated by a Neo-Ricardian Model," in *The First Urban Churches 2: Roman Corinth*, ed. James R. Harrison and L. L. Welborn, WGRWSup 8 (Atlanta: SBL Press, 2016), 69–70.

⁷³ E.g., Moo, *Romans*, 3. According to Rom 16:22, the letter was written down by a certain Tertius, who also sends his personal greetings to the Roman congregation: ἀσπάζομαι ὑμᾶς ἐγὼ Τέρτιος ὁ γράψας τὴν ἐπιστολὴν ἐν κυρίῳ. L. L. Welborn argues that Tertius may have been a slave in the wealthy household of Gaius, given that Tertius was a common Latin name for slaves. Welborn, "Inequality in Roman Corinth," 67–68. If so, Tertius would be an additional figure with

the same person.⁷⁴ However, there is some debate about the role of Gaius in the Corinthian Christian congregation. Some scholars take ξένος in Rom 16:23 to mean "host," suggesting therefore that Gaius was a prominent and wealthy member of the Corinthian Christian congregation, who gave Paul a place to stay and in whose lodgings the Christian assembly regularly gathered.⁷⁵ However, others have argued that ξένος should be here understood in a sense of "guest," proposing instead that Gaius was a member of the *Roman* Christian congregation who stayed with Paul and the Corinthian congregation on his visit to Corinth.⁷⁶ In either case, what matters here is that Gaius appears to have been a well-known Christ-follower not only in Corinth but also in Rome, which, along with his name, suggests close affiliation with the capital of the empire.⁷⁷

In Rom 16:23, Paul also extends greetings to the Roman Christians from a certain Erastus,⁷⁸ whom he describes as ὁ οἰκονόμος τῆς πόλεως, often translated as "the city treasurer" (e.g., NRSV, NASB), although the precise meaning and function of οἰκονόμος in this context remains unclear.⁷⁹ Despite the ambivalence of the term

---

close ties to both the Corinthian and Roman congregations. However, Alan Cadwallader has argued that the name Tertius does not yet point to affiliations with Rome, and that Tertius was more likely a slave of Greek heritage in a local Corinthian household. Alan H. Cadwallader, "Tertius in the Margins: A Critical Appraisal of the Secretary Hypothesis," *NTS* 64 (2018): 381–87.

⁷⁴ E.g., Welborn, "Inequality in Roman Corinth," 70.

⁷⁵ E.g., Meeks, *The First Urban Christians*, 57; Moo, *Romans*, 935; Welborn, "Inequality in Roman Corinth," 71.

⁷⁶ John Kloppenborg points out, for example, that Gaius was one of the most common names at the time. Thus, unless this Gaius was intimately familiar to the Roman congregation, Paul would not have mentioned him to the Romans without any further identity markers. Kloppenborg, therefore, believes Gaius to have been a member of the Roman congregation visiting Corinth. John S. Kloppenborg, "Gaius the Roman Guest," *NTS* 63 (2017): 534–49; also, Kloppenborg, *Christ's Associations*, 85–86.

⁷⁷ However, some biblical scholars have proposed that while the section of Rom 16:1–23 may have been composed in Corinth, it was not intended for Roman Christians but to another congregation (perhaps that of Ephesus). E.g., Blasi, *Social Science*, 116–18. If this were the case, Gaius's affiliation with Rome would be questionable. However, most biblical scholars take Rom 16:1–23 as belonging with the rest of the letter to the Romans and I follow this assumption here.

⁷⁸ 2 Tim 4:20 also associates the name Erastus with the city of Corinth, although there is no additional information about this person here.

⁷⁹ Some have argued that the Erastus of Rom 16:23 should be identified with the Erastus mentioned in an inscription discovered in 1929 by the theater of Corinth, which reads: "Erastus for his aedileship laid (the pavement) at his own expense." See discussion in Colin G. Kruse, *Paul's Letter to the Romans* (Grand Rapids: Eerdmans, 2012), 462–64. According to John Kloppenborg,

οἰκονόμος here, however, it seems that it had something to do with the administration of the affairs of the city (of Corinth), no matter how local or limited. If so, Erastus would have been in some capacity responsible for the public devotion of the imperial cult, and as we have seen, *capite velato* was an important component of that. Thus, more than anyone else mentioned here, Erastus would have had a reason to participate in certain acts of worship in an appropriate manner for the imperial cult—*capite velato*.[80] While this conjecture can be no more than speculation, it is nevertheless noteworthy that so many of the named individuals in Paul's letters that are associated with Corinth bear latinized names or are in other ways associated with Rome. It suggests that the Christian congregation in Corinth had an influential Roman presence (especially if it consisted of only around ten people at the time of Paul, as some scholars have proposed[81]). If, therefore, any of such members with affiliations to Rome wished to emphasize their Roman-ness, we expect *capite velato* to have featured.

---

an aedile was "in high public office, since in the political structure of Corinth as a Roman colony, the two aediles elected yearly were responsible for the maintenance of public streets and buildings and were junior only to the two *duoviri* who administered the colony." Kloppenborg, *Christ's Associations*, 190. An aedile was therefore someone of considerable wealth and status. However, Kloppenborg firmly rejects the idea that the Erastus of the inscription should be equated with the Erastus of 1 Cor 16:23. On the other hand, L. L. Welborn has suggested that Erastus of 1 Cor 16:23 could very well have been an aedile, whether or not the inscription is about him. Welborn, "Inequality in Roman Corinth," 72–73. John Goodrich, on the other hand, has proposed that Erastus's title οἰκονόμος suggests that he was a municipal quaestor, a treasure magistrate. John K. Goodrich, "Erastus, *Quaestor* of Corinth: The Administrative Rank of ὁ οἰκονόμος τῆς πόλεως (Rom 16.23) in an Achaean Colony," *NTS* 56 (2010): 90–115. However, Goodrich's argument has been criticized for misrepresenting the available evidence. E.g., Alexander Weiss, "Keine Quästoren in Korinth: Zu Goodrichs (und Theißens) These über das Amt des Erastos (Röm 16.23)," *NTS* 56 (2010): 576–81. And Goodrich has responded to this criticism with an acknowledgment of having made mistakes in the interpretation of the evidence. John K. Goodrich, "Erastus of Corinth (Romans 16.23): Responding to Recent Proposals on His Rank, Status, and Faith," *NTS* 57 (2011): 583–93.

[80] Appointed officials in Roman Corinth were expected to show loyalty to the emperor, and the organization of and exemplary participation in the imperial cult were effective means to demonstrate this. See, for example, John K. Chow, "Patronage in Roman Corinth," in *Paul and Empire: Religion and Power in Roman Imperial Society*, ed. Richard A. Horsley (Harrisburg, PA: Trinity Press International, 1997), 110–13.

[81] E.g., Richard Last, "The Neighborhood (*vicus*) of the Corinthian *ekklēsia*: Beyond Family-Based Descriptions of the First Urban Christ-Believers," *JSNT* 38 (2016): 402.

4.2.3 The Venue of Prayer, the Venue of Prophecy

Most readers of 1 Cor work with an assumption that with 1 Cor 11:2, Paul begins a completely new section in his letter, shifting his focus specifically to problems associated with the public worship of the Corinthian Christian congregation. Gordon Fee claims, for example, that with 1 Cor 11:1, Paul concludes his discussion on "pagan worship" and, with 1 Cor 11:2, turns his attention to "items of abuse in [the Christian] assemblies."[82] Joseph Fitzmyer concurs, suggesting that with 1 Cor 11:2, Paul moves to another topic entirely, which has to do with the "conduct of Christians in their cultic assemblies."[83] Even Anthony Thiselton, who admonishes "virtually all [other] commentators" for ignoring "the fundamental continuity between the arguments and themes of 8:1–11:1 and the application of these very same themes ... in 11:2–14:40," nevertheless begins a completely new section of his commentary on 1 Cor at 1 Cor 11:2 with the title that includes the words "public worship."[84]

The assumption regarding 1 Cor 11:2–16 is, therefore, that the issue of head-coverings pertains exclusively to the context of Christian gatherings, and we have seen in Chapter 1 how such an assumption plays out in the interpretations of this passage. It is understandable why 1 Cor is read in this way: the words "praying" and "prophesying" in 1 Cor 11:2–16 appear in close proximity to Paul's subsequent discussion about the *deipnon* of the Lord (1 Cor 11:17–34), the use of *charismata* (1 Cor 12), and the conduct of the gathered assembly in relation to speaking in tongues and prophesying (1 Cor 14), which creates an impression that the context for "praying or prophesying" in 1 Cor 11:2–16 must also be the gathering of the

---

[82] Fee, *First Corinthians: Revised*, 542. See also, John Coolidge Hurd, *The Origin of 1 Corinthians* (London: SPCK, 1965), 182; Garland, *1 Corinthians*, 512; Gardner, *1 Corinthians*, 474–75; Dunn, *The Theology of Paul the Apostle*, 588; Kathy Ehrensperger, "The Question(s) of Gender: Relocating Paul in Relation to Judaism," in *Paul within Judaism: Restoring the First-Century Context to the Apostle*, ed. Mark D. Nanos and Magnus Zetterholm (Minneapolis: Fortress Press, 2015), 249; Jill E. Marshall, "Paul, Plutarch and Gender Dynamics of Prophecy," *NTS* 65 (2019): 217.

[83] Fitzmyer, *First Corinthians*, 405. Fitzmyer points to 1 Cor 11:16, in which Paul mentions ἐκκλησία, as proof that 1 Cor 11:2–16 is concerned with behavior solely in the context of Christian cultic assemblies. Fitzmyer, *First Corinthians*, 406. The same line of reasoning is also taken in David K. Lowery, "The Head Covering and the Lord's Supper in 1 Corinthians 11:2–34," *BSac* 143 (1986): 157. However, as we shall see, Paul's use of ἐκκλησία in 1 Cor 11:16 does not yet demonstrate that the Christian ἐκκλησία is the sole context of Paul's instructions regarding praying and prophesying (see Chapter 5).

[84] Thiselton, *Corinthians*, 799.

Christians in an assembly. However, on a closer examination, there does not seem to be as strong of a connection between 1 Cor 11:2–16 and what follows it as is made out to be.

For example, nowhere in 1 Cor 11:2–16 does Paul specify the context for "praying or prophesying," which is in contrast to the immediately following passage, where Paul repeatedly uses the phrase "when you come together" as a context of his instructions:

> But I do not praise you in commanding this [the following], that when you come together (συνέρχεσθε) it is not for the better but for the worse. For first of all, I hear that when you come together in an assembly (συνερχομένων ὑμῶν ἐν ἐκκλησίᾳ) there are divisions among you and I believe this in part.... When you then come together in the same place (συνερχομένων οὖν ὑμῶν ἐπὶ τὸ αὐτό), it is not to eat the Lord's *deipnon*.... If anyone is hungry, let them eat at home, so that you do not come together (συνέρχησθε) for judgment. (1 Cor 11:17–18, 20, 34)

Paul's repetition in this passage of "when you come together," which is set in antithesis to "at home" (ἐν οἴκῳ), suggests that it is only at 1 Cor 11:17 that Paul switches his focus solely on the gathering together of the Corinthian Christian congregants, which then appears to be the default setting until the end of 1 Cor 14 (συνέρχησθε is again repeated at 1 Cor 14:26, for example).

This way of reading 1 Cor squares well with Dennis Smith's important work on the nature of early Christian gatherings. Smith has convincingly argued that just like the gatherings of other "religious people and sectarian groups in the ancient world," so also the assemblies of early Christians followed the format of a Greco-Roman banquet.[85] The banquet began with "a full-course dinner"—or *deipnon*, which is the term that also Paul uses in 1 Cor 11:20–21 (κυριακὸν δεῖπνον vs. ἴδιον δεῖπνον)—and was followed by a symposium, which consisted of an "extended period of entertainment and conversation."[86] Smith argues that in 1 Cor 11:17–14:40, therefore, Paul first addresses the *deipnon* part of the Christian banquet and then the symposium part, and that he does so by following the Greco-Roman literary traditions regarding banquets.[87] For example, "encomia or conversations in praise of love were ... standard in the symposium tradition," and we see

---

[85] Smith, *From Symposium to Eucharist*, 174.
[86] Smith, *From Symposium to Eucharist*, 178, 201.
[87] Smith, *From Symposium to Eucharist*, 203.

that Paul also includes an ode to love (1 Cor 13) in his instructions to the Corinthians about their gatherings.[88]

If the Christian banquet is the context that governs Paul's instructions in 1 Cor 11:17–14:40, and does so in the order of the banquet (*deipnon* followed by symposium), then 1 Cor 11:2–16 falls outside of that purview. This is not to say that there are no overlapping themes or concerns, but only to point out that the context of Paul's instructions in 1 Cor 11:2–16 should not therefore be limited to *only* the Christian banquet (or to the gathering of Corinthian Christians in a formal assembly). There were other potential venues where Corinthian Christians could pray and access divine (fore)knowledge. Most obviously, there was the privacy of one's own home, which appears to be the context of prayer in 1 Cor 7:5, for example. But 1 Cor 11:2–16 is also preceded by Paul's mention of two other venues that the Corinthian Christians seem to have frequented, and which may have, therefore, served as locations for the Corinthians' praying and prophesying activities: a home of an "unbeliever" (1 Cor 10:27) and a "temple of an idol" (εἰδωλεῖον, 1 Cor 8:10). Even though Paul's language in both of these passages is hypothetical—"if any of the unbelievers invites you [to a meal] and you wish to go"; and, "if anyone sees you ... reclining in an idol's temple"—it nevertheless appears that the "believers" and "unbelievers" regularly mingled at these locations (in addition to the Christian assemblies, which, according to 1 Cor 14:22–25, seem to have been regularly frequented by the "unbelievers").

Any banquet in the home of an "unbeliever" or at a "temple of an idol" would have been accompanied by prayers, the pouring of libations, and occasionally also divination (particularly in the temples).[89] If the "unbeliever" happened to be a

---

[88] Smith, *From Symposium to Eucharist*, 211. Mikael Parsons and Michael Wade Martin have argued that Paul's *encomium* on love in 1 Cor 13 is typical of how the *encomia* were composed in the contemporaneous literature, in *Ancient Rhetoric and the New Testament: The Influence of Elementary Greek Composition* (Waco, TX: Baylor University Press, 2018), 216–18.

[89] Recall T. J. Lang's argument, discussed in the previous chapter, that "unbelievers" in the Corinthian correspondence should not be understood as "outsiders," but as those with intimate ties to the Christ associations who did not think it necessary to disassociate themselves from their non-Christian cultic involvements. But whether we follow Lang, and take "unbelievers" as "deviant insiders," or whether we think of them more in terms of "outsiders"— as in Paul Trebilco, "Creativity at the Boundary: Features of the Linguistic and Conceptual Construction of Outsiders in the Pauline Corpus," *NTS* 60 (2014): 185–94—a meal at a home of an "unbeliever" would, in either interpretation, likely have included pouring of libations and prayers addressed to household gods or tutelary deities.

Roman or if the temple was associated with Roman worship,[90] then the above activities—praying, pouring of libations, and divination—would have been conducted *capite velato*, as we have established. Thus, the Corinthian Christians who frequented Roman households or attended banquets in Roman temples would have felt pressure to participate in these rituals that accompanied banquets in the customary way—with a covered head. And it is entirely possible that this custom of praying and accessing divine knowledge with a covered head was then transferred also into the Christian meetings, perhaps even as a result of pressure exerted by the visiting Roman "unbelievers" on the Christian neophytes. If so, Paul's placement of his discussion about head-coverings between 1 Cor 8:1–11:1—in which focus is on idolatry—and 1 Cor 11:17–14:40—in which focus is on the Christian assemblies in session—may demonstrate that 1 Cor 11:2–16 serves a transitory function between the two contexts. That is, before Paul goes on to deal specifically with the "when you come together" or the conduct during Christian banquets, he wants to address the issue of praying and accessing divine (fore)knowledge with (or without) a covered head that finds expression in both contexts: in the venues dominated by the so-called unbelievers and in the venues of the Christian assemblies.

This way of reading 1 Cor may also explain the apparent discrepancy between 1 Cor 11:2–16, in which it is taken for granted that women pray and access divine (fore)knowledge, and 1 Cor 14:34–35, in which women are instructed to be silent during the assemblies (ἐν ταῖς ἐκκλησίαις σιγάτωσαν). If we take 1 Cor 14:34–35 as original to Paul's letter (and this is a matter of much debate[91]), then we find these

---

[90] Kathy Ehrensperger has argued that "Corinth as a Roman colony privileged Roman deities as the officially practiced cults," and so in the public arena, Roman forms of worship appear to have been dominant in first-century Corinth. Kathy Ehrensperger, "Between Polis, Oikos, and Ekklesia," 108–9.

[91] Some biblical scholars insist that there is enough text-critical evidence to demonstrates that 1 Cor 14:34–35 is an interpolation. E.g., Philip B. Payne, "Fuldensis, Sigla for Variants in Vaticanus, and 1 Cor 14.34–5," *NTS* 41 (1995): 240–62; idem., "MS. 88 as Evidence for a Text Without 1 Cor 14.34–5," *NTS* 44 (1998): 152–58; idem., *Man and Woman*, 228–66; idem., "Vaticanus Distigme-obelos Symbols Marking Added Text, Including 1 Corinthians 14.34–5," *NTS* 63 (2017): 604–25; Fee, *First Corinthians: Revised*, 780–92. While the presentation of 1 Cor 14:34–35 is certainly odd in some manuscripts—e.g., these verses are placed after 1 Cor 14:40—many biblical scholars remain hesitant to declare these verses an interpolation on text-critical grounds, since such manuscript oddities (quite late in most cases) do not yet clearly point towards this conclusion. Furthermore, Payne's interpretation of the manuscript evidence regarding these verses has also been heavily criticized. E.g., Richard G. Fellows, "Are There Distigme-Obelos

verses in the context of Paul's instructions specifically concerning the symposium part of the banquet, and so Paul's displeasure here may only be with Christian women asking questions during the symposium. Traditionally, the symposium part of the Greek or Roman banquet was dominated by male conversation, and women participation was viewed with suspicion (women at the banquets were often there for entertainment purposes only).[92] In general, Greek and Roman men perceived themselves as more qualified to take part in conversations on subjects that women were thought to be ignorant of, and so criticism of the participation of women at dinner parties was common.[93] Furthermore, silence was often thought to be virtuous on a woman—"silence gives grace to a woman" wrote Aristotle, for example (*Pol.* 1.1260a)[94]—and silence was also thought appropriate for those not yet qualified to converse on matters of importance.[95] Thus, Paul may

---

Symbols in Vaticanus?" *NTS* 65 (2019): 246–51; Jan Krans, "Paragraphos, Not Obelos, in Codex Vaticanus," *NTS* 65 (2019): 252–57; Jorunn Økland, "The Celebrity Paratexts: The 1 Corinthians 14 Gloss Theory before and after *The Corinthian Women Prophets*," in *After the Corinthian Women Prophets: Reimagining Rhetoric and Power*, ed. Joseph A. Marchal (Atlanta: SBL Press, 2021), 73–93. Most of the early influential manuscripts, including P46, place these verses in their current location without any indication that they should not belong there. Thus, text-critical scholars have called for caution in pronouncing 1 Cor 14:34–35 an interpolation on purely text-critical grounds. E.g., D. C. Parker, *An Introduction to the New Testament Manuscripts*, 275–76. They suggest that the apparent discrepancy with 1 Cor 11:2–16 is a far stronger indicator of interpolation than text-critical evidence. E.g., David Trobisch, "The Need to Discern Distinctive Editions of the New Testament in the Manuscript Tradition," in *The Textual History of the Greek New Testament: Changing Views in Contemporary Research*, ed. Klaus Wachtel and Michael W. Holmes (Atlanta, GA: Society of Biblical Literature, 2011), 46. However, if it can be shown that 1 Cor 11:2–16 and 1 Cor 14:34–35 can both have their place in the same letter without contradiction, then there is one less reason for taking 1 Cor 14:34–35 as an interpolation—although I must admit that these verses fit very awkwardly into 1 Cor 14, and so there will always remain that reason to claim that they do not belong there.

[92] Ekkehard W. Stegemann and Wolfgang Stegemann, *The Jesus Movement: A Social History of Its First Century*, trans. O. C. Dean, Jr. (Minneapolis: Fortress Press, 1999), 370–71; Smith, *From Symposium to Eucharist*, 208.

[93] E.g., MacDonald, *The Power of Children*, 115–16; Susan E. Hylen, *Women in the New Testament World* (New York: Oxford University Press, 2019), 135–36.

[94] For other ancient statements on the virtue of women's silence see, Armin D. Baum, "Paul's Conflicting Statements on Female Public Speaking (1 Cor. 11:5) and Silence (1 Cor. 14:34–35)," *TynBul* 65 (2014): 253–54.

[95] Aulus Gellius relays an interesting example of this in relation to how discipleship operated in the school of Pythagoras: "Then, when he [Pythagoras] had thus examined a man and found him suitable, he at once gave orders that he should be admitted to the school and should keep

have thought of the Corinthian Christian women as not yet fully equipped to participate in conversations of the Christian symposiums, and thus advises them to pursue understanding by asking questions of their husbands at home.[96] 1 Cor 14:34–35 may therefore address a particular issue (i.e., asking questions) regarding married women (or those with "own men at home") in the context of specifically the *Christian* symposium.[97] If so, 1 Cor 14:34–35 and 1 Cor 11:2–16 do not address the same concern nor context at all. While 1 Cor 14:34–35 may be about a particular speech-act in a specific context, 1 Cor 11:2–16 is about *ritual* acts *wherever* these were performed. But for all we know, 1 Cor 14:34–35 could very well be a non-Pauline interpolation (see above), in which case the apparent discrepancy between the two texts is not Pauline and therefore not relevant to the *Sitz im Leben* of 1 Cor 11:2–16. In any case, the bottom line here is that the context of 1 Cor 11:2–16 is not solely the "when you gather together," but the Corinthian Christians may have

---

silence for a fixed period of time; this was not the same for all, but differed according to his estimate of the man's capacity for learning quickly. But the one who kept silent listened to what was said by others; he was, however, religiously forbidden to ask questions, if he had not fully understood, or to remark upon what he had heard. Now, no one kept silence for less than two years, and during the entire period of silent listening they were called ἀκουστικοί or "auditors." But when they had learned what is of all things the most difficult, to keep quiet and listen, and had finally begun to be adepts in that silence which is called ἐχεμυθία or "continence in words," they were then allowed to speak, to ask questions, and to write down what they had heard, and to express their own opinions" (*Noct. att.* 1.9 [Rolfe]). It is noteworthy that the candidates were specifically forbidden to ask questions for at least two years. Asking questions seems to be an issue also in 1 Cor 14:34–35. However, the relevance of this anecdote by Aulus Gellius on 1 Cor 14:34–35 is questionable, since Gellius speaks about the distant past from his perspective, and thus we do not know whether in the first century CE or later such methods of discipleship were even practiced.

[96] A study of a cache of papyri from the relevant time period (e.g., Roman imperial rule of Egypt) pertaining to Arsinoe, Egypt, concludes that of the landowners, 96% of men signed the documents related to the lease of land themselves, while 80% of female landowners did so. In regards to land renters, however, about a third of men signed the lease documents themselves, while there are no examples of female renters signing the documents themselves. Sabine R. Huebner, *Papyri and the Social World of the New Testament* (Cambridge: Cambridge University Press, 2019), 79–80. If this is representative of Roman colonies at large, we can say that women's basic literacy was near non-existent at lower social strata at the time of Paul, while a number of men who owned no land still had some basic literacy skills. In a mixed assembly, therefore, there would have been disproportionally more women who could not read nor write at all, and who for this reason were dependent on others (statistically, men) for these skills.

[97] For an overview of the various proposals in biblical scholarship of how 1 Cor 14:34–35 should be read in light of 1 Cor 11:2–16, see, for example, Baum, "Paul's Conflicting Statements," 248–51. See also, Ehrensperger, "The Question(s) of Gender," 256.

prayed and accessed divine (fore)knowledge in any number of venues, such as in their own homes, in the homes of "unbelievers," and in Roman temples of Corinth.[98]

4.2.4 *Capite velato* and Shame

If any of the Corinthian Christian congregants of Roman background continued to practice *capite velato* in any of the above-mentioned venues—whether because it was expected, or it felt right, or it helped stress their Roman-ness—then Paul's association of this custom with shame would have caused some problems. That is, we expect an early Christ-follower to have been connected to the wider society in a number of ways—through ancestry, ethnicity, clan, place of residence, association, guild, client-patron relationship, cult, profession, and so on. The earliest Christian congregations were not isolated communities cut off from the influence of and connection to the world outside of their own gatherings.[99] Thus, based on the expectations of the time, a first-century Corinthian Christian (of whatever ethnic background) had numerous social obligations to attend to outside of the association of Christ-followers. For example, it was expected that kin and other close social relations visited each other's homes to honor members of (extended) family, for coming-of-age parties, for funerary rites, and for commemoration of dead ancestors, to name just a few notable reasons.[100] Also, in some Greco-Roman associations and guilds it was customary to communally celebrate whenever a member got married or had a child or purchased land, and fines were imposed upon those members who failed to participate in these events.[101] And any individual in a client

---

[98] Here is where I part ways with Dennis Smith. Smith considers 1 Cor 14:34–35 an "anomaly" and is willing to entertain the possibility that it is an interpolation mainly on the basis that women's "equal participation in the symposium is clearly indicated in 1 Cor 11:2–16." Smith, *From Symposium to Eucharist*, 207. Unfortunately, Smith fails to follow his own proposed reading of 1 Cor here. It does not really make sense for Paul to address the Christian symposium before *deipnon* only to return to speaking of it after. Considering that there are no clear indicators in 1 Cor 11:2–16 itself that limit the context of the instructions only to the symposium part of the banquet (as discussed above), it seems more reasonable to hold that while the context of the instructions preserved in 1 Cor 14:34–35 may be limited to the Christian symposium only, this is not the case with 1 Cor 11:2–16.

[99] E.g., Dunn, *Theology of Paul the Apostle*, 695.

[100] Janet H. Tulloch, "Women Leaders in Family Funerary Banquets," a contributing chapter in *A Woman's Place: House Churches in Earliest Christianity*, by Carolyn Osiek and Margaret Y. MacDonald (Minneapolis: Fortress Press, 2006), 168; Dolansky, "Household and Family," 177–79, 182–83.

[101] Kloppenborg, *Christ's Associations*, 36, 157–58.

relationship to a patron had to ensure that his or her patron was appropriately honored in social events and at other times.[102]

The main part of the gatherings that took place for any of the above reasons was the banquet. In fact, to host a banquet for one's social relations needed no other reason than a wish to socialize, and so banquets were a frequent form of social interaction (and appears to have been the format of also the early Christian gatherings, as discussed above). Banquets in which conversation on matters of importance between friends or acquaintances was the main reason of the gathering had ideally fewer participants—Aulus Gellius, for example, recommends that the number of partakers should be between three to nine (*Noct. att.* 13.11). Familial gatherings for celebrations or commemorations may have been somewhat larger in number, while the gatherings of occupational guilds could at times exceed a hundred participants, and imperial banquets were frequented by hundreds of invitees (Suetonius informs us, for example, that emperor Claudius's banquets entertained 600 guests each time, *Claud.* 32.1).[103] In each case, an invitation to a banquet was a privilege *and* an obligation, because an invitation afforded an opportunity to strengthen social ties with one's social equivalents, to fulfil one's social duty to extended family and to dead ancestors, for sustenance (e.g., meat), and to honor one's social superiors—and in the case of social superiors, to be honored.[104] Furthermore, an invitation to a banquet of a social superior did not usually go unnoticed by one's uninvited social rivals, and so participation afforded an opportunity to get ahead if one made the best of the occasion.[105]

While dining, conversation, entertainment, honor, and socialization were the most important components of the banquet, "gods were never very far away," as Richard Ascough observes, "and were often acknowledged through specific rituals, particularly libations and prayers."[106] Pouring of libations and prayers allowed

---

[102] Chow, "Patronage in Roman Corinth," 121–24.

[103] Kloppenborg, *Christ's Associations*, 111–13.

[104] Richard S. Ascough, "Communal Meals," in *The Oxford Handbook of Early Christian Ritual*, ed. Risto Uro, et al. (Oxford: Oxford University Press, 2019), 207–11. However, a banquet was not always a pleasant experience for the one who was socially inferior to the host but who needed to fulfill his or her social duty in the hope of some future benefit. Juvenal, for example, satirizes such occasions in which an invitee to a banquet is willing to be subjected to all manner of abuse and maltreatment in the faintest of hopes that some benefit, no matter how small, will accrue (*Sat.* 5.12–173). See also, Meeks, *The First Urban Christians*, 68.

[105] Ascough, "Communal Meals," 207–11.

[106] Ascough, "Communal Meals," 215.

participants to affirm their (shared) "religious commitments."[107] The Romans at such banquets would have been expected to pour libations and offer prayers *capite velato*, as we have established, and failure to do so would have been taken notice of by the host, by one's peers, and by one's social superiors and inferiors. Furthermore, many of the social and household gatherings (e.g., for the commemoration of dead ancestors) were not confined to the banquet hall only, but also contained rites at public places, such as at altars on street corners, in local temples, or at other local shrines.[108] And then there were the city-wide celebrations of important events, such as imperial games, imperial birthdays, coronations of emperors, and the like.[109] The performance of rites at public places and on public occasions could be observed by anyone,[110] and a failure to perform these rites in an expected manner was thus publicly visible.

It has already been pointed out that Romans were particularly scrupulous in matters of worship. Great care was taken to prevent or to eliminate mistakes in the performance of rituals in order not to offend the gods.[111] Plutarch recounts, for example, how a particular Roman sacrifice was repeated thirty times because mistakes in the performance prevented the completion of the ritual. Plutarch gives this as a pertinent example of the "piety of the Romans towards the gods" (τοιαύτη μὲν εὐλάβεια πρὸς τὸ θεῖον 'Ρωμαίων, *Cor.* 25.3). It seems that in the mind of a Roman, scrupulousness in matters of worship was intimately tied to the success and stability of the empire. Paul's contemporary Latin writer Valerius Maximus puts it this way:

> No wonder therefore if the indulgence of the gods has persisted, ever watchful to augment and protect an imperial power by which even minor items of religious significance are seen to be weighed with such scrupulous care; for never should our community be thought to have averted its eyes from the most meticulous practice of religious observances.[112] (*Memorable Doings and Sayings*, 1.1.8 [Shackleton Bailey])

Due to such sentiments, exactness in matters of worship was not only a concern of the state but also of the *patres familias*. A dutiful Roman head of household would have wanted to ensure that important social values, such as harmony and

---

[107] Ascough, "Communal Meals," 216.
[108] Dolansky, "Household and Family," 177–79.
[109] Chow, "Patronage in Roman Corinth," 107–8.
[110] Raja, "Ancient Sanctuaries," 146.
[111] See also, Ehrensperger, *Paul at the Crossroads of Cultures*, 182–83.
[112] See also, Dihle, *Greek and Latin Literature*, 85; Ehrensperger, "Between Polis, Oikos, and Ekklesia," 109–10.

piety, were promoted and established in the household, and following a traditional script in regards to the performance of rituals was an effective way to do that.[113] A household member or a visitor who in open defiance failed to follow the script in regards to the performance of rituals would have thus been a source of disharmony and would have demonstrated unwelcome impiousness.[114] Most importantly, willful neglect of such matters would have been perceived as open dishonor and violation of trust.[115] Thus, if *capite velato* was an important component of ritual performances in household worship, at banquets, or at local shrines, then an uncovered head on a Roman praying, sacrificing, pouring libation, or seeking divination in these contexts would have been an unwelcome sight.[116] In worst-case scenarios, going against cultural expectations in regards to the worship of the gods could have led to social ostracism and denial of access to previously available resources, perhaps even to life's basic necessities, such as food, shelter, and clothing.[117]

Thus, Paul's negative assessment of a man praying and accessing divine (fore)knowledge with a covered head—or more specifically, with something "down from the head"—would have caused consternation for a Roman, as taking this seriously was not a simple matter of praying differently from here onwards, but it risked severing important social ties, the consequences of which could have been dire. A Roman cut off from his or her previous social ties—because of an unwillingness to participate in something customary now deemed shameful—would have been increasingly more reliant on other members of the Christ association for life's basic needs, but the problem may in fact have been exacerbated if fellow Christ-followers of Roman background failed to act in the same manner. For example, if some Corinthian congregants of Roman background saw no

---

[113] Dolansky, "Household and Family," 171; Ehrensperger, "Between Polis, Oikos, and Ekklesia," 116.

[114] E.g., T. J. Lang, "Trouble with Insiders," 992.

[115] Schwiebert, "Honoring the Divine," 33.

[116] As Kathy Ehrensperger notes, "the *mors maiorum*, the practices/traditions of the ancestors, were the decisive factor in Roman self-perception." Ehrensperger, *Paul at the Crossroads of Cultures*, 78. Considering that *capite velato* was traced to the forefather of all Romans, Aeneas, this practice must have been important indeed.

[117] In the words of Kathy Ehrensperger: "In addition to the general significance of cult practice and that of sacrifice in particular, a key function of public sacrifices, certainly from the Early Principate onwards, was to secure the well-being of the empire (and its embodiment the emperor). Failing to participate in this 'order of the world' and its maintenance was not merely considered anti-social, but viewed as an actual threat to the very existence of 'this world' by exposing it to the risk of chaos." Ehrensperger, *Paul at the Crossroads of Cultures*, 185.

problem in praying with a covered head in the various venues mentioned above, and even considered it dishonorable not to do so, they would have continued to have access to social benefits and resources, which they may not have wished to now share with the "bad" Romans (and so some get drunk while others go hungry; cf. 1 Cor 11:21). Thus, a simple ritual gesture, if left unperformed, could have become a cause of conflict with major repercussions for the well-being of Christ-following individuals and for the unity of the entire Christian congregation.

I am fully aware of the speculative nature of the above scenario. My intention here is not to argue that the non-performance of *capite velato* in Corinth led precisely to the above-described circumstances. I merely wish to highlight that the performance and non-performance of rituals affect human cognition and group dynamics, as CSR theorizes, and so we cannot take Paul's claim that praying with a covered head is shameful for a man lightly in the context of first-century Corinth. It is important to recognize that such a statement is predicted by CSR to have been weighty for those who had been used to praying *capite velato*, who valued this ritual gesture as a cultural symbol, and who feared that the non-performance of it led to terrible consequences for one's personal well-being, as well as for the welfare of the state. Of those people, therefore, Paul is not only asking for a different posture in prayer, but for a complete alteration to worldview, lifestyle, and social relationships.

This way of reading 1 Cor 11:4 squares well with Jason Lamoreaux's interpretation of Paul's instructions in the immediately preceding 1 Cor 8–10:

> In asking the Corinthians to abstain from idol meat, Paul does not simply ask the knowledgeable to avoid idolatry or contamination from such things. First, he asks them to trust him with ritual authority. They must accept his claims about right and wrong action and ritual failure. Second, if ritual is an indicator of identity, Paul is asking—commanding, really—the knowledgeable to distance themselves from familial activities and their ties to households outside of the Jesus group. For the knowledgeable, it was vitally important to continue such familial and patronal ties. So what Paul demanded of them amounted to social violence, an act that would cut them off from social, as well as material, resources.... So what Paul asked of the knowledgeable was not simply a cognitive shift in perspective but rather a somatic shift that would place them outside the circles of people they knew and, perhaps, to whom they were very closely related. Here, Paul called for the splitting of families, friends, and patron-client relationships. There was a

genuine violence embodied in Paul's demands that aimed at fealty to a new group, the Jesus group, at the expense of all other social ties.[118]

If Lamoreaux's assessment of 1 Cor 8–10 is correct (and I think it is), then Paul's claim that a covered head on a man during praying and prophesying is shameful is a fitting continuation of 1 Cor 8–10: just as in 1 Cor 8–10, one of Paul's objectives in 1 Cor 11:2–16 seems to be to weaken the Corinthian congregants' social ties with and dependence on "outsiders," and conversely, to strengthen the relationships *within* the Christ association, all the while reminding his addressees of his claim to (ritual) authority on matters of Christian conduct.[119] A Roman hearing this, therefore, faced a dilemma: either to accept the (ritual) authority of Paul and stop performing *capite velato* (and consuming idol meat), thus risking social ostracism and denial of access to social resources, or to ignore the (ritual) authority of Paul and risk going against the founder of the Corinthian Christ association. In the next chapter, I will argue that 1 Cor 11:2–16 suggests that some Corinthian Christians had already taken Paul seriously on the question of head-coverings, even more seriously than Paul had envisioned, which had then led to some unanticipated consequences that required Paul's follow-up intervention.

4.3 Conclusion

Rituals affect human minds and human relationships—this is the most important take-away from this chapter. And while cognitive scientists of religion do not

---

[118] Jason T. Lamoreaux, "Ritual Negotiation," in *Early Christian Ritual Life*, ed. Richard E. DeMaris, Jason T. Lamoreaux, and Steven C. Muir (New York: Routledge, 2018), 143. Richard Horsley has argued for a similar reading of 1 Cor 8–10: "For Paul the sharing of 'food offered to idols' was not an issue of ethics, but of the integrity and survival of the Corinthians' assembly as an exclusive alternative community to the dominant society and its social networks. In his concern to 'build up' the assembly of saints over against the networks of power relations by which the imperial society was constituted, he could not allow those who had joined the assembly to participate in the sacrificial banquets by which those social relations were ritually established.... For the members of the new alternative community that meant cutting themselves off from the very means by which their previously essential socio-economic relations were maintained." Richard A. Horsley, "1 Corinthians: A Case Study of Paul's Assembly as an Alternative Society," in *Paul and Empire: Religion and Power in Roman Imperial Society*, ed. Richard A. Horsley (Harrisburg, PA: Trinity Press International, 1997), 248–49. See also, Ehrensperger, "Between Polis, Oikos, and Ekklesia," 119–21.

[119] Richard Horsley suggests that 1 Cor 5–6, in which "Paul insist[s] that the Corinthian assembly conduct its own affairs autonomously, in complete independence of 'the world,'" also participates in this rhetoric. Horsley, "1 Corinthians," 245.

always agree on *how* or *why* they do so, their hypotheses have been built upon testable and verifiable observations, which allows us to apply their theories also on ancient data about rituals that can no longer be observed in situ. As *capite velato* should be counted among ritualized behaviors, I have, in this chapter, discussed the possible effects of its performance on human cognition and on group dynamics through the lens of CSR theories. I have suggested, among other things, that *capite velato* appears to have functioned as an excellent transmitter of religious traditions and doctrines in Roman society; that its performance would have allowed Romans to instinctively trust and cooperate with one another; and that the non-performance of it may have been unthinkable to a Roman because of the close association of *capite velato* with the brain's hazard-precaution system, and because of the potential social costliness (such as social ostracism) that the neglect of this custom would have brought about.

Given, then, that the Corinthian Christian congregation seems to have held in its number members with affiliations to Rome, Paul's claim that it is shameful for men to pray with a covered head would have been heard by these members as a radical call for abandonment of current social ties and for alteration to one's lifestyle, since a principled non-performance of *capite velato* would have kept them from participating in banquets and other social events outside of the Christ association. That Paul in 1 Cor 11:2–16 had in mind also venues outside of the Christian gatherings is suggested by the placement of this text between Paul's discussion about consumption of idol meat in the homes of "unbelievers" and temples (1 Cor 8–10) and Paul's focus on problems associated solely with the Corinthian Christian gatherings for their banquets (1 Cor 11:17–14:40).

I want to emphasize here, in conclusion to this chapter, that this radicalness of Paul's statement that praying with a head-covering causes shame for (Roman) men needs to be taken seriously in the study of 1 Cor 11:2–16, since based on the predictions of CST, (radical) bans are costly to an individual but crucial to the survival of the social group that adheres to them. Thus, any ban, whether adhered to or ignored, would affect individuals and groups to whom they apply or to whom they are addressed. If group survival is at stake, adherence to group's peculiar rituals and bans can enhance the chances of survival. In the next chapter, I will argue that some Corinthian Christians appear to have taken the survival of the Corinthian Christ association seriously, and that they had responded to Paul's (ritual) authority with utmost earnestness, leading to an unforeseen problem with the ban on head-coverings that required Paul to explain himself more thoroughly.

5. Shame on Christ, Shame on Man, and Shame on Woman

Exegesis of 1 Cor 11:2–16 in Light of *capite velato*

Having demonstrated that *capite velato* was a widespread Roman ritual gesture at the time of Paul and that Paul's statement deeming it shameful for men to pray and access divine (fore)knowledge with a head-covering would have been heard by Romans as a radical call to alter their way of life, we are now prepared to conduct a detailed exegetical examination of 1 Cor 11:2–16 for any clues as to what may have been going on in the Corinthian congregation in relation to *capite velato*. The main question that consumes us here is the one that biblical scholars, who have likewise argued for *capite velato* as background of 1 Cor 11:2–16, have failed to satisfactorily answer (see section 1.6): why does Paul associate the performance of *capite velato* with shame in regards to men, but does not do so in regards to women, even though both men and women of Roman background prayed and accessed divine (fore)knowledge with covered heads? In this chapter, I propose, based on a close reading of 1 Cor 11:2–16, that certain members of the Christ association in Corinth had begun to argue that since Christians of Roman background were not to pray or access divine (fore)knowledge with a garment over the head, no-one else should have anything in their hair or on their head during these activities either. This, however, posed a problem for those women (especially of non-Roman background) who wished to keep a garment or a veil over the head as a sign of marital faithfulness or who wished to put pins, ribbons, or hairnets on their head to keep the hair in place. Paul sympathized with the concerns of these women and offered several arguments as to why it was shameful for men to pray with a garment over the head, but not so for women.

5.1 Opening Praise of the Corinthians (1 Cor 11:2)

Curiously, Paul begins the passage of 1 Cor 11:2–16 with a praise of the Corinthian Christians: "And I praise you because you have remembered me in everything and are keeping the traditions just as I handed them to you (Ἐπαινῶ δὲ ὑμᾶς ὅτι πάντα[1] μου μέμνησθε καί, καθὼς παρέδωκα ὑμῖν, τὰς παραδόσεις κατέχετε)." Such praise at this stage of the letter appears odd, since there seems to be no good reason to praise the Corinthian believers. All throughout the letter, Paul finds fault with the conduct and opinions of the Corinthian congregation, and 1 Cor 11:3–16 seems no different—here also Paul seems to take issue with the conduct of the Corinthians, this time in relation to how they pray and prophesy. Thus, for a long time, readers of this passage took Paul's opening praise to be ironic or sarcastic—that Paul meant the exact opposite of what he wrote down.[2] This view has lost traction in recent times and for good reasons—Paul's emphatic assertion in the immediately following section of the letter (1 Cor 11:17), that he cannot praise the Corinthian congregation for their behavior during the *kyrion deipnon*, suggests that the praise in 1 Cor 11:2 was not meant as irony.[3]

Yet, most biblical scholars are still reluctant to take Paul's praise of the Corinthians here at face value. Thus, the most popular current explanation in biblical scholarship of Paul's praise in 1 Cor 11:2 is that it functions as a *captatio benevolentiae*, a rhetorical strategy common in ancient letter writing and oratory, in which the author or speaker attempts to get the addressee(s) on his or her side through flattery or praise (usually at the start of a letter or speech). It is suggested, therefore, that Paul's praise in 1 Cor 11:2–16 should not be taken as entirely genuine, but as a rhetorical ploy to "placate [the Corinthian believers] so that they will

---

[1] The word πάντα here is in the accusative which has raised some questions about its relation to the main verb ἐπαινῶ and the personal pronoun μου in the genitive. Anthony Thiselton has suggested that πάντα here is "an adverbial or modal accusative of respect," and so it should be understood in the sense of "unfailingly" (i.e., you have kept me in mind unfailingly). Thiselton, *The First Epistle to the Corinthians*, 810. David Garland has argued against this view, however, suggesting instead that πάντα should be taken here as "an accusative of respect or reference"—"in all things." Garland, *1 Corinthians*, 512. I have followed Garland in my translation.

[2] See Thiselton, *The First Epistle to the Corinthians*, 810.

[3] E.g., Hurley, "Did Paul Require Veils?" 191–92; Francis Watson, "The Authority of the Voice: A Theological Reading of 1 Cor 11.2–16," *NTS* 46 (2000): 526.

be receptive to critical advice."[4] Yet, the question remains: why would Paul employ the rhetorical strategy of *captatio benevolentiae* here at 1 Cor 11:2 of all places? The letter is filled with Paul's criticism of the Corinthians and at times Paul takes a strong opposite stance to the ideas and practices of his addressees. In comparison to some such passages, 1 Cor 11:3–16 comes across as mild, especially considering that Paul's main goal here appears to be to fill a gap in the Corinthian Christians' knowledge ("but I want you to know...," 1 Cor 11:3), rather than to explicitly rebuke them. Thus, it is not clear from the context why Paul would need to "placate" the Corinthians at this stage of the letter. Furthermore, in the immediately following section of the letter, Paul has no reservations about introducing his displeasure at the inappropriate behavior of the Corinthians with a refusal of praise, which makes *captatio benevolentiae* as a rhetorical strategy at 1 Cor 11:2 seem like a waste of ink.[5]

Considering the above, I concur with those scholars who have argued that 1 Cor 11:2 should be read as Paul's genuine praise of the Corinthians for something about their conduct or ideas that pleased Paul.[6] Ann Jervis has suggested, for example, that 1 Cor 11:2 "is Paul's acknowledgement that he carries much of the blame for the practice that he is in the process of rebuking. His converts are holding on to what they have been taught."[7] Troels Engberg-Pedersen had earlier

---

[4] Margaret M. Mitchell, *Paul and the Rhetoric of Reconciliation: An Exegetical Investigation of the Language and Composition of 1 Corinthians* (Louisville, KY: Westminster/John Knox Press, 1991), 260. See also, Hans Conzelmann, *1 Corinthians*, trans. James W. Leitch, ed. George W. MacRae (Philadelphia: Fortress Press, 1975), 182; John P. Meier, "On the Veiling of Hermeneutics (1 Cor 11:2–16)," *CBQ* 40 (1978): 215; Schrage, *Der erste Brief an die Korinther (1 Kor 6,12–11,16)*, 499; Raymond F. Collins, *First Corinthians*, SP 7 (Collegeville, MN: The Liturgical Press, 1999), 395; James W. Thompson, "Creation, Shame and Nature in 1 Cor 11:2–16: The Background and Coherence of Paul's Argument," in *Early Christianity and Classical Culture: Comparative Studies in Honor of Abraham J. Malherbe*, ed. John T. Fitzgerald, Thomas H. Olbricht, and L. Michael White, NovTSup 110 (Boston: Brill, 2003), 243; and Garland, *1 Corinthians*, 513.

[5] See also, Troy W. Martin, "Veiled Exhortations Regarding the Veil: Ethos as the Controlling Proof in Moral Persuasion (1 Cor 11:2–16)," in *Rhetoric, Ethic, and Moral Persuasion in Biblical Discourse*, ed. Thomas H. Olbricht and Anders Eriksson (New York: T&T Clark, 2005), 259–61.

[6] This is not to say that Paul does not flatter here. On the contrary, πάντα and καθώς seem to be hyperboles, as there is no good reason to believe that the Corinthians were as meticulous in following Paul as he gives them credit for. Yet, I do not think that these hyperboles in themselves devalue ἐπαινῶ.

[7] L. Ann Jervis, "But I Want You to Know ...": Paul's Midrashic Intertextual Response to the Corinthian Worshipers (1 Cor 11:2–16)," *JBL* 112 (1993): 238.

argued in a similar fashion, suggesting that 1 Cor 11:2 indicates that in the rest of this passage, Paul "is not blaming [the Corinthian Christians] for the behavior they have hitherto adopted for the precise reason that in that behavior they have been conforming to something he himself taught them."[8] But what could these "traditions" have been that Paul had passed on to the Corinthian congregation, the keeping of which by the Corinthians had led to a problematic situation that required Paul's follow-up clarification?

In the undisputed letters of Paul, the noun παράδοσις is only used twice—once in 1 Cor 11:2 and once in Gal 1:14. In the latter text, Paul speaks of his past zealousness towards his ancestral customs (περισσοτέρως ζηλωτὴς ὑπάρχων τῶν πατρικῶν μου παραδόσεων), and so παράδοσις in this context may refer to any number of practices and beliefs.[9] Given, therefore, the general nature of this term and the lack of usage of it in Paul's undisputed letters, παράδοσις in 1 Cor 11:2 tends to be interpreted by biblical scholars in a way that corresponds to their overall understanding of the text. For example, Chapter 1 demonstrated that one of the most popular readings in biblical scholarship of 1 Cor 11:2–16 holds that certain women in the Corinthian congregation had begun removing their customary head-coverings due to their (mis)understanding of Paul's teaching preserved in Gal 3:28—that in Christ all were one and that the categories of "male" and "female" were "no longer" (οὐκ ἔνι ἄρσεν καὶ θῆλυ· πάντες γὰρ ὑμεῖς εἷς ἐστε ἐν Χριστῷ Ἰησοῦ)—and so, correspondingly, one of the most popular interpretations of παράδοσις in this context is that it refers to a teaching of Paul akin to Gal 3:28.[10]

---

[8] Troels Engberg-Pedersen, "1 Corinthians 11:16 and the Character of Pauline Exhortation," *JBL* 110 (1991): 681.

[9] David DeSilva suggests, for example, that "Paul probably indicates hereby the oral traditions that were accepted by the Pharisaic school as an authoritative complement to the written Torah." DeSilva, *Galatians*, 144. If so, the "traditions" here could number in the hundreds, encompassing a wide range of practices and beliefs.

[10] E.g., Jervis, "But I Want You to Know," 234–35; Mary Rose D'Angelo, "Veils, Virgins, and the Tongues of Men and Angels: Women's Heads in Early Christianity," in *Women, Gender, Religion: A Reader*, ed. Elizabeth A. Castelli (New York: Palgrave, 2001), 394–95; Thiselton, *The First Epistle to the Corinthians*, 811. Jill Marshall, taking the plural of "traditions" in 1 Cor 11:2 seriously, has suggested that besides the teaching of "an affirmation of the dissolution of social differences" (cf. Gal 3:28) that Paul had passed on to the Corinthians, he had also taught them that "the head of every man is Christ," and that in the communication of 1 Cor 11:2–16, therefore, Paul modified both of these teachings in parallel. Jill E. Marshall, "Uncovering Traditions in 1 Corinthians 11:2–16," *NovT* 61 (2019): 74–75. I fail to see, however, why Paul would want to connect and address two seemingly disparate traditions in one paragraph, and Marshall's arguments

Since I have argued, however, that *capite velato* should be taken as subject matter of 1 Cor 11:2–16, I propose that the "traditions" that Paul has in mind here are concerned with certain customs associated with praying and accessing of divine (fore)knowledge that Paul presented to the Christian neophytes in Corinth. While Paul generally shows little concern for any postures or formularies associated with praying and prophesying in the undisputed letters, as I have shown in Chapter 3, it does not mean that Paul did not think it necessary to correct ways of praying and prophesying that he found problematic. For example, we can imagine that if any of the newly joined members to the Christ association were praying in a way that stressed their Roman-ness or their allegiance to Rome or their status as (prominent) citizens of Rome by demonstratively covering their heads with outer garments, Paul may have found it damaging to the unity and cooperation of the culturally mixed assembly. Thus, it is not difficult to envisage that Paul in such a scenario would have encouraged praying without a garment over the head, and that he would have passed it on as one of the "traditions."

If the initial content of this custom that Paul passed on to the Corinthians had anything to do with the discouragement of *capite velato*, then Paul's follow-up communication indicates that something in the Corinthians' implementation of this ban must have caused concern for Paul. I propose that the rest of Paul's argument suggests that some in the congregation wished to ban not only *capite velato* during praying and prophesying, but all forms of head-coverings, which in turn caused a conflict that Paul had not envisioned, and which required him not only to defend his initial position, but also to respond to the problematic development that had arisen in this regard.

---

are not convincing to me. Some other scholars, on the other hand, tend to see in "traditions" a reference to a larger body of teachings. C. K. Barrett, for example, suggests that Paul has in mind here "the central truths of the Christian faith" more generally. See, C. K. Barrett, *A Commentary on the First Epistle to the Corinthians*, HNTC (New York: Harper & Row, 1968), 247. David Garland likewise takes "traditions" here in a more general sense, but in reference to specifically Paul's teachings (*1 Corinthians*, 512), and Gordon Fee argues that "traditions" cover all the practices mentioned in 1 Cor 11–14 (*First Corinthians: Revised*, 552). However, a general reference to a body of teachings, whether particularly of Paul or of a wider group, seems odd in the context of 1 Cor 11:2–16, as the passage deals specifically with customs associated with praying and prophesying.

5.2 Hierarchy of Heads: Foundational Premise (1 Cor 11:3–6)

Paul follows his opening praise with a statement that appears to address a shortcoming in how the Corinthians had followed his traditions: "But I want you to know that of every man the head is Christ, but the head of woman [is] the man, and the head of Christ [is] God" (Θέλω δὲ ὑμᾶς εἰδέναι ὅτι παντὸς ἀνδρὸς ἡ κεφαλὴ ὁ Χριστός ἐστιν, κεφαλὴ δὲ γυναικὸς ὁ ἀνήρ, κεφαλὴ δὲ τοῦ Χριστοῦ ὁ θεός). In modern biblical scholarship, this statement has caused the most controversy in relation to the interpretation of 1 Cor 11:2–16. The main issue of contention here has to do with the meaning of the metaphorical "head." For decades in the second half of the twentieth century, biblical scholars debated fiercely over the meaning of the term without reaching a consensus.[11]

The beginnings of this debate can be traced to a short 1954 article by Stephen Bedale, in which it was argued (rather carelessly and superficially) that metaphorical "head" in Pauline literature should be understood in a sense of "source" or "beginning of," and so in 1 Cor 11:3, Paul's point is that God is the source of Christ, Christ of man, and man of woman (at creation).[12] This idea appealed to several subsequent biblical scholars, who developed Bedale's argument further,[13] but such

---

[11] So much so that Anthony Thiselton in his 2000 commentary on 1 Cor confesses: "The translation of this verse has caused more personal agony and difficulty than any other in the epistle, not least because the huge array of research literature and lexicographical data which presses controversially and polemically for diverse translations of κεφαλή, in which each of three main views finds powerful and well-informed advocates." Thiselton, *The First Epistle to the Corinthians*, 811.

[12] Stephen Bedale, "The Meaning of κεφαλή in the Pauline Epistles," *JTS* 5 (1954): 211–15.

[13] E.g., Barrett, *First Epistle to the Corinthians*, 248–49; Bruce, *1 and 2 Corinthians*, 103; Scroggs, "Paul and the Eschatological Woman," 298–300 (esp. n. 41); Berkeley Mickelsen and Alvera Mickelsen, "What Does *Kephalē* Mean in the New Testament?" in *Women, Authority and the Bible*, ed. Alvera Mickelsen (Downers Grove, IL: InterVarsity Press, 1986), 97–110; Catherine C. Kroeger, "Head," in *Dictionary of Paul and His Letters*, ed. Gerald F. Hawthorne, Ralph P. Martin, and Daniel G. Reid (Downers Grove, IL: InterVarsity Press, 1993), 375–77; Horsley, *1 Corinthians*, 153; Fee, *First Corinthians: Revised*, 555–56. Paul Gardner has recently pointed out, however, that many of the subsequent interpreters, who have followed Bedale, have not actually given due consideration to Bedale's own conclusions regarding the implication of his study on 1 Cor 11:3. That is, whereas most subsequent interpreters emphasize that "source" as a metaphorical meaning of "head" in Paul absolves 1 Cor 11:3 of all ideas of subordination, Bedale himself did not think so. For Bedale, this text of Paul still carried the idea that one is in a subordinate relationship to his or her "head"—that is, to his or her "source" or "beginning." See discussion in Gardner, *1 Corinthians*, 480–85.

a development also elicited a strong reaction from some quarters of biblical scholarship, in which it was firmly held that the metaphorical "head" in Paul stands for "authority over" (i.e., God has authority over Christ, Christ over man, and man over woman).[14] The debate was then complicated further by a third proposal, which posited that the metaphorical "head" in Paul should be understood in a sense of "pre-eminence" (i.e., God's pre-eminence exceeds Christ's, Christ's man's, and man's woman's).[15] By the turn of the 21st century, the lines were firmly drawn, and since no consensus had been reached, the debate quieted down. In his 2010 review of the debate, Michael Lakey adjudged the discussion on the meaning of metaphorical "head" to have "arrived at deadlock,"[16] and the decade or so since Lakey's assessment has not produced any major scholarly breakthroughs on the matter either.

The fierceness with which the debate has been conducted makes it seem like the meaning of the metaphorical "head" is absolutely crucial to the interpretation of 1 Cor 11:2–16; that its definition should be regarded as a central question on which the exegesis of this passage hinges. However, on a closer look at how this debate has played out, it becomes clear that the interpretation of 1 Cor 11:2–16 is of secondary concern for most of the participants (if it is even a concern at all). Michael Lakey has demonstrated how the debate around the metaphorical "head" in biblical scholarship has been fueled in large part by modern (American) evangelical concerns about "gender roles" at (Christian) homes (husband and wife) and in churches (leadership structures).[17] Thus, the main underlying issue that this debate

---

[14] E.g., Wayne Grudem, "Does κεφαλη ("Head") Mean "Source" or "Authority over" in Greek Literature? A Survey of 2336 Examples," *TJ* 6 (1985): 38–59; Joseph A. Fitzmyer, "Another Look at κεφαλη in 1 Corinthians 11.3," *NTS* 35 (1989): 503–11; Wayne Grudem, "The Meaning of κεφαλή ("Head"): An Evaluation of New Evidence, Real and Alleged," *JETS* 44 (2001): 25–65.

[15] E.g., Richard S. Cervin, "Does Κεφαλή Mean "Source" or "Authority over" in Greek Literature? A Rebuttal," *TJ* 10 (1989): 85–112; A. C. Perriman, "The Head of a Woman: The Meaning of κεφαλη in 1 Cor. 11:3," *JTS* 45 (1994): 602–22; Thiselton, *The First Epistle to the Corinthians*, 812–22; Garland, *1 Corinthians*, 516. Richard Cervin's article prompted Wayne Grudem to respond with a lengthy defense of the position that "head" has the metaphorical meaning of "authority over." Wayne Grudem, "The Meaning of Κεφαλή ("Head"): A Response to Recent Studies," *TJ* 11 (1990): 3–72.

[16] Michael Lakey, *Image and Glory of God: 1 Corinthians 11:2–16 as a Case Study in Bible, Gender and Hermeneutics*, LNTS 418 (New York: T&T Clark, 2010), 33.

[17] Lakey, *Image and Glory of God*, 1–7. See also, Shelly Matthews, "'To Be One and the Same with the Woman Whose Head is Shaven': Resisting the Violence of 1 Corinthians 11:2–16 from the Bottom of the Kyriarchal Pyramid," in *Sexual Violence and Sacred Texts*, ed. Amy Kalmanofsky (Eugene, OR: Wipf & Stock, 2017), 35.

revolves around is not concerning the historical circumstances that could have given rise to Paul's arguments in 1 Cor 11:2–16 (there is very little interest in that), but whether women can assume leadership roles in modern Christian congregations or not, and whether a modern Christian husband has God-ordained authority over his wife in domestic affairs or not. Thus, while much of the debate appears historically oriented (e.g., philological studies of κεφαλή), the arguments also betray influence of and interest in certain modern assumptions about biblical texts (e.g., inerrancy of Christian Scriptures), church tradition, church dogma (e.g., Trinity[18]), contemporary social norms, and contemporary politics that have little to do with the historical context of Paul's world.

Thus, in this debate, 1 Cor 11:3 has not been generally treated as a constitutive part of Paul's complex argument in relation to a real situation in Corinth, but more as an independent maxim about relationships that is applicable (with explanation) to modern situations. My interest here, however, is solely with the possible *historical* circumstances that could have given rise to Paul's argument in 1 Cor 11:2–16. I have suggested that Paul's main concern in this text is about a practice that had to do with *literal* heads, and that it is this concern that then governs his whole argument. I propose, therefore, that in order to understand how Paul may have employed the metaphorical "head" in the foundational premise of his argument, we should read 1 Cor 11:3 from the perspective of its historical context—that is, within the framework of *capite velato*.[19]

5.2.1 "Of Every Man the Head is Christ" and *capite velato*

Having introduced this concept of the hierarchy of heads as something that the Corinthians should be aware of, Paul moves on to demonstrate what this all implies. First, Paul states that "every man, who prays or prophesies having something down from the head, dishonors his [literal as well as metaphorical] head" (πᾶς ἀνὴρ

---

[18] Lakey has shown how the theology of Trinity became crucial in interpreting 1 Cor 11:3 in this debate, since it was believed that if Paul's statement "head of Christ is God" could be explained through the concept of Trinity, then the idea that "the head of woman is the man" could also be understood from this perspective. Lakey, *Image and Glory of God*, 37–69.

[19] At the apex of this debate about the meaning of the metaphorical "head" in Paul, Craig Keener called on all the parties to recognize that they were all in a sense right: the metaphorical "head" can take any of the meanings proposed, and so the quest should not be about finding some universal meaning of the metaphorical "head" that applies to all Pauline texts equally, but that each context should determine what meaning is in view. Keener, *Paul, Women and Wives*, 33–35. On this point, see also, Martina Böhm, "1 Kor 11,2–16: Beobachtungen zur paulinischen Schriftrezeption und Schriftargumentation im 1. Korintherbrief," *ZNW* 97 (2006): 216.

5.2 Hierarchy of Heads: Foundational Premise (1 Cor 11:3–6)

προσευχόμενος ἢ προφητεύων κατὰ κεφαλῆς ἔχων καταισχύνει τὴν κεφαλὴν αὐτοῦ, 1 Cor 11:4). It is generally agreed that the first mention of κεφαλή in this statement refers solely to man's physical head, but that the second mention of κεφαλή refers first and foremost to man's metaphorical head introduced in 1 Cor 11:3—that is, to Christ.[20] Paul's basic point here is, therefore, that if a man has something down from his head (κατὰ κεφαλῆς ἔχων) during the activities of praying and of accessing divine (fore)knowledge, he shames Christ.

As Chapter 2 demonstrated, κατὰ κεφαλῆς ἔχων was in the contemporary Greek literature used for a particular appearance—a garment over the head—and depending on the context, this appearance could be associated with either honor or shame. For example, Plutarch speaks of κατὰ κεφαλῆς ἔχων in connection to προσκυνεῖν τοὺς θεούς (lit. "to make obeisance to the gods," see sections 2.1.1 and 2.3.4) and Virgil introduces the appearance of *capite velato* in his *Aeneid* as an important component of *honore deorum* (see section 2.2.1). A direct connection is therefore drawn between human heads and the gods, and we can imagine that Paul's contemporary Romans understood *capite velato* precisely in this manner—their covering of the head during certain acts of reverence directly honored the gods. In light of this, Paul's placement of Christ as the direct head of man, in between man and God, is of significance. As was discussed in Chapter 2, Romans were expected to remove their garments off the head if they happened to meet those of honor (τοῖς ἀξίοις τιμῆς ἀπαντῶντες as per Plutarch, see section 2.1.1). Failure to do so brought dishonor to one's social superiors. This raises an intriguing possibility that Paul presents Christ here as man's social superior, who must be honored by the removal of the garment off the head (if it happens to be on), as per the Roman custom, and that this honoring of Christ with an uncovered head during praying and accessing of divine (fore)knowledge, therefore, takes precedence over the honoring of the god(s) with a covered head. It is noteworthy, for example, that the argument on the hierarchy of heads does not follow a logical sequence. We would expect the hierarchy to start at the highest point and move in logical steps to the lowest, or vice versa, but Paul begins with the relationship from the middle section—man in relation to Christ. This suggests that Paul gives this hierarchy of heads a place of prominence in relation to the topic of discussion at

---

[20] E.g., Jason David BeDuhn, "'Because of the Angels': Unveiling Paul's Anthropology in 1 Corinthians 11," *JBL* 118 (1999): 299; Thiselton, *The First Epistle to the Corinthians*, 827–28; Garland, *1 Corinthians*, 513–14; Heil, *The Rhetorical Role of Scripture*, 179–80; Lakey, *Image and Glory of God*, 104–5; Jantsch, "Einführung," 21.

hand.²¹ The central issue, therefore, appears to be Christ's dishonor in relation to a man "having down from the head."

If so, this would present a clever way of dealing with possible Roman counter-arguments against the initial ban on *capite velato* that does not devalue Roman customs but takes them seriously.²² That is, if any of the Corinthian Christians of Roman background objected that a covered head during praying and prophesying honored the god(s) (including Paul's god)—or if any of their "unbelieving" relations pointed it out to them—Paul would not need to deny it. Rather, Paul can highlight that this same appearance that honors the gods also dishonors one's social superiors as per their own customs, and for a Christ-following man there is no-one that requires more immediate social honor than his resurrected and interceding (cf. Rom 8:34) *kyrios* and Messiah, Jesus.²³ For a Roman who claimed Christ as his *kyrios*, therefore, this argument would have provided a reason not to engage in *capite velato* during praying and accessing of divine (fore)knowledge, all the while maintaining that he adhered to the customs of his *ethnos* (although it would not have been perceived so from the outside, see Chapter 4).

5.2.2 "The Head of Woman is the Man" and *capite velato*

We now turn to the most vexing problem of 1 Cor 11:2–16 for the *capite velato* hypothesis: why does Paul claim that "every woman who prays or prophesies with an uncovered head shames her [literal as well as metaphorical] head" (πᾶσα δὲ γυνὴ προσευχομένη ἢ προφητεύουσα ἀκατακαλύπτῳ τῇ κεφαλῇ καταισχύνει τὴν κεφαλὴν αὐτῆς, 1 Cor 11:5a), if *capite velato* was also practiced by Roman women? Should not the performance of it by Christ-following women equally have perturbed

---

²¹ Jill Marshall has also argued that Paul's placement of Christ-man relationship at the front of this hierarchy of heads gives it priority, and that it therefore has something to do with what Paul had initially taught the Corinthians. Jill Marshall, "Uncovering Traditions," 79.

²² Mark Finney has argued that since "Paul is only now giving *theological* justification for his views [in 1 Cor 11:3] perhaps demonstrates that during his time in Corinth his theological reflection upon the uncovered head of the man may not have been fully formed or elucidated, or perhaps that he was misunderstood." Finney, "Honour, Head-coverings and Headship," 48. I suspect that the situation may have been more complicated than that. For example, Paul in 1 Cor 11:2–16 may also be reacting to counter-arguments (real or imagined) against his initial position, as well as to some unforeseen applications of his traditions that he found problematic (see further below).

²³ "Our *kyrios* Jesus Christ" is a common phrase in Paul's letters to the Corinthians (e.g., 1 Cor 1:2; 1:7; 1:8; 1:9; 1:10; 5:4; 9:1; 15:31; 15:57; 16:23; 2 Cor 1:3; 8:9; 11:31). And in 1 Cor 8:5–6, Paul specifically highlights that even though there are "many gods and many lords, for us there is one God, the father, ... and one *kyrios*, Jesus Christ."

Paul? In order to be in a position to answer these questions, we need to take a closer look at women's head-covering practices at the time of Paul.

The question of women's head-coverings in antiquity is a much more complicated issue than the question of men's head-coverings. First of all, most (if not all) of the relevant literary entries on women's head-coverings from the time period in question were authored by men. By modern standards, many of these men espoused misogynistic views, and so it is difficult for modern scholars to draw a line between what should be considered prescriptive and ideological, and what descriptive and real. As Kelly Olson points out, male discourse on women's appearances "often specified an ideal moral system, not necessarily social practice."[24] For many ancient male authors, the ideal was that (respectable) women should be as inconspicuous as possible, out of public view and confined to their own quarters in their domestic dwellings.[25] The ideal public appearance of a woman, therefore, was such that she should be as covered up as possible in order not to be seen or observed.[26] Consider, for example, the following entry of Dio Chrysostom (ca. 40–120 CE) from the end of the first century CE about certain customs of Tarsus he had taken notice of:

> Indeed, then, in the past your city was famous for orderly behavior and for temperance, and such were the men it raised. However, now I fear the opposite to be the case, so that your city may be named alongside any other [disorderly city]. And yet, many of the [customs] that still remain demonstrate the moderation and austerity of past conduct. Of such is the one concerning the clothing of women (τὴν ἐσθῆτα τῶν γυναικῶν), that they should dress and go about in such a manner that no one may see any part of them, neither of the face nor of the rest of the body, and that they should see nothing but the road ahead. (*1 Tars.* 48)

The above quote is sometimes referenced in biblical scholarship on 1 Cor 11:2–16 as proof that women in antiquity were in general covered of the head.[27] However, there is no reason to believe that *all* women of first-century Tarsus—and by extension, of the whole of the Mediterranean region—were completely covered

---

[24] Olson, *Dress and the Roman Woman*, 11.

[25] Craig Keener lists several examples of how this ideal was presented in literary sources in his *Paul, Women and Wives*, 22–24. We must keep in mind, however, that most of these idealistic prescriptions concerned women of status, since little regard was shown for female slaves, for example, who were rather treated as property or chattel, not equally human. E.g., Jennifer A. Glancy, *Slavery in Early Christianity* (New York: Oxford University Press, 2002), 41.

[26] E.g., Lloyd Llewellyn-Jones, *Aphrodite's Tortoise: The Veiled Woman of Ancient Greece* (Swansea, UK: The Classical Press of Wales, 2003), 1; Olson *Dress and the Roman Woman*, 31.

[27] E.g., Finney, "Honour, Head-coverings and Headship," 35.

whenever outside of their homes. It is much more plausible that Dio Chrysostom engages here in prescriptive rhetoric that stems from his own views about what is ideal. The archaeological evidence we have of women's heads from the relevant time period and region, for example, contradicts such statements, as most portraits of women have hair on display.[28] Thus, this major discrepancy between literary ideals and artistic ideals regarding the appearances of women's heads calls for caution in how we reconstruct reality.[29] The whole issue is much more complex than saying either that women were generally covered of the head (based on literary ideals) or that women were generally not covered of the head (based on artistic ideals). Literary ideals must certainly have influenced women's behavior, but so must have artistic ideals, and thus, the whole issue regarding head-coverings may have been much more individual than scholarship has generally allowed for.

That being said, it does nevertheless appear that it was *more* common for women to be covered of the head in antiquity than for men to be so. This seems especially true in regards to the eastern provinces of the empire.[30] However, Plutarch's observation concerning certain Roman customs suggests that the same was generally true of Romans as well:

> Why do the sons bury their parents being completely covered (συγκεκαλυμμένοι), but the daughters [do so] with bare heads and loosed hair (γυμναῖς ταῖς κεφαλαῖς καὶ ταῖς κόμαις λελυμέναις;)? Is it because it is necessary for males to honor the forefathers as gods, but for daughters to mourn [them] as dead—the custom, having assigned what is fitting for each, produces what is suitable from both? Or is that which is not customary proper for mourning, as it is more customary for women to be covered and men to be uncovered in public (συνηθέστερον δὲ ταῖς μὲν γυναιξὶν ἐγκεκαλυμμέναις, τοῖς δ' ἀνδράσιν ἀκαλύπτοις εἰς τὸ δημόσιον προϊέναι;)? (*Quaest. rom.* 14 [267a–b])

Here Plutarch is unsure why Roman men and women buried their parents with contrasting appearances of the head. He ponders whether *capite velato* may have had something to do with it in case of men, which the women then complemented with an appearance fitting for mourning,[31] but he also wonders whether during burial ceremonies it was simply the case that that which was customary in normal

---

[28] Thompson, "Hairstyles, Head-coverings, and St. Paul," 107–13; Olson, *Dress and the Roman Woman*, 35–36, 41.

[29] Olson, *Dress and the Roman Woman*, 34–35.

[30] E.g., Llewellyn-Jones, *Aphrodite's Tortoise*.

[31] It seems that loosening the hair during mourning was a common posture of grieving women, as it is often mentioned in ancient literature (e.g., Livy, *Ab urbe cond.* 1.26.2; Juvenal, *Sat.* 3.212–213; Apuleius, *Metam.* 8.8). However, uncut (and unkempt) hair (and beard) appears also to have been a sign of mourning for Roman men (e.g., Suetonius, *Aug.* 23.2).

5.2 Hierarchy of Heads: Foundational Premise (1 Cor 11:3–6)

circumstances was reversed. Yet, Plutarch does not claim with the latter that Roman women were universally covered, while Roman men were universally uncovered—συνηθέστερον only suggests that one was a more common sight than the other.

In Chapter 2, I discussed the possible reasons why Roman men may have wished to cover their heads with an outer garment outside of liturgical settings. I pointed out that there is evidence that outer garments were useful as head-coverings in case of foul weather and for concealment of identity, and that garments were also drawn over the head in face of death. It is reasonable to assume that Roman women covered their heads with an outer garment for these same reasons. However, there were also additional reasons for (some) Roman women to cover their heads with an outer garment. For example, one of the virtues that those Roman women embraced, who had only been married once, was *pudicitia*. Susan Treggiari explains that "*pudicitia*, inadequately translated 'chastity', connotes in a wife sexual fidelity and love towards her husband. The abstraction was worshipped by women who had been married only once, *univirae*. These receive special praise on tombstones and in literature."[32] Interestingly, the personified Pudicitia always has an outer garment or a veil drawn over the head in Roman art (see Figure 5.1 for an example). Thus, it is reasonable to suppose that those women, who wished to express the importance of *pudicitia* for them, dressed more often in a manner that the personified *Pudicitia* displayed—with an outer garment or a veil over the head. In that case, covered head on a woman would indeed have been a more frequent sight among Romans than a covered head on a man.

Expressing commitment to fidelity and marriage through the covering of the head with an outer garment or a veil seems to have been even more pronounced in Greek culture.[33] And Philo's remark that it was customary (ἔθος) for "blameless" (ἀναίτιος) Jewish wives to wear a head-covering (ἐπίκρανον) as a symbol of modesty (τὸ σύμβολον τῆς αἰδοῦς) suggests that the same was true of Jewish culture (*Spec. Laws* 3.56).[34] Thus, while it is unreasonable to suppose that all women in antiquity

---

[32] Susan Treggiari, "Marriage and Family," in *A Companion to Latin Literature*, ed. Stephen Harrison (Malden, MA: Blackwell, 2005), 381.

[33] Llewellyn-Jones, *Aphrodite's Tortoise*, 121–54.

[34] The later rabbinic material also mentions women's head-coverings. For example, in Gen. Rab. 17:8, a question is posed as to why women must always have their heads covered, to which an answer is given that it is because of the transgression of the first woman. For discussion on this and other similar rabbinic references see, for example, Judith R. Baskin, *Midrashic Women: Formations of the Feminine in Rabbinic Literature* (Hanover, NH: Brandeis University Press, 2002),

were meticulously covered of the head whenever outside of their homes (as some ancient male authors perhaps wished), it does seem that there was an important social group in all the relevant cultures—(elite) married women—for whom covering the head with an outer garment or a veil was a much more frequent and dearer habit due to its symbolism.

Figure 5.1: Personified Pudicitia from the Flavian era. Her head is covered with either her garment or a veil. However, her hair as well as her crown remain visible. This is generally how Pudicitia was portrayed in Roman art. Musei Vaticani, inv. 2284.

---

68. See also, D'Angelo, "Veils, Virgins, and the Tongues," 398–99. Yet, just how much such a late and clearly ideological stance portrays Jewish day-to-day life in first-century Jerusalem, Alexandria, Rome, or Corinth, is up for debate. It seems hardly credible that all Jewish women at all times had their heads completely covered.

5.2 Hierarchy of Heads: Foundational Premise (1 Cor 11:3–6) 257

If this was in broad strokes the state of affairs regarding head-coverings in antiquity, we can see why problems could have arisen in a culturally mixed social group seeking or enforcing uniformity. That is, if the Corinthian Christ association included Roman men and women, who prayed and prophesied with a garment over the head in honor of the gods, Greek (and Jewish and other eastern) men, who did not do so, and Greek and Jewish (and Roman) married women, who always wore a garment (or a veil) over the head whenever outside of their homes, how could uniformity be achieved in ritual matters related to head-coverings? Supposing that Paul had asked the Romans not to perform *capite velato* during praying and accessing of divine (fore)knowledge—a reasonable request given its symbolism—those Greek and Jewish married women who always had their heads covered with a garment would, for example, technically be in the pose of *capite velato* during these ritual acts, even if they did not themselves think of it in that way. Furthermore, a Roman married woman could easily have by-passed a ban on *capite velato* by claiming that her head was covered with a garment during praying or prophesying not because of *capite velato*, but because of *pudicitia*—thus avoiding the same social stigma that befell those Romans who took the ban on *capite velato* seriously. Given that all these complexities were possible, I propose, therefore, that after Paul left Corinth, some (Romans) began to argue for uniformity in how the Christian neophytes were to pray and access divine (fore)knowledge, so that, as per the "traditions" of Paul, all—regardless of sex, *ethnos*, and social status—were to participate in these ritual acts with an uncovered head in the name of unity.

But the question of what counts as an "uncovered head" on a woman may not have been a straight-forward one. If a Roman man removed a garment or a cap from his head, he would most likely have been completely "uncovered" of the head, without anything else remaining on his head or in his hair. But women generally wore long hair, which tended to be arranged into different hairstyles with the aid of various accessories,[35] such as hair pins,[36] hairnets, ribbons or fillets (e.g.,

---

[35] Not everyone had the means and the leisure to tend to their hair with care, but some certainly did. Juvenal in his *Satires*, for example, pokes fun at those Roman women who were spending a fortune and a lot of time on doing up their hair. Juvenal mocks them for appearing unrecognizably tall as a result (*Sat.* 6.486–511). Juvenal is clearly exaggerating here, but his exaggeration must be based on some kernel of truth, suggesting, then, that some Roman women did in fact spend a lot of time and money on intricate and elaborate hairdos which had to be kept in place with various hair accessories.

[36] Hundreds of hairpins made of ivory or bone have been unearthed in the site of ancient (Roman) Corinth alone. Thompson, "Hairstyles, Head-Coverings, and St. Paul," 106.

vittae),[37] cloth bandages, and the like. Some such accessories covered the hair to a large extent or even completely (e.g., a *mitra* or *mitella*, a headwrap of eastern origins, which could be wrapped around the hair so as to create a turban on the head).[38] Furthermore, unlike men (in general), women sometimes added jewelry and other ornaments into their hair as part of their hairdos.[39] All these accessories and decorations could then be covered with the edge of an outer garment[40] or a

---

[37] Kelly Olson has argued that a respectable Roman woman was expected to have her hair bound with fillets whenever she was out of doors. Olson, *Dress and the Roman Woman*, 25, 38–39. The most well-known types of fillets were called *vittae*, and these were especially associated with young Roman girls. Olson, *Dress and the Roman Woman*, 16, 18.

[38] Olson, *Dress and the Roman Woman*, 53; Ria Berg, "Dress, Identity, Cultural Memory: *Copa* and *Ancilla Cauponae* in Context," in *Gender, Memory, and Identity in the Roman World*, ed. Jussi Rantala (Amsterdam: Amsterdam University Press, 2019), 209. There is an interesting entry on the *mitella* in Apuleius's novel *Metamorphoses*. In the relevant scene, a Thracian bandit named Haemus recounts how he escaped death: "'I put on a woman's flowery robe with loose billowy folds, covered my head with a woven turban (*mitellaque textile contecto capite*), and wore a pair of those thin white shoes that ladies wear. Then, disguised and under cover of the weaker sex, and riding on the back of a donkey loaded with ears of barley, I passed right through the lines of hostile soldiers. Thinking I was a donkey-woman, they allowed me free passage, for even then my beardless cheeks glistened with the smoothness of boyhood'" (*Metam.* 7.8 [Hanson]). It is interesting to note here that in the attempt to conceal his identity, Haemus did not hide his face completely, as would be expected, but let it be seen. What passed him off as a woman were certain articles of clothing, which also included the textile *mitella* that covered the head. Apuleius may have therefore thought that women of eastern provinces were easily recognizable by such headgear.

[39] Olson, *Dress and the Roman Woman*, 20, 99.

[40] According to Kelly Olson, Roman matrons—those who were legally married to Roman citizens—wore the *stola* that was covered with a *palla*, a large rectangular cloth which could be drawn over the head whenever necessary. Olson, *Dress and the Roman Woman*, 27–30, 33. However, *palla* is not the only known "wrap" of ancient Roman women. Olson also points out that terms such as *ricinium, palliola, amictus, amiculum, amictorium*, and *cyclas* in Roman literature all seem to refer to a similar piece of clothing. *Ricinium* appears to have been especially associated with widows, and *cyclas* seems to have been a "wrap" for wealthy women, as it is described to have been embroidered with gold. However, it is more difficult to determine the exact nature of these latter items of clothing, as we possess less information on these in the primary sources than we do on *palla*. Olson, *Dress and the Roman Woman*, 42, 51. Greek women (and men) also wore their outer garments in a way that these could be drawn over the head (and face) whenever necessary. Terms such as ἱμάτιον (often used in Greek sources to also describe the Roman toga, see Chapter 2), φᾶρος, πέπλος, ἐπίβλημα, περίβλημα, and ἐπιβόλαιον are all used in reference to an outer garment (for both women and men) that in addition to enveloping the body could also be drawn over the head or wrapped around it. Llewellyn-Jones, *Aphrodite's Tortoise*, 26.

cap⁴¹ or a veil,⁴² and veils could also be placed on top of garments or caps and in turn further ornamented with jewelry and the like. Thus, a woman's "head-covering" could have multiple layers, with each layer in a sense a "head-covering" in its own right.⁴³ At what stage, then, can a woman be said to be ἀκατακαλύπτῳ τῇ κεφαλῇ ("with uncovered head")? Is a woman "uncovered of the head" when she removes a mantle, or a cap, or a veil (or all of the above) off her head but leaves hair accessories in place, even though these may cover most or all of her head? Or is a woman only truly "uncovered" if there is nothing in and on her hair?

If any of the (Roman) men in the Corinthian congregation began to argue that an appropriately uncovered head during praying and accessing of divine (fore)knowledge was one that had nothing on it, not even a hairpin, then that would have certainly caused major consternation for women (and their male relations), regardless of their cultural belonging or social status. That some Corinthian men were on this trajectory of thinking about women's heads is suggested by Paul's comments in 1 Cor 11:5b–6: "For it [an uncovered head] is the same as if she were shaven. For if a woman is not covered, let her be shorn, but if it is shameful for a woman to be shorn or shaven, let her be covered" (ἓν γάρ ἐστιν καὶ τὸ αὐτὸ τῇ ἐξυρημένῃ. εἰ γὰρ οὐ κατακαλύπτεται γυνή, καὶ κειράσθω· εἰ δὲ αἰσχρὸν γυναικὶ τὸ κείρασθαι ἢ ξυρᾶσθαι, κατακλυπτέσθω). It is important to note here that all the main verbs regarding the behavior of women are either in the middle or in the passive voice, which suggests to me that it was not the women themselves who were advocating for a certain appearance, but rather the men. Thus, I read Paul's argument here as a challenge to the main instigators of the position that all members of the

---

⁴¹ For example, Roman freedwomen, just like freedmen, were given a cap known as *pileus* on their manumission (see also section 2.1). However, Kelly Olson has argued that Roman women generally did not wear hats due to the nature of their hairstyles. Olson, *Dress and the Roman Woman*, 53. Caps as head-coverings may have been more popular with poorer women (see below).

⁴² *Rica* and *marfotium* are known Latin terms for "veil"—piece of cloth intended for the covering of the head (and face)—that Roman women seem to have made use of. Olson, *Dress and the Roman Woman*, 53–54. The Greek literary sources preserve a number of terms for "veil," the most common of which are τὸ κρήδεμνον, ἡ καλύπτρα (or καλύπτρη), and τὸ κάλυμμα. The precise nature of these "veils" and how they were distinguished from one another is a debated matter, but it seems that their primary function was to cover the head. See discussion in Llewellyn-Jones, *Aphrodite's Tortoise*, 28–35.

⁴³ The number of layers seems to have depended on one's status and wealth. Poorer women (those who had to do manual labor) tended to wear less layers on their heads—perhaps only a cap to protect them from the elements and to keep their hair in place. Thompson, "Hairstyles, Head-coverings, and St. Paul," 111; Olson, *Dress and the Roman Woman*, 35.

Christ association should have a uniform appearance of the head during praying and prophesying, to think through their reasoning to its logical conclusion—if uniformity of appearance is truly sought after, then the hair of women should be either shaven off or cropped short in the typical manner of how men's heads appeared. Only then can the appearance of Christian congregants said to be uniform during praying and accessing of divine (fore)knowledge.

Such a challenge should certainly have made the instigators think twice about what they were advocating. A shaven or shorn head on a woman was not a sight that many men found acceptable. It is interesting to note, for example, that the adjective αἰσχρόν, that Paul uses here to describe the effect of a shaven or shorn head on a woman, can mean "shameful" or "dishonoring" (in a moral sense), as well as "ugly" (in terms of appearance).[44] That at least some Roman men found such an appearance on a woman ugly finds humorous expression in Apuleius, for example:

> However—though it is forbidden to mention this and I hope that such a horrible illustration of this point will never occur—if you were to strip the hair from the head of the most extraordinary and beautiful woman and rob her face of its natural decoration, even if she were descended from heaven, born out of the sea, and raised by the waves, even, I say, if she were Venus herself, surrounded by the whole chorus of Graces and accompanied by the entire throng of Cupids, wearing her famous girdle, breathing cinnamon, and sprinkling balsam—if she came forth bald she could not attract even her husband Vulcan. (*Metam.* 2.8 [Hanson])

Even though in this context, the protagonist Lucius openly confesses to being particularly attracted to women's hair (*Metam.* 2.9–10), he was scarcely the only one to share the sentiment expressed above, that even the most beautiful woman—or goddess, for that matter—could not have been attractive to her husband (let alone anyone else) if she shaved her head.

However, lack of hair on a woman was not only a matter of beauty ideals. Such an appearance could also be considered shame-inducing not only on the woman herself but also (and especially) on her male relations. There is an interesting example of this in the *Acts of Thomas*, a tale that was probably composed sometime during the third century CE in the eastern borderlands of the empire (although the individual stories included in the work may have come from an earlier time

---

[44] LSJ, s.v. "αἰσχρός."

period).⁴⁵ In the relevant scene, a woman by the name of Mygdonia hears the apostle Thomas preach and believes as a result. This angers Mygdonia's husband Charisius, who succeeds in imprisoning Thomas. However, when Charisius returns home to dine and have sex with Mygdonia, he finds her with shorn hair and rent clothes. Charisius is aghast at this appearance and laments the fact that the beautiful body of his wife "from virginity" had been destroyed, and that he, whom the whole nation had honored, is now humiliated, having become a laughing-stock (Acts Thom. 114–115).⁴⁶ Although this story is set in an exotic place from the reader's perspective (India), it is reasonable to suppose that the author is nevertheless here evoking emotions that most male readers of the target audience could relate to—shame at the shaven appearance of one's wife.⁴⁷

It is therefore likely that most Corinthian congregants would have agreed with Paul that a shaven or shorn head on a woman was αἰσχρόν—ugly and shameful⁴⁸—in which case they would have had to reevaluate their reasoning for calling on all to pray and prophesy "uncovered" of the head. That is, even though some of the Corinthian congregants may have thought that in requiring all to pray and prophesy with nothing on the head, they were following Paul's "traditions" in the name of unity, they now had to contend with Paul's corrective that true uniformity in regards to the appearances of heads—that all appear as men—would not lead to

---

⁴⁵ This is the thesis of Susan Myers regarding the provenance and dating of *Acts of Thomas*. See, Susan E. Myers, "Revisiting Preliminary Issues in the Acts of Thomas," *Apocrypha* 17 (2006): 95–112. Jan Bremmer has also dated the book to the third century, and has suggested Edessa to be the most likely place of its composition. Jan N. Bremmer, "The *Acts of Thomas*: Place, Date and Women," in *The Apocryphal Acts of Thomas*, ed. Jan N. Bremmer (Leuven: Peeters, 2001), 74–77.

⁴⁶ I have followed the edition of Han J. W. Drijvers here: "The Acts of Thomas," in *New Testament Apocrypha*, ed. Wilhelm Schneemelcher, trans. R. McL. Wilson (Louisville, KY: Westminster John Knox, 2003), 2:322–411.

⁴⁷ Antti Marjanen has suggested that a cropped head on a woman signaled that the woman had "shut herself outside the ordinary female ways of life, such as marriage and child-bearing. Thus, it clearly meant denial of all sexual life." Antti Marjanen, *The Woman Jesus Loved: Mary Magdalene in the Nag Hammadi Library and Related Documents* (New York: Brill, 1996), 48. If that was the case, a woman cutting off her hair would most certainly be humiliating to the woman's husband.

⁴⁸ Suetonius relays how Augustus had an actor by the name of Stephanio, a Roman citizen, beaten with rods and banished because he had provided a service to a matron—a married woman—who had cut her hair short in a boyish manner (*in puerilem habitum circumtonsam matronam*). Suetonius explains that Augustus did this to curb the licentiousness (*licentia*) of actors (*Aug.* 45.4). Thus, it appears that in Roman society, it may have been considered shameful for a Roman citizen to even associate with a short-haired woman.

the desired outcome, but to shame for all involved. I propose, therefore, that 1 Cor 11:2–16 should be read as: a) Paul's refutation of the Corinthian position that all should pray and prophesy "uncovered"; and b) his explanation of why in praying and prophesying the ideal is not uniform appearance, but rather distinction between the sexes.

It is important to note that in regards to the appearance of men's heads, Paul is very specific about what is shameful—"having down from the head"—but in regards to the appearance of women's heads, Paul is much more general in his language: κατακαλύπτω, for example, does not specify the nature of the head-covering. If Paul's choice of language here is intentional, then we could argue that in principle, Paul had no issue with men donning other head-coverings during praying and accessing of divine (fore)knowledge, but that his sole concern was with *capite velato*—with the garment hanging down from the head. And conversely, the lack of specification in regards to the nature of women's head-coverings may suggest that Paul left that up to each individual to decide based on their social standing, cultural belonging, age, and marital status. The main principle for Paul seems to be that an "uncovered" head on a woman—one that is stripped of everything—shames a woman herself[49] and a woman's metaphorical head—the man, whether it be her husband, father, or owner[50]—and that this is universally so. However, Paul's solution of "let her be covered" should not therefore be read as a command for all women to be meticulously covered in the manner of Dio Chrysostom's fantasy (see above), but as a call to let women keep their heads appropriately adorned

---

[49] As Alicia Batten points out, "adornment was a means by which females could assert their standing (as well as that of their husband) and seek honor in the community." Batten, "Neither Gold nor Braided Hair," 490.

[50] Some have argued that the words ἀνήρ and γυνή in 1 Cor 11:3–5 should only (or principally) be understood in the sense of "husband" and "wife," and so Paul's instructions in regards to women's head-coverings only (or principally) address married women whose metaphorical heads are their own husbands. E.g., Gail Paterson Corrington, "The 'Headless Woman': Paul and the Language of the Body in 1 Cor 11:2–16," *PRSt* 18 (1991): 225; Keener, *Paul, Women and Wives*, 35–36; Dunn, *The Theology of Paul the Apostle*, 591; Winter, *After Paul Left Corinth*, 126–27; Preston T. Massey, "Gender Versus Marital Concerns: Does 1 Corinthians 11:2–16 Address the Issues of Male/Female or Husband/Wife?" *TynBul* 64 (2013): 239–56; Gardner, *1 Corinthians*, 480. However, I take ἀνήρ and γυνή here to be more general references to "man" and "woman." So also, Conzelmann, *1 Corinthians*, 184; Finney, "Honour, Head-coverings and Headship," 50–51; Fee, *First Corinthians: Revised*, 560–61. Yet, Jorunn Økland's point, that even though γυνή can refer to any woman, the paradigmatic γυνή in ancient literature is "wife," is well worth keeping in mind. Økland, *Women in Their Place*, 14. On this, see also, Fitzmyer, *First Corinthians*, 413.

during praying and prophesying in relation to their social standing, marital status, age, and *ethnos*—but most importantly, in relation to the honor of their metaphorical head.⁵¹ And while for some women this may have meant a meticulous covering of the head, for others it may have only meant keeping their hair done up with the aid of hair accessories in a manner appropriate for their social status (e.g., Roman girls and their *vittae*).⁵²

5.2.3 Summary

Based on the above presented evidence of men's and women's head-covering practices in antiquity, and on the discussion so far of Paul's argument in 1 Cor 11:2–6, I propose, therefore, the following *Sitz im Leben* to have given rise to this passage: during his initial stay in Corinth, Paul discouraged the performance of *capite velato*, but having departed, he heard (or read) reports about certain developments in regards to the ban on *capite velato* that disturbed him. On the one hand, some Corinthian Christians of Roman background may have forcefully counter-argued against Paul's initial instructions, while others may have taken him seriously to the

---

⁵¹ Kelly Olson notes that it was a common assumption in ancient literature that "women dressed to please men." Olson, *Dress and the Roman Woman*, 108. Thus, a married woman's clothing in relation to her head, for example, depended a lot on her husband's wishes. Consider, for example, the following anecdote told by Paul's contemporary Valerius Maximus: "Rugged too was the marital brow of C. Sulpicius Galus. He divorced his wife because he learned that she had walked abroad with head uncovered (*capite aperto*). The sentence was abrupt, but there was reason behind it. 'To have your good looks approved,' says he, 'the law limits you to my eyes only. For them assemble the tools of beauty, for them look your best, trust to their closer familiarity. Any further sight of you, summoned by needless incitement, has to be mired in suspicion and crimination'" (*Memorable Doings and Sayings*, 6.3.10 [Shackleton Bailey]). While this Gallus lived in the early second century BCE and Valerius Maximus deems his punishment of divorce in the case of his wife's public appearance with an uncovered head overly harsh, the sentiment expressed here that a woman's beauty should only be for the eyes of her husband may have been shared by many first-century men, which would have then influenced how their wives dressed. At the same time, however, Carolyn Osiek and Margaret MacDonald have argued that veiling proper was much less common in Rome during the first century CE than elsewhere in the empire, and also less common than it had been in prior times. They argue that evidence shows that beginning with the first century BCE, the independence and public visibility of Roman women had been growing not only in Rome but also in the provinces, and this influenced how women dressed for public. Carolyn Osiek and Margaret Y. MacDonald, *A Woman's Place: House Churches in Earliest Christianity* (Minneapolis: Fortress Press, 2006), 8, 23–24. While this may have indeed been a general trend at the time of Paul, it does not mean that it was a universal one.

⁵² As David Garland notes, "the command 'let her be covered' (11:6) communicates different things in different cultures." Garland, *1 Corinthians*, 510.

point that they had implemented (or had attempted to do so) a rule that all, regardless of their sex, *ethnos*, or social status, should pray and access divine (fore)knowledge with absolutely nothing on their heads. Since in all likelihood such developments would have caused great disturbance among particularly non-Roman women of the congregation (and their male relations),[53] Paul needed to defend his initial "tradition," while at the same time curbing the excessive application of it. In his proposed solution to mitigate the problems that the Corinthian Christ-followers had with the ban on *capite velato* and its application, Paul presented the idea of hierarchy of heads, which then allowed him to argue that *capite velato*, if performed by men, shamed Christ, while a completely uncovered head on a woman shamed man (and herself). Thus, while *capite velato* was not fitting for a Christ-follower, the opposite—uniformly uncovered heads during praying and prophesying—was not appropriate either. The Corinthians, therefore, had to compromise for the sake of unity over uniformity.

5.3 Because of Creation: First Supportive Argument (1 Cor 11:7–10a)

In the rest of the passage of 1 Cor 11:2–16, Paul attempts to bolster his main argument with various supportive arguments, the number and variety of which may demonstrate that Paul lacked confidence in the ability of his main argument alone to convince the addressees. His first supportive argument focuses on the creational differences between men and women:

---

[53] Paul mentions two women with whom he may have been personally acquainted with, who seem to have been connected to the Corinthian congregation one way or another, and who may have been quite prominent: Chloe—from whose associates Paul receives word about the Corinthian frictions (1 Cor 1:11)—and Phoebe—who seems to have been a leader or a patroness of a Christ association in nearby Kenchreai, and to whom Paul may have entrusted the carrying of his letter to the Romans (Rom 16:1–2). We do not know Paul's relationship with Chloe nor whether Chloe herself was even a member of the Corinthian congregation, but Paul does seem to place a lot of trust in Phoebe, even commanding the Roman congregation to meet her every need. See discussion in, for example, Meeks, *The First Urban Christians*, 59–60. It is not unreasonable to suppose that if women like Phoebe—whom Paul valued and who seems to have held authority in an association of Christians and perhaps in the society at large—felt affronted by certain men (of lower status) wishing to strip them of their head-coverings or hair accessories during praying and prophesying, they would have made their feelings known to Paul, and that Paul would have taken the matter seriously.

5.3 Because of Creation: First Supportive Argument (1 Cor 11:7–10a)

Ἀνὴρ μὲν γὰρ οὐκ ὀφείλει κατακαλύπτεσθαι τὴν κεφαλὴν εἰκὼν καὶ δόξα θεοῦ ὑπάρχων· ἡ γυνὴ δὲ δόξα ἀνδρός ἐστιν. οὐ γάρ ἐστιν ἀνὴρ ἐκ γυναικὸς ἀλλὰ γυνὴ ἐξ ἀνδρός. καὶ γὰρ οὐκ ἐκτίσθη ἀνὴρ διὰ τὴν γυναῖκα ἀλλὰ γυνὴ διὰ τὸν ἄνδρα. διὰ τοῦτο ὀφείλει ἡ γυνὴ ἐξουσίαν ἔχειν ἐπὶ τῆς κεφαλῆς. (1 Cor 11:7–10a)

> For indeed, a man does not have an obligation to cover the head, being the image and honor of God, but the woman is the honor of man—for man is not of woman, but woman [is] from man, and man was not created for the woman, but woman for the man. For this reason, the woman is obliged to have authority over the head.

The μὲν γάρ at the beginning of this argument suggests that it was intended to provide immediate support to the preceding claim that *capite velato*, if performed by a man during praying and prophesying, shamed Christ, while a completely uncovered head on a woman during these same activities shamed men, and so both were inappropriate. Yet, these verses present a number of curiosities that have made it difficult for interpreters to draw precise connections between Paul's main argument and this supportive argument on creational differences. For example, while verse 3 introduces Christ as man's metaphorical head (in between God and man), who is directly shamed by what man does with his physical head, verse 7 omits Christ altogether, and draws a direct connection between man and God in relation to "honor"[54] (most interpreters argue that δόξα, which usually is translated as "glory," has the meaning of "honor" or "repute" in this context[55]).

Such a discrepancy may demonstrate that Paul only came up with this idea of the hierarchy of heads to deal with the particular problem of *capite velato* but that he otherwise thought like most ancients that (the male) humans bore the responsibility of honoring the gods directly. For example, just before Paul picks up the question about head-coverings, he calls on the Corinthians to do everything for the honor of God (πάντα εἰς δόξαν θεοῦ ποιεῖτε, 1 Cor 10:31). Thus, while this idea that Christ is man's immediate social superior may have worked for the specific point that man must not have a garment over the head during praying and prophesying, it does not appear that crucial for Paul in general. And it does seem that Paul is dealing with more general concepts regarding head-coverings in verses 7–9

---

[54] Several scholars have expressed surprise at this omission of Christ. E.g., Fee, *First Corinthians: Revised*, 568, 570.

[55] E.g., Corrington, "The 'Headless Woman'," 226; Keener, *Paul, Women and Wives*, 33; Horsley, *1 Corinthians*, 155; Thiselton, *The First Epistle to the Corinthians*, 835; Gillian Beattie, *Women and Marriage in Paul and His Early Interpreters* (New York: T&T Clark, 2005), 48; Fee, *First Corinthians: Revised*, 520; Jantsch, "Einführung," 33–35; Marshall, "Uncovering Traditions," 83.

than he is in verses 4–6.⁵⁶ For example, in his claim in verse 7, that a man is not obligated to cover the head, Paul uses the general verb κατακαλύπτω, as opposed to the more specific phrase κατὰ κεφαλῆς ἔχων used in verse 4. Thus, in verses 7–9, Paul may have moved beyond the specific contexts of praying and prophesying to argue in general terms that, given man's status in creation, he has no obligation⁵⁷ to cover his head with anything at any time—that whenever a man does cover his head, he should be under no coercion to do so, because he himself is "God's honor," and no covering of the head can enhance that honor.⁵⁸

Yet, whatever the exact reasons for omitting Christ in verses 7–9, Paul does seem to offer support here to the other idea presented in verses 3–6—that "the head of woman is the man" (which may therefore be his main aim here). That is, in Paul's understanding of the creation account that he presents in these verses, man is God's image and honor, while woman is man's honor, because she was created from man and for man. Thus, just like in verse 3, a woman is denied a direct link to God's honor or shame, her direct link is rather to man's honor or shame, and is so from the beginning. But as scholars point out, Paul does not seem to be referencing one particular creation account here, but is rather combining several ideas together into his own version of what happened at creation. Thus, for example, although LXX Gen 1:27 reads that God created *the human* or *humanity* (ὁ ἄνθρωπος) in his image as "male and female" (ἄρσεν καὶ θῆλυ ἐποίησεν αὐτούς), Paul seems to understand this from the perspective of LXX Gen 2, in which "the human" (ὁ ἄνθρωπος) is at first only a man, Adam, for whose pleasure and companionship a woman is created only after other creatures fail to satisfy the man's needs.⁵⁹ At the same time, however, LXX Gen 1–2 says nothing of δόξα ("honor")

---

⁵⁶ As Jason BeDuhn notes in regards to verses 7–9: "Paul has moved into very generic argumentation here." BeDuhn, "'Because of the Angels'," 306.

⁵⁷ The οὐκ ὀφείλει here is sometimes taken in the sense of "must not" or "ought not," but several scholars point out that it is better to understand οὐκ ὀφείλει here as "is not obligated to" or "is not under obligation to." E.g., Barrett, *First Epistle to the Corinthians*, 252; BeDuhn, "'Because of the Angels'," 300.

⁵⁸ This is especially so if we consider θεοῦ in δόξα θεοῦ as objective genitive. As John Paul Heil explains: "On the other hand, it [θεοῦ] can also be taken as an objective genitive, so that man is the 'glory of God' in the sense that as the man he was created to be he renders honor or gives glory to the Creator." Heil, *The Rhetorical Role of Scripture*, 181.

⁵⁹ See also, Thiselton, *The First Epistle to the Corinthians*, 834; Garland, *1 Corinthians*, 522–23; Jonathan D. Worthington, *Creation in Paul and Philo: The Beginning and Before*, WUNT 317 (Tübingen: Mohr Siebeck, 2011), 151–57; David Lincicum, "Genesis in Paul," in *Genesis in the New Testament*, ed. Maarten J. J. Menken and Steve Moyise, Library of New Testament Studies 466 (New York: Bloomsbury, 2012), 102; Fee, *First Corinthians: Revised*, 570.

5.3 Because of Creation: First Supportive Argument (1 Cor 11:7–10a)

in relation to creation, even though for Paul this is a very important idea here. Yet, other sources from Second Temple period do speak of Adam as God's glory and of woman as man's glory (often in connection to creation), and so it seems that Paul was influenced by such ruminations about creation and about creational differences.[60] Thus, while it is impossible to pinpoint one particular presentation of creation as the main source that Paul follows here, Paul's mix of ideas about creation seems intended to support the basic point made earlier, that there is an inherent difference in how men and women accrue shame and honor—the "pivotal cultural values in the Mediterranean"[61]— and how they distribute it.

Yet, what confuses scholars at this stage of Paul's argument is the conclusion that Paul draws from the above premise regarding creational differences, that "for this reason, a woman is obliged to have authority over the head" (1 Cor 11:10a). Considering that Paul's conclusion from the same premise regarding men is that they have no obligation to cover the head (1 Cor 11:7), we expect Paul to conclude the opposite regarding women—that they have an obligation to cover the head—but Paul does not do so. Rather, Paul seems to claim here that creational differences provide a woman with a prerogative (or even moral duty[62]) to maintain

---

[60] See, for example, Heil, *The Rhetorical Role of Scripture*, 173–74; Julie Newberry, "Paul's Allusive Reasoning in 1 Corinthians 11.7–12," *NTS* 65 (2019): 47; Luise Schottroff, *1 Corinthians*, trans. Everett R. Kalin (Stuttgart: Kohlhammer, 2022), 210–11.

[61] This phrase is from Zeba Crook, in whose assessment the veracity of this statement is commonly agreed to be "beyond question." Zeba Crook, "Honor, Shame, and Social Status Revisited," *JBL* 128 (2009): 591. However, what constituted "honor" and what constituted "shame" varied based on location, culture, social standing, gender, age, and so on. E.g., Richard L. Rohrbaugh, "Honor," in *The Ancient Mediterranean Social World: A Sourcebook*, ed. Zeba A. Crook (Grand Rapids: Eerdmans, 2020), 64, 66–67. But in any case, if it was perceived that one's honor had been breached, it was a very serious matter throughout the region. 1 Cor 11:2–16 suggests that Paul and (some of) the Corinthians had differing opinions about what constituted "honor" and what "shame" in the context of head-coverings, and that it was this lack of common ground on this matter that had then caused issues with the implementation of Paul's ban on *capite velato*.

[62] Both Jason BeDuhn and Joseph Fitzmyer point out that here the verb ὀφείλω has the connotation of "moral duty" or "moral debt." BeDuhn, "Because of the 'Angels'," 303; Fitzmyer, *First Corinthians*, 416.

control over her own (literal) head[63] or to have power over it on her own terms.[64] But how should this be understood in the context in which Paul also communicates the command "let her be covered" (1 Cor 11:6)? If covering the head is ideal, how can a woman exercise control over her own head?

Due to these apparent difficulties in reconciling 1 Cor 11:10a with 1 Cor 11:5–6, a number of scholars reject the most natural meaning of διὰ τοῦτο ὀφείλει ἡ γυνὴ ἐξουσίαν ἔχειν ἐπὶ τῆς κεφαλῆς, and find ways to read the phrase as expressing the need for a woman to have a head-covering on, whether as a sign of someone else's

---

[63] Hans Förster has recently proposed that "head" in 1 Cor 11:10a should also be understood in its metaphorical sense as in 1 Cor 11:5, and so Paul's point here is that because of creational differences, women have (sexual) control over men (their metaphorical heads). For this reason, they should be covered during praying and prophesying in order not to exercise that (sexual) control over praying and prophesying men. Hans Förster, "The 'Power on the Head' of a Woman: A New Appraisal of 1 Corinthians 11:10 and its Variants," in *The New Testament in Antiquity and Byzantium: Traditional and Digital Approaches to its Texts and Editing; A Festschrift for Klaus Wachtel*, ed. H. A. G. Houghton, David C. Parker, and Holger Strutwolf, ANTF (Boston: Walter de Gruyter, 2019), 135–46. Despite its novelty, however, the argument fails to convince for the simple reason that if "head" in 1 Cor 11:10 is taken as metaphorical, so should the parallel "head" in 1 Cor 11:7 be taken as metaphorical, but it makes little sense for Paul to argue that men are not obligated to cover *Christ* because they themselves are the image and honor of God. It is much more likely, therefore, that 1 Cor 11:10 refers to a woman's literal head.

[64] Many biblical scholars have pointed out that this is the most natural meaning of ὀφείλει ἡ γυνὴ ἐξουσίαν ἔχειν ἐπὶ τῆς κεφαλῆς, despite how odd it sounds in the context in which Paul has also given the imperative "let her be covered" (1 Cor 11:6). Thus, for example, Craig Keener argues that the "only normal way to read the Greek phrase is to read it that the woman has 'authority over her own head,'" and so Paul here "emphasizes that it is the woman's right to choose what she will wear" (*Paul, Women and Wives*, 38); Jason BeDuhn asserts that ἐξουσία in such a grammatical construct suggests "the individual's right and freedom to act, the individual's control over objects, persons, or situations" ("Because of the 'Angels'," 303); David Garland claims that what "best fits standard Greek grammar" here is the option in which 'authority' means 'the right to do something' or 'to have control,' and ἐπί plus the genitive means 'over.' This option takes the phrase to mean that the woman is 'to have authority over her head': that is, she is to exercise control over her head or to have control of her head" (*1 Corinthians*, 525); Joseph Fitzmyer points out that "in all the other instances [in the NT] it [the grammatical construct ἐξουσίαν ἔχειν] has an act[ive] meaning, 'have the right to control something or do something'" (*First Corinthians*, 417); Julie Newberry proposes that "ἔχειν ἐξουσίαν ἐπί refers to the woman's own exercise of authority, either in controlling her head/hair by covering/binding it or in having the right/authority to cover or uncover her head as she chooses" ("Paul's Allusive Reasoning," 51); and Luise Schotroff understands ἐξουσία here as "the power that women have to deal responsibly with their own heads" (*1 Corinthians*, 210). See also, Fee, *First Corinthians: Revised*, 575–76; Westfall, *Paul and Gender*, 34–36.

5.3 Because of Creation: First Supportive Argument (1 Cor 11:7–10a)

(e.g., her husband's) authority over her[65] or as a symbol of her own authority to perform certain tasks, such as prophesying or praying in public, that she otherwise cannot perform.[66] However, nowhere in 1 Cor 11:2–16 is a woman's head-covering treated as a sign or a symbol of something else, and so Paul does not provide us with the vocabulary that would allow us to amend the text of 1 Cor 11:10 to include the word "sign" or "symbol" in it.[67] Thus, rather than amending the text to make it fit with this or that hypothesis, we must allow the text to have its most natural meaning and amend our hypotheses in response to that.

If we allow 1 Cor 11:10a to read that a woman must have control over her own head, then it implies that this power had been taken from women of the Corinthian congregation.[68] Thus, the most natural way of reading 1 Cor 11:10a aligns well

---

[65] E.g., Margaret E. Thrall, *I and II Corinthians* (New York: Cambridge University Press, 1965), 80; D'Angelo, "Veils, Virgins, and the Tongues," 391–92; Winter, *After Paul Left Corinth*, 131.

[66] This view gained ascendancy after the 1964 publication of Morna D. Hooker's influential article on 1 Cor 11:10, in which the argument was made that Paul found head-coverings on a woman during praying or prophesying necessary because: a) given that a woman was man's glory, the head-covering functioned as concealment of man's glory in the presence of God; and b) the head-covering served as a sign to all that a woman had the right to prophesy and pray in public. Morna D. Hooker, "Authority on Her Head: An Examination of I Cor. xi. 10," *NTS* 10 (1964): 415–16. Hooker's argument finds endorsement in, for example, Barrett, *First Epistle to the Corinthians*, 254–55; Bruce, *1 and 2 Corinthians*, 106; Dunn, *The Theology of Paul the Apostle*, 590; and (less directly) Watson, "The Authority of the Voice," 525. See also, Hurley, "Did Paul Require Veils?" 208. Dale Martin has, on the other hand, suggested that the head-covering on a woman served as a sign of both, her own authority (to veil herself), as well as her subordination. Dale B. Martin, *The Corinthian Body* (New Haven: Yale University Press, 1995), 246. And Anthony Thiselton has expanded Hooker's thesis by suggesting that not only was a head-covering on a woman a sign of her authority to prophesy or pray, but it also allowed a woman the chance to go anywhere in security; without head-coverings, women were vulnerable. Thiselton, *The First Epistle to the Corinthians*, 839.

[67] The editors of the NRSV have also come to realize this. The original NRSV (1989) translates 1 Cor 11:10 as "for this reason a woman ought to have a symbol of authority on her head," but the recently updated version (NRSVue, 2021) omits "a symbol of," and suggests in a footnote that the phrase "ought to have authority over her head" should be understood in a sense of "have freedom of choice regarding her head."

[68] Some have argued that 1 Cor 11:10a suggests that women themselves had lost control over their heads, and so the phrase should be read as Paul's demand for women to regain control over their heads. E.g., L. J. Lietaert Peerbolte, "Man, Woman, and the Angels in 1 Cor 11:2–16," in *The Creation of Man and Woman: Interpretations of the Biblical Narratives in Jewish and Christian Traditions*, ed. Gerard P. Luttikhuizen (Boston: Brill, 2000), 87. While this is a possible

with the hypothesis I have provided so far in regards to the *Sitz im Leben* behind 1 Cor 11:2–16, without creating a contradiction with verses 5–6. That is, I have argued that 1 Cor 11:2–6 suggests that certain influential members of the Corinthian congregation wished to strip everything off of women's heads during praying and prophesying—a development that Paul found problematic—and so 1 Cor 11:10a can be read as Paul's continued affirmation that women have the right to decide for themselves how to dress their heads in relation to honor, and that they should not be coerced into completely uncovering their heads (implied in verse 6, see above). It should also be pointed out that Paul's language here at verse 10 may be purposefully vague, as he may not want to specify *how* women should dress their heads, given the variance based on culture or ethnicity, marital status, or age. However, as demonstrated above, at least the (elite) married women would have wanted to keep something in their hair or on their heads whenever in public, so Paul's vague statement, that a woman has authority over her head, would have been heard by these women in the context of this conflict over *capite velato* as a permission to keep dressing their hair and heads as they had been used to in response to societal or cultural expectations, which for them included veils and garments as head-coverings. Thus, Paul's main point in 1 Cor 11:7–10a appears to be that, due to creational differences, men have no obligation to cover their heads because they themselves are the honor of God, and women should not be coerced into stripping their heads of everything, because they have the right to dress their heads (and hair) appropriately in relation to the honor of their metaphorical head[69] (which could mean different things in different circumstances). In this sense, 1 Cor 11:7–10a provides a fitting continuation to the arguments of 1 Cor 11:2–6, despite some differences in emphasis.

5.4 "Because of the Angels" (1 Cor 11:10b)

The phrase "because of the angels" (διὰ τοὺς ἀγγέλους, 1 Cor 11:10b), that immediately follows the above-discussed argument on creational differences (1 Cor 11:7–10a), is without a doubt the most enigmatic element in the whole of 1 Cor 11:2–16.

---

connotation of "to have authority over," it seems that the main emphasis is rather on a woman's ability to do as is fitting in regards to her head (as discussed above), which suggests that some *external* forces were preventing women from doing so.

[69] Julie Newberry has suggested, for example, that the διὰ τοῦτο at the beginning of 1 Cor 11:10a refers specifically back to the claim that woman is man's honor (verse 7). Newberry, "Paul's Allusive Reasoning," 52. If so, there is an intimate connection between the idea that a woman must have authority over her head and her status as man's honor.

The abruptness with which this short phrase enters the argument, coupled with the lack of any explanatory remarks, makes it very difficult to understand its purpose and meaning in Paul's overall reasoning about head-coverings during praying and prophesying. While the διά here suggests that it is somehow connected to the previous argument, the connection is not obvious. What have "the angels" got to do with a woman's obligation to have authority over the head? Or with creational differences? Or with head-coverings? Besides, "angel" is not a self-explanatory term, as it can refer to widely different beings, for which reason the definition must be gleaned from the context, but Paul has left no obvious clues regarding the identity of "the angels" in the context of 1 Cor 11:2–16 (although he clearly expects the Corinthians to understand his reference[70]). There are thus a number of equally appealing scholarly proposals regarding the identity of "the angels" in 1 Cor 11:10b, and in this section, we will examine the most popular ones in order to determine whether one or another of these suggestions makes the most sense in light of the hypothesis that I have thus far provided.

5.4.1 "The Angels" as "the Watchers"

One of the earliest and most enduring proposals identifies "the angels" in 1 Cor 11:10b with the beings referenced in Gen 6:1–4, who mated with "the daughters of men." In the Hebrew text (MT) these beings are described as בני־האלהים—"sons of the god(s)"—and some versions of the LXX translate the phrase literally: οἱ υἱοὶ τοῦ θεοῦ. However, the Greek translation of Gen 6:2 preserved in Codex Alexandrinus (fifth century CE), for example, has instead οἱ ἄγγελοι τοῦ θεοῦ ("the angels of God").[71] It is likely that this rendering was influenced by the Second Temple Enochian tradition (e.g., *Book of the Watchers* and *Jubilees*), which developed the brief reference made to בני־האלהים in Gen 6:1–4 into a more extensive narrative about angelic beings known as "the Watchers,"[72] how they lusted after human

---

[70] There are three other (passing) references to "angels" in 1 Cor, and so Kevin Sullivan wonders whether "the cumulative effect of the four Corinthian passages might suggest more than a passing interest in the presence of angels in the community." Kevin Sullivan, *Wrestling with Angels: A Study of the Relationship Between Angels and Humans in Ancient Jewish Literature and the New Testament* (Boston: Brill, 2004), 170. If so, Paul may have held prolonged discussions with the Corinthians about "the angels," and for this reason expects his brief and passing reference in this context to be intelligible to them, but we simply do not know.

[71] Susan Brayford, *Genesis*, Septuagint Commentary Series (Boston: Brill, 2007), 260.

[72] For a fuller list of writings from the Second Temple period that reference this motif see, for example, Loren T. Stuckenbruck, *The Myth of Rebellious Angels: Studies in Second Temple Judaism and New Testament Texts*, WUNT 335 (Tübingen: Mohr Siebeck, 2014), 2.

women and how they corrupted humanity as a result.[73] These ideas about angels were also popular in certain circles of early Christianity, as evidenced most clearly, for example, by the *Pseudo-Clementine Homilies*.[74]

Some biblical scholars have argued, therefore, that given these popular ideas about the lustful angels, one of Paul's worries with women praying or prophesying without head-coverings was that it allowed these lustful (or evil) angelic beings access to the congregation through the uncovered heads of women when they were in an ecstatic state, and thus head-coverings on women were for Paul prophylactic measures against such unwelcome intrusions (or intruders).[75] However, while there is no denying that "the angels" in 1 Cor 11:10b can, in principle, be defined as the Watchers of the Enochian tradition, there are a number of problems with this line of interpretation. First, it requires us to read διὰ τοῦτο ὀφείλει ἡ γυνὴ ἐξουσίαν ἔχειν ἐπὶ τῆς κεφαλῆς in 1 Cor 11:10a as saying that women have an obligation to

---

[73] Brayford, *Genesis*, 261. See also, John J. Collins, "Watcher," in *Dictionary of Deities and Demons in the Bible*, ed. Karel van der Toorn, Bob Becking, and Pieter W. van der Horst, second edition (Leiden: Brill, 1999), 893–95; Annette Yoshiko Reed, *Fallen Angels and the History of Judaism and Christianity: The Reception of Enochic Literature* (New York: Cambridge University Press, 2005), 27–28, 30–34.

[74] For a summary of relevant passages see, Matt Jackson-McCabe, *Jewish Christianity: The Making of the Christianity-Judaism Divide*, AYBRL (New Haven: Yale University Press, 2020), 157–58. These ideas are also present in, for example, Acts Thom. 32; *The Pseudo-Titus Epistle*, see, Aurelio de Santos Otero, "The Pseudo-Titus Epistle," in *New Testament Apocrypha*, ed. Wilhelm Schneemelcher, trans. R. McL. Wilson (Louisville, KY: Westminster John Knox, 2003), 2:60; *The Secret Book According to John*, see, Bentley Layton, trans., *The Gnostic Scriptures*, second edition, AYBRL (New Haven: Yale University Press, 2021), 59; and a number of early church fathers (see, Reed, *Fallen Angels*, 149). In some of the so-called gnostic texts, such as the *Reality of Rulers* and *On the Origin of the World*, certain angelic beings are also described as lusting after the first created woman, Eve, so much so that they rape her. See, Layton, *The Gnostic Scriptures*, 100; Hans-Gebhard Bethge and Bentley Layton, trans., "On the Origin of the World (II,5 and XIII,2)," in *The Nag Hammadi Library in English*, ed. James M. Robinson (New York: HarperCollins, 1990), 182–83.

[75] I have tried to summarize the various nuances of this line of argument, although not all of the proponents of such an identification of "the angels" in 1 Cor 11:10b would subscribe to the entirety of my summary. But see, Conzelmann, *1 Corinthians*, 189; Corrington, "The 'Headless Woman'," 230–31; Martin, *The Corinthian Body*, 242–44, 248; Lietaert Peerbolte, "Man, Woman, and the Angels," 88–91; Loren T. Stuckenbruck, "Why Should Women Cover Their Heads Because of the Angels? (1 Corinthians 11:10)," *SCJ* 4 (2001): 232; Beattie, *Women and Marriage in Paul*, 49; Guy Williams, *The Spirit World in the Letters of Paul: A Critical Examination of the Role of Spiritual Beings in the Authentic Pauline Epistles*, FRLANT 231 (Göttingen: Vandenhoeck & Ruprecht, 2009), 270–79. See also, Troels Engberg-Pedersen, *Cosmology and Self in the Apostle Paul: The Material Spirit* (New York: Oxford University Press, 2010), 93–94.

wear head-coverings, but as discussed above, this is not what the text says. Rather, the most natural meaning of this phrase presents a woman with a prerogative to have control over her head. And while for some women this may have meant meticulous covering of the head, this was not necessarily the case for all women that Paul addresses. Thus, the question here should not be as to why a woman should be covered of the head because of the angels, but as to why a woman should have control over the head because of the angels. And the latter concern is not as easily answered by identifying "the angels" as "the Watchers."

Second, up to this point, Paul has not identified an uncovered head on a woman as an object of lust, but he has rather deemed it αἰσχρόν, ugly and an object of shame—repulsive rather than sexually arousing. Thus, the main concern with an uncovered head on a woman seems to lie elsewhere than it being an object of lust. And third, "the Watchers" line of interpretation supposes that Paul required women to be so meticulously covered that even the angelic beings would not be aroused (let alone humans), but there is no evidence that this is how women generally dressed their heads. It seems that even if head-coverings were worn in antiquity by women, facial features were still observable in most cases, if not also part or most of the hairdo (see Chapter 2 and above). Besides, the Enochian tradition regarding the בני־האלהים does not specify that the Watchers lusted after women specifically because of their uncovered heads. On the contrary, in some presentations of this myth, the Watchers became enamored with human women because of how they adorned their heads (presumably with jewelry and various headgear, e.g., T. Reu. 5:6–7). Thus, we cannot be sure that Paul would have thought of covered heads (but uncovered faces) as a universal solution to the problem of angelic lust.

5.4.2 "The Angels" as Guardians of Worship

Another popular line of interpretation takes "the angels" here to be holy beings, who are the guardians of worship (order). They thus ensure either that "conventions of modesty" are followed in the worship of God[76] or that worship of God is conducted in an appropriate manner (men with uncovered heads and women with covered heads).[77] Yet, while there is no doubt that in certain contexts, "the angels" were understood as holy beings who participated with humans in the worship of God, it is not clear that this is what Paul has in mind here. First, the immediately preceding argument (1 Cor 11:7–10a) does not address the idea of "worship" but

---

[76] E.g., Garland, *1 Corinthians*, 529.

[77] E.g., Gardner, *1 Corinthians*, 494.

rather creational differences and how these relate to honor and shame. Second, while the wider context does indeed speak of the activities of praying and prophesying, I have argued that Paul does not confine these acts of worship to the Christian gatherings only, but that he has in mind other venues as well, such as the "temples of idols," where these activities were performed (with head-coverings on, see Chapter 3). Thus, it is unlikely that Paul thought of angels here as holy beings of God, who would also frequent the temples of idols to observe whether praying and accessing of divine (fore)knowledge was performed there *capite velato* or not, or whether women were stripped of their customary head-coverings or not.

A more nuanced argument in this line of interpretation can be found in the works of Joseph Fitzmyer. Taking the Qumranic references to angelic presence in the assemblies of God as the starting point, Fitzmyer proposes that with "the angels," Paul has in mind those holy beings who were imagined to ensure that no bodily defects, which included the uncovered heads of women, appeared in the presence of God.[78] However, there is no evidence that Paul considered uncovered heads on women bodily defects that should not come into the presence of God (nor is there evidence that even the Qumranites did so).[79] In fact, there is no evidence that Paul considered *any* bodily defect (lameness, blindness, etc.) unworthy of God's presence, as some of the Qumranites seem to have done.

Cecilia Wassen, however, has offered a more comprehensive treatment of 1 Cor 11:10b in light of the Dead Sea Scrolls, taking into account not only Qumranic references to angelic presence in God's assemblies, but also the references to angelic presence at creation, which is the theme of 1 Cor 11:7–10a. In light of these references, Wassen proposes that in 1 Cor 11:10b, Paul calls on the congregants to imitate the appearance of angels, their holy co-worshipers, after whose likeness the first male, Adam, was created. Given, then, that long hair was the most visible distinguishing feature of the females, Paul's point in 1 Cor 11:10 is that the Corinthian female congregants should have their long hair covered in order to appear more like the male angels who were present.[80] While Wassen rightly takes the theme of creation as the immediate context of διὰ τοὺς ἀγγέλους seriously, her conclusion

---

[78] Joseph A. Fitzmyer, "A Feature of Qumran Angelology and the Angels of I Cor. XI. 10," *NTS* 4 (1957): 48–58. See also, Fitzmyer, *First Corinthians*, 419.

[79] See also, Williams, *The Spirit World in the Letters of Paul*, 269–70.

[80] Cecilia Wassen, "'Because of the Angels': Reading 1 Cor 11:2–16 in Light of Angelology in the Dead Sea Scrolls," in *The Dead Sea Scrolls in Context: Integrating the Dead Sea Scrolls in the Study of Ancient Texts*, ed. Armin Lange, Emanuel Tov, and Matthias Weigold (Boston: Brill, 2011), 2:748–54.

nevertheless presumes that what Paul says in 1 Cor 11:10a is that women must be so meticulously covered that their long hair cannot be seen, but as I have repeatedly pointed out, this is not what 1 Cor 11:10a says. If we follow the most natural meaning of 1 Cor 11:10a—that women ought to have control over their heads—then it makes little sense to argue that this is so because they must imitate the physical appearance of the male angels.

5.4.3 "The Angels" as Creators or as Guardians of Creation Order

Given that 1 Cor 11:7–10a focuses on creation and creational differences, many biblical scholars have taken the appended διὰ τοὺς ἀγγέλους as continuation of that theme. One strand in this line of interpretation suggests that "the angels" here are a reference to "guardians of creation order"—holy beings of God who ensure that creational differences fixed at creation are maintained in the congregations of God.[81] However, it is not clear how such an understanding of "the angels" fits with Paul's preceding argument. This identification of "the angels" as guardians of creation order suggests that we should take διὰ τοὺς ἀγγέλους as an appended threat or warning, rather than as an explanation. But it seems to me that the force of διά in relation to the preceding argument is more explanatory than threatening. Besides, it is unclear how the angels should be imagined as maintaining that creation order, particularly outside of the Christian assemblies.

For this reason, a more promising hypothesis in regards to the identity of "the angels" in 1 Cor 11:10b in relation to creation posits them to have been active participants in the creation of humanity, particularly in the "rupture" of the original *Anthropos* into male and female.[82] Several early Christian texts or thinkers attribute the creation of humans to the activity of some type of angelic beings, rather than to God (or Christ).[83] The most fascinating example of this is found in the *Acts of*

---

[81] E.g., Hooker, "Authority on Her Head," 412–13; Thrall, *I and II Corinthians*, 80; Barrett, *First Epistle to the Corinthians*, 254; Bruce, *1 and 2 Corinthians*, 106; Böhm, "1 Kor 11,2–16," 228–29.

[82] So BeDuhn, "Because of the 'Angels'," 308–9.

[83] For example, *The Secret Book According to John* lists a number of angelic beings who were each responsible for the creation of one particular part of the body—Barbar for the right nipple, Kharkha for the left knee, and so on—or for the creation of particular traits or abilities of humans—Arkhendekta for perception, and so on. Interestingly, at the end of this creation account, *The Secret Book According to John* refers its readers to the *Book of Zoroaster* for more information on these angelic beings. See, Layton, *The Gnostic Scriptures*, 45–51. *Gospel of Judas* also attributes the creation of Adam and Eve to certain angelic beings. See, Bart D. Ehrman and Zlatko Pleše,

Paul, which in some manuscripts preserves a supposed letter of the Corinthian congregation to Paul and Paul's reply to it (commonly referred to as *3 Corinthians*). Some scholars date the composition of these apocryphal letters to as early as the beginning of the second century CE, and some early Christian circles attached great importance to this supposed correspondence of Paul with the Corinthians, as they incorporated these letters independently of the *Acts of Paul* into their versions of Christian Scriptures as authentically Pauline.[84]

In this correspondence, the Corinthians complain to Paul that certain men had come to Corinth, Simon and Cleobius, who had taught them, among other things, that "the world is not of God, but of the angels."[85] In his reply, "Paul" repeatedly emphasizes that God the Father is the creator of the world and of man, condemning all who say that "heaven and earth and all that in them is are not works of the Father" as "children of wrath," from whose teaching the Corinthians should flee.[86] Is it possible that the composer(s) of this fictional correspondence purposefully chose the Corinthian congregation as the community which struggled with the "correct" understanding of creation, because in the popular or historical imagination of the early Christians, the roots of understanding creation as an act of angels were traced to Corinth, particularly to Paul's communication with the Corinthians? If this were indeed the case, it would certainly strengthen the idea that both the original Paul and the original Corinthian Christians understood "the angels" in 1 Cor 11:10b as somehow responsible for the creational differences laid out in 1 Cor 11:7–10a. However, it is more likely that the forgers of this correspondence chose Corinth not because of any teachings associated with the original

---

The Apocryphal Gospels: Texts and Translations (New York: Oxford University Press, 2011), 407. And a claim is made by Clement of Alexandria that the early second-century Christian teacher Valentinus taught that the angels had created Adam, while Irenaeus claims that another early second-century Christian teacher, Basilides of Alexandria, taught that the angels had created the world and everything in it. See, Layton, *The Gnostic Scriptures*, 234–35, 423. Beliefs about the involvement of angelic beings in creation are also present in Qumran literature. E.g., Benjamin G. Wold, *Women, Men, and Angels: The Qumran Wisdom Document Musar LeMevin and Its Allusions to Genesis Creation Traditions* (Tübingen: Mohr Siebeck, 2005), 180–82.

[84] See, for example, Gerard Luttikhuizen, "The Apocryphal Correspondence with the Corinthians and the Acts of Paul," in *The Apocryphal Acts of Paul and Thecla*, ed. Jan N. Bremmer (Kampen, Netherlands: Kok Pharos, 1996), 75–81.

[85] I have followed Wilhelm Schneemelchers's translation of the *Acts of Paul* here. See, Wilhelm Schneemelcher, trans., "The Acts of Paul," in *New Testament Apocrypha*, ed. Wilhelm Schneemelcher, trans. R. McL. Wilson (Louisville, KY: Westminster John Knox, 2003), 2:237–63.

[86] Schneemelcher, "The Acts of Paul," 255.

Christian congregation there, but for the simple reason that the authentic Corinthian correspondence mentions several letters that had no longer survived, thus giving the forgery a higher chance of being accepted as authentic.[87]

Nevertheless, if we take Paul's mention of "the angels" in 1 Cor 11:10b as reference to angelic participation in the creation of man and woman, regardless of whether *3 Corinthians* has anything to do with the memory of the original congregation that Paul established, it would serve as a fairly sensible explanation for why a woman should have control over her head. That is, Paul's point would be that these creational differences, that set no obligation on a man to be covered of the head, but set an obligation on a woman to have control over her own head in relation to the honor of her metaphorical head (man), are due to the creative agency of angels—and not the product of some mishap of God—that still need to be respected. The problem with this line of interpretation, however, is that nowhere else does Paul attribute the creation of the world or of humans to angelic beings, and in the immediately following argument in 1 Cor 11:2–16, Paul unabashedly attributes the origin of everything (presumably also of creational differences) to God (τὰ δὲ πάντα ἐκ τοῦ θεοῦ, 1 Cor 11:12; cf. also Rom 1:25). Thus, while this line of reasoning perhaps best explains the connection between "the angels" and the preceding argument regarding creational differences, it is difficult to reconcile with Paul's immediately following claim that "everything is from God," and with Paul's overall theology of creation.

5.4.4 "The Angels" as Spies or Messengers

The basic meaning of ἄγγελος is "one that announces," and thus ἄγγελος can also be used in reference to human messengers or envoys (as, for example, in Jas 2:25). Some biblical scholars have argued, therefore, that "the angels" of 1 Cor 11:10b should not be read as a reference to divine or semi-divine beings but rather as a reference to certain people, who (may have) frequented the Christian gatherings in Corinth. Jerome Murphy-O'Connor has argued, for example, that Paul's point here is that "practices at Corinth should not shock envoys from other churches,"[88] while Bruce Winter has suggested that Paul warns the Corinthians here to be careful in following social conventions because of the governmental spies who

---

[87] Caleb Webster, "Trapped in a Forgerer's Rhetoric: *3 Corinthians*, Pseudepigraphy, and the Legacy of Ancient Polemics," in *"Non-Canonical" Religious Texts in Early Judaism and Early Christianity*, ed. Lee Martin McDonald and James H. Charlesworth (New York: T&T Clark, 2012), 156.

[88] Murphy-O'Connor, "1 Corinthians 11:2–16 Once Again," 271–72.

frequent their gatherings in search of compromising material.[89] While I do not agree with the hypotheses of either Murphy-O'Connor nor Winter as far as the *Sitz im Leben* behind 1 Cor 11:2–16 is concerned (see sections 1.4.8 and 1.6.8), their suggestion that we should think of "the angels" here in terms of human beings is worth considering.

For example, given that *capite velato* was an important Roman ritual gesture, addressing it negatively in a letter may have been a somewhat dangerous undertaking (especially for a provincial). If Paul worried that his letter(s) could end up at the hands of government officials, he would have worded his argument here in a way as to not appear seditious (could this be a reason why we have so many exegetical difficulties in 1 Cor 11:2–16?).[90] It may be, therefore, that at 1 Cor 11:10b, Paul uses ἄγγελος as a (pre-arranged?) code in reference to those who were hostile to Paul and to his cause, and who sought ways to shut down the Corinthian operation. Roman men ignoring *capite velato* and Roman, Greek, and Jewish women being stripped against their will of whatever they were wearing in their hair and on their heads would certainly have provided any hostile detractors with plenty of ammunition to eradicate the Christ-association of Corinth. We should keep in mind, for example, that if any of the Corinthian congregants argued for uniformity of appearance *whenever* one prayed or accessed divine knowledge, the rule would have also applied to wives of "unbelievers" during domestic devotions or social banquets. We can only imagine the horror and shame that a wife would have brought on her husband and on all the guests present if she unstripped her head completely for prayer in these circumstances. This certainly would have caused a

---

[89] Winter, *After Paul Left Corinth*, 136–38; Winter, *Roman Wives, Roman Widows*, 90. Winter's argument is endorsed in Blasi, *Social Science*, 68 n. 144.

[90] Quite a few biblical scholars have argued that Paul may have been wary of his letters ending up at the hands of Roman authorities, and so his letters should be read with this awareness. However, Laura Robinson has recently pointed out that "scholars have yet to find solid historical evidence that the first-century Roman world was the kind of environment where a private citizen such as Paul would be at risk for the surveillance and prosecution of [his] speech." Laura Robinson, "Hidden Transcripts? The Supposedly Self-Censoring Paul and Rome as Surveillance State in Modern Pauline Scholarship," *NTS* 67 (2021): 57. In conclusion of her own assessment of the available evidence in this regard, Robinson states that "[t]he evidence simply is not on our side if we wish to posit that Paul lived in fear that his words would be used against him in court." Robinson, "Hidden Transcripts?" 72. While I agree with this caution of Robinson, I would say that unlike most of what Paul writes about, 1 Cor 11:2–16 specifically addresses a *Roman* custom (and an important one at that), which some in the Corinthian congregation may have still practiced. Thus, there may be extra reason here for Paul to tread carefully.

scandal that would have made it very difficult for Christians to co-exist peacefully with their non-Christian neighbors.

Thus, it would make sense for Paul to address this concern at some point in 1 Cor 11:2–16, and 1 Cor 11:10b is a potential candidate for this. Paul's comments in 1 Cor 11:10 should in this case be read in the following sense: "because of creational differences, women are obligated to have control over their heads (in relation to the honor of man), and because of the hostile forces (who look for ways to rid themselves of our presence)." However, despite the appeal of this line of interpretation, it fits very awkwardly into the general flow of Paul's argument: Paul follows his account of creation and creational differences in 1 Cor 11:7–10a with an immediate qualification of this argument in 1 Cor 11:11–12 (see below), and an unexplained reference to governmental spies in the midst of it just seems too out of place, even for Paul. Besides, grasping all of the above-mentioned connotations from such a throwaway phrase seems like asking too much of his original addressees.

5.4.5 "The Angels" as Mediators

Another role that the angelic beings are given in Second Temple (and early Christian) literature is worth considering here: the angels as mediators of human prayers to god(s) and of divine (fore)knowledge to humans.[91] And this belief that certain (quasi-)divine beings (such as the *daimones*) communicated messages to humans (from gods) for the purpose of guidance (particularly through "signs") and human prayers to gods was also held in some ancient Greek and Roman circles, such as in certain philosophical schools.[92] While some biblical scholars have made note of this in their interpretation of 1 Cor 11:10,[93] this mediating role of angels has generally not been given the serious attention it deserves, even though Paul specifically addresses the activities of praying and accessing of divine (fore)knowledge in 1 Cor 11:2–16. Here we will, therefore, consider whether there are any possible reasons

---

[91] Many references could be given here, but compositions such as Daniel, Zechariah, 1 Enoch, Ascension of Isaiah, and Tobit stand out as particularly conspicuous examples of such angelic activity. Interestingly, the third-century Christian scholar Origen valued the book of Tobit precisely for what it taught about the angels, particularly that the angels were presented there as mediating the prayers of human beings to God. See, Daniel J. Harrington, "The Old Testament Apocrypha in the Early Church and Today," in *The Canon Debate*, eds. Lee Martin McDonald and James A. Sanders (Peabody, Ma: Hendrickson, 2002): 202.

[92] E.g., Dale B. Martin, *Inventing Superstition: From the Hippocratics to the Christians* (Cambridge, MA: Harvard University Press, 2004), 99–106.

[93] E.g., Lietaert Peerbolte, "Man, Woman, and the Angels," 90–91.

for why Paul would have wanted to highlight the mediating role of angels at this stage of the argument.

One possibility is that if by "the angels" Paul had in mind divine messengers, who mediated prayers and divine (fore)knowledge to and from God (or gods), and who were thought of as males, he may have wished to stress the idea that *whenever* and *wherever* humans prayed or accessed divine (fore)knowledge, they were in the presence of (male) messengers of divine origin who were ready to receive prayers to deliver to God or to impart some (fore)knowledge from God. Thus, a woman who had been stripped of her customary head-coverings during praying or accessing of divine (fore)knowledge was not only a source of shame for herself and for her husband, father, guardian, or owner, but also for the male divine messengers, who in these moments were at their service (just as a man shamed Christ, his lord, whenever he prayed or accessed divine knowledge *capite velato*). If this was indeed Paul's reasoning here, his claim that women must have control over their heads because of "the angels" makes sense—due to creational differences women must have the ability to dress their hair and heads in relation to the honor of their metaphorical head, because the mediating angels who are in communication with them also expect this.

The biggest problem with this line of interpretation regarding "the angels" is that Paul nowhere else attaches such a mediating role to angels. Rather, in regards to prayer and "prophesying," Paul considers "the Spirit" to have this mediating role (e.g., Rom 8:26; Gal 4:6; 1 Cor 12–14). Thus, we would have to assume that Paul had communicated this role of angels to the Corinthians either through a now lost letter or orally. However, given how prevalent this understanding of the *function* of angels was in Second Temple literature, and how ancient Romans and Greeks viewed (semi-)divine messenger figures, it seems like the idea of mediation should have been tacitly acknowledged as belonging to angelic activity by both Paul and his Corinthian addressees.

5.4.6 Summary Analysis

Given that "the angels" can be a reference to a number of different beings or to different roles of these beings, it is very difficult to make sense of διὰ τοὺς ἀγγέλους in its own right. Any definition of διὰ τοὺς ἀγγέλους has to be dependent on one's interpretation of the entirety of this passage on head-coverings, and especially on the preceding clause that a woman must have authority over the head. Since this preceding clause has often been interpreted as Paul's command for women to be meticulously covered of the head, the definitions of "the angels" have often focused on such beings for whom the uncovered heads of women would have been a problem one way or another (e.g., the Watchers, guardians of worship, etc.). However, if we take this preceding clause to be Paul's affirmation that women have the right to dress their heads as fitting in regards to the honor of their male relations, then these interpretations of "the angles" are inadequate. I propose that in the context of the *Sitz im Leben* that I have argued to be behind 1 Cor 11:2–16, it makes the most sense to take "the angels" in 1 Cor 11:10b as Paul's reference to the role of these (semi-)divine beings as mediators of prayers and divine knowledge. That is, it may be that Paul reminds the Corinthians that just like a man must be cognizant of the presence of Christ, his *kyrios*, when he prays or accesses divine (fore)knowledge, so must he be cognizant that when a woman prays or accesses divine (fore)knowledge, she interacts with divine male beings in whose presence she must have the right to dress as is befitting her. Paul may want to stress that the male angelic beings certainly do not require women to be stripped of their head-coverings and hair accessories in order for them to pray or to receive divine knowledge, so the Corinthian instigators should not argue for the contrary.

5.5 "Nevertheless": Paul's Qualification (1 Cor 11:11–12)

Paul follows his presentation of the creational differences with the following remark: "Nevertheless, neither woman without man nor man without woman in the Lord, because just as the woman [is] from the man, so also the man [is] through the woman, but all things [are] from God" (πλὴν οὔτε γυνὴ χωρὶς ἀνδρὸς οὔτε ἀνὴρ χωρὶς γυναικὸς ἐν κυρίῳ· ὥσπερ γὰρ ἡ γυνὴ ἐκ τοῦ ἀνδρός, οὕτως καὶ ὁ ἀνὴρ διὰ τῆς γυναικός· τὰ δὲ πάντα ἐκ τοῦ θεοῦ). Many biblical scholars have pointed out the strong adversative effect of πλήν that begins 1 Cor 11:11–12, and so these verses have been described as either Paul's corrective, qualification, mitigation, a caveat, clarification, concession, or the like in relation to the preceding 1 Cor 11:7–10.[94]

Torsten Jantsch has suggested that perhaps Paul added these words at the end of his argument on creational differences because of his fear that his ideas would be excessively applied by his addressees if not checked.[95] Considering that my hypothesis regarding the *Sitz im Leben* behind 1 Cor 11:2–16 posits that the whole of

---

[94] E.g., Engberg-Pedersen, "1 Corinthians 11:16," 683; Horsley, *1 Corinthians*, 155; Collins, *First Corinthians*, 403; Garland, *1 Corinthians*, 529; Wassen, "'Because of the Angels'," 750; Edsall, "Greco-Roman Costume," 144; Fee, *First Corinthians: Revised*, 577; Newberry, "Paul's Allusive Reasoning," 54.

[95] Jantsch, "Einführung," 54. See also, Watson, "The Authority of the Voice," 527.

this passage should be read as Paul's attempt to correct an excessive application of a tradition regarding praying and accessing of divine (fore)knowledge, Jantsch's suggestion seems reasonable. That is, if Paul had already experienced that some of his addressees were especially zealous in pursuing his teachings to extreme ends, he may have feared that this correction of his would be treated in the same way. Thus, Paul lets his audience know that "in the Lord" a woman is not separate (entity) from a man, and vice versa,[96] because neither can come into existence without the other, and because the origins of both are ultimately traced back to God. This would then have ideally served as a safeguard for Paul against anyone taking his argument, that man was created for the honor of God and woman for the honor of man, too far—for example, to the point of forcing women into doing *whatever* a man found "honorable" to him without any regard for a woman's own honor.[97]

5.6 Analogy from Nature: Second Supportive Argument (1 Cor 11:13–15)

After the above qualification, but before another supportive argument is given, Paul poses a rhetorical question: "Judge among yourselves: is it proper for an uncovered woman to pray to God?" (Ἐν ὑμῖν αὐτοῖς κρίνατε· πρέπον ἐστὶν γυναῖκα ἀκατακάλυπτον τῷ θεῷ προσεύχεσθαι;). As has often been pointed out, the question here is phrased in a way that it expects the addressees to give an unequivocal "no" for an answer.[98] In other words, Paul expects his readers to agree with him that it is improper or unseemly[99] for an "uncovered" (of the head) woman to pray to God.

---

[96] The basic meaning of the preposition χωρίς with the genitive is "without," but χωρίς with the genitive can also take the sense of "separate from" or "differently from" or "independently of" (LSJ, s.v. "χωρίς").

[97] Notice that "woman" begins both clauses in 1 Cor 11:11–12, whereas in the previous arguments, "man" is always discussed first (and so it is also in the next argument, see below). Perhaps it shows where Paul's emphasis lies in these verses—that *a woman* is not separate from man "in the Lord." Gordon Fee has also taken notice of this reversal and has suggested that this further demonstrates that 1 Cor 11:11–12 should be read as Paul's qualification of his previous argument. Fee, *First Corinthians: Revised*, 578.

[98] E.g., Barrett, *First Epistle to the Corinthians*, 256; Heil, *The Rhetorical Role of Scripture*, 186; Fee, *First Corinthians: Revised*, 581.

[99] It seems that already by the time of Cicero in the mid-first century BCE, the neuter participle form of the verb πρέπω that Paul employs in 1 Cor 11:13, πρέπον, was being used as a technical term for a particular form of conduct or way of life, and as the Greek equivalent to the Latin *decorum*. Cicero explains the meaning of *decorum* and πρέπον as follows: "For to employ reason

5.6 Analogy from Nature: Second Supportive Argument (1 Cor 11:13–15)

That being said, it is nevertheless noteworthy that Paul even raises such a rhetorical question at this stage of the argument. Does Paul's appeal to his addressees' own sense of propriety ("judge among yourselves"), right after a major qualification of an argument Paul himself has raised, show that Paul was not that confident in the persuasiveness of his supportive argument on creational differences? Perhaps, but regardless, the main takeaway here is that the way Paul phrases his rhetorical question suggests that Paul was at least confident that, if nothing else, his readers would have enough moral decency to conclude with him that it was not πρέπον for a woman to pray to God while stripped of everything off her head.

But just to be sure, Paul provides yet another supportive argument in demonstration of the validity of his position on praying and prophesying with or without head-coverings: "Does not the nature herself teach you that if a man has long hair, it is dishonorable to him, but if a woman has long hair, it is an honor to her? Because the hair has been given in place of a wraparound"[100] (οὐδὲ ἡ φύσις αὐτὴ

---

and speech rationally, to do with careful consideration whatever one does, and in everything to discern the truth and to uphold it—that is proper. To be mistaken, on the other hand, to miss the truth, to fall into error, to be led astray—that is as improper as to be deranged and lose one's mind. And all things just are proper; all things unjust like all things immoral, are improper" (Cicero, *Off.* 1.27 [93–94] [Miller]).

[100] "Wraparound" or "covering" such as an ancient mantle that could be thrown about the body and the head is the most well-attested meaning of the noun περιβόλαιον. Troy Martin has proposed, however, that περιβόλαιον in 1 Cor 11:15 should be understood in a sense of "testicle," and so Paul's point is that instead of testicles, which the men have (and cover up), women have been given long hair (which they need to cover up). Troy W. Martin, "Paul's Argument from Nature for the Veil in 1 Corinthians 11:13–15: A Testicle Instead of a Head Covering," *JBL* 123 (2004): 75–84. However, I think Martin has misread (or misrepresented) the primary sources that he uses to support his claim. For example, one of the main pieces of evidence that Martin refers to is a sentence found in a tragedy of Euripides (5th century BCE): ἐπεὶ δὲ σαρκὸς περιβόλαι' ἐκτησάμην ἡβῶντα (*Herc. fur.* 1269). In his literal translation of this phrase, Martin provides the following: "After I received [my] bags of flesh, which are the outward signs of puberty…". This is an acceptable translation, but Martin then says the following: "A dynamic translation of [this] clause would be: 'After I received my testicles (περιβόλαια), which are the outside signs of puberty.'" Martin, "Paul's Argument from Nature," 77. The problem here is that Martin has taken only half of the euphemism "coverings of flesh"—a more literal translation of σαρκὸς περιβόλαι'—as on its own representing the body parts "testicles," but this is a careless maneuver. We cannot isolate περιβόλαια here—in order for this word to have anything to do with "testicles," it has to remain in the genitival relationship with "flesh." On its own, περιβόλαια retains the meaning "coverings" or "wraparounds" also in this phrase from Euripides. Thus, this quote from Euripides does not prove that περιβόλαιον (singular!) was used on its own as a reference to "testicle,"

διδάσκει ὑμᾶς ὅτι ἀνὴρ μὲν ἐὰν κομᾷ ἀτιμία αὐτῷ ἐστιν, γυνὴ δὲ ἐὰν κομᾷ δόξα αὐτῇ ἐστιν; ὅτι ἡ κόμη ἀντὶ περιβολαίου δέδοται[101]). As discussed in Chapter 1, these verses (1 Cor 11:14–15) are thought by some interpreters to indicate the subject matter of the entire passage—length or style of hair. The main impetus for this position comes from the phrase ὅτι ἡ κόμη ἀντὶ περιβολαίου δέδοται, which is taken by these scholars to indicate that Paul here notifies his readers that he has been talking about hair "instead of" (ἀντὶ) head-coverings all along (see section 1.4).

However, as I have already demonstrated in section 1.4.8, the so-called hair theory regarding verses 4–6 is not viable, and so verses 14–15 must have a different

---

and Martin provides no other primary source in which περιβόλαιον on its own is so used. Besides, in a text that speaks of covered and uncovered heads, we expect περιβόλαιον to have its most natural meaning—"covering"—and not be euphemism, which would have been lost on most readers. For other criticisms of Martin's position, see also, Mark Goodacre, "Does περιβόλαιον Mean 'Testicle' in 1 Corinthians 11:15?" *JBL* 130 (2011): 391–96; Jantsch, "Einführung," 56–59. However, see also, Troy W. Martin, "Περιβόλαιον as 'Testicle' in 1 Corinthians 11:15: A Response to Mark Goodacre," *JBL* 132 (2013): 453–65, in which Martin specifically responds to Goodacre's criticism.

[101] Some influential manuscripts, such as Codex Sinaiticus and Codex Vaticanus, add here αὐτῇ ("to her"), but αὐτῇ is missing in the earlier P46, for example. Thus, the question of whether αὐτῇ should be taken as original to the letter or as a later addition is the most debated text-critical issue of 1 Cor 11:2–16. The cumulative effect of the traditional text-critical criteria of "shorter reading is to be preferred," "earlier manuscript evidence is to be preferred," and "the more difficult reading for the scribe is to be preferred"—the text without αὐτῇ makes less immediate sense than the text with its inclusion—points towards αὐτῇ being a later addition. For discussion on these text-critical criteria see, for example, Bruce M. Metzger, *A Textual Commentary on the Greek New Testament*, 2nd ed (Stuttgart: Deutsche Bibelgesellschaft, 1994), 10*–14*; Eldon Jay Epp, "Traditional 'Canons' of New Testament Textual Criticism: Their Value, Validity, and Viability—or Lack Thereof," in *The Textual History of the Greek New Testament: Changing Views in Contemporary Research*, ed. Klaus Wachtel and Michael W. Holmes (Atlanta: Society of Biblical Literature, 2011): 92–125, esp. 104. On the other hand, however, it has also been shown that P46 tends to omit words, particularly "conjunctions and particles, articles, and pronouns" (which αὐτῇ is). See, James R. Royse, "The Early Text of Paul (and Hebrews)," in *The Early Text of the New Testament*, ed. Charles E. Hill and Michael J. Kruger (Oxford: Oxford University Press, 2012), 183. Thus, it is difficult for interpreters of 1 Cor 11:2–16 to decide on the originality of αὐτῇ, with some opting for inclusion (e.g., Collins, *First Corinthians*, 413), while others prefer omission (Thiselton, *The First Epistle to the Corinthians*, 843–44). I personally think the text without αὐτῇ to be more original, because the shorter reading makes more sense in light of the *capite velato* hypothesis (see below), but would make less sense to someone for whom the text only addresses *women*—and as will be shown in the next chapter, most readers by the second century CE understood the pericope to solely address women. Thus, it seems more reasonable to suppose that an early scribe added αὐτῇ in order to align the text more closely with the dominant interpretation of the entire passage.

5.6 Analogy from Nature: Second Supportive Argument (1 Cor 11:13–15)

function in Paul's overall argumentation than indicating the subject matter of the pericope. Indeed, most biblical scholars take these verses to be Paul's argument by analogy[102]—that is, Paul presents something that is commonly observable in everyday life[103] as somehow applicable (by way of analogy) on the question of whether men and women should or should not wear head-coverings during praying and accessing of divine (fore)knowledge. Most often, this analogy is understood in the following sense: the "natural" appearance of short hair on a man indicates that a head-covering is not necessary for him, while the "natural" appearance of long hair on a woman indicates that a head-covering is a necessity for her—in other words, nature teaches the appropriate appearances regarding head-coverings through the typical appearances of hair on men and women.[104]

While this is one way that the above analogy may be understood, I propose that an alternative interpretation may be more fitting here. Given that Paul has argued that men and women should not have a uniform appearance during the activities of praying and prophesying because of creational differences (which affect how men and women accrue and distribute shame and honor), Paul's statement, that long hair is a woman's honor but a man's shame, may be taken as a

---

[102] E.g., Bruce, *1 and 2 Corinthians*, 108; Watson, "The Authority of the Voice," 533; Garland, *1 Corinthians*, 518; Fee, *First Corinthians: Revised*, 585.

[103] This is how most biblical scholars understand "nature" (ἡ φύσις) here—how things are or how things have been (ordered). E.g., Keener, *Paul, Women and Wives*, 42; Thiselton, *The First Epistle to the Corinthians*, 844–45; Winter, *After Paul Left Corinth*, 131; Garland, *1 Corinthians*, 509, 530; Beattie, *Women and Marriage in Paul*, 53; Fitzmyer, *First Corinthians*, 420; Fee, *First Corinthians: Revised*, 583; Gardner, *1 Corinthians*, 495–96. The following passage from the Stoic philosopher Epictetus (ca. 50–135 CE) is often referenced in biblical scholarship on 1 Cor 11:14–15 as indicating this: "Come, let us leave the chief works of nature (τὰ ἔργα τῆς φύσεως), and consider merely what she does in passing. Can anything be more useless than the hairs on a chin? Well, what then? Has not nature used even these in the most suitable way possible? Has she not by these means distinguished between the male and the female? Does not the nature (ἡ φύσις) of each one among us cry aloud forthwith from afar, "I am a man; on this understanding approach me, on this understanding talk with me; ask for nothing further; behold the signs"? Again, in the case of women, just as nature has mingled in their voice a certain softer note, so likewise she has taken the hair from their chins…. Wherefore, we ought to preserve the signs which God has given; we ought not to throw them away; we ought not, so far as in us lies, to confuse the sexes which have been distinguished in this fashion" (*Diatr.* 1.16.9–14 [Oldfather]). For Epictetus it is "natural" that men have hair on their chins and so they should not remove it, while it seems that for Paul it is "natural" that men have short hair and women have long hair on their heads.

[104] E.g., Conzelmann, *1 Corinthians*, 190; Bruce, *1 and 2 Corinthians*, 108; Stuckenbruck, "Why Should Women Cover Their Heads," 219; Belleville, "Κεφαλή and the Thorny Issue of Headcovering," 221; Fee, *First Corinthians: Revised*, 585.

further demonstration of that idea. That is, Paul may be saying here that just as long hair can be either shameful or honorable, depending on whether it is a man or a woman that wears it, so it is with having a garment over the head—the honor or shame associated with this head-covering depends on whether it is a man or a woman who has a head-covering on. If this is the case, the phrase ὅτι ἡ κόμη ἀντὶ περιβολαίου δέδοται should be read as Paul's indication that he has intended the statement regarding long hair to serve as an analogy applicable to the issue about head-coverings: "long hair [that brings either shame or honor depending on one's sex] has been given [by me] in place of [or: as an analogy for[105]] a wraparound [which brings either honor or shame during praying and accessing of divine (fore)knowledge depending on one's sex]."

5.7 Example of Others: Third Supportive Argument (1 Cor 11:16)

Paul concludes his discussion on head-coverings in the following manner: "But if anyone determines to be contentious, we do not have such a custom, neither [do] the assemblies of God" (Εἰ δέ τις δοκεῖ φιλόνεικος εἶναι, ἡμεῖς τοιαύτην συνήθειαν οὐκ ἔχομεν οὐδὲ αἱ ἐκκλεσίαι τοῦ θεοῦ). As many scholars have pointed out, Paul's final argument betrays a certain lack of confidence in his hitherto argumentation.[106] Perhaps Paul found some of the arguments of his opponents potent, and is thus unsure whether a theological argument regarding differences between men and women that he has presented, is enough to convince his addressees. For example, if some of the Corinthians had raised an argument that for the sake of unity of all believers, all women of the Christ association should pray and access divine (fore)knowledge with a bare head, just as Roman men had been required to do (by Paul), Paul may have found it a praiseworthy approach, because he also shared the sentiment that all believers should be in unity. In any case, Paul does seem to concede here that the "lovers of victory" (lit. of φιλόνεικος[107]) in the Corinthian congregation had yet more ammunition at their disposal for continued resistance, and so it is for this reason that Paul presents himself and the congregations of God as examples of a different mode of conduct.

---

[105] As Gordon Fee explains, ἀντί "ordinarily serves for the concept of replacement—one thing instead of another." Fee, *First Corinthians: Revised*, 584. In essence, this is what analogy is—one thing instead of another, but for the purpose of illuminating or explaining the latter.

[106] E.g., Conzelmann, *1 Corinthians*, 191; BeDuhn, "Because of the 'Angels'," 315.

[107] E.g., Thiselton, *The First Epistle to the Corinthians*, 847; Garland, *1 Corinthians*, 531.

There is some debate around the antecedent of συνήθεια ("custom"), however. Some have suggested that when Paul says that "we do not have such a custom," he means that he and his co-workers (and the assemblies of God) do not have the custom of being "contentious," and thus Paul, alongside his accomplices, leaves the decision regarding head-coverings up to the Corinthian congregation here (cf. "judge among yourselves," 1 Cor 11:13).[108] While this is a possible interpretation of 1 Cor 11:16, I am not convinced that this is how Paul ends his argument here. I prefer the traditional reading, that "custom" refers to the subject matter of 1 Cor 11:2–16, and so I propose that in light of the *capite velato* hypothesis that I have provided, Paul concludes here that he, his co-workers, and other Christian congregations do not have the custom of stripping women of their head-coverings for moments of prayer and accessing of divine (fore)knowledge, as the Corinthians wish to do. Thus, even though Paul may show some hesitancy here about whether his arguments are convincing enough, he ends with perhaps the most potent counter-argument of all: no-one else among Christ associations does what the Corinthians propose to do (or have done).

5.8 Conclusion

I have suggested that in 1 Cor 11:2–16, Paul addresses a problem that had arisen in regards to his previous teaching on *capite velato*, the Roman custom of praying and of accessing divine (fore)knowledge with a garment over the head. I have proposed that this passage indicates that some influential members in the Corinthian congregation had begun to argue for the uniformity of appearances during praying and prophesying in response to Paul's ban on *capite velato*, requiring all members, regardless of their sex, ethnicity, age, and (marital) status, to pray and prophesy with absolutely nothing in their hair or on their heads. This created problems in the congregation especially for those (non-Roman) married women who always wore something in their hair or on their heads whenever in a public space. Paul thus found this development troublesome, and penned 1 Cor 11:2–16 to curb the excessive application of his teaching, while defending his initial position regarding *capite velato*. Basing his argument on the concept of the hierarchy of heads God-Christ-man-woman, Paul provides several reasons for why men have no obligation to cover their heads and why they should not do so in the context of praying and prophesying with a garment, and why women should have control over their heads and not be stripped of their head-coverings during praying and prophesying. Most

---

[108] E.g., Engberg-Pedersen, "1 Corinthians 11:16," 684–86; Jantsch, "Einführung," 59–60.

crucially, Paul finds that having a garment hanging from the head during praying and prophesying shames man's immediate social superior (as per Roman customs), his *kyrios* Jesus the Messiah, while a woman's head, if stripped of all hair accessories and head-coverings, shames the woman herself, her male relations, and the male angels who mediate prayers and divine (fore)knowledge. Paul's underlying worry, therefore, seems to be that the Corinthian insistence on uniformity of appearances leads to shame for all involved, and for this reason, he discourages them from pursuing this any further. In all this, however, a nagging question remains: if this is how 1 Cor 11:2–16 should be interpreted, why do we lack evidence that this passage was so understood by the earliest readers? This is the question we will now turn to.

6. Women as Scapegoats

How the Interpretive Framework of *capite velato* Was Lost Sight of in the Early Christian Readings of 1 Cor 11:2–16

I have argued thus far, that in 1 Cor 11:2–16, Paul addresses the Roman ritual gesture of *capite velato* and the problems surrounding the implementation of its ban in the Corinthian congregation. But the *capite velato* line of interpretation is a fairly novel one—only recently have some biblical scholars argued with any conviction for the relevance of this ritual gesture on 1 Cor 11:2–16 (despite Michaelis suggesting already in the eighteenth century that *capite velato* was indirectly related to 1 Cor 11:2–16, see section 1.2.3). This recent scholarly interest in *capite velato* as an interpretive framework of 1 Cor 11:2–16 has no doubt been driven by the availability of larger and more accessible databases on archaeological finds and ancient literary texts, which have allowed scholars to perceive how widespread the ritual gesture of *capite velato* was at the time of Paul. Yet, while the surviving statues, drawings, and carvings, together with the various Greek and Latin texts, demonstrate that it was a common Roman practice to cover the head with a garment during praying, divination, and sacrificing, and would thus have been known to Paul and his addressees, none of the earliest interpreters of 1 Cor portray any awareness of a connection between *capite velato* and 1 Cor 11:2–16, even though this text talks about covered and uncovered heads in the context of praying and prophesying. In this chapter, therefore, I present the earliest surviving engagements with 1 Cor 11:2–16, and discuss the possible reasons why *capite velato* as an interpretive framework was lost sight of.

6.1 The Letter of 2 Corinthians

Biblical scholars are in general agreement that the composition known today as 2 Corinthians is authentically Pauline and a follow-up communication with the

Corinthian congregation after 1 Cor.[1] It is also generally agreed that 2 Cor was written within a relatively short space of time after the composition of 1 Cor (perhaps even within one to two years). It thus provides us a window (albeit a very small one) into Paul's relationship with the Corinthian congregation shortly after 1 Cor had been received by the congregants in Corinth. And what is immediately clear in reading 2 Cor is that the general tone of the letter is rather different than that of 1 Cor. For example, while in 1 Cor, Paul seems to speak from the position of authority, confidently laying out the behavioral and dogmatic norms that the Corinthian believers should adhere to, in 2 Cor, Paul seems to speak rather from the position of one whose authority has been seriously challenged, resorting even at times to self-promotion and vituperative language against rivals.

It is not entirely clear what had caused such a shift in tone, but there are some hints in 2 Cor that a major fallout had happened between Paul and the Corinthians after the Corinthians had received 1 Cor. For example, 2 Cor 2:1–11 seems to suggest that a certain individual within the congregation personally challenged Paul[2] to which Paul reacted with a (now lost) "letter of tears" (2:4), and perhaps even with a "painful visit" (2:1).[3] While this particular conflict appears to have been

---

[1] There is some debate, however, whether 2 Cor should be taken as one letter or as an edited document consisting of two or three or even more letters. See discussion in, for example, Fredrick J. Long, *Ancient Rhetoric and Paul's Apology: The Compositional Unity of 2 Corinthians* (Cambridge: Cambridge University Press, 2004), 1–17; Harris, *Second Corinthians*, 8–51; Ivar Vegge, *2 Corinthians—a Letter about Reconciliation: A Psychological, Epistolographical and Rhetorical Analysis* (Tübingen: Mohr Siebeck, 2008), 9–33; Ivor H. Jones, "Rhetorical Criticism and the Unity of 2 Corinthians: One 'Epilogue', or More?" *NTS* 54 (2008): 496–524; Troels Engberg-Pedersen, "Paul's Temporal Thinking: 2 Cor 2.14–7.4 as Paraenetic Autobiography," *NTS* 67 (2021): 157–80. What matters for our purposes is that 2 Cor is a subsequent communication of Paul to the Corinthians after 1 Cor, and the question of whether it was sent as one letter or as multiple letters has thus no bearing on my arguments here.

[2] For a long time, this individual was identified as the incestuous man of 1 Cor 5, but most biblical scholars of the 20th and 21st century are in agreement that 2 Cor 2 speaks of a different individual with whom Paul had a conflict *after* 1 Cor had been composed. For a research history on this question, see, for example, L. L. Welborn, *An End to Enmity: Paul and the 'Wrongdoer' of Second Corinthians*, BZNW 185 (Berlin: Walter de Gruyter, 2011), 3–22.

[3] This idea that Paul visited Corinth in between writing 1 Cor and 2 Cor rests mostly on the word πάλιν ("again") in 2 Cor 2:1. Stephen Carlson has recently argued, however, that πάλιν in 2 Cor 2:1 cannot be taken as evidence of that. Stephen C. Carlson, "On Paul's Second Visit to Corinth: Πάλιν, Parsing, and Presupposition in 2 Corinthians 2:1," *JBL* 135 (2016): 597–615. It is more likely, therefore, that Paul only sent a (now lost) letter in the interim but did not visit the Corinthians personally.

somewhat resolved by the time of the writing of 2 Cor (cf. 2 Cor 7),[4] another conflict appears to have been still ongoing: certain individuals seemingly from outside of Corinth had undermined Paul's authority and his credentials, and had won some support from the Corinthian congregation (cf. 2 Cor 10–13).[5] John Barclay proposes that these individuals had raised a question as to whether Paul was "genuine" (δόκιμος, cf. 2 Cor 13:5–7), and that they had done so most likely in response to some of the things that Paul had written about in 1 Cor that they found disagreeable.[6] But whatever the exact reason for this undermining of Paul's authority, 2 Cor does suggest that Paul and the Corinthians had experienced a major decline of trust in their relationship in the time period between Paul's initial visit to Corinth and his last surviving written communication to them.

In this context, it is interesting to observe what topics covered in 1 Cor are picked up again in 2 Cor, and which topics are relegated to the margins or fall completely out of view. Most conspicuous of course is Paul's defense of his apostleship, which receives some treatment in 1 Cor (e.g., ch. 9) but which dominates 2 Cor (e.g., chs. 3–4, 10–13). Perhaps intimately tied to this is the question of the collection of funds for "the saints" in Jerusalem, which is discussed only in passing in 1 Cor (16:1–4), but which in 2 Cor requires Paul's elongated explanation (2 Cor 8–9). On the flip side, Paul's warning against idolatry, that receives a fair bit of space in 1 Cor (e.g., chs. 8 and 10), is only mentioned in a short reminder in 2 Cor 6:14–7:1. And all other highlighted topics in 1 Cor (e.g., inner conflicts, sexual immorality, lawsuits, marriage, head-coverings, *deipnon* of the Lord, spiritual gifts and the

---

[4] In 2 Cor 7, Paul claims that the Corinthians felt "godly sorrow" in response to a letter he had sent them, and that this sorrow had led them to "repentance." The generally conciliatory tone of the context in which this claim is found, has led scholars to believe that the conflict recounted in 2 Cor 2 had been mostly solved by the time of the writing of 2 Cor. However, B. G. White has recently argued that Paul's language in 2 Cor 7 actually suggests that the Corinthians continued to harbor feelings of grief or bitterness over the conflict between Paul and this unnamed individual among them, which suggests that it had not been solved by the time of the writing of 2 Cor. See, B. G. White, "The Varieties of Pain: Re-examining the Setting and Purpose of 2 Corinthians with Paul's λυπ- Words," *JSNT* 43 (2020): 147–72.

[5] The precise identity of Paul's opponents in 2 Cor 10–13 has been a hotly debated matter in biblical scholarship. For an overview of the various proposals see, for example, N. H. Taylor, "Apostolic Identity and the Conflicts in Corinth and Galatia," in *Paul and His Opponents*, ed. Stanley E. Porter (Boston: Brill, 2005), 118–19; L. L. Welborn, "Paul's Caricature of his Chief Rival as a Pompous Parasite in 2 Corinthians 11.20," *JSNT* 32 (2009): 39–41.

[6] John M. G. Barclay, "Deviance and Apostasy: Some Applications of Deviance Theory to First-Century Judaism and Christianity," in *Pauline Churches and Diaspora Jews*, by John M. G. Barclay, WUNT (Tübingen: Mohr Siebeck, 2011), 138.

nature of Christian gatherings, and resurrection) receive insignificant or no attention at all in 2 Cor. Clearly, the focus of Paul has shifted from providing authoritative counsel on matters of conduct and belief to fighting for a position even to be heard or to be taken seriously by the Corinthian believers.

It is entirely possible, then, that some of the things that Paul had written about in 1 Cor were rejected or ignored by the Corinthian congregation, as Paul's credentials and authority were being questioned.[7] One of those rejected or ignored teachings may have been the instructions about *capite velato*,[8] and given that Paul's focus was now on winning back the support of the Corinthian congregation, he may have made a calculated decision not to address head-coverings again in order not to antagonize his addressees any further on the question of *capite velato*.[9] Thus, even though the conflict over head-coverings in the Corinthian congregation may have resolved on its own accord one way or another, with or without the help of Paul, the specific instructions of 1 Cor 11:2–16 may have nevertheless been forgotten or ignored until a much later time when Paul's letters began to circulate in a collection, by which time the original *Sitz im Leben* for these instructions was no longer known. This may help explain why in no other early Christian source is there even a hint of any customs associated with head-coverings during praying or prophesying until a century later (!), when Irenaeus quotes a modified version of 1 Cor 11:10 (see below).

That no other early Christian community or early Christian writer until the middle of the second century portrays any anxiety about praying or prophesying with or without head-coverings suggests that no independent (Pauline) tradition circulated in this regard, and that 1 Cor 11:2–16 may be, therefore, Paul's address of a very specific problem on a local level. But as I have pointed out, it is possible that

---

[7] See, for example, Pickett, "Conflicts at Corinth," 114–16, 132.

[8] Recently, L. L. Welborn has argued at length that the "wrongdoer" of 2 Cor 2 should be identified with the wealthy and influential Gaius, the "host" to Paul and to the Corinthian congregation, who had taken exception to some of the things Paul had done and also to what he had said in 1 Cor. L. L. Welborn, *An End to Enmity*, 23–484. While this hypothesis is quite speculative, it is nevertheless possible that some of those Corinthians with whom Paul was in conflict were of Roman background, as there seems to have been a number of Romans in the Christ association of Corinth (see section 4.2.2). If, then, Paul's credentials and authority came to be questioned, it is easy to see how those of Roman background could have ignored or rejected Paul's instructions specifically regarding Roman customs.

[9] Mary D'Angelo has suggested that Paul's decision not to revisit the issue of head-coverings in 2 Cor may demonstrate "his discretion in response to [the Corinthians'] rejection of his strictures." D'Angelo, "Veils, Virgins, and the Tongues," 399.

the addressees of this personalized message themselves never gave it much thought. Thus, the bottom line here is that, despite 1 Cor 11:2–16 being most likely intelligible to its *original* readers, the first surviving engagements with it from a century later and onwards may have already lost all knowledge of the original problem of the Corinthian congregation that gave rise to this passage, because no oral tradition had originated from Corinth around this pericope and spread to other Christian communities. This possibility needs to be kept in mind as we engage with the earliest interpreters of 1 Cor 11:2–16.

6.2 The Letter to the Romans

As was discussed in Chapter 4, it is generally held that Paul wrote his letter to the Romans from Corinth (see section 4.2.2). If so, this would mean that at some point in time after writing (some portions or all of) 2 Cor, Paul visited Corinth again, and Rom 16:23 suggests that Paul continued to have some powerful allies in this city (e.g., Erastus, the city "manager," and Gaius, "host" to the congregation). This suggests, then, that even if Paul had not won over the entire congregation, he had made peace with some of its influential members. But the question remains: did Paul have to make some concessions in order to regain his authority or to reconcile with his allies? In other words, did Paul have to soften his stance on some of the issues that he had addressed in 1 Cor, for example? It is impossible to know, since we possess no communication between Paul and the Corinthians after 2 Cor. But it is noteworthy, for example, that Paul appears to be on good terms with Erastus, because if Erastus was in any capacity involved in the administrator of the city of Corinth, he would most likely have been responsible to a certain degree of the organization of the imperial worship or with the worship of local deities. If so, it would have been impossible for him to follow Paul's instructions concerning idolatry exactly as spelled out in 1 Cor 8–11 (including the issue of head-coverings, see section 4.2.2). While this all is speculative, it is nevertheless worth keeping in mind the possibility that Paul had to rethink some of the things he had taught the Corinthians in order to maintain good relationships with certain influential members of the Corinthian congregation, and to allow these members to exercise their influence in the wider community. After all, it was most likely from Corinth that Paul issued the following directive to the Roman Christians:

> Let every soul subordinate to higher powers ... for the powers that are, are appointed by God.... Return, therefore, to everyone what is owed. To the one [who is owed] tribute, tribute. To the one [who is owed] duty, duty. To the one [who is owed] reverence, reverence. To the one [who is owed] honor, honor (τῷ τὴν τιμὴν τὴν τιμήν)." (Rom 13:1, 7)

Despite the tendentious nature of my line of argument here, we must nevertheless be cognizant of the fact that Paul continued to communicate with the Corinthians after 1 Cor and 2 Cor had been written, and since we do not have access to these subsequent communications, we must be careful in taking 1 Cor and 2 Cor as the final word in the correspondence between Paul and the Corinthians. Much could have changed in the relationship between Paul and the Corinthians (especially after 1 Cor), which could have affected also how Paul thought about certain matters, including, perhaps, how he viewed the issue of head-coverings during praying and accessing of divine (fore)knowledge.

6.3 The Household Codes and the Pastoral Epistles

Modern biblical scholarship is in general agreement that Ephesians and the Pastoral Epistles (1 Timothy, 2 Timothy, and Titus) were not authored by Paul (directly), but that they were rather later productions of some disciples of Paul or of Pauline "schools," which used Paul's name to address certain concerns in the changing landscape of Christian congregations' engagement with the outside world.[10] Thus, these letters give us some insight into how Paul was remembered or appropriated a generation or two after his passing, and how his teachings had been absorbed (either through oral tradition, circulating collection of tractates, or both). What interests us here is that these letters present Paul as someone who took great interest in how Christian households and congregations should be managed, and in the proper place of women in both of these realms. Such a focused interest in these matters stands out, because in the authentic Pauline literature, Paul is ambivalent about such things (especially if we count 1 Cor 14:34–35, which demands silence from women during Christian gatherings, as a later interpolation, but see discussion on this in section 4.2.3). In general, the authentic Paul counts women as fellow apostles, coworkers, patronesses, and missionaries, portraying little if any of that unease on the question of women's involvement in ecclesial affairs or in household management that seems to underlie much of the Pastorals, for example.

---

[10] In a recent assessment of the state of biblical scholarship on the question of authorship of the so-called deutero-Pauline letters, Margaret MacDonald claims that most scholars take Ephesians and the Pastoral Epistles to be works of a later generation and not of the authentic Paul, whereas the authorship of other letters of the deutero-Pauline collection is a much more contested matter. Margaret Y. MacDonald, "The Deutero-Pauline Letters in Contemporary Research," in *The Oxford Handbook of Pauline Studies*, ed. Matthew V. Novenson and R. Barry Matlock (Oxford: Oxford University Press, 2022), 259.

In light of this, it is important to note that these later texts address two ideas that Paul makes use of in his argument in 1 Cor 11:2–16, but in both cases, the ideas have been reworked to serve different aims. First, recall that in 1 Cor 11:3, Paul presents the idea that "of every man the head is Christ" and that "the head of woman is the man" to argue that men and women accrue and distribute shame and honor differently in relation to how their heads are dressed during praying and prophesying (see section 5.2). We find these ideas about headship referenced again in Eph 5:21–24:

> Subordinate to one another in the fear of Christ—the women to their own husbands as to the lord (αἱ γυναῖκες τοῖς ἰδίοις ἀνδράσιν ὡς τῷ κυρίῳ[11]), because man is the head of the woman (ὅτι ἀνήρ ἐστιν κεφαλὴ τῆς γυναικὸς), as also Christ is the head of the assembly, he [is] the savior of the body. But as the assembly subordinates to Christ, thus also the women [should subordinate] to the husbands in everything (οὕτως καὶ αἱ γυναῖκες τοῖς ἀνδράσιν ἐν παντί).

While there are certainly some similarities here with 1 Cor 11:3, there are also some crucial differences that should be noted. For example, while the emphasis in 1 Cor 11:3 is on the headship of Christ over man, since it is discussed first and also finds application in Paul's subsequent argument (see section 5.2.1), here in Eph 5, the emphasis is clearly on the headship of man over woman, and the idea of Christ's headship (over "assembly," rather than over "every man") is used only as a supportive argument to what is the author's main point: women should subordinate to their husbands. Also, the phrase κεφαλὴ δὲ γυναικὸς ὁ ἀνήρ ("but the head of woman is the man") in 1 Cor 11:3 is quite general in regards to the relationship between "woman" and "man"—it does not specify, for example, that the relationship here is between husband and wife (see section 5.2.2). In Eph 5, however, man's headship over woman is phrased in a way to suggest that the main concern is specifically with the relationship between husband and wife: ἀνήρ ἐστιν κεφαλὴ τῆς γυναικός ("a man is head of *the* woman," i.e., his wife).

For the authentic Paul, then, this idea that Christ is the head of man and man is the head of woman served as a foundational premise to argue that men and women accrue and distribute shame and honor differently, so that when a man

---

[11] This is how this clause appears in P46 and Codex Vaticanus, but many influential manuscripts add ὑποτασσέσθωσαν ("let them be subordinate") after γυναῖκες or after ἀνδράσιν, which then adds further emphasis to the idea of subordination. It has been recently argued that the longer reading is the more original. See, for example, Peter J. Gurry, "The Text of Eph. 5.22 and the Start of the Ephesian Household Code," *NTS* 67 (2021): 560–81; Joey McCollum, "The Intrinsic Probability of τοῖς ἰδίοις ἀνδράσιν ὑποτασσέσθωσαν in Eph. 5.22," *JSNT* 46 (2024): 556–78.

prays or accesses divine (fore)knowledge with a garment over the head, he shames Christ (and himself), while if a woman prays or accesses divine (fore)knowledge stripped of her head-covering(s), she brings shame on the males present (and herself). The author of Ephesians, however, alters this concept of headship (and the language used) to argue (in the name of Paul) that women should subordinate themselves to their own husbands *in everything*, just as the Christian assembly does in relation to its head, Christ. The aims and emphases of the two authors in using the headship concept are therefore rather different,[12] and based on Paul's qualification of his argument in 1 Cor 11:11–12 (see section 5.5), I am not sure Paul would have subscribed to this Ephesian alteration of the headship concept. But as we shall see, the Ephesian alteration became a lens through which 1 Cor 11:3 came to be read in the early church, beginning with the second century CE.

Second, recall that in 1 Cor 11:7–10, Paul appeals to the priority of man in creation to argue that a man has no obligation to cover his head because he is God's honor, while a woman must have control over her head because she is man's honor (see section 5.3). In 1 Tim 2:11–14, this idea that man was created first is also employed, but in service of a rather different aim: "A woman must learn in silence, in all subordination. I command a woman not to teach nor to have authority over man, but to be in silence. For Adam was formed first, then Eve. And Adam was not deceived, but the woman, having been deceived, came into transgression." Here the author of 1 Tim connects the formation of Eve after Adam with the transgression of "woman" (notice that Eve is not mentioned in this clause but a generic reference to "woman" is made instead), which is then used to support the idea that a woman must be silent, must not teach a man, and must not have authority over a man. Thus, woman's secondary status in creation of humanity is in 1 Tim 2 cast in an entirely negative light, without any caveats whatsoever. This is in stark contrast to 1 Cor 11:2–16, however, in which Paul qualifies his argument on the priority of man in creation with a claim that "in the Lord," a woman is not separate from man (1 Cor 11:11–12, see section 5.5).

---

[12] Jill Marshall has also demonstrated how in comparison to 1 Cor 6:12–7:7, Eph 5:21–33 presents an "opposing view" in regards to "sex and marriage," even though their respective conclusions are "based on shared cultural resources, including recitation of Gen 2:24 ('the two shall be one flesh') and the metaphor of community as body." Jill E. Marshall, "Community is a Body: Sex, Marriage, and Metaphor in 1 Corinthians 6:12–7:7 and Ephesians 5:21–33," *JBL* 134 (2015): 834. This then serves as another example of how Eph 5 reworks certain concepts that Paul makes use of in 1 Cor to reach a rather different conclusion to the authentic Paul.

6.3 The Household Codes and the Pastoral Epistles

Furthermore, it is also worth pointing out that when the authentic Paul discusses the deception of Eve, the focus is on the serpent and its "craftiness" (πανουργία), rather than on Eve (or "woman") and her transgression (2 Cor 11:3). And nowhere in authentic Paul is Adam absolved of his guilt (e.g., Rm 5:14), contrary to what 1 Tim seems to imply,[13] nor does the authentic Paul use the creation or fall narratives to limit women's ability to speak. Thus, we see that this concept of priority of man in creation, which is used in authentic Paul (with caveats) in support of instructing how *both* men and women must act, has been employed in 1 Tim to limit the independence, visibility, and freedom of expression of *only* the women.

It is not entirely clear why the Household Codes and the Pastorals present (or appropriate) Paul in such a way. Some have suggested that since Christians in the later decades of the first century (and beyond) were more conspicuously present in many major centers of the Roman Empire, there was increasing pressure (at times even hostile) to conform to the societal norms in matters of household management and organization of public assemblies.[14] Thus, certain influential individuals or groups of second or third-generation Christians may have felt pressured to limit the influence of women in Christian households and congregations to make their associations more palatable to the society at large, and used Paul's name for their aim.[15] Others have suggested, regarding specifically the Pastorals, that these

---

[13] This idea that "woman" is responsible for sin predates both 1 Tim and the authentic Paul. For example, Sir 25:24 from the second century BCE claims that "from a woman is the beginning of sin, and because of her, we all die." See, Alicia J. Batten, "Gender," in *The Ancient Mediterranean Social World: A Sourcebook*, ed. Zeba A. Crook (Grand Rapids: Eerdmans, 2020), 144. Given that this idea that "woman" is the main (or even the sole) culprit in regards to the "beginning of sin" was in circulation at the time of Paul, it is all the more noteworthy that Paul does not focus on that in his description of the origins of sin.

[14] See, for example, MacDonald, *The Power of Children*, 5; Osiek and MacDonald, *A Woman's Place*, 234.

[15] How much such ideals reflected the real situation in Christian homes and assemblies is of course a different matter. For example, even in these later letters some women are highlighted for their positive roles in Christian mission (e.g., Nympha in Col 4:15, Lois and Eunice in 2 Tim 1:5). Thus, it is entirely possible that, despite the anxiety some (men) felt about women's active and open participation in Christian mission, many women nevertheless continued to flout the societal norms that these men held dear in order to spearhead the rapidly growing movement. See, for example, MacDonald, *The Power of Children*, 8, 100. However, it seems that as time went on, these ideals of the Household Codes and the Pastorals gained in influence since, in the words of Carolyn Osiek and Margaret MacDonald, "as we move beyond Paul's day, incidental references

may have been composed in the early decades of the second century CE largely in response to certain tales about women's involvement in Pauline mission (such as the story of Paul and Thecla) that were circulating in some contemporary Christian circles.[16] Thus, the purpose of the composers of these letters was to rescue Paul's legacy from what they thought were blasphemous portraits of him. But whatever the exact circumstances of the origins of the Household Codes and the Pastorals, starting with the second century CE, these writings were increasingly thought of as authoritative and authentic communications of Paul. Thus, the rest of the Pauline corpus (including 1 Cor) came to be read in conjunction with (and through) the ideas and ideals of the Household Codes and the Pastorals. But, as we shall see below, reading 1 Cor 11:2–16 through the lens of such ideas and ideals gives the passage a rather different tone than it has on its own accord.

6.4 Valentinians according to Irenaeus

The first clear reference to 1 Cor 11:2–16 appears in Irenaeus's (ca. 130–202 CE) engagement with a Valentinian creation myth, in which a modified version of 1 Cor 11:10 is cited. Valentinus (ca. 100–180 CE) had been an influential Christian

---

to 'real' women become rarer and women's identities increasingly become constructs operating through such literary genres as apology, martyrology, and novelistic accounts." Osiek and MacDonald, *A Woman's Place*, 229. Concerning the second century CE, for example, we find a much higher number of positive evaluations regarding women as participants and leaders in Christian mission in the writings relegated to the margins or vilified by the heresiologists (e.g., some of the Nag Hammadi tracts), than we do in the writings of the so-called Church Fathers. See, for example, Marjanen, *The Woman Jesus Loved*, 216. Also, in the latter half of the second century CE, one of the stock accusations of heresiologists against their opponents was that they granted women too much authority in Christian matters (e.g., administration of baptism), suggesting perhaps that women at large had been excluded from positions of authority in the "mainstream" church. E.g., Judith M. Lieu, *Marcion and the Making of a Heretic: God and Scripture in the Second Century* (New York: Cambridge University Press, 2015), 397. Thus, even if the Household Codes and the Pastorals do not reflect the reality of the environments in which they were composed, they certainly seem to have shaped the reality of the later generations of Christians. See also, Huebner, *Papyri*, 58–59, 62.

[16] E.g., Dennis Ronald MacDonald, *The Legend and the Apostle: The Battle for Paul in Story and Canon* (Philadelphia: Westminster Press, 1983), 54–77; Bart D. Ehrman, *Lost Christianities: The Battles for Scripture and the Faiths We Never Knew* (New York: Oxford University Press, 2003), 39. On the other hand, Adela Yarbro Collins has argued that 1 Timothy was most likely a reaction against Marcion's teachings about the evils of marriage, and his laxness concerning leadership and visibility of women in Christian congregations of the early second century CE. Adela Yarbro Collins, "The Female Body as Social Space in 1 Timothy," *NTS* 57 (2011): 155–75.

teacher in mid-second century Rome, where he reportedly also led his own school of instruction (one of his foremost students appears to have been a certain Ptolemy).[17] Unfortunately, we have access to only fragments of the ideas of Valentinus and his student Ptolemy, and this only through the writings of those who were adversarial towards them, so caution must be exercised in determining exactly who taught what and why.[18] For example, even though the reference to 1 Cor 11:10 appears in Irenaeus's engagement with Ptolemy specifically, he throughout his presentation uses the more general "they," without further specifying his interlocutors. Thus, it is more practical for our purposes here to speak of Valentinians as a general group of followers of Valentinus *as so constructed* by Irenaeus, and not attempt to trace the various ideas Irenaeus attributes to this group to one individual or another.[19]

In the context where the reference to 1 Cor 11:10 appears, Irenaeus is in the midst of presenting a creation myth that he claims the Valentinians to have held. At this particular point, the focus is on the formation of a being known as Achamoth ("higher wisdom's thinking," *Haer.* 1.4.1). When Achamoth comes to her senses after being formed, she is emptied of Christ, and so she begins searching for him (*Haer.* 1.4.1). However, she is unsuccessful, and so through her fear, grief, and tears, she becomes the creator of matter and thus the world (*Haer.* 1.4.2). After a while, however, Christ, who has returned to the fullness, sends a savior to her in the company of angels. Upon their meeting, "Achamoth was ashamed before him and put on a veil (κάλυμμα) out of shame" (*Haer.* 1.4.5).[20] Irenaeus then continues on with the retelling of this Valentinian creation myth, but returns later to list the scriptural texts that the Valentinians had supposedly amassed in support of this myth:

> The fact that the savior appeared to her [Achamoth] while she was outside the fullness and had the appointed lot of an aborted fetus, is—they say—spoken of by Paul in 1 Corinthians: "Last of all, as to an aborted fetus, he appeared also to me" (1 Cor 15:8). The advent of the savior with his comrades before Achamoth is likewise shown by him in the

---

[17] Layton, *The Gnostic Scriptures*, 341.

[18] However, many scholars now hold that a number of tracts in the Nag Hammadi Library should be classified as "Valentinian." E.g., Risto Auvinen, *Philo's Influence on Valentinian Tradition*, SPhiloM 10 (Atlanta: SBL Press, 2024), 27. Yet, how much of that was authored by Valentinus himself, or by any of his closest followers, is not known.

[19] On this, see also, Carl Johan Berglund, *Origen's References to Heracleon: A Quotation-Analytical Study of the Earliest Known Commentary on the Gospel of John*, WUNT 450 (Tübingen: Mohr Siebeck, 2020), 17–33.

[20] Translation in Layton, *The Gnostic Scriptures*, 358.

same epistle, when he says "A woman ought to have a veil on her head, because of the angels" (Δεῖ τὴν γυναῖκα κάλυμμα ἔχειν ἐπὶ τῆς κεφαλῆς διὰ τοὺς ἀγγέλους / *Oportere mulierem velamen habere in capite propter Angelos*, 1 Cor 11:10). The fact that Achamoth put on a veil out of shame when the savior came to her, was shown by Moses putting a veil on his face (Ex 34:33).[21] (*Haer.* 1.8.2)

What interests us here the most is the wording of 1 Cor 11:10 that Irenaeus presents. There is overwhelming manuscript support for the Greek text of 1 Cor 11:10 that reads: διὰ τοῦτο ὀφείλει ἡ γυνὴ ἐξουσίαν ἔχειν ἐπὶ τῆς κεφαλῆς διὰ τοὺς ἀγγέλους. No early Greek manuscript replaces ἐξουσία with κάλυμμα in 1 Cor 11:10, as in the above quotation of Irenaeus; only in some later Latin and Bohairic translations of the NT, and in the biblical quotations of some Church Fathers (most notably, Hippolytus of Rome[22]), does "veil" feature in this verse instead of "authority." Thus, the κάλυμμα version of 1 Cor 11:10 does not appear to be a scribal "corruption" of the text, since it leaves no separate trail in the earliest Greek manuscripts, but seems to have circulated at first independently and outside of the Greek NT manuscripts until the Latin and Bohairic renditions of the NT incorporated it. But that does not mean that we must credit the Valentinians with the origin of this alternate reading. It is noteworthy, for example, that Irenaeus does not fault the Valentinians for reading 1 Cor 11:10 in this way, even though he does not hold back in his

---

[21] Translation (with modifications) from Layton, *The Gnostic Scriptures*, 367. Greek text from PG 7:524b; Latin text from PG 7:523b.

[22] Hippolytus of Rome (third century CE) is an enigmatic figure in Christian history. Not much is known about him, and there is controversy about the writings that have been attributed to him. Some scholars have argued, for example, that the "Hippolytus" of the commentaries on biblical books is a different figure to the "Hippolytus" of some other treatises, and that the association with Rome is not secure in either case. See discussion in, for example, Joel Marcus, "Israel and the Church in the Exegetical Writings of Hippolytus," *JBL* 131 (2012): 390–92. However, it does appear that the *Commentary on Daniel*, in which 1 Cor 11:10 is quoted, may be traced to a Hippolytus of the early third century CE who was connected to Rome. Marcus, "Israel and the Church," 391. In any case, in this commentary on Daniel, "Hippolytus" claims that the accusers, who unveiled Susanna, committed an evil act, "for the apostle says: 'the woman must have a veil upon the head because of the angels'" (τοῦ γὰρ ἀποστόλου εἰπόντος ἡ γυνὴ κάλυμμα ὀφείλει ἔχειν ἐπὶ τῆς κεφαλῆς διὰ τοὺς ἀγγέλους). Greek text from G. N. Bonwetsch and M. Richard, eds., *Kommentar zu Daniel*, GCS (Berlin: Akad. Verl., 2000), 56. We see here that there are some syntactical and grammatical differences between Irenaeus's and Hippolytus's quotations of 1 Cor 11:10, but κάλυμμα plays the same role in both renditions. If, then, the *Commentary on Daniel* is indeed the work of a third-century CE Hippolytus who was connected to Rome, we would have an additional early example originating from Rome in which κάλυμμα features in 1 Cor 11:10. It may show, therefore, that this reading was particularly popular in that geographic region, but we cannot be sure, since Hippolytus cannot be securely located there.

criticism of their positions otherwise. It may be, then, that Irenaeus (and other contemporaries) in principle shared the Valentinian reading of this verse, but we cannot be sure.

In any case, this modification indicates that some early Christians understood 1 Cor 11:2–16 to include a reference to κάλυμμα, even if the physical texts they read of this passage did not have this word. Yet, it is not entirely clear why 1 Cor 11:2–16 came to be read this way. There appear to be no hints in 1 Cor 11:2–16 itself that Paul's main concern was with κάλυμμα—a piece of clothing intended for the covering of the head (and of the face) that was especially associated with women's dress. The only piece of clothing that 1 Cor 11:2–16 mentions is περιβόλαιον (11:15), which was a mantle (or more precisely, "wraparound") that *both* men and women could use to "envelope" their bodies, and if necessary, also their heads (see Chapter 5). But regardless of the exact reasons why κάλυμμα came to be incorporated into 1 Cor 11:10, that 1 Cor 11:2–16 came to be associated with κάλυμμα strongly affected how later readers then understood the text. The focus shifted to a piece of clothing that was first and foremost associated with women's dress, the purpose of which was not only to cover the head but also the face. Thus, beginning with the end of the second century CE, many interpreters of this passage focused their attention solely on the necessity for women to cover their heads and faces (see below).

6.5 Theodotus according to Clement of Alexandria

Clement of Alexandria's own engagement with 1 Cor 11:2–16 will be discussed momentarily, but here mention should be made of Clement's notebook *Excerpta ex Theodoto*, which includes Clement's notes about the teachings of a certain Theodotus. This Theodotus seems to have been a second-century Valentinian, but not much is known of him.[23] What concerns us here is an excerpt that is somewhat similar in content to the above quoted portion of the creation myth that Irenaeus attributed to the Valentinians:

> When Wisdom beheld him, she recognized that he was similar to the Light who had deserted her, and she ran to him and rejoiced and worshiped and, beholding the male angels (τοὺς δὲ ἄρρενας ἀγγέλους) who were sent out with him, she was abashed and put on a veil (κατηδέσθη καὶ κάλυμμα ἐπέθετο). Through this mystery Paul commands the women to wear power on their heads on account of the angels (Διὰ τοῦτο τοῦ μυστηρίου

---

[23] Auvinen, *Philo's Influence*, 38.

ὁ Παῦλος κελεύει τὰς γυναῖκας φορεῖν ἐξουσίαν ἐπὶ τῆς κεφαλῆς διὰ τοὺς ἀγγέλους).[24] (*Exc.* 44)

Notice that in Theodotus's version of this creation myth (as presented by Clement), Wisdom puts on a veil out of shame because of the presence of male angels, whereas in the version that Irenaeus presents, Achamoth veils because she feels shame in the presence of the savior.[25] Thus, Theodotus's version appears more closely tied to 1 Cor 11:10, as it specifically makes mention of (male) angels.

What is also interesting here is that ἐξουσία is retained in the specific reference to 1 Cor 11:10, as in the manuscript tradition. However, the context makes it clear that ἐξουσία is nevertheless understood in the sense of κάλυμμα—1 Cor 11:10 is even presented as Paul's command for women "to wear" (φορέω) authority upon the head, even though this is not what we find in the manuscript tradition. Yet, it is impossible to know whether it is Clement who retains ἐξουσία in his reference to 1 Cor 11:10 or whether this is a version of 1 Cor 11:10 that Clement already finds in Theodotus.[26] In any case, this excerpt is a further demonstration that those Christians, who were associated with Valentinus, understood 1 Cor 11:10 as speaking of women wearing veils on their heads (and over their faces), and made use of this reading of 1 Cor 11:10 in their theology of the origins of the world. And it is also worth pointing out that neither Irenaeus nor Clement protested against this reading of 1 Cor 11:10.

6.6 Clement of Alexandria

Clement of Alexandria (ca. 150–215 CE) was for a time in charge of instructing Christian neophytes in Alexandria on matters of Christian belief and conduct upon their entrance into the community,[27] and it is no surprise, then, that his

---

[24] Greek text and English translation in Robert Pierce Casey, ed., *The Excerpta ex Theodoto of Clement of Alexandria* (London: Christophers, 1934), 70–71.

[25] For a more in-depth comparison of these two versions of the creation myth, see, Auvinen, *Philo's Influence*, 40–42.

[26] Risto Auvinen notes that it is possible that this whole section of the *Excerpta* which deals with the creation myth of Theodotus, was "an independent summary or even an extant copy of the primary source text itself." Auvinen, *Philo's Influence*, 39, 43.

[27] Some scholars of early Christianity speak of a "catechetical school" in this context, but there is debate about how institutionalized Clement's instructions actually were. While there is little doubt about Clement's involvement with instructing baptizands, caution should be exercised in determining the precise nature of this "office." For a concise overview of this debate, see,

writings are full of specific instructions concerning appropriate Christian conduct. What concerns us here are Clement's teachings about proper attire for Christian men and women because it is in this context that a reference to 1 Cor 11:2–16 appears. In his *Paedagogus* (*Christ the Educator*), Clement reserves considerable space for a discussion on this topic. Clement's underlying principle on this matter seems to be that the only purpose of clothing is to cover the body for protection against cold and heat, and so clothing should not be expensive nor ostentatious, but must be plain, simple, and inexpensive (*Paed.* 2.10.102–106). And thus, Clement believes that men and women should essentially wear similar (παραπλήσιος) clothes, except that women should additionally wear a covering that conceals their eyes (εἰ δὲ καὶ σκέπην ταύτην παραληπτέον, καθ' ἣν κρύπτειν ὄμματα θηλειῶν χρεών), because of their weakness (διὰ τὴν ἀσθένειαν, *Paed.* 2.10.106–107). Clement then claims that women "have been commanded" (κεκώλυται) thus to cover their heads and to conceal their faces (ἐγκεκαλύφθαι δὲ καὶ τὴν κεφαλὴν καὶ τὸ πρόσωπον ἐπεσκιάσθαι προστέτακται), but also adds that this required "covering" (τό παραπέτασμα, lit. "curtain") must not be purple in color because that color inflames lusts and brings unwanted attention to that which must remain inconspicuous (*Paed.* 2.10.114–115).

In this context, Clement does not specify who had commanded women to be thus covered, but when Clement later returns to the question of women's head-coverings in his *Paedagogus*, he does reference 1 Cor 11:13, which suggests that 1 Cor 11:2–16 features in the background of also these earlier comments. In this later context, Clement discusses how men and women should dress modestly (κοσμίως) for the gatherings of the Christians, which for women, according to Clement, also means being completely covered (κεκαλύφθω τὰ πάντα). Clement argues that it is necessary for a woman to be so in order that she not become a cause for her own "stumble" (οὔποτε αὐτὴ σφαλήσεται). Furthermore, by not bearing her face (τὸ πρόσωπον ἀπογυμνουμένη), but covering it with a "veil" (τὴν ἀμπεχόνην θεμένη), she also prevents anyone else from sinning. According to Clement, "this is what the Word wishes, that 'it is proper for her to pray having been veiled'" (τοῦτο γὰρ ὁ λόγος βούλεται ἐπεὶ πρέπον αὐτῇ ἐγκεκαλυμμένη προσεύχεσθαι, *Paed.* 3.11.79).

"The Word," that Clement of Alexandria refers to here in his argument for women to cover their heads and faces, is clearly 1 Cor 11:13. However, Clement does not actually quote 1 Cor 11:13 but paraphrases its content—what in Paul is a

---

for example, Henny Fiskå Hägg, *Clement of Alexandria and the Beginnings of Christian Apophaticism* (New York: Oxford University Press, 2006), 55–59; Piotr Ashwin-Siejkowski, *Clement of Alexandria: A Project of Christian Perfection* (New York: T&T Clark, 2008), 31–37.

rhetorical question is turned into a statement of fact by Clement, using his own wording, although the general idea is still recognizably 1 Cor 11:13. That Clement paraphrases 1 Cor 11:13, instead of quoting it from a manuscript, allows us better access to his understanding of 1 Cor 11:2–16 in general. For example, Clement opts to use the verb ἐγκαλύπτω in his paraphrase of 1 Cor 11:13, while the manuscript tradition presents this verse with the adjective ἀκατακάλυπτος. While both of these words share the same καλυπτ- root, ἐγκαλύπτω was more readily used to describe complete hiddenness (of head *and* face), and was also associated with feelings of shame, whereas κατακαλύπτω, that Paul throughout 1 Cor 11:2–16 employs as a remedy for ἀκατακάλυπτος, was used in a much more general sense of "to cover."[28] Thus, we see that Clement understood Paul to have commanded women to completely cover their heads and faces, and believed that this had to do with women's weakness and their proclivity to sin and to be the cause of sin, ideas that are not found in 1 Cor 11:2–16 itself.

There is yet another engagement with 1 Cor 11:2–16 that may be traced to Clement of Alexandria. In a much later biblical commentary of a certain Oecumenios (perhaps from the sixth century CE), several quotes are claimed to have been taken from Clement's *Hypotyposeis*, a work that has itself not survived but which appears to have been Clement's commentary on biblical writings.[29] One of these quotes that Oecumenios presents as Clement's, deals with the enigmatic διὰ τοὺς ἀγγέλους of 1 Cor 11:10:

"Διὰ τοὺς ἀγγέλους." ἀγγέλους φησὶ τοὺς δικαίους καὶ ἐναρέτους. κατακαλυπτέσθω οὖν, ἵνα μὴ εἰς πορνείαν αὐτοὺς σκανδαλίσῃ· οἱ γὰρ ὄντως καὶ ἐν οὐρανοῖς ἄγγελοι καὶ κατακεκαλυμμένην αὐτὴν βλέπουσιν. Οὕτως ὁ Κλήμης ἐν τετάρτῳ Ὑποτυπώσεων.[30]

"'Because of the angels.' He [Paul] says the angels [to be] righteous and virtuous. Let her be covered then, so that she does not cause them to stumble into fornication.[31] For the

---

[28] LSJ, s.v. "ἐγκαλύπτω" and "κατακαλύπτω."

[29] Hägg, *Clement of Alexandria*, 62.

[30] Greek text from Otto Stählin, ed., *Band 3 Stromata. Buch VII und VIII: Excerpta ex Theodoto – Eclogae propheticae quis dives salvetur – Fragmente* (Leipzig: J.C. Hinrichs'she Buchhandlung, 1909), 195.

[31] As discussed in section 1.4.8, πορνεία has been notoriously difficult to translate and define in biblical scholarship. However, it seems that "fornication" is an appropriate translation of this term in relation to Christian writings from at least the second century CE onwards, because *fornicatio* came to be used as the Latin equivalent of πορνεία, and so πορνεία was increasingly defined from this perspective. E.g., Kyle Harper, "*Porneia*: The Making of a Christian Sexual Norm," *JBL* 131 (2011): 379–83.

angels also in heaven likewise see her covered." Thus says Clement in the fourth [book of] *Hypotyposeis*.

If this quote is indeed Clement's, as Oecominius claims, then it shows that Clement understood διὰ τοὺς ἀγγέλους as a reference to the righteous and virtuous heavenly angels, who could be tempted into sin by uncovered women. Thus, Clement appears quite anxious about how much chaos an uncovered face on a woman could cause not only in the congregations of Christians, but also in the heavenly realms. Such an anxiety about how women should appear in regards to their heads is unmatched in the surviving Christian sources predating Clement, but is shared by Clement's contemporary, Tertullian, to whom we turn next.

6.7 Tertullian

Of the surviving early Christian writings, Tertullian's (ca. 155–220) literary output is the first to preserve an elongated engagement with 1 Cor 11:2–16. It is also the first to do so in Latin. Tertullian's prolonged and sustained interest in the interpretation of 1 Cor 11:2–16 revolves around the question of whether this passage demands virgins to also be covered of the head or only the married women. This matter seems to have been quite important for Tertullian, because even though he addresses this issue fairly comprehensively in one of his earlier works, *De oratione* (*Prayer*), he returns to the topic later in his career several more times.[32] One of these later treatments was apparently written in Greek, but it has not survived.[33] This is unfortunate, as it would be fascinating to analyze Tertullian's references to and quotations of Greek 1 Cor 11:2–16 in comparison to how the text has been preserved in the available Greek NT manuscripts and in comparison to how he deals with the passage in Latin. However, we do seem to possess his latest and most comprehensive treatment on the matter, *De virginibus velandis* (*The Veiling of Virgins*), and so here we will summarize Tertullian's main arguments made in this treatise, analyze his use of 1 Cor 11:2–16, and problematize some of his claims.

In the opening statements of *De virgibinus velandis*, Tertullian explains that his main aim in this work is to demonstrate that "it is proper that our virgins be veiled from when they reach puberty" (*Virg.* 1.1).[34] Given that Tertullian had

---

[32] While there is some controversy surrounding the chronology of Tertullian's writings, it seems that *De oratione* is Tertullian's earliest surviving engagement with 1 Cor 11:2–16. See discussion in Geoffrey D. Dunn, *Tertullian* (New York: Routledge, 2004), 5, 96–97.

[33] Dunn, *Tertullian*, 97, 101.

[34] Translations of *De virgibinus velandis* are taken from Dunn, *Tertullian*, 101–15.

already argued for this position in *De oratione*, it appears that this particular stance had garnered much controversy and was met with resistance, prompting Tertullian to then respond with even more arguments, including a more detailed exegesis of 1 Cor 11:2–16. Interestingly, in his introductory remarks, Tertullian argues that his addressees should not be so preoccupied with custom, but should allow the Paraclete to reveal new truths (*Virg.* 1.4–7). This suggests that the custom in Carthage (where Tertullian operates) had thus far been that it was not mandatory for virgin women to cover their heads, and Tertullian admits as much: "But still, among us until recently more tolerance was being shown for each custom. The matter had been entrusted to personal choice, such that each [virgin] had resolved either to be covered or to be exposed" (*Virg.* 3.1). Thus, it appears that it was Tertullian himself who was spearheading a movement to have all the women cover up their heads, and that his was a minority position still at the time of the writing of *De virginibus velandis*.

At the same time, however, Tertullian claims that it was the custom of some other churches in Africa and Greece to veil their virgins (*Virg.* 2.1). Tertullian particularly highlights the example of the church in Corinth, which he claims did so in his day (*Virg.* 8.4). We have no independent verification that this was so; for all we know, Tertullian may have claimed this solely for rhetorical purposes without any actual knowledge of what the church in Corinth (or in some other place) was up to. In any case, this bit of information allows Tertullian to argue, then, that this new light, that the Paraclete was wishing to impart (through Tertullian) on the believers in Carthage about the veiling of virgins, was actually also an ancient custom that could be traced to apostolic origins (*Virg.* 2.1; 8.4). In fact, Tertullian goes so far as to suggest that 1 Cor 11:16 (in which Paul addresses those who wish to be argumentative) demonstrates that already Paul faced opposition on the question of whether virgins should be veiled, meaning that 1 Cor 11:2–15 should be read as Paul's argument that virgins, like other women, should indeed be veiled (*Virg.* 8.4).

Tertullian makes use of almost every clause in 1 Cor 11:2–16 to prove his point. He argues, for example, that "if the head of a woman is a man, certainly [he is head] of a virgin" and "if it is a disgrace for a woman to be shaved or cropped, [it is] especially so for a virgin" (*Virg.* 7.1). Also, "if the glory of a man is a woman, how much more [is] a virgin"; "if a woman [is] from a man and for a man, that rib of Adam was at first a virgin"; and "if a woman ought to have authority on her head, even more rightly [ought] the virgin" (*Virg.* 7.2). Furthermore, Tertullian argues that "the angels" referenced in 1 Cor 11:10 are the fallen angels of Gen 6:2–4, who lusted after human women, and who must therefore have lusted especially after virgins: "Can anyone presume that such angels have desired the already defiled bodies and the relics of human lust instead of being even more on fire for virgins, whose youthful freshness even excuses human lust?" (*Virg.*7.2). Finally, he argues that since Paul deems "cascading hair" as "the honor of a woman ..., certainly this is especially a mark of distinction for a virgin" (*Virg.* 7.4).

Interestingly, in building his thesis that female virgins must be veiled, Tertullian does not ignore Paul's comments about men in 1 Cor 11:2–16:

> Certainly the obverse of all these [arguments] means that a man may not veil his head, because he has not obtained by nature a great display of hair, because to be shaved or cropped is not felt to be a disgrace for him, because it was not on account of him that the angels deviated, because [he is] 'the glory and the image of God', [and] because 'Christ [is] his head'. (*Virg.* 8.1)

However, Tertullian's main point in referencing Paul's comments about men is to demonstrate that these are widely accepted as true for an adult man as they are for "a boy," and so Paul's comments about women must likewise be applicable for both, married women as well as virgins (*Virg.* 8.1).

Yet, what is fascinating about Tertullian reading 1 Cor 11:2–16 as also Paul's command that "a man may not veil his head," is that Tertullian appears to be familiar with the Roman ritual gesture of *capite velato*. In his *Apologeticus* (*Apology*), which is addressed to the "magistrates of the Roman Empire" (*Apol.* 1.1), Tertullian exclaims:

> Looking up to heaven the Christians—with hands outspread (*minibus expansis*), because innocent, with head bare (*capite nudo*) because we do not blush, yes! and without one to give the form of words, for we pray from the heart,— are ever making intercession for all the emperors. (*Apol.* 30.4 [Glover])

It is clear that Tertullian here contrasts how Christians pray with how Romans pray:

> This apologetic description evidently contrasts Christian and Roman prayer practices: *minibus expansis*, which means 'stretched out crosswise', is opposed to the raising of the arms above the head while turning the palms upside; praying 'with bare head' (*capite nudato*) is opposed to the particularly Roman custom of covering the head with the hem of the toga. Tertullian's assertion that Christians prayed without prompters was of particular interest to interpreters, as the use of prompters is widely attested to in Roman religion as well.[35]

---

[35] Klinghardt, "Prayer Formularies for Public Recitation," 2.

Considering, then, the pride that Tertullian takes in (male) Christians praying with a bare head, and his awareness of Paul's instructions that men should not veil, it is possible that these two were connected in Tertullian's mind. However, in none of the surviving literary works does Tertullian actually make that connection obvious. In his exegesis of 1 Cor 11:2–16, Tertullian is so preoccupied with the question of whether female virgins must be covered of the head that he refers to Paul's instructions about men only in passing and mainly to support his main point that female virgins must be covered of the head. Nevertheless, what Tertullian's comment about Christian prayer postures and practices suggests is that by the end of the second century CE, there had developed a tradition among some (only male?) Christians to purposefully pray with a bare head, so as to distinguish from Roman prayer postures and practices. It is entirely possible that at least some such Christians justified their behavior with reference to 1 Cor 11:4, but unfortunately, we possess no sources from this time period in which this is made explicit.

For example, Cyprian of Carthage (ca. 210–258 CE), who was the next-generation intellectual leader in the Christian community of Carthage after Tertullian, also expresses his aversion to *capite velato*, but likewise does so without an explicit reference to 1 Cor 11:4:

> Your head has remained free from the impious and wicked veil with which the captive heads of those who sacrificed were there veiled (*Ab impio sceleratoque velamina, quo illie velabantur sacrificantium capita captiva, caput vestrum liberum mansit*); your brow, pure with the sign of God, could not bear the crown of the devil (*diaboli coronam*), but reserved itself for the Lord's crown.[36] (*Laps.* 2)

Apparently, the Christian community in Carthage at the time of Cyprian had experienced a bout of persecution, during which the Christians were forced to sacrifice in the Roman manner—*capite velato*. Cyprian heaps praise on those who did not cover their heads with "the impious and wicked veil," which he also deems "the crown of the devil." Cyprian thus takes a very strong stance against *capite velato*, but there is no appeal to 1 Cor 11:4 here.

Perhaps by the time of Tertullian (and Cyprian), it was simply self-evident to these Christians that they should not worship in the manner of "pagans," and so this principled decision (for men) not to cover their heads with an outer garment during prayer needed no additional scriptural proof. The case with women's head-coverings, however, seems to have been much more complex, and despite Tertullian's claim that he had Paraclete and custom on his side, his comments suggest

---

[36] Latin text from PL 4:466c; English translation from *ANF* 5.437.

that most everyone else had a rather different view on the matter, including on the interpretation of 1 Cor 11:2–16. For example, in one place in *De virginibus velandis*, Tertullian bemoans the fact that some (presumably married) women would not even cover "during the psalms, or at any mention of God," and would only "place a fringe or a piece of cloth or whatever thread they like over the top their head" when they were about to pray (*Virg.* 17.4). This comment suggests that some women saw no reason to cover their heads (nor eyes) at all times, and that they had interpreted 1 Cor 11:2–16 as instructing women to place something on their heads *only* at the time of prayer, but that this something did not need to cover the head fully, let alone the face. Some other women apparently did cover their heads more regularly, but not in the manner of Tertullian's liking, as they left too much of the head and the neck to be seen (*Virg.* 17.1–2). Interestingly, in castigating these women, Tertullian does not appeal to Christian custom nor scriptures, but calls their attention to recent "revelations," in which it was shown to "a certain sister of ours" in a dream that an appropriate head-covering also covers the neck (*Virg.* 17.3).

However, despite his appeal to Paul, custom, and revelations, it does not appear that Tertullian was particularly successful in convincing his addressees that married women as well as virgins should be meticulously covered of the head (including of the face and of the neck). For example, only a few decades after Tertullian's treatises on this question appeared, Cyprian also addressed the issue of Christian women's (and particularly the virgins') appearances in Carthage. Cyprian instructs the Christian virgins not to braid nor dye their hair, not to dress their hair sumptuously, not to wear ornaments and necklaces that hide the neck, not to pierce their ears, not to wear purple, and not to wear make-up (this last bit he especially highlights for married women and widows as well, *Hab. virg.* 5, 9, 12, 14–16). In none of this does Cyprian mention veils. This is noteworthy, considering that for Tertullian, for example, the simple solution to all of the above problems with women's appearances was for them to be veiled (*Cult. fem.* 2.7), but this solution does not seem to cross Cyprian's mind. This suggests, then, that despite Tertullian's appeals, the Christian virgins in Carthage had not taken him seriously. In fact, Cyprian even has to chastise those virgins who were frequenting public baths, where they were seen naked by men and themselves saw naked men (*Hab. virg.* 19).[37] It shows, then, that some Christian women at the time of Cyprian felt

---

[37] Cyprian was not the only early Christian author who had an issue with (Christian) women visiting Roman baths, which suggests that it was widely practiced, and not only something that

perfectly comfortable not only with their unveiled heads but also in full nakedness in front of strangers. It appears, therefore, that Tertullian's dire warnings about lusting men and fallen angels (cf. *Virg.* 7.3–4) had not registered with these women.

Ironically, however, Tertullian's minority position on the issue of the veiling of virgins survived in all its verbosity for the consumption of much later generations of Christians, who imbued Tertullian (and Clement of Alexandria) with authority on biblical interpretation and on Christian conduct. Unfortunately, we can only guess the views of Tertullian's opponents from his own comments, but we do not have access to their arguments in writing. However, some early Christian writings do preserve hints of alternate viewpoints regarding women's veiling. For example, there is a story in the *Acts of Thomas*, in which a bride about to be married meets the Lord, believes, and as a result removes her veil. When her parents (the king and the queen) challenge her over this act, she replies: "I do not veil myself because the mirror [veil] of shame is taken from me, and I am no longer ashamed or abashed, because the work of shame and bashfulness has been removed far from me" (Acts Thom. 14).[38] Here, the veil is viewed negatively, and the removal of it is hailed as positive, a contrary evaluation to that of Tertullian and Clement of Alexandria.

However, biblical scholarship has traditionally given preferential treatment to the arguments and exegeses of Tertullian and Clement of Alexandria on this question, as they have been viewed to represent "orthodox" or "authoritative" views on the matter. Yet, Tertullian's own writings evidence that there was actually no consensus on the question of women's head-coverings nor on the interpretation of 1 Cor 11:2–16 within his Christian community at the end of the second and at the beginning of the third century CE. Alternate views existed and seem to have won the day for the next few decades at least in Carthage, Tertullian's stronghold. We must be constantly reminded of this fact, because it is tempting for biblical scholars to jump to the first full surviving interpretation of 1 Cor 11:2–16 and think that this represented tradition or consensus on the matter, whereas in reality, it may have been nothing more than ruminations of a man in the minority, who was not heeded in his own day.

---

a small group of Carthagean Christian virgins did. See, Robin Jensen, *Living Water: Images, Symbols, and Settings of Early Christian Baptism* (Boston: Brill, 2011), 159–62.

[38] Translation from Drijvers, "The Acts of Thomas," 344.

6.8 Origen

As we have seen already, the question regarding the identity of "the angels" in 1 Cor 11:10 seems to have been of particular interest to the early readers of 1 Cor 11:2–16. "The Valentinians" thought of these beings as the primordial companions of the savior, Clement of Alexandria imagined them to have been righteous heavenly beings with potential to "stumble" at the sight of uncovered women, and Tertullian viewed them as fallen angels who were lusting after Christian women, particularly after virgins. Origen (ca. 185–253 CE) also weighs in on this debate:

> And angels are present in the church—at least in that church that deserves them and belongs to Christ. This is the reason why women are commanded to have "a veil on their heads" when they pray, because of the angels (*propterea orantibus feminis praecipitur, ut habeant velamen super caput propter angelos*). Which angels? Clearly those who aid the holy ones and rejoice in the church.[39] (*Hom. Luc.* 23.8)

Unfortunately, Origen's homilies on Luke have only survived in Jerome's Latin translation of them,[40] so we do not know how closely Origen's original Greek version resembled the Greek NT manuscripts. For example, in Jerome's translation here, the noun *velamen* ("veil") is used, but we do not know whether Origen used κάλυμμα, like some "Valentinians" had done (and perhaps also Irenaeus), κατακαλύπτω, like it was in the Greek NT manuscripts, or ἐγκαλύπτω, the preferred verb of Clement of Alexandria. In any case, Origen's identification of "the angels" here resembles Clement of Alexandria's take on the matter, although unlike Clement, Origen does not provide a reason as to why women must then be veiled because of these helpful beings in their midst. But Origen's question of "which angels?" suggests that he may have been aware of alternate interpretations of "the angels" (e.g., Tertullian's identification of them as fallen lustful beings), and so his own comment was intended to dismiss such views.

6.9 *Dialogue between a Montanist and an Orthodox*

Most early engagements with 1 Cor 11:2–16 take the subject matter of this passage to be concerned with literal head-coverings. However, in a tractate known as *Dialogue between a Montanist and an Orthodox*, an allegorical interpretation of 1 Cor 11:2–16 is also preserved. Although this tractate was anonymously written,

---

[39] English translation from Joseph T. Lienhard, trans., *Origen. Homilies on Luke. Fragments on Luke*, FC 94 (Washington, D.C.: The Catholic University of America Press, 1996), 101.

[40] On this, see, Lienhard, *Origen*, xxxii–xxxvi.

Didymus the Blind (ca. 313–398 CE) has most often been associated with its authorship. At the very least, he seems to have known of this work, and so the composition of *Dialogue* can be dated to somewhere in the fourth century CE.⁴¹ I reproduce here in full the portion of this debate between a Montanist and an Orthodox that deals with 1 Cor 11:2–16, as it is quite instructive:

> The Montanist: Why do you reject the holy women Maximilla and Priscilla and say that women are not allowed to prophesy? Did not Philip also have four daughters who prophesied (Acts 21:9)? And was Deborah not a prophetess (Judg 4:4)? And if it is not [permissible] for women to prophesy or pray, would the apostle say: any woman who prays or prophesies with her head unveiled (Πᾶσα γυνὴ προσευχομένη ἢ προφητεύουσα ἀκατακαλύπτῳ τῇ κεφαλῇ;)? But if women pray, let them also prophesy.
>
> The Orthodox: We do not reject the prophecies of women: the holy Mary also prophesied when she said: henceforth all generations will call me blessed (Luke 1:48). As you said yourself, Philip had four daughters who prophesied, and Mary, the sister of Aaron, prophesied (Exod 15:20). But we do not allow them to speak in the churches (1 Cor 14:34), nor to have authority over men (1 Tim 2:12), in that books are written in their names—for this is the meaning of their praying and prophesying with unveiled head (τοῦτο γάρ ἐστιν ἀκατακαλύπτως αὐτὰς προσεύχεσθαι καὶ προφητεύειν), and [the apostle did not allow woman to do it because it] dishonored her head, that is, the man (καὶ οὖν κατῄσχυνε τὴν κεφαλὴν τουτέστι(ν) τὸν ἄνδρα). Mary, the holy Mother of God, was surely capable of writing books in her own name, was she not? But she did not do it, so as not to dishonor her head, by having authority over men (1 Tim 2:12).
>
> The Montanist: So praying or prophesying with unveiled head means writing books (Τὸ γὰρ ἀκατακαλύπτῳ τῇ κεφαλῇ προσεύχεσθαι ἢ προφητεύειν ἐστὶ τὸ μὴ γράφειν βιβλία;)?
>
> The Orthodox: Exactly.
>
> The Montanist: Then if the holy Mary says, Henceforth all generations will call me blessed, does she say this as one unveiled (ἀνακεκαλυμμένως), that is, as one speaking freely, or not?
>
> The Orthodox: She has the Gospel writer as a veil (κάλυμμα). She has not written the Gospel in her own name.
>
> The Montanist: You should not take allegorical interpretations for authoritative teaching.
>
> The Orthodox: But the holy Paul most certainly used allegory to confirm his teachings when he said, Abraham had two wives. Now this is an allegory: these women are two covenants (Gal 4:24). But for the sake of argument let us allow that the veil of the head is not meant as an allegory. If you want to dismiss all allegory, answer this for me: if a

---

⁴¹ See, William Tabbernee, *Montanist Inscriptions and Testimonia: Epigraphic Sources Illustrating the History of Montanism* (Macon, GA: Mercer University Press, 1997), 354–55.

woman is poor and has nothing with which to veil herself (καὶ μὴ ἔχῃ, τί κατακαλύπτεται), must she refrain from praying and prophesying?

The Montanist: Can she be so poor as to have nothing with which to cover herself (ὡς μὴ ἔχειν τί σκεπάσεται;)?

The Orthodox: We have often seen women so poor as not to have anything with which to cover themselves (σκεπάσονται). But since you refuse to admit that women can be so poor that they have nothing with which to cover themselves (σκεπάσονται), what do you do in the case of those who are being baptized? Are those who are being baptized not required to pray? And what do you say in the case of men, who often cover their heads (σκεπαζομένων τὴν κεφαλήν) because of illness. Do you forbid them from praying and prophesying?

The Montanist: During the time when such a man prays or prophesies, he uncovers (ἀνακαλύπτεται).

The Orthodox: Must he not pray constantly in order to obey the apostle who teaches him to pray constantly (1 Thess 5:17)? And are you also counseling the woman who is being baptized not to pray?

The Montanist: So the reason you do not accept Priscilla and Maximilla is that they wrote books?

The Orthodox: Not for this reason alone, but also because they were false prophetesses, as their leader Montanus was a false prophet.

The Montanist: And what leads you to conclude that they were false prophetesses?

The Orthodox: Did they not teach the same things as Montanus?

The Montanist: Yes.

The Orthodox: We have shown that Montanus taught things contrary to divine Scripture, and so these women must be rejected along with him.[42]

The debate here centers on the question of whether women are allowed to prophesy. The Montanist accuses the Orthodox of rejecting women prophets and points out, among other things, that 1 Cor 11:2–16 takes it for granted that women prophesy. The Orthodox denies the accusation, but takes exception to how the Montanist interprets 1 Cor 11:2–16. The Orthodox claims that 1 Cor 11:2–16 cannot literally speak about praying and prophesying with head-coverings, because poor women and those being baptized cannot cover their heads, but are still expected to pray, while men who are ill need to cover their heads even though they are to also pray

---

[42] English translation (with some modifications) from Judith L. Kovacs, ed. and trans., *1 Corinthians: Interpreted by Early Christian Commentators* (Grand Rapids: Eerdmans, 2005), 180–82. Greek text from Ronald E. Heine, *The Montanist Oracles and Testimonia* (Macon, GA: Mercer University Press, 1989), 124–27.

constantly. Thus, according to the Orthodox, the passage must be read allegorically, and so what Paul actually forbids in this text is for women to write books. This interpretive maneuver allows the Orthodox to then accept the prophecies of women like Mary, whose prophetic utterances were known only through the writings of the (male) evangelist Luke, and reject the prophecies of the Montanist prophetesses Maximilla and Priscilla, who had apparently written books.

This is a novel interpretation of 1 Cor 11:2–16, and it is interesting that it is associated here with "orthodox" Christianity. Traditionally, "orthodoxy" on this matter has been afforded to the likes of Clement of Alexandria and Tertullian, who, as we have seen, argued that Paul in 1 Cor 11:2–16 required all females to be completely covered of the head and of the face (whenever in public) because of how much damage an uncovered head on a woman could cause in the Christian congregations and in heaven. Yet, the *Dialogue* demonstrates that this anxiety about uncovered heads on women that some (Christian) men felt was not as deeply shared in some other circles of Christianity. The Orthodox of the *Dialogue* is more concerned about women writing books than he is with them wearing head-coverings. He takes it for granted, for example, that when women are being baptized, they have nothing on their heads, and that some women cannot even afford such items of clothing with which to cover their heads. The Montanist, on the other hand, does seem to take Paul's instructions in 1 Cor 11:2–16 more literally, and so it is possible that in these circles of Christianity, women who were welcomed to prophesy, were nevertheless asked to be covered when doing so. However, the *Dialogue* does not give too much space to the Montanist interpretation of 1 Cor 11:2–16 beyond the Montanist's caution that this passage should not be read allegorically, and so we do not know exactly how Paul's instructions regarding head-coverings were implemented in the Christian communities that encouraged and welcomed women prophets.

6.10 John Chrysostom

We end where we began—with John Chrysostom. In Chapter 1, I discussed Chrysostom's proposal that 1 Cor 11:2–16 addresses certain Greek customs in regards to hair and head-coverings that the Corinthians practiced that Paul found problematic, and I demonstrated that there is no merit to Chrysostom's hypothesis, as the available evidence does not support it. In the closing of the current chapter, however, I want to present a particular interpretive strategy of Chrysostom's that he makes use of in his sermon on this passage, since this way of reading the text became a standard for a long time. That is, Chrysostom reads 1 Cor 11:2–16 in conjunction with and through 1 Tim 2:11–14 and Eph 5:21–24 (e.g., PG 61:215a–216a), the two passages, discussed above, that appropriate and rework some of Paul's ideas from 1 Cor 11:2–16 (see section 6.3). Chrysostom assumes all these passages to be inspired writings of Paul and that they therefore address the same issue—subjection of woman. Due to this, Chrysostom claims that Paul wished women to always dress in a way that symbolized their subjection to man (e.g., PG 61:220b), and this, therefore, is also the purpose of women wearing head-coverings (which Chrysostom identifies as mantles and veils). As we have seen, however, Paul never claims a woman's head-covering to be a symbol of subjection, and if we remove 1 Tim 2 and Eph 5 as the lenses through which to read 1 Cor 11:2–16, nothing compels us to interpret Paul as doing so. Chrysostom's commentary on this passage is therefore a fitting example of how the lenses through which 1 Cor 11:2–16 is read, dictates what the passage is thought to address.

6.11 Conclusion

There are clear reasons why the interpretive framework of *capite velato* was lost sight of in the early Christian engagements with 1 Cor 11:2–16. First, Paul's instructions may have already been ignored or rejected by the very people to whom they were addressed, as conflict over Paul's authority took center stage. Considering that there is nothing in any other Christian source that even remotely resembles the "traditions" of 1 Cor 11:2–16 from the first hundred years after the composition of 1 Cor, we can be fairly certain that no independent (Pauline) tradition was in circulation in this regard.

Second, within decades after Paul's death, certain individuals or groups had reworked some of the ideas that Paul in 1 Cor 11:2–16 based his arguments on: Christ's headship over man, man's headship over woman, and priority of man in creation. I have shown how these concepts, that Paul employed to argue that man and woman accrue and distribute shame and honor differently, were reworked to justify women's subjugation and their forced silence, all in Paul's name. These later reworkings, however, had an enormous influence on how 1 Cor 11:2–16 came to be read, since it became a standard assumption that all of these texts were authentically Pauline and addressed the same issue. Thus, focus was shifted from the conduct of *both*, men and women, to the problematic conduct of *only* women.

Third, some early readers replaced ἐξουσία with κάλυμμα in 1 Cor 11:10, even though the Greek manuscripts appear not to have given them a reason for this alteration. Because of this change, however, the verse that otherwise reads as an affirmation for women to have control over their heads, was now read as a demand for women to have a *veil* on their heads. This way of understanding the text appears to have become dominant, which therefore reinforced this idea that Paul in 1 Cor 11:2–16 was particularly concerned with *women's* veils even further.

Fourth, some early Christian intellectuals exhibited great anxiety about the seductive power of women's appearances, and their solution to this was to limit the visibleness of women. They interpreted 1 Cor 11:2–16 through these anxieties, and found in it a ready ally for their mission to cover up all women beyond recognition and beyond a possibility of arousal (even in heaven). Even though in their own day and age, these men may have been in the minority, their readings became authoritative, especially as asceticism became one of the defining features of Christianity.

It is easy to see why with each coating of these interpretive layers on 1 Cor 11:2–16, *capite velato* as an interpretive framework was not entertained, even though the ritual gesture of *capite velato* was well known to many Christians at least until the third century CE. In this work, however, I have attempted to peel back these interpretive layers and read 1 Cor 11:2–16 not with feelings of anxiety about the seductive power of women's uncovered heads, not with κάλυμμα as the subject matter, and not through 1 Tim 2:11–14 and Eph 5:21–24, but as a message addressed to those men and women, who were intimately familiar with praying and accessing divine (fore)knowledge with a garment over the head. And despite the earliest surviving readings of 1 Cor 11:2–16 not being on my side on this issue, I retain that *capite velato* as an interpretive framework best explains Paul's arguments in this passage.

7. Conclusions

It is unfortunate that we do not have access to the report of "Chloe's people" (cf. 1 Cor 1:11) nor to the letter(s) that the Corinthians sent to Paul (cf. 1 Cor 7:1) nor to the now lost letters that Paul sent to the Corinthians (cf. 1 Cor 5:9; 2 Cor 2:4). And it is a pity that no one kept a record of Paul's face-to-face conflict management with the Corinthian congregation during his last visit(s) with them. We would be in a much better position to make sense of why Paul said the things that he did in his surviving letters, including why he addressed the issue of head-coverings the way that he did. Nearly two thousand years of confused scholarship on this passage of 1 Cor 11:2–16 has demonstrated that we could do with some extra resources.

But we have to do with what we have, and imagine the rest. And what we have is enough to generate reasonable hypotheses. For starters, we have a text that in P46, for example, is a page and a half long. The words in this text are arranged in a way that creates easily discernible thought patterns, and so we can be confident that the intention of the author of this passage was to communicate sensible ideas to the addressees. We can also clearly make out that one of the main foci of this passage is concerned with "covered" and "uncovered" heads during the activities of praying and prophesying. This is quite a specific topic, which allows us to set this text in comparison with material that is similarly specific about appearances during devotional acts.

In fact, the phrase κατὰ κεφαλῆς ἔχων, that is employed in this passage, is so peculiar that its relatively rare use in contemporary sources points to a very specific appearance: an outer garment over the head. And there is plenty of evidence that praying, sacrificing, and accessing of divine (fore)knowledge with an outer garment over the head was widely practiced by Romans in all corners of the empire from at least the time of Augustus until well into the third century CE. We find mention of this practice in several Greek and Latin texts and also in Josephus, and we find it depicted on monuments, statues, altars, walls, and domestic statuettes in Italy, Greece, and other territories of the former empire. There is, therefore, a strong reason to entertain the possibility that 1 Cor 11:2–16 belongs with this pool of material. And this is what this thesis has been all about—an attempt to read 1 Cor 11:2–16 in light of the available evidence on *capite velato*, the Roman ritual gesture of covering the head with the edge of an outer garment when praying, sacrificing, or seeking divine (fore)knowledge.

But this exercise requires a fair bit of imagination. It is not self-evident why Paul would discourage men from performing *capite velato* during praying and accessing of divine (fore)knowledge but would not do so in regards to women, even though Roman women also worshiped their gods with covered heads. But with the aid of some theories that cognitive scientists of religion have put forward concerning ritual behavior, in addition to the evidence we have of head-coverings in antiquity, of the make-up of first-century Roman Corinth, and of the Christ association located there, I have imagined the following scenario: When Paul first visited Corinth, some influential men of Roman background (e.g., Gaius) joined the Christ association that Paul was establishing there. These men had been used to praying, sacrificing, and accessing divine (fore)knowledge with a covered head. This way of worshiping indicated to everyone else that they were Roman. In a cultural hodgepodge of first-century Corinth, exhibiting one's Roman-ness had clear social benefits. When these men (and their families) then joined the Christ association, they continued to worship in a Roman manner—whether during assemblies, in their homes, at banquets, on street corners, or in Roman temples—in full display of their status in society. This, however, caused some friction in the fledgling movement that counted in its number also those that were of non-Roman background, such as those of Judean heritage and Greek heritage. Paul, therefore, decided to address the matter by requesting those with affiliations to Rome to cease practicing *capite velato* for the sake of the unity of the congregation, intending his congregants to adhere to his "traditions" also outside of their own gatherings. And then he left.

After Paul's departure, some began questioning Paul's reasoning behind his request for *capite velato* not to be performed, while others, on the other hand, took Paul's instructions seriously, and began arguing that not only should *Romans* stop performing *capite velato*, but that all those who claimed allegiance to the Christ association of Corinth—including women of every ethnicity, marital status, and age—should from now on pray and access divine (fore)knowledge with absolutely nothing on their heads or in their hair wherever that took place. This way, the Corinthian Christ association would be in uniformity in regards to the question of how to pray and access divine (fore)knowledge. This development, however, greatly disturbed some female members of the congregation and also their husbands, because for these women, covering the head symbolized their faithfulness to their husbands and longevity of their marriages. They made their concerns known.

Against this backdrop, Paul's comments in 1 Cor 11:2–16 can be reasonably explained. That is, Paul both affirms and bolsters his initial stance on why *capite velato* should not be performed, while he also explains why this idea that all of the congregants, including non-Roman women, should be stripped of everything off their heads for prayer and accessing of divine (fore)knowledge is not an acceptable development of his traditions. Paul bases his argument on the idea that men and women have different metaphorical heads, which then affects how their literal heads relate to honor and shame. Thus, a man who is God's honor because he was created first, has no obligation to cover his literal head with anything, because he cannot enhance that honor through such actions. On the contrary, by covering his literal head during praying and prophesying, he instead brings dishonor on his metaphorical head, *kyrios* Jesus the Messiah, who is his immediate social superior—a sentiment that Romans would have, in principle, agreed with, as it was customary for them to remove their garments off the head when meeting persons of honor.

In Paul's view this does not affect women, however. Paul's arrangement of the metaphorical heads in a hierarchical relationship of God-Christ-man-woman allows him to argue that a woman's immediate concern is rather with the honor of man, from whom and for whom she was created. She cannot, therefore, be stripped of her head-coverings and hair accessories during prayer and accessing of divine (fore)knowledge, because that dishonors her male relations, as well as the male angels who mediate her prayers to God and God's (fore)knowledge to her. Thus, she must have the right to dress her head in connection to the honor of her male relations. In support of this argument, Paul points to the natural way men and women grow their hair—what is shameful on one, is honorable on the other. And thus, it is also perfectly reasonable for Paul that men and women pray and access divine (fore)knowledge with contrasting appearances of the head.

It appears, however, that the letter which Paul sent to the Corinthians with these and other instructions deepened an ongoing conflict over Paul's authority on matters of conduct and belief. Some in the congregation challenged Paul outright, while others were persuaded by some traveling missionaries not to imbue Paul with absolute authority. Paul responded with letters and visits to mend his relationship with the congregation and to win back full confidence of the

Corinthian believers. We do not know how successful he was, but it seems that in this struggle for the Corinthians' allegiance, some of the issues that Paul had addressed in 1 Cor, including his instructions on head-coverings, were either ignored, forgotten about, or solved unceremoniously, whether in line with Paul's instructions or in some other manner. Either way, no other early Christian community or Christian author appears to have been familiar with any Christian or Pauline tradition about head-coverings during praying or prophesying, which suggests that none circulated independently.

But by the considerably later time when Paul's letters began to be copied and passed around in a collection, certain compositions known as the Letter to the Ephesians and the First Letter to Timothy had been added that claimed to have been written by Paul himself, although that seems unlikely to have been the case. These later letters portrayed Paul as someone who took great interest in how Christian households and congregations were to be managed and in the place of women in these realms—that they should be in subjection to their husbands in everything, that they should be silent during congregational meetings, and should never teach nor have authority over a man. In arguing for this, these letters made use of certain concepts that Paul had relied on in his argument in 1 Cor 11:2–16, but reworked them to fit their agenda. Even later readers, however, who took this collection of writings as all authentically Pauline, assumed, therefore, that all these texts spoke of the same concerns—a necessity of a woman's subjection to her husband and of her invisibility during the gatherings. Increasingly more interpreters then began to read 1 Cor 11:2–16 as addressing first and foremost a problem with the Corinthian women overstepping their God-ordained limits. This assumption became so entrenched that it remains the most dominant reading of this passage to this day. However, the last one hundred years of biblical scholarship has demonstrated that interpreting 1 Cor 11:2–16 with this assumption does not lead to a coherent explanation of Paul's argument.

I propose, therefore, that we not read 1 Cor 11:2–16 through the lens of Eph 5:21–24 and 1 Tim 2:11–14, but that we peel back these later interpretive layers and attempt to understand the passage in its own right. And when we do so, we find that there are strong linguistic and thematic links with *capite velato*, a gesture that must have been known to Paul and the Corinthians in the middle of the first century CE. In this thesis, I have argued that when *capite velato* is taken as an interpretive framework of 1 Cor 11:2–16, a certain coherency appears in Paul's argument, which it otherwise lacks. It then allows us to recharacterize 1 Cor 11:2–16 not as "obscure" and "peevish," as much of modern biblical scholarship has come to think of it (see Introduction), but as Paul's thoughtful, considerate, innovative, and practical response to a reaction that his traditions had elicited. But whether the Corinthians thought of these instructions in these terms is another matter entirely, as is the question of whether this passage has any relevance or applicability in modern times.

Bibliography

Ancient sources

The Ante-Nicene Fathers. Edited by Alexander Roberts and James Donaldson. 1885–1887. 10 vols. Repr., Peabody, MA: Hendrickson, 1994.
Appian. *Roman History.* Vol. 3: *The Civil Wars, Books 1–3.26.* Translated by Horace White. LCL. Cambridge, MA: Harvard University Press, 1913.
Apuleius. *Metamorphoses (The Golden Ass).* Translated by J. Arthur Hanson. LCL. 2 vols. Cambridge, MA: Harvard University Press, 1989–1996.
Aristotle. *Politics.* Translated by H. Rackham. LCL. Cambridge, MA: Harvard University Press, 1932.
Bethge, Hans-Gebhard and Bentley Layton, trans. "On the Origin of the World (II,5 and XIII,2)." Pages 170–89 in *The Nag Hammadi Library in English.* Edited by James M. Robinson. New York: HarperCollins, 1990.
Bonwetsch, Georg Nathanael, and Marcel Richard, eds. *Kommentar zu Daniel.* Bd. 1, T. 1 of *Hippolyt Werke,* 2nd ed. GCS, N.F. 7. Berlin: Akad. Verl.; De Gruyter, 2000.
Casey, Robert Pierce, ed. *The Excerpta ex Theodoto of Clement of Alexandria.* London: Christophers, 1934.
Catullus, Tibullus. *Catullus. Tibullus. Pervigilium Veneris.* Translated by F. W. Cornish, J. P. Postgate, J. W. Mackail. Revised by G. P. Goold. LCL. Cambridge, MA: Harvard University Press, 1913.
Cicero. *On Duties.* Translated by Walter Miller. LCL. Cambridge, MA: Harvard University Press, 1913.
Cicero. *On Old Age. On Friendship. On Divination.* Translated by W. A. Falconer. LCL. Cambridge, MA: Harvard University Press, 1923.
Cicero. *On the Nature of the Gods. Academics.* Translated by H. Rackham. LCL. Cambridge, MA: Harvard University Press, 1933.
Cicero. *Pro Archia. Post Reditum in Senatu. Post Reditum ad Quirites. De Domo Sua. De Haruspicum Responsis. Pro Plancio.* Translated by N. H. Watts. LCL. Cambridge, MA: Harvard University Press, 1923.
Clement of Alexandria. *Paedagogus.* PG 8. Edited by J.-P. Migne. Paris, 1857.
Cyprian. *De habitu virginum.* PL 4. Edited by J.-P. Migne. Paris, 1844.
Cyprian. *De lapsis.* PL 4. Edited by J.-P. Migne. Paris, 1844.
De Jonge, M., ed. *The Testaments of the Twelve Patriarchs: A Critical Edition of the Greek Text.* Leiden: Brill, 1978.
De Santos Otero, Aurelio, trans. "The Pseudo-Titus Epistle." Pages 53–74 in vol. 2 of *New Testament Apocrypha.* Edited by Wilhelm Schneemelcher. Translated by R. McL. Wilson. Louisville, KY: Westminster John Knox, 2003.

Dio Cassius. *Roman History*. Vol 4: *Books 41–45*. Translated by Earnest Cary, Herbert B. Foster. LCL. Cambridge, MA: Harvard University Press, 1916.

Dio Chrysostom. *Discourses 31–36*. Translated by J. W. Cohoon, H. Lamar Crosby. LCL. Cambridge, MA: Harvard University Press, 1940.

Dionysius of Halicarnassus. *Roman Antiquities*. Vol. 1: *Books 1–2*. Translated by Earnest Cray. LCL. Cambridge, MA: Harvard University Press, 1937.

Dionysius of Halicarnassus. *Roman Antiquities*. Vol. 2: *Books 3–4*. Translated by Earnest Cray. LCL. Cambridge, MA: Harvard University Press, 1939.

Dionysius of Halicarnassus. *Roman Antiquities*. Vol. 7: *Books 11–20*. Translated by Earnest Cray. LCL. Cambridge, MA: Harvard University Press, 1950.

Drijvers, Han J. W., trans. "Acts of Thomas." Pages 322–411 in vol. 2 of *New Testament Apocrypha*. Edited by Wilhelm Schneemelcher. Translated by R. McL. Wilson. Louisville, KY: Westminster John Knox, 2003.

Ehrman, Bart D., and Zlatko Pleše. *The Apocryphal Gospels: Texts and Translations*. New York: Oxford University Press, 2011.

Epictetus. *Discourses, Books 1–2*. Translated by W. A. Oldfather. LCL. Cambridge, MA: Harvard University Press, 1925.

Euripides. *Bacchanals. Madness of Hercules. Children of Hercules. Phoenician Maidens. Suppliants*. Translated by Arthur S. Way. LCL. New York: The MacMillan Co., 1912.

Gellius, Aulus. *Attic Nights*. Translated by John C. Rolfe. LCL. 3 vols. Cambridge: Harvard University Press, 1927.

Herodotus. *The Persian Wars*. Vol. 2: *Books 3–4*. Translated by A. D. Godley. LCL. Cambridge, MA: Harvard University Press, 1921.

Herodotus. *The Persian Wars*. Vol. 3: *Books 5–7*. Translated by A. D. Godley. LCL. Cambridge, MA: Harvard University Press, 1922.

Herodotus. *The Persian Wars*. Vol. 4: *Books 8–9*. Translated by A. D. Godley. LCL. Cambridge, MA: Harvard University Press, 1925.

Historia Augusta. Vol. 1. Translated by David Magie. Revised by David Rohrbacher. LCL. Cambridge, MA: Harvard University Press, 2022.

John Chrysostom. *Homiliae in epistulam i ad Corinthios*. PG 61. Edited by J.-P. Migne. Paris, 1862.

Josephus. Translated by Henry St. J. Thackeray et al. LCL. 10 vols. Cambridge: Harvard University Press, 1926–1965.

Juvenal, Persius. *Juvenal and Persius*. Translated by G. G. Ramsay. LCL. Cambridge, MA: Harvard University Press, 1928.

Kovacs, Judith L, ed. and trans. *1 Corinthians: Interpreted by Early Christian Commentators*. Grand Rapids: Eerdmans, 2005.

Layton, Bentley, trans. *The Gnostic Scriptures*. Second edition. AYBRL. New Haven: Yale University Press, 2021.

Lewis, Naphtali, and Meyer Reinhold, eds. *Roman Civilization, Sourcebook II: The Empire*. New York: Harper & Row, 1966.

Lienhard, Joseph T., trans. *Origen. Homilies on Luke. Fragments on Luke*. FC 94. Washington, D.C.: The Catholic University of America Press, 1996.

Livy. *History of Rome*. Vol 1: *Books 1–2*. Translated by B. O. Foster. LCL. Cambridge, MA: Harvard University Press, 1919.

Livy. *History of Rome.* Vol 2: *Books 3–4.* Translated by B. O. Foster. LCL. Cambridge, MA: Harvard University Press, 1922.
Livy. *History of Rome.* Vol 3: *Books 5–7.* Translated by B. O. Foster. LCL. Cambridge, MA: Harvard University Press, 1924.
Livy. *History of Rome.* Vol 4: *Books 8–10.* Translated by B. O. Foster. LCL. Cambridge, MA: Harvard University Press, 1926.
Livy. *History of Rome.* Vol 11: *Books 38–39.* Translated by Evan T. Sage. LCL. Cambridge, MA: Harvard University Press, 1936.
Lucian. *How to Write History. The Dipsads. Saturnalia. Herodotus or Aetion. Zeuxis or Antiochus. A Slip of the Tongue in Greeting. Apology for the "Salaried Posts in Great Houses." Harmonides. A Conversation with Hesiod. The Scythian or The Consul. Hermotimus or Concerning the Sects. To One Who Said "You're a Prometheus in Words." The Ship or The Wishes.* Translated by K. Kilburn. LCL. Cambridge, MA: Harvard University Press, 1959.
Lucian. *The Passing of Peregrinus. The Runaways. Toxaris or Friendship. The Dance. Lexiphanes. The Eunuch. Astrology. The Mistaken Critic. The Parliament of the Gods. The Tyrannicide. Disowned.* Translated by A. M. Harmon. LCL. Cambridge, MA: Harvard University Press, 1936.
Lucretius. *On the Nature of Things.* Translated by W. H. D. Rouse. Revised by Martin F. Smith. LCL. Cambridge, MA: Harvard University Press, 1924.
Ovid. *Fasti.* Translated by James G. Frazer. Revised by G. P. Goold. LCL. Cambridge, MA: Harvard University Press, 1931.
Ovid. *Metamorphoses.* Vol. 1: *Books 1–8.* Translated by Frank Justus Miller. Revised by G. P. Goold. LCL. Cambridge, MA: Harvard University Press, 1916.
Pausanias. *Description of Greece.* Vol. 3: *Books 6–8.21.* Translated by W. H. S. Jones. LCL. Cambridge, MA: Harvard University Press, 1933.
Philo. *Every Good Man is Free. On the Contemplative Life. On the Eternity of the World. Against Flaccus. Apology for the Jews. On Providence.* Translated by F. H. Colson. LCL. Cambridge, MA: Harvard University Press, 1941.
Philo. *On Abraham. On Joseph. On Moses.* Translated by F. H. Colson. Cambridge, MA: Harvard University Press, 1935.
Philo. *On Flight and Finding. On the Change of Names. On Dreams.* Translated by F. H. Colson, G. H. Whitaker. LCL. MA: Harvard University Press, 1934.
Philo. *On the Confusion of Tongues. On the Migration of Abraham. Who is the Heir of Divine Things? On Mating with the Preliminary Studies.* Translated by F. H. Colson, G. H. Whitaker. LCL. Cambridge, MA: Harvard University Press, 1932.
Philo. *On the Creation. Allegorical Interpretation of Genesis 2 and 3.* Translated by F. H. Colson, G. H. Whitaker. LCL. Cambridge, MA: Harvard University Press, 1929.
Philo. *On the Decalogue. On the Special Laws, Books 1–3.* Translated by F. H. Colson. Cambridge: Harvard University Press, 1937.
Philo. *On the Embassy to Gaius. General Indexes.* Translated by F. H. Colson. Index by J. W. Earp. LCL. Cambridge, MA: Harvard University Press, 1962.
Philo. *On the Special Laws, Book 4. On the Virtues. On Rewards and Punishments.* Translated by F. H. Colson. LCL. Cambridge, MA: Harvard University Press, 1939.
Plautus. *Amphitryon. The Comedy of Asses. The Pot of Gold. The Two Bacchises. The Captives.* Translated by Paul Nixon. LCL. Cambridge, MA: Harvard University Press, 1916.

Pliny. *Natural History*. Vol. 1: *Books 1–2*. Translated by H. Rackham. LCL. Cambridge, MA: Harvard University Press, 1938.

Pliny. *Natural History*. Vol. 2: *Books 3–7*. Translated by H. Rackham. LCL. Cambridge, MA: Harvard University Press, 1942.

Pliny. *Natural History*. Vol. 5: *Books 17–19*. Translated by H. Rackham. LCL. Cambridge, MA: Harvard University Press, 1950.

Pliny. *Natural History*. Vol. 8: *Books 28–32*. Translated by W. H. S. Jones. LCL. Cambridge, MA: Harvard University Press, 1963.

Plutarch. *Lives*. Vol. 1: *Theseus and Romulus. Lycurgus and Numa. Solon and Publicola*. Translated by Bernadotte Perrin. LCL. Cambridge, MA: Harvard University Press, 1914.

Plutarch. *Lives*. Vol. 2: *Themistocles and Camillus. Aristides and Cato Major. Cimon and Lucullus*. Translated by Bernadotte Perrin. LCL. Cambridge, MA: Harvard University Press, 1914.

Plutarch. *Lives*. Vol. 3: *Pericles and Fabius Maximus. Nicias and Crassus*. Translated by Bernadotte Perrin. LCL. Cambridge, MA: Harvard University Press, 1916.

Plutarch. *Lives*. Vol. 4: *Alcibiades and Coriolanus. Lysander and Sulla*. Translated by Bernadotte Perrin. LCL. Cambridge, MA: Harvard University Press, 1916.

Plutarch. *Lives*. Vol. 5: *Agesilaus and Pompey. Pelopidas and Marcellus*. Translated by Bernadotte Perrin. LCL. Cambridge, MA: Harvard University Press, 1917.

Plutarch. *Lives*. Vol. 6: *Dion and Brutus. Timoleon and Aemilius Paulus*. Translated by Bernadotte Perrin. LCL. Cambridge, MA: Harvard University Press, 1918.

Plutarch. *Lives*. Vol. 7: *Demosthenes and Cicero. Alexander and Caesar*. Translated by Bernadotte Perrin. LCL. Cambridge, MA: Harvard University Press, 1919.

Plutarch. *Lives*. Vol. 8: *Sertorius and Eumenes. Phocion and Cato the Younger*. Translated by Bernadotte Perrin. LCL. Cambridge, MA: Harvard University Press, 1919.

Plutarch. *Lives*. Vol. 10: *Agis and Cleomenes. Tiberius and Gaius Gracchus. Philopoemen and Flamininus*. Translated by Bernadotte Perrin. LCL. Cambridge, MA: Harvard University Press, 1921.

Plutarch. *Lives*. Vol. 11: *Aratus. Artaxerxes. Galba. Otho. General Index*. Translated by Bernadotte Perrin. LCL. Cambridge, MA: Harvard University Press, 1926.

Plutarch. *Moralia*. Vol. 3: *Sayings of Kings and Commanders. Sayings of Romans. Sayings of Spartans. The Ancient Customs of the Spartans. Sayings of Spartan Women. Bravery of Women*. Translated by Frank Cole Babbitt. LCL. Cambridge, MA: Harvard University Press, 1931.

Plutarch. *Moralia*. Vol. 4: *Roman Questions. Greek Questions. Greek and Roman Parallel Stories. On the Fortune of the Romans. On the Fortune or the Virtue of Alexander. Were the Athenians More Famous in War or in Wisdom?* Translated by Frank Cole Babbitt. LCL. Cambridge, MA: Harvard University Press, 1936.

Plutarch. *Moralia*. Vol. 5: *Isis and Osiris. The E at Delphi. The Oracles at Delphi No Longer Given in Verse. The Obsolescence of Oracles*. Translated by Frank Cole Babbitt. LCL. Cambridge, MA: Harvard University Press, 1936.

Quintilian. *The Orator's Education*. Vol. 1: *Books 1–2*. Translated by Donald A. Russell. LCL. Cambridge, MA: Harvard University Press, 2002.

Sallust. *Fragments of the Histories. Letters to Caesar*. Translated by John T. Ramsey. LCL. Cambridge, MA: Harvard University Press, 2015.

Schneemelcher, Wilhelm, trans. "The Acts of Paul." Pages 237–63 in vol. 2 of *New Testament Apocrypha*. Edited by Wilhelm Schneemelcher. Translated by R. McL. Wilson. Louisville, KY: Westminster John Knox, 2003.
Seneca. *Epistles*. Vol. 2: *Epistles 66–92*. Translated by Richard M. Gummere. LCL. Cambridge, MA: Harvard University Press, 1920.
Seneca. *Epistles*. Vol. 3: *Epistles 93–124*. Translated by Richard M. Gummere. LCL. Cambridge, MA: Harvard University Press, 1925.
Stählin, Otto, ed. *Band 3 Stromata. Buch VII und VIII: Excerpta ex Theodoto - Eclogae propheticae quis dives salvetur - Fragmente*. Leipzig: J.C. Hinrichs'she Buchhandlung, 1909.
Suetonius. *Lives of the Caesars*. Translated by J. C. Rolfe. LCL. 2 vols. Cambridge: Harvard University Press, 1914.
Tacitus. *Annals: Books 13–16*. Translated by John Jackson. LCL. Cambridge, MA: Harvard University Press, 1937.
Tertullian, Minucius Felix. *Apology. De Spectaculis. Minucius Felix: Octavius*. Translated by T. R. Glover, Gerald H. Rendall. LCL. Cambridge, MA: Harvard University Press, 1931.
Valerius Flaccus. *Argonautica*. Translated by J. H. Mozley. LCL. Cambridge, MA: Harvard University Press, 1934.
Valerius Maximus. *Memorable Doings and Sayings*. Translated by D. R. Shackleton Bailey. LCL. 2 vols. Cambridge, MA: Harvard University Press, 2000.
Varro. *On the Latin Language*. Vol. 1: *Books 5–7*. Translated by Ronald G. Kent. LCL. Cambridge, MA: Harvard University Press, 1938.
Velleius Peterculus. *Compendium of Roman History. Res Gestae Divi Augusti*. Translated by Frederick W. Shipley. LCL. Cambridge, MA: Harvard University Press, 1924.
Virgil. *Eclogues. Georgics. Aeneid: Books 1–6*. Translated by H. Rushton Fairclough. Revised by G. P. Goold. Cambridge, MA: Harvard University Press, 1916.
Xenophon. *Anabasis*. Translated by Carleton L. Brownson. Revised by John Dillery. LCL. Cambridge, MA: Harvard University Press, 1998.

Literature

Arnold, Russell C. D. "Qumran Prayer as an Act of Righteousness." *JQR* 95 (2005): 509–29.
Ascough, Richard S. "Communal Meals." Pages 204–19 in *The Oxford Handbook of Early Christian Ritual*. Edited by Risto Uro, Juliette J. Day, Richard E. DeMaris, and Rikard Roitto. Oxford: Oxford University Press, 2019.
Ashwin-Siejkowski, Piotr. *Clement of Alexandria: A Project of Christian Perfection*. New York: T&T Clark, 2008.
Aune, David E. "Prayer." Pages 245–64 in *The Oxford Handbook of Early Christian Ritual*. Edited by Risto Uro, Juliette J. Day, Richard E. DeMaris, and Rikard Roitto. Oxford: Oxford University Press, 2019.
—. *Prophecy in Early Christianity and the Ancient Mediterranean World*. Grand Rapids: Eerdmans, 1983.
Auvinen, Risto. *Philo's Influence on Valentinian Tradition*. SPhiloM 10. Atlanta: SBL Press, 2024.
Barclay, John M. G. *Paul and the Gift*. Grand Rapids: Eerdmans, 2015.
—. *Pauline Churches and Diaspora Jews*. WUNT 275. Tübingen: Mohr Siebeck, 2011.

Barrett, C. K. *A Commentary on the First Epistle to the Corinthians*. HNTC. New York: Harper & Row, 1968.

Barrett, Justin L. *Cognitive Science, Religion, and Theology: From Human Minds to Divine Minds*. West Conshohocken, PA: Templeton Press, 2011.

Bartman, Elizabeth. *Portraits of Livia: Imaging the Imperial Woman in Augustan Rome*. New York: Cambridge University Press, 1999.

Baskin, Judith R. *Midrashic Women: Formations of the Feminine in Rabbinic Literature*. Hanover, NH: Brandeis University Press, 2002.

Batten, Alicia J. "Gender." Pages 141–58 in *The Ancient Mediterranean Social World: A Sourcebook*. Edited by Zeba A. Crook. Grand Rapids: Eerdmans, 2020.

—. "Neither Gold nor Braided Hair (1 Timothy 2.9; 1 Peter 3.3): Adornment, Gender and Honour in Antiquity." *NTS* 55 (2009): 484–501.

Baum, Armin D. "Paul's Conflicting Statements on Female Public Speaking (1 Cor. 11:5) and Silence (1 Cor. 14:34–35)." *TynBul* 65 (2014): 247–74.

Beale, G. K. "The Background of ἐκκλησία Revisited." *JSNT* 38 (2015): 151–68.

Beard, Mary, John North, and Simon Price. *Religions of Rome: A History*. New York: Cambridge University Press, 1998.

Beattie, Gillian. *Women and Marriage in Paul and His Early Interpreters*. New York: T&T Clark, 2005.

Bedale, Stephen. "The Meaning of κεφαλή in the Pauline Epistles." *JTS* 5 (1954): 211–15.

BeDuhn, Jason David. "'Because of the Angels': Unveiling Paul's Anthropology in 1 Corinthians 11." *JBL* 118 (1999): 295–320.

Bell, Catherine. *Ritual Theory, Ritual Practice*. Oxford: Oxford University Press, 2009.

Belleville, Linda L. "Κεφαλή and the Thorny Issue of Headcovering in 1 Corinthians 11:2–16." Pages 215–32 in *Paul and the Corinthians: Studies on a Community in Conflict; Essays in Honour of Margaret Thrall*. Edited by Trevor J. Burke and J. Keith Elliott. Boston: Brill, 2003.

Benda-Weber, Isabel. "Non-Greek Headdresses in the Greek East." Pages 95–114 in *Tiarae, Diadems and Headdresses in the Ancient Mediterranean Cultures: Symbols and Technology*. Edited by Carmen Alfaro Giner, Jónatan Ortiz García, and María Antón Peset. Valencia: SEMA, 2014.

Berg, Ria. "Dress, Identity, Cultural Memory: *Copa* and *Ancilla Cauponae* in Context." Pages 203–38 in *Gender, Memory, and Identity in the Roman World*. Edited by Jussi Rantala. Amsterdam: Amsterdam University Press, 2019.

Berglund, Carl Johan. *Origen's References to Heracleon: A Quotation-Analytical Study of the Earliest Known Commentary on the Gospel of John*. WUNT 450. Tübingen: Mohr Siebeck, 2020.

Bieber, Margarete. "The Development of Portraiture on Roman Republican Coins." *ANRW* 1 (1974): 871–98.

Billroth, Gustav. *A Commentary on the Epistles of Paul to the Corinthians*. Translated by W. Lindsay Alexander. Vol. 1. Edinburgh: Thomas Clark, 1837.

Biró, Tamás. "Is Judaism Boring? On the Lack of Counterintuitive Agents in Jewish Rituals." Pages 120–43 in *Mind, Morality and Magic: Cognitive Science Approaches in Biblical Studies*. Edited by István Czachesz and Risto Uro. New York: Routledge, 2014.

Black, Mark C. "1 Cor. 11:2–16—A Reinvestigation." Pages 191–218 in vol. 1 of *Essays on Women in Earliest Christianity*. Edited by Carroll D. Osburn. Joplin, MO: College Press, 1993.

Blasi, Anthony J. *Social Science and the Christian Scriptures: Sociological Introductions and New Translation.* Vol. 1. Eugene, OR: Wipf & Stock, 2017.
Blenkinsopp, Joseph. "The Formation of the Hebrew Bible Canon: Isaiah as a Test Case." Pages 53–67 in *The Canon Debate*. Edited by Lee Martin McDonald and James A. Sanders. Peabody, MA: Hendrickson, 2002.
Böhm, Martina. "1 Kor 11,2–16: Beobachtungen zur paulinischen Schriftrezeption und Schriftargumentation im 1. Korintherbrief." *ZNW* 97 (2006): 207–34.
Bookidis, Nancy. "Religion in Corinth: 146 B.C.E. to 100 C.E." Pages 141–64 in *Urban Religion in Roman Corinth*. Edited by Daniel N. Schowalter and Steven J. Friesen. Cambridge, MA: Harvard University Press, 2005.
Boschung, Dietrich. "Reliefs: Representation of Marcus Aurelius' Deeds." Pages 305–14 in *A Companion to Marcus Aurelius*. Edited by Marcel van Ackeren. Chichester, UK: Wiley-Blackwell, 2012.
Boyer, Pascal. *Religion Explained: The Evolutionary Origins of Religious Thought*. New York: Basic Books, 2001.
Boyer, Pascal, and Pierre Liénard. "Whence Collective Rituals? A Cultural Selection Model of Ritualized Behavior." *American Anthropologist* 108 (2006): 814–27.
—. "Why Ritualized Behavior? Precaution Systems and Action Parsing in Developmental, Pathological, and Cultural Rituals." *Behavioral and Brain Sciences* 29 (2006): 1–19.
Bradshaw, Paul F. *Daily Prayer in the Early Church: A Study of the Origin and Early Development of the Divine Office*. Repr., Eugene, OR: Wipf and Stock, 2008.
Brayford, Susan. *Genesis*. Septuagint Commentary Series. Boston: Brill, 2007.
Bremmer, Jan N. "The *Acts of Thomas*: Place, Date and Women." Pages 74–90 in *The Apocryphal Acts of Thomas*. Edited by Jan N. Bremmer. Leuven: Peeters, 2001.
Brown II, A. Philip. "Chrysostom and Epiphanius: Long Hair Prohibited as Covering in 1 Corinthians 11:4, 7." *BBR* 23 (2013): 365–76.
Bruce, F. F. *1 and 2 Corinthians*. Repr., Grand Rapids: Eerdmans, 1984.
Bulbulia, Joseph. "Charismatic Signalling." *JSRNC* 3 (2009): 518–51.
Bulbulia, Joseph, and Richard Sosis. "Signalling Theory and the Evolution of Religious Cooperation." *Religion* 41 (2011): 363–88.
Buzov, Marija. "The Imperial Cult in Dalmatia." *Classica et Christiana* 10 (2015): 67–96.
Cadwallader, Alan H. "Tertius in the Margins: A Critical Appraisal of the Secretary Hypothesis." *NTS* 64 (2018): 381–87.
Carlson, Stephen C. "On Paul's Second Visit to Corinth: Πάλιν, Parsing, and Presupposition in 2 Corinthians 2:1." *JBL* 135 (2016): 597–615.
Cervin, Richard S. "Does Κεφαλή Mean 'Source' or 'Authority over' in Greek Literature? A Rebuttal." *TJ* 10 (1989): 85–112.
Chester, Stephen J. "Divine Madness? Speaking in Tongues in 1 Corinthians 14.23." *JSNT* 27 (2005): 417–46.
Chow, John K. "Patronage in Roman Corinth." Pages 104–25 in *Paul and Empire: Religion and Power in Roman Imperial Society*. Edited by Richard A. Horsley. Harrisburg, PA: Trinity Press International, 1997.
Clark, Anna F. "Nasica and *Fides*." *ClQ* 57 (2007): 125–31.
Clarke, John R. *Art in the Lives of Ordinary Romans: Visual Representation and Non-Elite Viewers in Italy, 100 B.C.–A.D. 315*. Berkeley: University of California Press, 2003.

Clinch, Alice. "Ecstasy and Initiation in the Eleusinian Mysteries." Pages 314–31 in *The Routledge Companion to Ecstatic Experience in the Ancient World*. Edited by Diana Stein, Sarah Kielt Costello, and Karen Polinger Foster. New York: Routledge, 2022.

Collins, Adela Yarbro. "The Female Body as Social Space in 1 Timothy." *NTS* 57 (2011): 155–75.

Collins, John J. "Watcher." Pages 893–95 in *Dictionary of Deities and Demons in the Bible*. Edited by Karel van der Toorn, Bob Becking, and Pieter W. van der Horst. Second edition. Leiden: Brill, 1999.

Collins, Raymond F. *First Corinthians*. SP 7. Collegeville, MN: The Liturgical Press, 1999.

Concannon, Cavan W. *'When You Were Gentiles': Specters of Ethnicity in Roman Corinth and Paul's Corinthian Correspondence*. New Haven: Yale University Press, 2014.

Conzelmann, Hans. *1 Corinthians*. Translated by James W. Leitch. Edited by George W. MacRae. Philadelphia: Fortress Press, 1975.

Cooley, Alison E., and M. G. L. Cooley. *Pompeii and Herculaneum: A Sourcebook*. Second edition. New York: Routledge, 2014.

Cope, Lamar. "1 Cor 11:2–16: One Step Further." *JBL* 97 (1978): 435–36.

Corbeill, Anthony. *Nature Embodied: Gesture in Ancient Rome*. Princeton: Princeton University Press, 2004.

Corrington, Gail Paterson. "The 'Headless Woman': Paul and the Language of Body in 1 Cor 11:2–16." *PRSt* 18 (1991): 223–31.

Cosgrove, Charles H. "A Woman's Unbound Hair in the Greco-Roman World, with Special Reference to the Story of the 'Sinful Woman' in Luke 7:36–50." *JBL* 124 (2005): 675–92.

Crook, Zeba. "Honor, Shame, and Social Status Revisited." *JBL* 128 (2009): 591–611.

Czachesz, István. *Cognitive Science and the New Testament: A New Approach to Early Christian Research*. Oxford: Oxford University Press, 2017.

D'Angelo, Mary Rose. "Veils, Virgins, and the Tongues of Men and Angels: Women's Heads in Early Christianity." Pages 389–419 in *Women, Gender, Religion: A Reader*. Edited by Elizabeth A. Castelli. New York: Palgrave, 2001.

Danylak, Barry N. *Paul and Secular Singleness in 1 Corinthians 7*. SNTSMS 184. New York: Cambridge University Press, 2024.

Dautzenberg, Gerhard. *Urchristliche Prophetie: Ihre Erforschung, ihre Voraussetzungen im Judentum und ihre Struktur im ersten Korintherbrief*. BWA(N)T. Stuttgart: Kohlhammer, 1975.

DeMaris, Richard E. "Introduction: With Respect to Ritual." Pages 1–16 in *Early Christian Ritual Life*. Edited by Richard E. DeMaris, Jason T. Lamoreaux, and Steven C. Muir. New York: Routledge, 2018.

DeSilva, David A. *The Letter to the Galatians*. NICNT. Grand Rapids: Eerdmans, 2018.

Dihle, Albrecht. *Greek and Latin Literature of the Roman Empire: From Augustus to Justinian*. Translated by Manfred Malzahn. New York: Routledge, 1994.

DiLuzio, Meghan J. *A Place at the Altar: Priestesses in Republican Rome*. Princeton: Princeton University Press, 2016.

Dolansky, Fanny. "Household and Family." Pages 171–86 in *The Oxford Handbook of Early Christian Ritual*. Edited by Risto Uro, Juliette J. Day, Richard E. DeMaris, and Rikard Roitto. Oxford: Oxford University Press, 2019.

—. "*Togam Virilem Sumere*: Coming of Age in the Roman World." Pages 47–70 in *Roman Dress and the Fabrics of Roman Culture*. Edited by Jonathan Edmonson and Alison Keith. Toronto: Toronto University Press, 2008.

Downs, David J. "Physical Weakness, Illness and Death in 1 Corinthians 11.30: Deprivation and Overconsumption in Pauline and Early Christianity." *NTS* 65 (2019): 572–88.

Du Toit, David S. "Status und Anstand als Schlüssel zum Verständnis von 1Kor 11,2–16: Argumentationslogische und sozialgeschichtliche Überlegungen." Pages 61–96 in *Frauen, Männer, Engel: Perspektiven zu 1Kor 11,2–16*. Edited by Torsten Jantsch. Göttingen: Neukirchener, 2015.

Duling, Dennis C. "Ethnicity and Paul's Letter to the Romans." Pages 68–89 in *Understanding the Social World of the New Testament*. Edited by Dietmar Neufeld and Richard E. DeMaris. New York: Routledge: 2010.

Dunn, Geoffrey D. *Tertullian*. New York: Routledge, 2004.

Dunn, James D. G. *Jesus Remembered*. Grand Rapids: Eerdmans, 2003.

—. *The Theology of Paul the Apostle*. Grand Rapids: Eerdmans, 1998.

Edmonson, Jonathan. "Public Dress and Social Control in Late Republican and Early Imperial Rome." Pages 21–46 in *Roman Dress and the Fabrics of Roman Culture*. Edited by Jonathan Edmonson and Alison Keith. Toronto: Toronto University Press, 2008.

Edsall, Benjamin A. "Greco-Roman Costume and Paul's Fraught Argument in 1 Corinthians 11.2–16." *JGRChJ* 9 (2013): 132–46.

Ehrensperger, Kathy. "Between Polis, Oikos, and Ekklesia: The Challenge of Negotiating the Spirit World (1 Cor 12:1–11)." Pages 105–32 in *The First Urban Churches 2: Roman Corinth*. Edited by James R. Harrison and L. L. Welborn. WGRWSup 8. Atlanta: SBL Press, 2016.

—. *Paul at the Crossroads of Cultures: Theologizing in the Space Between*. LNTS 456. New York: Bloomsbury T&T Clark, 2013.

—. "The Question(s) of Gender: Relocating Paul in Relation to Judaism." Pages 245–76 in *Paul within Judaism: Restoring the First-Century Context to the Apostle*. Edited by Mark D. Nanos and Magnus Zetterholm. Minneapolis: Fortress Press, 2015.

Ehrman, Bart D. *Lost Christianities: The Battles for Scripture and the Faiths We Never Knew*. New York: Oxford University Press, 2003.

—. "The Text as Window: New Testament Manuscripts and the Social History of Early Christianity." Pages 803–30 in *The Text of the New Testament in Contemporary Research: Essays on the Status Quaestionis*. Edited by Bart D. Ehrman and Michael W. Holmes. Second edition. Boston: Brill, 2013.

Eisenbaum, Pamela. *Paul Was not a Christian: The Original Message of a Misunderstood Apostle*. New York: HarperCollins, 2009.

Elsner, Jaś. *Imperial Rome and Christian Triumph: The Art of the Roman Empire AD 100–450*. New York: Oxford University Press, 1998.

Elsner, John. "Cult and Sculpture: Sacrifice in the Ara Pacis Augustae." *JRS* 81 (1991): 51–60.

Engberg-Pedersen, Troels. "1 Corinthians 11:16 and the Character of Pauline Exhortation." *JBL* 110 (1991): 679–89.

—. *Cosmology and Self in the Apostle Paul: The Material Spirit*. New York: Oxford University Press, 2010.

—. "Paul's Temporal Thinking: 2 Cor 2.14–7.4 as Paraenetic Autobiography." *NTS* 67 (2021): 157–80.

Epp, Eldon Jay. "Traditional 'Canons' of New Testament Textual Criticism: Their Value, Validity, and Viability—or Lack Thereof." Pages 79–128 in *The Textual History of the Greek New Testament: Changing Views in Contemporary Research*. Edited by Klaus Wachtel and Michael W. Holmes. Atlanta: Society of Biblical Literature, 2011.

Eyl, Jennifer. *Signs, Wonders, and Gifts: Divination in the Letters of Paul.* New York: Oxford University Press, 2019.

Falk, Daniel K. "Qumran Prayer Texts and the Temple." Pages 106–26 in *Sapiential, Liturgical and Poetical Texts from Qumran: Proceedings of the Third Meeting of the International Organization for Qumran Studies, Published in Memory of Maurice Baillet.* Edited by Daniel K. Falk, F. García Martínez, and Eileen M. Schuller. Boston: Brill, 2000.

Fantham, Elaine. "Covering the Head at Rome: Ritual and Gender." Pages 158–71 in *Roman Dress and the Fabrics of Roman Culture.* Edited by Jonathan Edmonson and Alison Keith. Toronto: Toronto University Press, 2008.

Fatum, Lone. "Image of God and Glory of Man: Women in the Pauline Congregations." Pages 56–137 in *Image of God and Gender Models in Judaeo-Christian Tradition.* Edited by Kari Elisabeth Børresen. Oslo: Solum Forlag, 1991.

Fee, Gordon D. *The First Epistle to the Corinthians: Revised Edition.* NICNT. Grand Rapids: Eerdmans, 2014.

Fejfer, Jane. *Roman Portraits in Context.* New York: Walter de Gruyter, 2008.

Fellows, Richard G. "Are There Distigme-Obelos Symbols in Vaticanus?" *NTS* 65 (2019): 246–51.

Finney, Mark. "Honour, Head-coverings and Headship: 1 Corinthians 11.2–16 in its Social Context." *JSNT* 33 (2010): 31–58.

Fishwick, Duncan. *The Imperial Cult in the Latin West: Studies in the Ruler Cult of the Western Provinces of the Roman Empire.* Vol. 2.1. New York: Brill, 1991.

Fitzmyer, Joseph A. "A Feature of Qumran Angelology and the Angels of I Cor. XI. 10." *NTS* 4 (1957): 48–58.

—. "Another Look at κεφαλή in 1 Corinthians 11.3." *NTS* 35 (1989): 503–11.

—. *First Corinthians: A New Translation with Introduction and Commentary.* New Haven: Yale University Press, 2008.

Flower, Harriet I. *The Dancing Lares and the Serpent in the Garden: Religion at the Roman Street Corner.* Princeton: Princeton University Press, 2017.

Flower, Harriet I., and Meghan J. DiLuzio. "The Women and the Lares: A Reconsideration of an Augustan Altar from the Capitoline in Rome." *AJA* 123 (2019): 213–36.

Forbes, Christopher. *Prophecy and Inspired Speech in Early Christianity and its Hellenistic Environment.* WUNT 2.75. Tübingen: J. C. B. Mohr (Paul Siebeck), 1995.

Förster, Hans. "The 'Power on the Head' of a Woman: A New Appraisal of 1 Corinthians 11:10 and its Variants." Pages 135–46 in The New Testament in Antiquity and Byzantium: Traditional and Digital Approaches to Its Texts and Editing; A Festschrift for Klaus Wachtel. Edited by H. A. G. Houghton, David C. Parker, and Holger Strutwolf. ANTF. Boston: Walter de Gruyter, 2019.

Foss, Pedar W. "Watchful *Lares*: Roman Household Organization and the Rituals of Cooking and Eating." Pages 197–218 in *Domestic Space in the Roman World: Pompeii and Beyond.* Edited by Ray Laurence and Andrew Wallace-Hadrill. Portsmouth, RI: *JRA*, 1997.

Frey, Jörg. "The Relativization of Ethnicity and Circumcision in Paul and His Communities." Pages 45–62 in *Paul within Judaism: Perspectives on Paul and Jewish Identity.* Edited by Michael Bird, Ruben A. Bühner, Jörg Frey, and Brian Rosner. WUNT 507. Tübingen: Mohr Siebeck, 2023.

Gardner, Paul D. *1 Corinthians.* Grand Rapids: Zondervan, 2018.

Garland, David E. *1 Corinthians.* BECNT. Grand Rapids: Baker Academic, 2003.

Gawlinski, Laura. "Dress and Ornaments." Pages 96–106 in *A Companion to the Archaeology of Religion in the Ancient World*. Edited by Rubina Raja and Jörg Rüpke. Chichester, UK: John Wiley & Sons, 2015.

Gielen, Marlis. "Beten und Prophezeien mit unverhülltem Kopf? Die Kontroverse zwischen Paulus und der korinthischen Gemeinde um die Wahrung der Geschlechtsrollen-symbolik in 1Kor 11,2–16." *ZNW* 90 (1999): 220–49.

Gill, David W. J. "The Importance of Roman Portraiture for Head-Coverings in 1 Corinthians 11:2–16." *TynBul* 41 (1990): 245–60.

Gladd, Benjamin L. *Revealing the Mysterion: The Use of Mystery in Daniel and Second Temple Judaism with Its Bearing on First Corinthians*. New York: Walter de Gruyter, 2008.

Glancy, Jennifer A. *Slavery in Early Christianity*. New York: Oxford University Press, 2002.

Godet, Frédéric Louis. *Commentary on St. Paul's First Epistle to the Corinthians*. Translated by A. Cusin. Vol 2. Edinburgh: T&T Clark, 1890.

Goodacre, Mark. "Does περιβόλαιον Mean 'Testicle' in 1 Corinthians 11:15?" *JBL* 130 (2011): 391–96.

Goodrich, John K. "Erastus of Corinth (Romans 16.23): Responding to Recent Proposals on His Rank, Status, and Faith." *NTS* 57 (2011): 583–93.

—. "Erastus, *Quaestor* of Corinth: The Administrative Rank of ὁ οἰκονόμος τῆς πόλεως (Rom 16.23) in an Achaean Colony." *NTS* 56 (2010): 90–115.

Gordon, Richard. "The Veil of Power: Emperors, Sacrificers and Benefactors." Pages 199–232 in *Pagan Priests: Religion and Power in the Ancient World*. Edited by Mary Beard and John North. Ithaca, NY: Cornell University Press, 1990.

Goulder, Michael. "Vision and Knowledge." *JSNT* 17 (1995): 53–71.

Grimes, Ronald L. *The Craft of Ritual Studies*. Oxford: Oxford University Press, 2013.

Grudem, Wayne. "Does κεφαλή ("Head") Mean "Source" or "Authority over" in Greek Literature? A Survey of 2336 Examples." *TJ* 6 (1985): 38–59.

—. "The Meaning of Κεφαλή ("Head"): A Response to Recent Studies." *TJ* 11 (1990): 3–72.

—. "The Meaning of κεφαλή ("Head"): An Evaluation of New Evidence, Real and Alleged." *JETS* 44 (2001): 25–65.

Gurry, Peter J. "The Text of Eph. 5.22 and the Start of the Ephesian Household Code." *NTS* 67 (2021): 560–81.

Hägg, Henny Fiskå. *Clement of Alexandria and the Beginnings of Christian Apophaticism*. New York: Oxford University Press, 2006.

Hahn, Frances Hickson. "Performing the Sacred: Prayers and Hymns." Pages 235–49 in *A Companion to Roman Religion*. Edited by Jörg Rüpke. Malden, MA: Blackwell, 2007.

Harland, Philip A. *Dynamics of Identity in the World of the Early Christians: Associations, Judeans, and Cultural Minorities*. New York: T&T Clark, 2009.

Harper, Kyle. "*Porneia*: The Making of a Christian Sexual Norm." *JBL* 131 (2011): 363–83.

Harrington, Daniel J. "The Old Testament Apocrypha in the Early Church and Today." Pages 196–210 in *The Canon Debate*. Edited by Lee Martin McDonald and James A. Sanders. Peabody, MA: Hendrickson Publishers, 2002.

Harris, Murray J. *The Second Epistle to the Corinthians*. NIGCT. Grand Rapids: Eerdmans, 2005.

Heil, John Paul. *The Rhetorical Role of Scripture in 1 Corinthians*. Atlanta: Society of Biblical Literature, 2005.

Heine, Ronald E. *The Montanist Oracles and Testimonia*. Macon, GA: Mercer University Press, 1989.

Hickson, Frances V. *Roman Prayer Language: Livy and the Aneid [sic] of Vergil*. Stuttgart: Teubner, 1993.
Hjort, Birgitte Graakjær. "Gender Hierarchy or Religious Androgyny? Male-Female Interaction in the Corinthian Community—A Reading of 1 Cor 11,2–16." *ST* 55 (2001): 58–80.
Hodge, Charles. *An Exposition of the First Epistle to the Corinthians*. New York: Robert Carter & Brothers, 1874.
Hoehner, Harold W. *Ephesians: An Exegetical Commentary*. Grand Rapids: Baker Academic, 2002.
Hooker, Morna D. "Authority on Her Head: An Examination of I Cor. xi. 10." *NTS* 10 (1964): 410–16.
Horsley, Richard A. "1 Corinthians: A Case Study of Paul's Assembly as an Alternative Society." Pages 242–52 in *Paul and Empire: Religion and Power in Roman Imperial Society*. Edited by Richard A. Horsley. Harrisburg, PA: Trinity Press International, 1997.
—. *1 Corinthians*. ANTC. Nashville: Abingdon Press, 1998.
Huebner, Sabine R. *Papyri and the Social World of the New Testament*. Cambridge: Cambridge University Press, 2019.
Hurd, John Coolidge. *The Origin of 1 Corinthians*. London: SPCK, 1965.
Hurley, James B. "Did Paul Require Veils or the Silence of Women? A Consideration of I Cor. 11:2–16 and I Cor. 14:33b–36." *WTJ* 35 (1973): 190–220.
Hvalvik, Reidar. "Praying with Outstretched Hands: Nonverbal Aspects of Early Christian Prayer and the Question of Identity." Pages 57–90 in *Early Christian Prayer and Identity Formation*. Edited by Reidar Hvalvik and Karl Olav Sandnes. WUNT 336. Tübingen: Mohr Siebeck, 2014.
Hylen, Susan E. *Women in the New Testament World*. New York: Oxford University Press, 2019.
Irons, William. "Religion as a Hard-to-Fake Sign of Commitment." Pages 292–309 in *Evolution and the Capacity for Commitment*. Edited by Randolph M. Nesse. New York: Russell Sage Foundation, 2001.
Isaksson, Abel. *Marriage and Ministry in the New Temple: A Study with Special Reference to Mt. 19:13–12 [sic] and 1. Cor. 11.3–16*. Lund: C.W.K. Gleerup, 1965.
Jackson-McCabe, Matt. *Jewish Christianity: The Making of the Christianity-Judaism Divide*. AYBRL. New Haven: Yale University Press, 2020.
Jantsch, Torsten. "Die Frau soll Kontrolle über ihren Kopf ausüben (1Kor 11,10): Zum historischen, kulturellen und religiösen Hintergrund von 1Kor 11,2–16." Pages 97–144 in *Frauen, Männer, Engel: Perspektiven zu 1Kor 11,2–16*. Edited by Torsten Jantsch. Göttingen: Neukirchener, 2015.
—. "Einführung in die Probleme von 1Kor 11,2–16 und die Geschichte seiner Auslegung." Pages 1–60 in *Frauen, Männer, Engel: Perspektiven zu 1Kor 11,2–16*. Edited by Torsten Jantsch. Göttingen: Neukirchener, 2015.
Jensen, Robin. *Living Water: Images, Symbols, and Settings of Early Christian Baptism*. Boston: Brill, 2011.
Jervis, L. Ann. "'But I Want You to Know...': Paul's Midrashic Intertextual Response to the Corinthian Worshipers (1 Cor 11:2–16)." *JBL* 112 (1993): 231–46.
Johnson, Franklin P. "Sculpture: 1896–1923." *Corinth* 9 (1931): 3–155.
Johnston, Sarah Iles. "Mysteries." Pages 98–111 in *Religions of the Ancient World: A Guide*. Edited by Sarah Iles Johnston. Cambridge: Harvard University Press, 2004.

Jokiranta, Jutta. "Ritual System in the Qumran Movement: Frequency, Boredom, and Balance." Pages 144–63 in *Mind, Morality and Magic: Cognitive Science Approaches in Biblical Studies*. Edited by István Czachesz and Risto Uro. New York: Routledge, 2014.

Jones, F. Stanley. "The Pseudo-Clementines." Pages 285–304 in *Jewish Christianity Reconsidered: Rethinking Ancient Groups and Texts*. Minneapolis: Fortress Press, 2007.

Jones, Ivor H. "Rhetorical Criticism and the Unity of 2 Corinthians: One 'Epilogue', or More?" *NTS* 54 (2008): 496–524.

Joyce, Lillian. "In the Footsteps of Augustus: Hadrian and the Imperial Cult." Pages 79–94 in *Emperors in Images, Architecture, and Ritual: Augustus to Fausta*. Edited by Francesco de Angelis. Boston: Archaeological Institute of America, 2020.

Kaše, Vojtěch. "Meal Practices." Pages 409–25 in *The Oxford Handbook of Early Christian Ritual*. Edited by Risto Uro, Juliette J. Davis, Richard E. DeMaris, and Rikard Roitto. Oxford: Oxford University Press, 2019.

Kazen, Thomas, and Rikard Roitto, *Revenge, Compensation, and Forgiveness in the Ancient World*. WUNT 515. Tübingen: Mohr Siebeck, 2024.

Keener, Craig S. *Paul, Women and Wives: Marriage and Women's Ministry in the Letters of Paul*. Peabody, MA: Hendrickson, 1992.

Ketola, Kimmo. "A Cognitive Approach to Ritual Systems in First-Century Judaism." Pages 95–114 in *Explaining Christian Origins and Early Judaism: Contributions from Cognitive and Social Science*. Edited by Petri Luomanen, Ilkka Pyysiäinen, and Risto Uro. Boston: Brill, 2007.

King, Karen L. *What is Gnosticism?* Cambridge, MA: Harvard University Press, 2003.

Klinghardt, Matthias. "Prayer Formularies for Public Recitation: Their Use and Function in Ancient Religion." *Numen* 46 (1999): 1–52.

Kloppenborg, John S. *Christ's Associations: Connecting and Belonging in the Ancient City*. New Haven: Yale University Press, 2019.

—. "Gaius the Roman Guest." *NTS* 63 (2017): 534–49.

Knohl, Israel. "Between Voice and Silence: The Relationship between Prayer and Temple Cult." *JBL* 115 (1996): 17–30.

Kochenash, Michael. "You Can't Hear 'Aeneas' without Thinking of Rome." *JBL* 136 (2017): 667–85.

Kraemer, Ross Shepard. "Ecstasy and Possession: The Attraction of Women to the Cult of Dionysus." *HTR* 72 (1979): 55–80.

—. *Her Share of the Blessings: Women's Religions Among Pagans, Jews, and Christians in the Greco-Roman World*. Oxford: Oxford University Press, 1992.

Krans, Jan. "Paragraphos, Not Obelos, in Codex Vaticanus." *NTS* 65 (2019): 252–57.

Kroeger, Catherine. "Head." Pages 375–77 in *Dictionary of Paul and His Letters*. Edited by Gerald F. Hawthorne, Ralph P. Martin, and Daniel G. Reid. Downers Grove, IL: InterVarsity Press, 1993.

—. "The Apostle Paul and the Greco-Roman Cults of Women." *JETS* 30 (1987): 25–38.

Kruse, Colin G. *Paul's Letter to the Romans*. Grand Rapids: Eerdmans, 2012.

Laird, Margaret L. "The Emperor in a Roman Town: The Base of the *Augustales* in the Forum at Corinth." Pages 67–116 in *Corinth in Context: Comparative Studies on Religion and Society*. Edited by Steven J. Friesen, Daniel N. Schowalter, and James C. Walter. Boston: Brill, 2010.

Lakey, Michael. *Image and Glory of God: 1 Corinthians 11:2–16 as a Case Study in Bible, Gender and Hermeneutics*. LNTS 418. New York: T&T Clark, 2010.

Lamoreaux, Jason T. "Ritual Negotiation." Pages 133–45 in in *Early Christian Ritual Life*. Edited by Richard E. DeMaris, Jason T. Lamoreaux, and Steven C. Muir. New York: Routledge, 2018.

Lamp, Kathleen S. *A City of Marble: The Rhetoric of Augustan Rome*. Columbia, SC: University of South Carolina Press, 2013.

Lang, Martin, and Radim Chvaja. "Hazard Precaution: Examining the Possible Adaptive Value of Ritualized Behavior." Pages 164–84 in *The Routledge Handbook of Evolutionary Approaches to Religion*. Edited by Yair Lior and Justin Lane. New York: Routledge, 2023.

Lang, T. J. "Trouble with Insiders: The Social Profile of the ἄπιστοι in Paul's Corinthian Correspondence." *JBL* 137 (2018): 981–1001.

Last, Richard. "Christ Worship in the Neighbourhood: Corinth's *ekklēsia* and its Vicinity (1 Cor 14.22–5)." *NTS* 68 (2022): 310–25.

—. "*Ekklēsia* outside the Septuagint and the *Dēmos*: The Titles of Greco-Roman Associations and Christ-Followers' Groups." *JBL* 137 (2018): 959–80.

—. "The Neighborhood (*vicus*) of the Corinthian *ekklēsia*: Beyond Family-Based Descriptions of the First Urban Christ-Believers." *JSNT* 38 (2016): 399–425.

Legare, Cristine H., and André L. Souza. "Evaluating Ritual Efficacy: Evidence from the Supernatural." *Cognition* 124 (2012): 1–15.

Liddell, Henry George, Robert Scott, and Henry Stuart Jones. *A Greek-English Lexicon*. 9th ed. with revised supplement. Oxford: Clarendon, 1996.

Lietaert Peerbolte, L. J. "Man, Woman, and the Angels in 1 Cor 11:2–16." Pages 76–92 in *The Creation of Man and Woman: Interpretations of the Biblical Narratives in Jewish and Christian Traditions*. Edited by Gerard P. Luttikhuizen. Boston: Brill, 2000.

Lietzmann, Hans. *An die Korinther I/II*. Tübingen: J. C. B. Mohr (Paul Siebeck), 1949.

Lieu, Judith M. *Marcion and the Making of a Heretic: God and Scripture in the Second Century*. New York: Cambridge University Press, 2015.

Lightfoot, John. "The Harmony, Chronicle, and Order, of the New Testament." Pages 2–368 in vol. 3 of *The Whole Works of the Rev. John Lightfoot, D. D.* Edited by John Rogers Pitman. 13 vols. London: J. F. Dove, 1822–1825.

Lincicum, David. "Genesis in Paul." Pages 99–116 in *Genesis in the New Testament*. Edited by Maarten J. J. Menken and Steve Moyise. LNTS 466. New York: Bloomsbury, 2012.

Linderski, Jerzy. "The Pontiff and the Tribune: The Death of Tiberius Gracchus." *Athenaeum* 90 (2002): 339–66.

Lisdorf, Anders. "The Conflict over Cicero's House: An Analysis of the Ritual Element in *De Domo Sua*." *Numen* 52 (2005): 445–64.

Llewellyn-Jones, Lloyd. *Aphrodite's Tortoise: The Veiled Woman of Ancient Greece*. Swansea, UK: The Classical Press of Wales, 2003.

Long, Fredrick J. *Ancient Rhetoric and Paul's Apology: The Compositional Unity of 2 Corinthians*. Cambridge: Cambridge University Press, 2004.

Lösch, Stefan. "Christliche Frauen in Corinth (1 Cor. 11, 2–16): Ein neuer Lösungsversuch." *TQ* 127 (1947): 216–61.

Lott, J. Bert. *The Neighborhoods of Augustan Rome*. New York: Cambridge University Press, 2004.

Lowery, David K. "The Head Covering and the Lord's Supper in 1 Corinthians 11:2–34." *BSac* 143 (1986): 155–63.

Luomanen, Petri. "How Religions Remember: Memory Theories in Biblical Studies and in the Cognitive Study of Religion." Pages 24–42 in *Mind, Morality and Magic: Cognitive Science Approaches in Biblical Studies*. Edited by István Czachesz and Risto Uro. New York: Routledge, 2014.

Luttikhuizen, Gerard. "The Apocryphal Correspondence with the Corinthians and the Acts of Paul." Pages 75–91 in *The Apocryphal Acts of Paul and Thecla*. Edited by Jan N. Bremmer. Kampen, Netherlands: Kok Pharos, 1996.

MacDonald, Dennis Ronald. *The Legend and the Apostle: The Battle for Paul in Story and Canon*. Philadelphia: Westminster Press, 1983.

—. *There Is No Male and Female: The Fate of a Dominical Saying in Paul and Gnosticism*. Philadelphia: Fortress Press, 1987.

MacDonald, Margaret Y. "The Deutero-Pauline Letters in Contemporary Research." Pages 258–79 in *The Oxford Handbook of Pauline Studies*. Edited by Matthew V. Novenson and R. Barry Matlock. Oxford: Oxford University Press, 2022.

—. *The Power of Children: The Construction of Christian Families in the Greco-Roman World*. Waco, TX: Baylor University Press, 2014.

MacGregor, Kirk R. "Is 1 Corinthians 11:2–16 a Prohibition of Homosexuality?" *BSac* 166 (2009): 201–16.

Maiden, Brett E. *Cognitive Science and Ancient Israelite Religion: New Perspectives on Texts, Artifacts, and Culture*. SOTSMS. New York: Cambridge University Press, 2020.

Marcus, Joel. "Israel and the Church in the Exegetical Writings of Hippolytus." *JBL* 131 (2012): 385–406.

Marjanen, Antti. *The Woman Jesus Loved: Mary Magdalene in the Nag Hammadi Library and Related Documents*. New York: Brill, 1996.

Marshall, Jill E. "Community is a Body: Sex, Marriage, and Metaphor in 1 Corinthians 6:12–7:7 and Ephesians 5:21–33." *JBL* 134 (2015): 833–47.

—. "Paul, Plutarch and Gender Dynamics of Prophecy." *NTS* 65 (2019): 207–22.

—. "Uncovering Traditions in 1 Corinthians 11:2–16." *NovT* 61 (2019): 70–87.

—. *Women Praying and Prophesying in Corinth: Gender and Inspired Speech in First Corinthians*. Tübingen: Mohr Siebeck, 2017.

Martin, Dale B. *Inventing Superstition: From the Hippocratics to the Christians*. Cambridge, MA: Harvard University Press, 2004.

—. *The Corinthian Body*. New Haven: Yale University Press, 1995.

Martin, Luther H. "The Promise of Cognitive Science for the Study of Early Christianity." Pages 35–56 in *Explaining Christian Origins and Early Judaism: Contributions from Cognitive and Social Science*. Edited by Petri Luomanen, Ilkka Pyysiäinen, and Risto Uro. Boston: Brill, 2007.

Martin, Troy W. "Paul's Argument from Nature for the Veil in 1 Corinthians 11:13–15: A Testicle Instead of a Head Covering." *JBL* 123 (2004): 75–84.

—. "Veiled Exhortations Regarding the Veil: Ethos as the Controlling Proof in Moral Persuasion (1 Cor 11:2–16)." Pages 255–73 in *Rhetoric, Ethic, and Moral Persuasion in Biblical Discourse*. Edited by Thomas H. Olbricht and Anders Eriksson. New York: T&T Clark, 2005.

—. "Περιβόλαιον as 'Testicle' in 1 Corinthians 11:15: A Response to Mark Goodacre." *JBL* 132 (2013): 453–65.

Martin, William J. "1 Corinthians 11:2–16: An Interpretation." Pages 231–41 in *Apostolic History and the Gospel: Biblical and Historical Essays Presented to F. F. Bruce on His 60th Birthday*. Edited by W. Ward Gasque and Ralph P. Martin. Grand Rapids: Eerdmans, 1970.

Mason, Steve. "Josephus and His Twenty-Two Book Canon." Pages 110–27 in *The Canon Debate*. Edited by Lee Martin McDonald and James A. Sanders. Peabody, MA: Hendrickson, 2002.

Massey, Preston T. "Gender Versus Marital Concerns: Does 1 Corinthians 11:2–16 Address the Issues of Male/Female or Husband/Wife?" *TynBul* 64 (2013): 239–56.

—. "Is There a Case for Elite Roman 'New Women' Causing Division at Corinth?" *RB* 118 (2011): 76–93.

—. "The Meaning of κατακαλύπτω and κατὰ κεφαλῆς ἔχων in 1 Corinthians 11.2–16." *NTS* 53 (2007): 502–23.

—. "Veiling among Men in Roman Corinth: 1 Corinthians 11:4 and the Potential Problem of East Meeting West." *JBL* 137 (2018): 501–17.

Matthews, Shelly. "'To Be One and the Same with the Woman Whose Head Is Shaven': Resisting the Violence of 1 Corinthians 11:2–16 from the Bottom of the Kyriarchal Pyramid." Pages 31–52 in *Sexual Violence and Sacred Texts*. Edited by Amy Kalmanofsky. Eugene, OR: Wipf & Stock, 2017.

McAndrew, Francis T. "Costly Signaling Theory." Pages 1525–32 in *Encyclopedia of Evolutionary Psychological Science*. Edited by Todd K. Shackelford and Viviana A. Weekes-Shackelford. Cham, Switzerland: Springer, 2021.

McCauley, Robert N., and E. Thomas Lawson. *Bringing Ritual to Mind: Psychological Foundations of Cultural Forms*. New York: Cambridge University Press, 2003.

McCollum, Joey. "The Intrinsic Probability of τοῖς ἰδίοις ἀνδράσιν ὑποτασσέσθωσαν in Eph. 5.22." *JSNT* 46 (2024): 556–78.

McDonald, Lee Martin. *The Formation of the Biblical Canon*. Vol. 1. New York: Bloomsbury T&T Clark, 2017.

Meeks, Wayne A. *The First Urban Christians: The Social World of the Apostle Paul*. New Haven: Yale University Press, 1983.

Meier, John P. "On the Veiling of Hermeneutics (1 Cor 11:2–16)." *CBQ* 40 (1978): 212–26.

Metzger, Bruce M. *A Textual Commentary on the Greek New Testament*. Second edition. Stuttgart: Deutsche Bibelgesellschaft, 1994.

Meyer, Heinrich August Wilhelm. *Critical and Exegetical Handbook to the Epistles to the Corinthians*. Edited by William P. Dickson. Translated by D. Douglas Bannerman. Vol. 1. Edinburgh: T&T Clark, 1877.

Michaelis, Johann David. *Introduction to the New Testament*. Fourth edition. Translated by Herbert Marsh. Vol. 4. London: Rivington, 1823.

Mickelsen, Berkeley and Alvera Mickelsen. "What Does *Kephalē* Mean in the New Testament?" Pages 97–110 in *Women, Authority and the Bible*. Edited by Alvera Mickelsen. Downers Grove, IL: InterVarsity Press, 1986.

Milgrom, Jacob. *Leviticus 17–22: A New Translation with Introduction and Commentary*. AB. New York: Doubleday, 2000.

Mitchell, Margaret. *Paul and the Rhetoric of Reconciliation: An Exegetical Investigation of the Language and Composition of 1 Corinthians*. Louisville, KY: Westminster/John Knox Press, 1991.

Moo, Douglas J. *The Epistle to the Romans*. NICNT. Grand Rapids: Eerdmans, 1996.

Mount, Christopher. "1 Corinthians 11:3–16: Spirit Possession and Authority in a Non-Pauline Interpolation." *JBL* 124 (2005): 313–40.

Muraoka, Takamitsu. *A Greek-English Lexicon of the Septuagint*. Leuven: Peeters, 2009.

Murphy-O'Connor, Jerome. "1 Corinthians 11:2–16 Once Again." *CBQ* 50 (1988): 265–74.

—. *Keys to First Corinthians: Revisiting the Major Issues*. Oxford: Oxford University Press, 2009.

—. "Sex and Logic in 1 Corinthians 11:2–16." *CBQ* 42 (1980): 482–500.

—. "The Non-Pauline Character of 1 Corinthians 11:2–16?" *JBL* 95 (1976): 615–21.

Myers, Susan E. "Revisiting Preliminary Issues in the Acts of Thomas." *Apocrypha* 17 (2006): 95–112.

Nasrallah, Laura. *An Ecstasy of Folly: Prophecy and Authority in Early Christianity*. Cambridge, MA: Harvard University Press, 2003.

Newberry, Julie. "Paul's Allusive Reasoning in 1 Corinthians 11.7–12." *NTS* 65 (2019): 43–58.

Nissinen, Martti. *Ancient Prophecy: Near Eastern, Biblical, and Greek Perspectives*. Oxford: Oxford University Press, 2017.

—. "Divination." Pages 319–33 in *The Oxford Handbook of Early Christian Ritual*. Edited by Risto Uro, Juliette J. Davis, Richard E. DeMaris, and Rikard Roitto. Oxford: Oxford University Press, 2019.

—. "Prophecy and Omen Divination: Two Sides of the Same Coin." Pages 341–51 in *Divination and Interpretation of Signs in the Ancient World*. Edited by Amar Annus. Chicago: The University of Chicago, 2010.

Nõmmik, Aldar. "'Is It Proper for an 'Uncovered' Woman to Pray to God?' (1 Cor 11:13): A Socio-Historical and Exegetical Examination of 1 Cor 11:2–16." MTh diss., The University of Edinburgh, 2016.

Novenson, Matthew V. "'God is Witness': A Classical Rhetorical Idiom in Its Pauline Usage." *NovT* 52 (2010): 355–75.

Økland, Jorunn. "The Celebrity Paratexts: The 1 Corinthians 14 Gloss Theory before and after *The Corinthian Women Prophets*." Pages 69–98 in *After the Corinthian Women Prophets: Reimagining Rhetoric and Power*. Edited by Joseph A. Marchal. Atlanta: SBL Press, 2021.

—. *Women in Their Place: Paul and the Corinthian Discourse of Gender and Sanctuary Space*. JSNTSup 269. New York: T&T Clark, 2004.

Olshausen, Hermann. *Biblical Commentary on St Paul's First and Second Epistles to the Corinthians*. Translated by John Edmund Cox. Edinburgh: T&T Clark, 1851.

Olson, Kelly. *Dress and the Roman Woman: Self-Presentation and Society*. New York: Routledge, 2008.

—. *Masculinity and Dress in Roman Antiquity*. New York: Routledge, 2017.

Osiek, Carolyn and Margaret Y. MacDonald. *A Woman's Place: House Churches in Earliest Christianity*. Minneapolis: Fortress Press, 2006.

Oster, Richard. "When Men Wore Veils to Worship: The Historical Context of 1 Corinthians 11.4." *NTS* 34 (1988): 481–505.

Østergaard, Jan Stubbe. "Reflections on the Typology and Context of the Richmond Caligula." Pages 50–54 in *New Studies on the Portrait of Caligula in the Virginia Museum of Fine Arts*. Edited by Peter J. M. Schertz and Bernard Frischer. Boston: Brill, 2020.

Padgett, Alan. "Paul on Women in the Church: The Contradictions of Coiffure in 1 Corinthians 11:2–16." *JSNT* 20 (1984): 69–86.

Pao, David W. "Gospel within the Constraints of an Epistolary Form: Pauline Introductory Thanksgivings and Paul's Theology of Thanksgiving." Pages 101–28 in *Paul and the Ancient Letter Form*. Edited by Stanley E. Porter and Sean A. Adams. Boston: Brill, 2010.

Parker, D. C. *An Introduction to the New Testament Manuscripts and Their Texts*. New York: Cambridge University Press, 2008.

Parsons, Mikeal C., and Michael Wade Martin. *Ancient Rhetoric and the New Testament: The Influence of Elementary Greek Composition*. Waco, TX: Baylor University Press, 2018.

Payne, Philip B. "Fuldensis, Sigla for Variants in Vaticanus, and 1 Cor 14.34–5." *NTS* 41 (1995): 240–62.

—. *Man and Woman, One in Christ: An Exegetical and Theological Study of Paul's Letters*. Grand Rapids: Zondervan, 2009.

—. "Ms. 88 as Evidence for a Text without 1 Cor 14.34–5." *NTS* 44 (1998): 152–58.

—. "Vaticanus Distigme-obelos Symbols Marking Added Text, Including 1 Corinthians 14.34–5." *NTS* 63 (2017): 604–25

Pearson, Birger A. "Mystery and Secrecy in Paul." Pages 287–302 in *Mystery and Secrecy in the Nag Hammadi Collection and Other Ancient Literature: Ideas and Practices; Studies for Einar Thomassen at Sixty*. Edited by Christian H. Bull, Liv Ingeborg Lied, and John D. Turner. Boston: Brill, 2012.

Peppard, Michael. *The Son of God in the Roman World: Divine Sonship in Its Social and Political Context*. New York: Oxford University Press, 2011.

Peppiatt, Lucy. *Women and Worship at Corinth: Paul's Rhetorical Arguments in 1 Corinthians*. Eugene, OR: Cascade Books, 2015.

Perriman, A. C. "The Head of a Woman: The Meaning of κεφαλή in 1 Cor. 11:3." *JTS* 45 (1994): 602–22.

Phillips, L. Edward. "Early Christian Prayer." Pages 570–86 in *The Oxford Handbook of Early Christian Ritual*. Edited by Risto Uro, Juliette J. Davis, Richard E. DeMaris, and Rikard Roitto. Oxford: Oxford University Press, 2019.

Pickett, Ray. "Conflicts at Corinth." Pages 113–37 in *Christian Origins*. Edited by Richard A. Horsley. Minneapolis: Fortress Press, 2010.

Raja, Rubina. "Ancient Sanctuaries." Pages 137–53 in *The Oxford Handbook of Early Christian Ritual*. Edited by Risto Uro, Juliette J. Davis, Richard E. DeMaris, and Rikard Roitto. Oxford: Oxford University Press, 2019.

Reed, Annette Yoshiko. *Fallen Angels and the History of Judaism and Christianity: The Reception of Enochic Literature*. New York: Cambridge University Press, 2005.

Reno, Joshua M. "Γυνὴ τοῦ Πατρός: Analytic Kin Circumlocution and the Case for Corinthian Adultery." *JBL* 135 (2016): 827–47.

—. "Pornographic Desire in the Pauline Corpus." *JBL* 140 (2021): 163–85.

Ridgway, Brunilde Sismondo. "Sculpture from Corinth." *Hesperia* 50 (1981): 422–48.

Rives, James B. *Religion in the Roman Empire*. Malden, MA: Blackwell, 2007.

—. "Roman Empire and Roman Emperor: Animal Sacrifice as an Instrument of Religious Convergence." Pages 523–40 in *Religious Convergence in the Ancient Mediterranean*. Edited by Sandra Blakely and Billie Jean Collins. Atlanta: Lockwood Press, 2019.

Robertson, Archibald, and Alfred Plummer. *A Critical and Exegetical Commentary on the First Epistle of St Paul to the Corinthians*. Second edition. Edinburgh: T&T Clark, 1914.

Robinson, Laura. "Hidden Transcripts? The Supposedly Self-Censoring Paul and Rome as Surveillance State in Modern Pauline Scholarship." *NTS* 67 (2021): 55–72.

Rohrbaugh, Richard L. "Honor." Pages 63–78 in *The Ancient Mediterranean Social World: A Sourcebook*. Edited by Zebra A. Crook. Grand Rapids: Eerdmans, 2020.

Roitto, Rikard. "Using Behavioral Sciences to Understand Early Christian Experiences of Conversion." Pages 43–60 in *Religious and Philosophical Conversion in the Ancient Mediterranean Traditions*. Edited by Athanasios Despotis and Hermut Löhr. Leiden: Brill, 2022.

Roth, Martha T. "Women and Law." Pages 144–74 in *Women in the Ancient Near East: A Sourcebook*. Edited by Mark Chavalas. New York: Routledge, 2014.

Röthlisberger, Daniel. "Die *capitis velatio* von Männern und ihre Bedeutung für 1 Cor. 11,4." *JAC* 55 (2012): 47–71.

Royse, James R. "The Early Text of Paul (and Hebrews)." Pages 175–203 in *The Early Text of the New Testament*. Edited by Charles E. Hill and Michael J. Kruger. Oxford: Oxford University Press, 2012.

Runesson, Anders. "The Question of Terminology: The Architecture of Contemporary Discussions on Paul." Pages 53–79 in *Paul within Judaism: Restoring the First-Century Context to the Apostle*. Edited by Mark D. Nanos and Magnus Zetterholm. Minneapolis: Fortress Press, 2015.

Russell, Amy. "The Altars of the Lares Augusti." Pages 25–51 in *The Social Dynamics of Roman Imperial Imagery*. Edited by Amy Russell and Monica Hellström. New York: Cambridge University Press, 2020.

Rybanska, Veronika. *The Impact of Ritual on Child Cognition*. New York: Bloomsbury Academic, 2020.

Sandnes, Karl Olav. "Prophecy—A Sign for Believers (1 Cor 14,20–25)." *Bib* 77 (1996): 1–15.

Scheid, John. "The Priest." Pages 55–84 in *The Romans*. Edited by Andrea Giardina. Translated by Lydia G. Cochrane. Chicago: Chicago University Press, 1993.

Schotroff, Luise. *1 Corinthians*. Translated by Everett R. Kalin. Stuttgart: Kohlhammer, 2022.

Schrage, Wolfgang. *Der erste Brief an die Korinther (1 Kor 6,12–11,16)*. EKKNT 7/2. Düsseldorf: Benziger, 1995.

Schuller, Eileen. "Petitionary Prayer and the Religion of Qumran." Pages 29–45 in *Religion in the Dead Sea Scrolls*. Edited by John J. Collins and Robert A. Kugler. Grand Rapids: Eerdmans, 2000.

Schüssler Fiorenza, Elisabeth. *In Memory of Her: A Feminist Theological Reconstruction of Christian Origins*. Tenth anniversary edition. New York: Crossroad, 1994.

—. "Women in the Pre-Pauline and Pauline Churches." *USQR* 33 (1978): 153–66.

Schwiebert, Jonathan. "Honoring the Divine." Pages 19–37 in *Early Christian Ritual Life*. Edited by Richard E. DeMaris, Jason T. Lamoreaux, and Steven C. Muir. New York: Routledge, 2018.

Scroggs, Robin. "Paul and the Eschatological Woman." *JAAR* 40 (1972): 283–303.

Setzer, Claudia. *Resurrection of the Body in Early Judaism and Early Christianity: Doctrine, Community, and Self-Definition*. Leiden: Brill, 2004.

Shantz, Colleen. "Emotion, Cognition, and Social Change: A Consideration of Galatians 3:28." Pages 251–70 in *Mind, Morality and Magic: Cognitive Science Approaches in Biblical Studies*. New York: Routledge, 2014.

—. *Paul in Ecstasy: The Neurobiology of the Apostle's Life and Thought*. New York: Cambridge University Press, 2009.

Sharp, Matthew T. *Divination and Philosophy in the Letters of Paul*. Edinburgh: Edinburgh University Press, 2023.
Silva, Moisés. *Philippians*. BECNT. Second edition. Grand Rapids: Baker Academic, 2005.
Smith, Dennis E. *From Symposium to Eucharist: The Banquet in the Early Christian World*. Minneapolis: Fortress Press, 2005.
Smith, Shively T. J. *Strangers to Family: Diaspora and 1 Peter's Invention of God's Household*. Waco, TX: Baylor University Press, 2016.
Sosis, Richard. "Costly Signaling: The ABCs of Signaling Theory and Religion." Pages 209–26 in *The Routledge Handbook of Evolutionary Approaches to Religion*. Edited by Yair Lior and Justin Lane. New York: Routledge, 2023.
—. "Religious Behaviors, Badges, and Bans: Signaling Theory and the Evolution of Religion." Pages 61–86 in *Evolution, Genes, and the Religious Brain*. Vol. 1 of *Where God and Science Meet: How Brain and Evolutionary Studies Alter Our Understanding of Religion*. Edited by Patrick McNamara. Westport, CT: Praeger, 2006.
—. "The Adaptionist-Byproduct Debate on the Evolution of Religion: Five Misunderstandings of the Adaptionist Program." *Journal of Cognition and Culture* 9 (2009): 315–32.
—. "The Adaptive Value of Religious Ritual." *American Scientist* 92 (2004): 166–72.
Stanley, Christopher D. *Paul and the Language of Scripture: Citation Technique in the Pauline Epistles and Contemporary Literature*. New York: Cambridge University Press, 1992.
Stegemann, Ekkehard W., and Wolfgang Stegemann. *The Jesus Movement: A Social History of Its First Century*. Translated by O. C. Dean, Jr. Minneapolis: Fortress Press, 1999.
Stendahl, Krister. *Paul among Jews and Gentiles and Other Essays*. Philadelphia: Fortress Press, 1976.
—. "Paul at Prayer." *Int* 34 (1980): 240–49.
Stone, Michael E. *Secret Groups in Ancient Judaism*. New York: Oxford University Press, 2019.
Stuckenbruck, Loren T. *The Myth of Rebellious Angels: Studies in Second Temple Judaism and New Testament Texts*. WUNT 335. Tübingen: Mohr Siebeck, 2014.
—. "Why Should Women Cover Their Heads Because of the Angels? (1 Corinthians 11:10)." *SCJ* 4 (2001): 205–34.
Sullivan, Kevin. *Wrestling with Angels: A Study of the Relationship Between Angels and Humans in Ancient Jewish Literature and the New Testament*. Boston: Brill, 2004.
Tabbernee, William. *Montanist Inscriptions and Testimonia: Epigraphic Sources Illustrating the History of Montanism*. Macon, GA: Mercer University Press, 1997.
Tambiah, S. J. "A Performative Approach to Ritual." *Proceedings of the British Academy* 65 (1981): 113–69.
Taylor, N. H. "Apostolic Identity and the Conflicts in Corinth and Galatia." Pages 99–128 in *Paul and His Opponents*. Edited by Stanley E. Porter. Boston: Brill, 2005.
Teehan, John. *In the Name of God: The Evolutionary Origins of Religious Ethics and Violence*. Chichester, UK: Wiley-Blackwell, 2010.
Theissen, Gerd. *Psychological Aspects of Pauline Theology*. Translated by John P. Galvin. Edinburgh: T&T Clark, 1987.
—. *The Religion of the Earliest Churches: Creating a Symbolic World*. Minneapolis: Fortress Press, 1999.
Thiselton, Anthony C. *The First Epistle to the Corinthians: A Commentary on the Greek Text*. NIGTC. Grand Rapids: Eerdmans, 2000.

Thompson, Cynthia L. "Hairstyles, Head-Coverings, and St. Paul: Portraits from Roman Corinth." *BA* 51 (1988): 99–115.

Thompson, James W. "Creation, Shame and Nature in 1 Cor 11:2–16: The Background and Coherence of Paul's Argument." Pages 237–57 in *Early Christianity and Classical Culture: Comparative Studies in Honor of Abraham J. Malherbe*. Edited by John T. Fitzgerald, Thomas H. Olbricht, and L. Michael White. NovTSup 110. Boston: Brill, 2003.

Thrall, Margaret E. *I and II Corinthians*. New York: Cambridge University Press, 1965.

Townsley, Gillian. "Gender Trouble in Corinth: Que(e)rying Constructs of Gender in 1 Corinthians 11:2–16." *The Bible and Critical Theory* 2/2 (2006): 17.1–17.14.

—. *The Straight Mind in Corinth: Queer Readings across 1 Corinthians 11:2–16*. Atlanta: SBL Press, 2017.

Trebilco, Paul. "Creativity at the Boundary: Features of the Linguistic and Conceptual Construction of Outsiders in the Pauline Corpus." *NTS* 60 (2014): 185–201.

—. "Why Did the Early Christians Call Themselves ἡ ἐκκλησία?" *NTS* 57 (2011): 440–60.

Treggiari, Susan. "Marriage and Family." Pages 372–84 in *A Companion to Latin Literature*. Edited by Stephen Harrison. Malden, MA: Blackwell, 2005.

Trobisch, David. "The Need to Discern Distinctive Editions of the New Testament in the Manuscript Tradition." Pages 43–48 in *The Textual History of the Greek New Testament: Changing Views in Contemporary Research*. Edited by Klaus Wachtel and Michael W. Holmes. Atlanta: Society of Biblical Literature, 2011.

Trompf, G. W. "On Attitudes Towards Women in Paul and Paulinist Literature: 1 Corinthians 11:3–16 and Its Context." *CBQ* 42 (1980): 196–215.

Tulloch, Janet H. "Women Leaders in Family Funerary Banquets." Pages 164–93 in *A Woman's Place: House Churches in Earliest Christianity*, by Carolyn Osiek and Margaret Y. MacDonald. Minneapolis: Fortress Press, 2006.

Turpin, Hugh and Jonathan A. Lanman, "Credibility Enhancing Displays (CREDs): When They Work and When They Don't." Pages 227–42 in *The Routledge Handbook of Evolutionary Approaches to Religion*. Edited by Yair Lior and Justin Lane. New York: Routledge, 2023.

Ulrich, Roger B. "Trajan Conducting Sacrifice." https://www.trajans-column.org/?page_id=1041.

Uro, Risto. "Cognitive Science in the Study of Early Christianity: Why It Is Helpful—and How?" *NTS* 63 (2017): 516–33.

—. *Ritual and Christian Beginnings: A Socio-Cognitive Analysis*. Oxford: Oxford University Press, 2016.

—. "The Interface of Ritual and Writing in the Transmission of Early Christian Traditions." Pages 62–76 in *Mind, Morality and Magic: Cognitive Science Approaches in Biblical Studies*. New York: Routledge, 2014.

Van Kooten, George H. "Ἐκκλησία τοῦ θεοῦ: The 'Church of God' and the Civic Assemblies (ἐκκλησίαι) of the Greek Cities in the Roman Empire; A Response to Paul Trebilco and Richard A. Horsley." *NTS* 58 (2012): 522–48

Van Voorst, Robert E. "Why Is There No Thanksgiving Period in Galatians? An Assessment of an Exegetical Commonplace." *JBL* 129 (2010): 153–72.

Varner, Eric R. *Mutilation and Transformation: Damnatio Memoriae and Roman Imperial Portraiture*. Boston: Brill, 2004.

Vearncombe, Erin K. "Rituals for Communal Maintenance." Pages 92–111 in *Early Christian Ritual Life*. Edited by Richard E. DeMaris, Jason T. Lamoreaux, and Steven C. Muir. New York: Routledge, 2018.

Vegge, Ivar. *2 Corinthians—a Letter about Reconciliation: A Psychological, Epistolographical and Rhetorical Analysis*. Tübingen: Mohr Siebeck, 2008.

Vermeule, Cornelius C. *Roman Imperial Art in Greece and Asia Minor*. Cambridge, MA: Harvard University Press, 1968.

Von Albrecht, Michael. *A History of Roman Literature: From Livius Andronicus to Boethius*. 2 vols. Leiden: Brill, 1997.

Von Mosheim, Johann Lorenz. *Erklärung des Ersten Briefes des heiligen Apostels Pauli an die Gemeinde zu Corinthus*. Flensburg: Korten, 1762.

Waaler, Erik. *The Shema and the First Commandment in First Corinthians: An Intertextual Approach to Paul's Re-Reading of Deuteronomy*. Tübingen: Mohr Siebeck, 2008.

Walker, Jr., William O. "1 Corinthians 11:2–16 and Paul's Views regarding Women." *JBL* 94 (1975): 94–110.

—. "The Vocabulary of 1 Corinthians 11.3–16: Pauline or Non-Pauline?" *JSNT* 35 (1989): 75–88.

Warrior, Valerie M. *Roman Religion*. Cambridge: Cambridge University Press, 2006.

Wassen, Cecilia. "'Because of the Angels': Reading 1 Cor 11:2–16 in Light of Angelology in the Dead Sea Scrolls." Pages 735–54 in volume 2 of *The Dead Sea Scrolls in Context: Integrating the Dead Sea Scrolls in the Study of Ancient Texts*. Edited by Armin Lange, Emanuel Tov, and Matthias Weigold. Boston: Brill, 2011.

Watson, Francis. "The Authority of the Voice: A Theological Reading of 1 Cor 11.2–16." *NTS* 46 (2000): 520–36.

Webster, Caleb. "Trapped in Forgerer's Rhetoric: *3 Corinthians*, Pseudepigraphy, and the Legacy of Ancient Polemics." Pages 153–61 in *"Non-Canonical" Religious Texts in Early Judaism and Early Christianity*. Edited by Lee Martin McDonald and James H. Charlesworth. New York: T&T Clark, 2012.

Weima, Jeffrey A. D. *1–2 Thessalonians*. BECNT. Grand Rapids: Baker Academic, 2014.

Weiss, Alexander. "Keine Quästoren in Korinth: Zu Goodrichs (und Theißens) These über das Amt des Erastos (Röm 16.23)." *NTS* 56 (2010): 576–81.

Weiss, Johannes. *Der erste Korintherbrief*. Göttingen: Vandenhoeck & Ruprecht, 1910.

Welborn, L. L. *An End to Enmity: Paul and the 'Wrongdoer' of Second Corinthians*. Berlin: Walter de Gruyter, 2011.

—. "Inequality in Roman Corinth: Evidence from Diverse Sources Evaluated by Neo-Ricardian Model." Pages 47–84 in *The First Urban Churches 2: Roman Corinth*. Edited by James R. Harrison and L. L. Welborn. WGRWSup 8. Atlanta: SBL Press, 2016.

—. "Paul's Caricature of his Chief Rival as a Pompous Parasite in 2 Corinthians 11.20." *JSNT* 32 (2009): 39–56.

Westfall, Cynthia Long. *Paul and Gender: Reclaiming the Apostle's Vision for Men and Women in Christ*. Grand Rapids: Baker Academic, 2016.

White, B. G. "The Varieties of Pain: Re-examining the Setting and Purpose of 2 Corinthians with Paul's λυπ- Words." *JSNT* 43 (2020): 147–72.

White, Claire. *An Introduction to the Cognitive Science of Religion: Connecting Evolution, Brain, Cognition, and Culture*. New York: Routledge, 2021.

Whitehouse, Harvey. *Modes of Religiosity: A Cognitive Theory of Religious Transmission*. Walnut Creek, CA: Altamira Press, 2004.

Wilkes, J. J. *Dalmatia*. London: Routledge and Kegan Paul, 1969.
Williams, Guy. *The Spirit World in the Letters of Paul: A Critical Examination of the Role of Spiritual Beings in the Authentic Pauline Epistles*. FRLANT 231. Göttingen: Vandenhoeck & Ruprecht, 2009.
Williams, Ritva H. "Accessing Divine Knowledge." Pages 55–72 in *Early Christian Ritual Life*. Edited by Richard E. DeMaris, Jason T. Lamoreaux, and Steven C. Muir. New York: Routledge, 2018.
Williams II, C. K. "The Refounding of Corinth: Some Roman Religious Attitudes." Pages 26–37 in *Roman Architecture in the Greek World*. Edited by Sarah Macready and F. H. Thompson. London: The Society of Antiquaries of London, 1987.
Winter, Bruce W. *After Paul Left Corinth: The Influence of Secular Ethics and Social Change*. Grand Rapids: Eerdmans, 2001.
—. *Roman Wives, Roman Widows: The Appearance of New Women and the Pauline Communities*. Grand Rapids: Eerdmans, 2003.
Wire, Antoinette Clark. *The Corinthian Women Prophets: A Reconstruction through Paul's Rhetoric*. Minneapolis: Fortress Press, 1990.
Witherington III, Ben. *Conflict and Community in Corinth: A Socio-Rhetorical Commentary on 1 and 2 Corinthians*. Grand Rapids: Eerdmans, 1995.
Wold, Benjamin G. *Women, Men, and Angels: The Qumran Wisdom Document Musar LeMevin and Its Allusions to Genesis Creation Traditions*. Tübingen: Mohr Siebeck, 2005.
Wood, Susan E. *Imperial Women: A Study in Public Images, 40 BC – AD 68*. Boston: Brill, 1999.
Woolf, Greg. "Posterity in the Arval *Acta*." Pages 64–84 in *The Future of Rome: Roman, Greek, Jewish and Christian Visions*. Edited by Jonathan J. Price and Katell Berthelot. New York: Cambridge University Press, 2020.
Worthington, Jonathan D. *Creation in Paul and Philo: The Beginning and Before*. WUNT 317. Tübingen: Mohr Siebeck, 2011.
Wright, Richard A. "Crisis Management and Boundary Maintenance: Gentile Christ-Followers, Multiple Identities, and Sacrificial Practices in Corinth." Pages 42–57 in *The Social Worlds of Ancient Jews and Christians: Essays in Honor of L. Michael White*. Edited by Jaimie Gunderson, Tony Keddie, and Douglas Boin. NovTSup 189. Boston: Brill, 2023.
Zanker, Paul. *The Power of Images in the Age of Augustus*. Translated by Alan Shapiro. Ann Arbor, MI: The University of Michigan Press, 1988.

Index of Ancient Literature

Hebrew Bible

Genesis
1–2	266
1–3	42, 46
1:27	266
2	266
2:7	42
6:1–4	271
6:2	271
6:2–4	306
44:5–15	194

Exodus
15:20	312
28:22	194
34:33	300

Leviticus
10:6	65
13:45	56–57, 59, 62, 64–65
16:8	194
19:26	192
21:10	65

Numbers
5:11–28	66
5:18	56–57, 59, 62, 64–66

Deuteronomy
18	194, 201
18:9–22	184, 187, 190, 195
18:10	192
18:10–11	190, 192
18:11	193
28:49	*170*

Joshua
18:10	194

Judges
4:4	312

First Chronicles
24:5	194

Proverbs
18:18	194

Isaiah
28:11–12	169, *170*

Jeremiah
5:15	*170*

Daniel 279

Jonah
1:7	194

Zechariah 279

Deuterocanonical Books

Sirach
25:24	297

Tobit 279

Pseudepigrapha

1 Enoch	271, 279

Ascension of Isaiah
          279

Book of Jubilees	271

Testaments of the Twelve Patriarchs
T. Naph. 8:8	161
T. Reu. 5:6–7	273

Ancient Jewish Writers

Josephus
Ag. Ap.
1.22 §§202–205
Ant.

2.2.2–3 §§11–151	194
2.10.1 §241	195
3.8.9 §§216–218	194
3.11.6 §270	66
4.8.13 §212	*160*
5.1.17 §60	191
6.5.6 §92	191
6.6.3 §115	*181*
6.6.5 §125	194
6.12.4 §254	*181*
6.14.2 §334	*181*, 194
6.14.2–4 §§327–342	194
7.4.1 §§72–73	*181*
8.4.2 §§109–110	*181*
8.9.1 §§232–234	*181*
8.11.1 §§266–267	*181*
8.15.6 §418	*181*
9.6.6 §139	*181*
9.8.3 §168	*181*
9.8.6 §§180–182	200
9.11.3 §242	*181*
10.1.3 §§13–14	*181*
10.2.1 §§28–29	200
10.2.2 §35	*181*
10.4.2 §§60–61	*181*
10.5.1 §79	*181*
10.7.2 §106	*181*
10.9.6 §§177–180	*181*
10.10.2 §194	194
10.11.7 §§267–269	*181*
11.4.5 §96	*181*
11.8.4 §§327–328	194
12.2.14 §§112–113	194
13.3.1 §64	*181*
13.10.7 §§299–300	*181*
13.11.2 §§311–313	182
13.12.1 §322	194
14.15.11 §451	194
14.15.11 §455	190–91
15.10.5 §379	182
17.3.3 §§345–346	182, 194
18.5.3 §125	193
18.6.7 §§195–202	193
18.6.9 §§216–217	195
18.8.6 §§285–288	191
19.1.13 §87	191
19.8.2 §346	193
20.5.1 §97	200
20.8.6 §§168–169	200

J. W.

1.2.8 §§68–69	*181*
1.17.4 §§331–332	190
1.19.4 §377	*191*
2.7.3–4 §§111–118	194
2.8.12 §159	182
3.7.25 §§258–259	194
3.8.3 §352	195
3.8.7 §§387–391	194
3.8.7 §391	*194*
4.4.5 §§ 286–287	191
4.6.3 §§386–388	*181*
6.5.2–3 §§285–288	191
6.5.3 §289	191
6.5.3 §290–291	191
6.5.3 §§292–294	192
6.5.3 §295	192
6.5.3 §§296–298	192
6.5.3 §299	192
6.5.3 §§300–309	192
6.5.4 §310	192

6.5.4 §§313–315	197		4.50–51	185
7.5.4 §§123–127	106		4.151	194
7.5.4 §128	106			
7.8.7 §349	187			

Life

42 §§208–211   194

Philo
Creation
19.58   194

Dreams
1.1–2   194

Embassy
14.109   195

Flaccus
186   187

Heir
265–266   184

Joseph
17.90   173
18.95   195
18.98   173
19.104   173
21.116   173
22.125   173
24.143   173
41.248   173
44.269   173

Moses
1.264–265   186
1.274   186
1.277   186
1.282–284   186
2.6   183, *196*
2.187   183
2.188–191   184

Spec. Laws
1.60–63   185
1.64–65   185
1.87   194
1.219   187
3.56   66, 255
4.48–49   185
4.48–52   *197*

New Testament

Matthew
24:7   202
24:29   202

Mark
13:24   202

Luke
1:48   312
7:36–50   67
21:25–28   202

Acts
1:26   194, 202
21:9   312

Romans
1:2   164
1:9   157
1:10   156
1:25   277
3:2   197
3:21   164
5:14   297
8:15   159
8:26   158, 280
8:26–27   158
8:34   252
11:3   164
11:25–26   198
12:6   164
12:6–8   165
12:12   156
13:1   293
13:7   293
14:6   158
15:30–32   156
16:1–2   264
16:1–23   228
16:22   227

16:23	228, *229*, 293	10:31	265
16:25–27	*164*	11–14	27, 164, 178, *247*
16:26	164	11:1	230
		11:2	230, 244–46
First Corinthians		11:2–14:40	230
1:2	27, *252*	11:3	46, 245, 248–51, 266, 295
1:4	155		
1:7	252	11:3–5	*262*
1:8	252	11:3–6	248, 266
1:9	252	11:3–16	244–45
1:10	252	11:4	46–48, 56–60, 62–63, 71–74, 76–78, 81, *84–85*, 98–99, 149, 240, 251, 308
1:11	264, *317*		
1:12	*53*		
1:14	227		
2:1	*166*	11:4–5	23, 30, 59, *61*, 66–67, 79–80, 151, 164, 178, 201, 203
2:2	27		
2:3	27		
2:9–10	200	11:4–6	266, 284
2:15	200	11:5	47–48, 56–57, 59–60, 62, 72, *268*
3:16–17	*170*		
5	290	11:5–6	46–47, 268, 270
5–6	241	11:5a	252
5:1	*52*	11:5b–6	59, 259
5:1–2	67	11:6	*56*, *263*, 268, 270
5:4	252	11:7	*63*, 265, 267, *268*, *270*
5:9	67, 317	11:7–9	265–66
6:12–20	67	11:7–10a	264–65, 270, 273–76, 279
6:12–7:7	296		
7:1	22, 317	11:7–10	42, 281, 296
7:1–7	*162*	11:7–12	*267*
7:5	161–62, 232	11:7a	46
8	291	11:7b	46
8–10	68, 240–42	11:7c	46
8–11	293	11:8–9	46
8:1–11:1	230, 233	11:10	25, 46, *61*, 62, 76, *268*, 269, 274, 279, 292, 299–302, 304, 306, 315
8:5–6	252		
8:10	232		
9	291		
9:1	*252*	11:10a	267, *268*, 269–70, 272, 275
10	291		
10:23	22	11:10b	270–72, 275–79, 281
10:27	232	11:11	46
10:27–29	*225*	11:11–12	279, 281, *282*, 296
10:30	158	11:12	277

11:13	44, 47, *282*, 287, 303–4	14:29–32	172–76, 178, 202–3
11:13–15	282	14:31	*174*
11:14	46, 56, 59, 63	14:33b–36	*57*
11:14–15	57, 59, 284	14:34	312
11:15	46, 59, 63, 99	14:34–35	233–35, *236*, 294
11:16	76, *246*, 286–87, 306	14:37–39	175
11:17	231, 244	14:39	175
11:17–18	231	14:40	*233*
11:17–34	230	15:8	299
11:17–14:40	231–33, 242	15:31	*252*
11:20	231	15:51–52	198
11:20–21	231	15:57	*252*
11:21	240	16:1–4	291
11:23–24	158	16:17	226
11:27–30	199	16:23	*252*
11:30	*199*		
11:34	231	**Second Corinthians**	
12	179, 230	1:3	*252*
12–14	164–65, 167, 174–76, 179–80, 200–201, 280	1:10–11	157
		1:20	159
		1:23	*157*
12:8–10	165	2	*291–92*
12:10	178	2:1	290
12:28	177	2:1–11	290
12:28–29	165, 169, 172, 178	2:4	290, 317
13	232	3–4	291
13:2	166–69, 175, 178–79	4:15	158
13:8–9	168, 178	6:14–7:1	291
14	165–67, 175, 177, 179, 230–31, *234*	6:16	*170*
		7	291
14:1–5	168, 177–78	8–9	291
14:2	167	8:9	*252*
14:6	167, 169, 173	9:11–12	158
14:16–17	159	10–13	291
14:20–25	*171*	11:3	297
14:21	*169*	11:5	198
14:21–25	169	11:31	*252*
14:22–25	*171*, 232	12:1–7	198
14:23	*171*	12:3	199
14:24–25	178	12:4	199
14:26	231	12:7–9	162
14:29	*173*	12:7–10	162
14:29–31	169	12:9	197
		12:12	199

13:5–7	291

Galatians
1:14	246
1:16–17	198
2:2	198
2:6	198
3:28	59, 246
4:6	159, 280
4:24	312

Ephesians
1:16–17	155
3:14	160
5:21–24	295, 315–16, 320
5:21–33	296
5:22	295

Philippians
1:3–4	155
1:8	157
1:19	156
4:6	157

Colossians
1:3	155
4:2–4	157
4:15	297

First Thessalonians
1:2–3	155
2:5	157
2:13	155
2:14–15	164
3:4	200
3:9	158
3:9–10	157
3:10	158
4:2–6	198
4:15–17	198
5:17	313
5:17–18	158
5:20	164

Second Thessalonians
1:3	155
2:13	155

First Timothy
2:8	160
2:9	51, 57
2:11–14	296, 315–16, 320
4:4–5	158

Second Timothy
1:3	155
1:5	297
2:11–14	296
2:12	312
4:20	228

Philemon
4–5	155
22	156

James
2:25	277

First Peter
3:3	51

Rabbinic Works

b. Ketub 72a–b	65
b. Sanh. 58b	65
Gen. Rab. 7:8	65
Gen. Rab. 17:8	255
m. B. Qam. 8:6	65
m. Ketub. 2:1	65
m. Sotah 1:5	65
Midr. Num. Rab. 9:16	65
t. Sotah 3:1	65
t. Sotah 5:5	65
Sifre Num. 11 on 5:18	65

Early Christian Writings

3 Corinthians	276–77

Index of Ancient Literature

Acts of Paul 275–76

Acts of Thomas
14 310
32 272
114–115 261

Clement of Alexandria
Exc.
44 302
Hyp. 304–5
Paed.
2.10.102–106 303
2.10.106–107 303
2.10.114–115 303
3.11.79 303

Cyprian of Carthage
Hab. virg.
5 309
9 309
12 309
14–16 309
19 309
Laps.
2 308

Dialogue between a Montanist and an Orthodox 311–13

Didache
3:4 202
8:2–3 160

Gospel of Judas 275

Hippolytus of Rome
Commentary on Daniel
300

Irenaeus
Haer.
1.4.1 299
1.4.2 299
1.4.5 299
1.8.2 300

John Chrysostom
Hom. 1 Cor. 26 30–32, 314–15

On the Origin of the World
272

Origen
Hom. Luc.
23.8 311

Pseudo-Clementine Homilies
272

Pseudo-Titus Epistle
272

Reality of Rulers 272

Secret Book According to John
272, 275

Tertullian
Apol.
1.1 307
30.4 307
Cult. fem.
7 309
Virg.
1.1 305
1.4–7 306
2.1 306
3.1 306
7.1 306
7.2 306–7
7.3–4 310
7.4 307
8.1 307
8.4 306
17.1–2 309
17.3 309

17.4 309

Greco-Roman Literature

Appian
Bell. civ.
1.2.16 103

Apuleius
Metam.
2.8 260
2.9–10 260
7.8 *258*
8.8 *254*
11.10 *52*

Aristotle
Pol.
1.1260a 234

Aulus Gellius
Noct. att.
1.9 *235*
1.19 189
5.6 82
6.4 82
7.7 83
9.2 31
10.15 82
13.11 *237*
13.22.1 90
13.23.1 153
19.9.9–11 *87*

Cicero
Div.
1.1 (1) 188
1.2 (2–3) *189–90*
1.2 (4) 189
Dom.
124 104
Nat. d.
1.20 (55) 188–89
1.20 (55–56) *196*
2.3 (10) *101–2*

2.65 (162–163) 189
3.2 (5) 94
3.6 (15) 102
Off.
1.27 (93–94) *283*
Sen.
10 (34) 85

Dio Cassius
Hist. Rom.
42.4.5 86

Dio Chrysostom
1 Tars.
48 253

Dionysius of Halicarnassus
Ant. rom.
2.72.1–9 100
3.70.1 97
3.71.5 98, 202
12.16.1–3 *92–93*
12.16.5 99
15.9.1–2 100

Epictetus
Diatr.
1.16.9–14 *285*

Euripides
Herc. fur.
1269 *283*

Herodotus
Hist.
4.79.3–4 51
7.57 *191*
7.111 *188*
8.135 *188*
9.93 *188*

Historia Augusta
Hist. Aug. Hadrian
26.6–7 106

Index of Ancient Literature

Juvenal
Sat.
3.212–213	*254*
5.12–173	*237*
6.314–319	*50*
6.385–397	*111, 202*
6.486–511	*257*
6.548–591	*196*

Livy
Ab urbe cond.
1.7.1	*193*
1.18.6–10	*95, 202*
1.20.1–6	*94*
1.26.2	*254*
1.26.6	*86*
1.26.13	*86*
1.32.5–14	*100*
1.32.6	*87*
1.36.3–5	*98, 202*
1.36.5	*98*
1.36.6	*98, 193*
3.10.7	*197*
3.49.5	*86*
4.12.10–11	*86*
4.20.7	*113*
5.13.5	*197*
5.21.16	*99*
8.9.4–8	*101–2*
8.9.9–8.10.9	*101*
10.7.4–5	*102*
10.7.9–10	*102–3*
10.7.10	*201*
39.13.8–14	*50*

Lucian
Astr.
23	*188*

Hesiod
8	*196*

Lucretius
De rerum natura
5.1194–1203	*108*

Ovid
Fast.
3.361–376	*96*

Metam.
1.381–383	*94*
1.384–415	*94*
1.558–560	*83*
3.690–731	*51*

Pausanias
Descr.
8.37.11	*188*

Plautus
Amph.
1092–1095	*107*
1095–1125	*108*

Pliny the Elder
Nat.
2.58 (148)	*192*
7.3 (33–35)	*191*
18.2 (6)	*83*
28.17 (60)	*85*

Plutarch
Aem.
3.1–2	*97*

Alex.
27.3–5	*188*

Brut.
17.3	*86*

Caes.
66.6	*86*

Cam.
32.5	*127*
42.5	*83*

Cat. Min.
5.3	*85*

Crass.
6.4	*84*

Cor.
23.1–2   86
25.3   238
Def. orac.
9 (414e)   *189*
Flam.
13.6   82
Marc.
5.4   82
28.1–3   *192*
Num.
7.2   95, 202
Pel.
16.3   *188*
Pomp.
8.2–3   84
40.4   84
Quaest. rom.
6 (266c)   83–84, 93
10 (266d–e)   110
11–12 (266e–f)   111
13 (266f–267a)   111
14 (267a–b)   84, 254
Reg. imp. apophth.
13 (200f)   85
Rom.
16.6   83
Ti. C. Gracch.
19.4   103

Quintilian
Inst.
2.13.13   87

Res Gestae Divi Augusti
12   115

Sallust
Hist.
5.16   84

Seneca
Ep.
67.9   101

114.6   87

Suetonius
Aug.
7.2   *113*
23.2   *254*
31.1   *189*
31.3–4   *113*
40.5   90
45.4   *261*
82.1   *85*
95.1–97.3   193
Cal.
51.1   87
Claud.
32.1   237
Galb.
18.3   83
Jul.
43.1   97
57.1   85
58.2   85
82.2   86
Nero
32.3   97
48.1   85
57.1   83
Tib.
69.1   *83*
Vit.
2.5   105

Tacitus
Ann.
15.37   77

Tibullus
Elegiae
1.2.29–32   50

Valerius Flaccus
Argonautica
5.95–97   94, 201

Valerius Maximus
Memorable Doings and Sayings
1.1.5   *106*
1.1.8   *238*
1.4.1–7 *193*
6.3.10   *263*
9.12e.1 *87*

Varro
Ling.

5.29.130 *109*

Virgil
Aen.
3.403–409 *92*
3.543–547 *92*

Xenophon
Anab.
3.2.8–9 *200*

Index of Modern Authors

Arnold, Russell C. D. 156
Ascough, Richard S. 237–38
Ashwin-Siejkowski, Piotr 303
Aune, David E. 153, 165
Auvinen, Risto 299, 301–2

Barclay, John M. G. 155, 175, 291
Barrett, C. K. 247–48, 266, 269, 275, 282
Barrett, Justin L. 216
Bartman, Elizabeth 124
Baskin, Judith R. 256
Batten, Alicia J. 51, 262, 297
Baum, Armin D. 234–35
Beale, G. K. 27
Beard, Mary 153
Beattie, Gillian 265, 272, 285
Bedale, Stephen 248
BeDuhn, Jason David 251, 266–68, 275, 286
Bell, Catherine 207–8
Belleville, Linda L. 52, 285
Benda-Weber, Isabella 83
Berg, Ria 258
Berglund, Carl Johan 299
Bieber, Margarete 124
Billroth, Gustav 36–37
Biró, Tamás 217
Black, Mark C. 46
Blasi, Anthony J. 223, 228, 278
Blenkinsopp, Joseph 182
Böhm, Martina 250, 275
Bookidis, Nancy 223
Boschung, Dietrich 137
Boyer, Pascal 209–11, 217–19
Bradshaw, Paul F. 155, 159–61

Brayford, Susan 271–72
Bremmer, Jan N. 261
Brown II, A. Philip 63
Bruce, F. F. 46, 248, 269, 275, 285
Bulbulia, Joseph 220–21
Buzov, Marija 132

Cadwallader, Alan H. 228
Carlson, Stephen C. 290
Cervin, Richard S. 249
Chester, Stephen J. 171
Chow, John K. 229, 237–38
Chvaja, Radim 218
Clark, Anna F. 105
Clarke, John R. 114, 121, 126–27, 144
Clinch, Alice 50
Collins, Adela Yarbro 298
Collins, John J. 272
Collins, Raymond F. 245, 281, 284
Concannon, Cavan W. 224
Conzelmann, Hans 245, 262, 272, 285–86
Cooley, Alison E. 128, 131
Cooley, M. G. L. 128, 131
Cope, Lamar 21
Corbeill, Anthony 105
Corrington, Gail Paterson 262, 265, 272
Cosgrove, Charles H. 67
Crook, Zeba 267
Czachesz, István 174, 206–7, 211, 216–17, 221, 225

D'Angelo, Mary Rose 246, 256, 269, 292
Danylak, Barry N. 162
Dautzenberg, Gerhard 173

DeMaris, Richard E. 207
DeSilva, David A. 159, 246
Dihle, Albrecht 84, 91, 224, 238
DiLuzio, Meghan J. 109, 127, 145
Dolansky, Fanny 88–89, 142, 236, 238–39
Downs, David J. 199
Du Toit, David S. 47
Duling, Dennis C. 226
Dunn, Geoffrey D. 305
Dunn, James D. G. 41, 159, 162, 165–66, 172, 225–26, 230, 236, 262, 269

Earl, D. C. 103
Edmonson, Jonathan 89–91
Edsall, Benjamin A. 44–45
Ehrensperger, Kathy 110–11, 121, 126, 148, 214, 223–24, 230, 233, 235, 238–39, 241
Ehrman, Bart D. 197, 298
Eisenbaum, Pamela 162
Elsner, Jaś 137
Elsner, John 114
Engberg-Pedersen, Troels 245–46, 272, 281, 287, 290
Epp, Eldon Jay 284
Eyl, Jennifer 188, 193, 196–97, 200

Falk, Daniel K. 160
Fantham, Elaine 85
Fatum, Lone 46
Fee, Gordon D. 35, 45, 49, 151, 169, 171–73, 179, 227, 230. 233, 247–48, 262, 265–66, 268, 281–82, 285–86
Fejfer, Jane 139–40
Fellows, Richard G. 233
Finney, Mark 74–76, 78, 81, 149, 252–53, 262
Fishwick, Duncan 126
Fitzmyer, Joseph A. 43–44, 65, 78, 171–73, 178, 230, 249, 262, 267–68, 274, 285
Flower, Harriet I. 126–27, 142, 144–45
Forbes, Christopher 176

Förster, Hans 268
Foss, Pedar W. 126
Frey, Jörg 226

Gardner, Paul D. 161, 166, 169, 171–72, 230, 248, 262, 273, 285
Garland, David E. 43, 171–73, 178, 223, 230, 244–45, 247, 249, 251, 263, 266, 268, 273, 281, 285–86
Gawlinski, Laura 121
Gielen, Marlis 59–60, 65, 78
Gill, David W. J. 72–73, 76, 81, 88
Gladd, Benjamin L. 167
Glancy, Jennifer A. 253
Godet, Frédéric Louis 39
Goodacre, Mark 284
Goodrich, John K. 229
Gordon, Richard 114, 116, 121
Goulder, Michael 198
Grimes, Ronald L. 208
Grudem, Wayne 249
Gurry, Peter J. 295

Hägg, Henny Fiskå 303–4
Hahn, Frances Hickson 148, 153–54
Harland, Philip A. 50, 221, 226
Harper, Kyle 304
Harrington, Daniel J. 279
Harris, Murray J. 157, 162, 290
Heil, John Paul 170–71, 251, 266–67, 282
Heine, Ronald E. 313
Hickson, Frances V. 153–54
Hjort, Birgitte Graakjær 68
Hodge, Charles 38, 70
Hoehner, Harold W. 160
Hooker, Morna D. 269, 275
Horsley, Richard A. 41, 241, 248, 265, 281
Huebner, Sabine R. 235, 298
Hurd, John Coolidge 230
Hurley, James B. 56–59, 244, 269
Hvalvik, Reidar 160
Hylen, Susan E. 234

Irons, William 220
Isaksson, Abel 55–59

Jackson-McCabe, Matt 272
Jantsch, Torsten 22, 61–62, 251, 265, 281, 284, 287
Jensen, Robin 310
Jervis, L. Ann 245–46
Johnson, Franklin P. 120, 135
Johnston, Sarah Iles 51
Jokiranta, Jutta 212, 216
Jones, F. Stanley 160
Jones, Ivor H. 290
Joyce, Lillian 136

Kaše, Vojtěch 158
Kazen, Thomas 154
Keener, Craig S. 46, 78, 250, 253, 262, 265, 268, 285
Ketola, Kimmo 212, 216
King, Karen L. 226
Klinghardt, Matthias 153–54, 307
Kloppenborg, John S. 227–29, 236–37
Knohl, Israel 156
Kochenash, Michael 114
Kraemer, Ross Shepard 51–52, 69
Krans, Jan 234
Kroeger, Catherine 68, 248
Kruse, Colin G. 228

Laird, Margaret L. 129
Lakey, Michael 249–51
Lamoreaux, Jason T. 240–41
Lamp, Kathleen S. 114, 127
Lang, Martin 218
Lang, T. J. 170–71, 225, 232, 239
Lanman, Jonathan A. 221–22
Last, Richard 27, 171, 229
Lawson, E. Thomas 215–17
Legare, Cristine H. 210
Liénard, Pierre 209–11, 217–19
Lietaert Peerbolte, L. J. 269, 272, 279
Lietzmann, Hans 70
Lieu, Judith M. 298

Lightfoot, John 32–25
Lincicum, David 266
Linderski, Jerzy 103–4
Lisdorf, Anders 104
Llewellyn-Jones, Lloyd 253–55, 258–59
Long, Fredrick J. 290
Lösch, Stefan 40, 49, 51, 57, 62
Lott, J. Bert 126–27
Lowery, David K. 230
Luomanen, Petri 215
Luttikhuizen, Gerrard 276

MacDonald, Dennis Ronald 41–42, 49, 298
MacDonald, Margaret Y. 121, 234, 263, 294, 297–98
MacGregor, Kirk R. 60
Maiden, Brett E. 26
Marcus, Joel 300
Marjanen, Antti 261, 298
Marshall, Jill E. 50, 52, 230, 246, 252, 265, 296
Martin, Dale B. 269, 272, 279
Martin, Luther H. 213–14
Martin, Michael Wade 232
Martin, Troy W. 245, 283–84
Martin, William J. 56
Mason, Steve 182
Massey, Preston T. 63, 65, 76–77, 88, 97, 262
Matthews, Shelly 249
McAndrew, Francis T. 220–21
McCauley, Robert N. 215–17
McCollum, Joey 295
McDonald, Lee Martin 183
Meeks, Wayne A. 223, 227–28, 237, 264
Meier, John P. 245
Metzger, Bruce M. 284
Meyer, Heinrich August Wilhelm 37–38, 70
Michaelis, Johann David 34–35, 49, 289
Mickelsen, Alvera 248
Mickelsen, Berkeley 248
Milgrom, Jacob 193–94

Mitchell, Margaret 245
Moo, Douglas J. 158, 165, 227–28
Mount, Cristopher 21
Murphy-O'Connor, Jerome 22, 58–60, 63, 78, 277–78
Myers, Susan E. 261

Nasrallah, Laura 189
Newberry, Julie 267–68, 270, 281
Nissinen, Martti 188–90
Nõmmik, Aldar 79
North, John 153
Novenson, Matthew V. 157

Økland, Jorunn 51, 234, 262
Olshausen, Hermann 37, 70
Olson, Kelly 88–91, 224, 253–54, 258–59, 263
Osiek, Carolyn 263, 297–98
Oster, Richard 71–72, 78, 81, 88, 149
Østergaard, Jan Stubbe 132–33

Padgett, Alan 21
Pao, David W. 155
Parker, D. C. 164, 234
Parsons, Mikeal C. 232
Payne, Philip B. 60–61, 151, 233
Pearson, Birger A. 167
Peppard, Michael 126–27, 193
Peppiatt, Lucy 21
Perriman, A. C. 249
Phillips, L. Edward 161
Pickett, Ray 224, 292
Plummer, Alfred 39–40
Price, Simon 153

Raja, Rubina 50, 224, 238
Reed, Annette Yoshiko 272
Reno, Joshua M. 67
Ridgway, Brunilde Sismondo 135
Rives, James B. 114, 126, 131, 140, 188
Robertson, Archibald 39–40
Robinson, Laura 278
Rohrbaugh, Richard L. 267

Roitto, Rikard 154, 225
Roth, Martha T. 75
Röthlisberger, Daniel 72, 83
Royse, James R. 284
Runesson, Anders 27
Russell, Amy 126–27
Rybanska, Veronika 210

Sandnes, Karl Olav 171
Scheid, John 114
Schotroff, Luise 268
Schrage, Wolfgang 61, 245
Schuller, Eileen 155–56
Schüssler Fiorenza, Elisabeth 41, 49, 51, 62
Schwiebert, Jonathan 121, 239
Scroggs, Robin 21, 248
Setzer, Claudia 224
Shantz, Colleen 199–200, 215, 223–24
Sharp, Matthew T. 162–63, 171, 173, 196–98
Silva, Moisés 157
Smith, Dennis E. 175, 231–32, 234, 236
Smith, Shively T. J. 156
Souza, André 210
Sosis, Richard 219–22
Stanley, Christopher D. 169–70
Stegemann, Ekkehard W. 234
Stegemann, Wolfgang 234
Stendahl, Krister 159, 171
Stone, Michael E. 50
Stuckenbruck, Loren T. 271–72, 285
Sullivan, Kevin 271

Tabbernee, William 312
Tambiah, S. J. 208
Taylor, N. H. 291
Teehan, John 220
Theissen, Gerd 42–43, 48, 52, 209, 225
Thiselton, Anthony C. 52, 162, 165–67, 171–73, 177, 226–27, 230, 244, 246, 248–49, 251, 265–66, 269, 284–86
Thompson, Cynthia L. 71–72, 76–77, 254, 257, 259

Thompson, James W. 245
Thrall, Margaret E. 269, 275
Townsley, Gillian 46, 66, 68–69
Trebilco, Paul 27, 232
Treggiari, Susan 255
Trobisch, David 234
Tromph, G. W. 21
Tulloch, Janet H. 236
Turpin, Hugh 221–22

Ulrich, Roger B. 136
Uro, Risto 174, 206–7, 211–12, 215, 217

Van Kooten, George H. 27
Van Voorst, Robert E. 155
Varner, Eric R. 134
Vearncombe, Erin K. 207
Vegge, Ivar 290
Vermeule, Cornelius C. 137
Von Albrecht, Michael 91–92, 106, 108, 121
Von Mosheim, Johann Lorenz 33–35

Waaler, Erik 160
Walker, Jr., William O. 21
Warrior, Valerie M. 153–54
Wassen, Cecilia 274, 281

Watson, Francis 244, 269, 281, 285
Webster, Caleb 277
Weima, Jeffrey A. 155, 158, 165
Weiss, Alexander 229
Weiss, Johannes 70
Welborn, L. L. 227–29, 290–92
Westfall, Cynthia Long 53, 75–77, 79, 268
White, B. G. 291
White, Claire 206
Whitehouse, Harvey 210–13, 215, 217–18
Wilkes, J. J. 132
Williams, Guy 272, 274
Williams, Ritva H. 188–89, 194, 197–98, 202
Williams II, C. K. 223
Winter, Bruce W. 73–74, 76–77, 81, 88, 223, 262, 269, 277–78, 285
Wire, Antoinette Clark 162
Witherington III, Ben 73, 77
Wold, Benjamin G. 276
Wood, Susan E. 124
Woolf, Greg 140
Worthington, Jonathan D. 266
Wright, Richard A. 225

Zanker, Paul 117, 121, 125, 140

Index of Subjects

abstinence 162
Acts of Paul 275–77
Acts of Thomas 260–61, 310
Adam 266–67, 274, 296–97
adultery (*see* sexual impropriety)
Aeneas 91–93, 113, *114*, 115–16, 128, 219
Aeneid 91–92, 114, 214, 251
Amphytrion (Plautus) 107
Ancus Marcius 100
androgyne 42
angels
– and creation 275–77
– and lust 306–7
– as guardians of worship 62, 273–75
– as human messengers 74, 277–79
– as mediators 279–81
– as Watchers 271–73
– identity of 270–71, 304–5
– in worship 42, 311
Antoninus Pius 137
Appian 103–4
Appius 85–86
Apuleius 260
Ara Pacis 113–16, 128, 202
Argonautica (Valerius Flaccus) 94
Arval Brothers (*see* priestly colleges)
assembly (*see* Christ association)
associations, Greco-Roman 236
Attus Navius 97–98, 202
Augustales 128–29
Augustus
– celebration of 224
– depictions of 127, 202
– on Ara Pacis 113–14, 117
– reign of 113

– rules of 90
– statues of 71–72, 116–17, 120–23, 128–29

Balaam 185–87
banquet
– *deipnon* of the Lord 199, 230–31
– etiquette 84
– format of 231–32, 237
– reasons for 237
– symposium 234–35
Battle of Sentinum 101
Battle of Vesuvius 101
Brutus 86

Caesar, Julius 85–86, 97, *114*
Caligula, Gaius 105, 132–33
Camillus 99
capite velato
– and Augustus 113–123
– and cognition 222–23
– and divination 95, 111–12, 201–2
– and gender 78, 115
– and honor 251
– and mishaps 99, 106
– and prayer 92–97, 100–102, 106–7
– and shame 264
– and women 72–73, 77–78, 145, 147–48
– as ritual 211
– definition of 82–83, 87
– description of 71, 106, 209
– in 1 Cor 11:2–16 71–80, 251–52
– in Greek 87–88
– in sacrificial scenes 78, 92–94, 97, 102–3, 127–30, 137, 139, 148

– spread of 48, 81–82
– symbolism of 72, 110
Capitol, Rome 102, 104, 201
Castor of Rhodes 110
Cato the Younger 85
charismata 165–66, 230
charismatic signaling 221–22
Christ association, of Corinth
– and homes 43, 75
– conflict with Paul 290–91
– make-up of 31, 226–29, 257
– rituals of 215
– unbelievers 171, 232–33, 236, 278
– uninitiated 170–71
– worship of 64, 172, 174, 202–3, 219, 230–31
Cicero 104
Claudius 133–34
Clement of Alexandria 29, 302–4
Codex Alexandrinus 271
cognition 26, 206–7, 211–12, 216
cognitive science of religion 26, 206
congregation (*see* Christ association)
consecratio 103–4
Corinth, city of
– administration of 228–29, 293
– and Roman influence 71, 223
– archaeology 71–72, 77
– forum 120, 128–29, 135
– history of 223
– make-up of 31, 225
– map of 122
Corinthian correspondence
– *captatio benevolentiae* 244–45
– catchphrases 22, 167
– irony 244
– praise 244
– thematic arrangement 230, 290–92
– timeline 289–90
Coriolanus, Marcius 86
cornucopia 142, 144
Costly Signaling Theory 219–22
covered face 33, 39–40
covered head
– and concealment 85–87
– and death 86
– and honor 251–52, 270
– and prayer 35
– and prostitutes 75
– and Roman priests 82
– and shame 32–33, 76, 296
– and slaves 75, 82
– and soldiers 82
– and virgins 305–7
– Latin terms of 87
– on man 84–88, 255
– on woman 40, 84, 253–57, 268–69, 309
creation 42, 264–67, 275–77, 282, 296, 299–300, 302
Crispus 227
cross-dressing (*see* transvestism)
culture
– boundaries of 224
– definition of 221
– Greek 60–61, 223, 255
– Jewish 60–61, 255
– Roman 60–61, 91, 222–23
custom, ancient
– Christian 73, 306
– Greek 31, 33–34, 36–39, 43–44, 48, 314
– Jewish 32–36, 40, 43–44, 48, 57, 72–73, 246
– Roman, 31, 34–36, 44, 48, 64, 72, 82, 84, 254
Cyprian of Carthage 308–9

Dea Dia 140
Decii 101–3, 153
Demeter (and Kore) 40, 51, 52, 55
Demetrius (associate of Pompey) 84
devotio 101–2
Didymus the Blind 312
Dio Chrysostom 253–54, 262
Dionysius of Halicarnassus 93, 98–100, 219
Dionysos, cult of 41, 52, 68–69

Index of Subjects

disheveled hair 34, 40–41, 49–53, 57, 61, 64–67, 254
divination
– astrology 195
– (bird) augury 95–98, 102–3, 127, 184–87, 192–93, 201–2
– brontologia 194
– casting lots 194
– definition of 188
– forbidden 185, 190
– haruspicy (or extispicy) 111–12, 184–85, 187, 202
– horoscopes 194
– hydromancy 194
– in Paul 196–201
– marvel interpretation 184–85, 190–92, 196, 199
– oleomancy 194
– omen interpretation 190–91, 201
– oracular 195–97
– Roman 110, 193, 202–3
– ventriloquism 193–94
divine knowledge, access of 183 (*see also* divination, prophecy)
dream interpretation *173*, 198

ekklēsia 27–28
emancipation
– of women 39–40, 42–43, 49
– of slaves 82–83
Enochian tradition 271–73
Erastus (of Corinth) 228–29, 293
eschatology, over-realized 59–60
Essenes 182
Eumachia 128, 130
Eve 42, 296–97
evolution 218–19
exegesis
– of John Chrysostom 32
– of 1 Cor 11:2–16 35, 243–87

Fasti (Ovid) 96
festivals
– Greek 34, 69
– Roman 90
fetials 100
fillet (*see* head-covering)
First Maccabees 182–83
flamen 137
flaminicae 109
freedom (*see* emancipation)
Flavians 136

Gaius (of Corinth) 227–28, 293
garment (outer)
– bottom edge of 103–5
– in 1 Cor 11 301
– purple 92, 96–97, 101
– Roman 90–91
– white 96–97
genius 126, 142–46
Great Antonine Altar 137
group dynamics 219–20, 222, 240

Hadrian 106, 136–38
hair (*see* disheveled hair, long hair, short hair)
hazard-precaution system 217–19
head, metaphorical 248–50, 270
head-covering
– cap 259
– fillet 83, 100, 257
– garland 83, 114–15
– *mitra* (or *mitella*) 258
– outer garment 42–44, 63, 83
– *pileus* 82
– priestly turban 58, 64–65
– protection of 43, *83*, 85
– purple 303
– veil (*see* veil)
Helenus, seer 92, 219
Herculaneum 123, 132
hierarchy of heads 46, 248–65, 295–96
Hippolytus of Rome *300*
Historia Augusta 106
homoeroticism, in antiquity 58–60, *66*
honor 265–67, 270, 282
Horatius 86

House of the Red Walls 142
House of Sutoria Primigenia 144
House of the Vettii 142
Household Codes 294–98

identity
– Christian 73, 225–26
– confusion 224
– of self 27
– of the Corinthian assembly 27
– Roman 205, 224–25, 229
image of God 42, 265–66
intercession 158
interpolation
– of 1 Cor 11:2–16 21–22
– of 1 Cor 14:34–35 233, *234*, 235, 294
– of Rom 16:25–27 *164*
Irenaeus 298–301
Isis
– cult of 41, 50, 52
– depiction of 52, 54
– priestess of 54

Jewish-Roman War, First 180, 191–92
John Chrysostom 29–32, 314–15
John Hyrcanus 181
Josephus 66, 105–6, 180–82, 190–93
Julia (daughter of Augustus) 131
Jupiter 95–96, 101–2, 107–8
Juvenal 111

knowledge 166–67
kyrios 252

lararia 141–42, 145
Lares 125–27, 141–44
libation, pouring of 94, 127–28, 139, 148, 210, 237–38
lituus 95, 202
Livia 113, 123–25
Livy 95–96, 98–99
long hair
– in 1 Cor 11:4 58
– on man 30–31, 56, 59–63, 66–67, 283

– on woman 59, 257, 274, 283, 285, 307
loose hair (*see* disheveled hair)
Lucius Verus 137, 139
Lucius Vitellius 105
Lucretius 108

madness, divine 51, 68, 184 (*see also* possession)
maenads 41, 50
Maimonides 32–33
Marcellus 131–32
Marcus Aurelius 137, 139, 141
Masinissa 85
Middle Assyrian Laws 75, 77
Modes of Religiosity Theory 211–15
modesty 33, 38
Montanism 312–14
Mopsus, diviner 94, 201
Moses 183–84
mourning rituals 67, 254–55
mystery 166–67
mystery cults 36, 40, 49–53, 61–62, 77, 213–14
mythology, Roman 91–94

Nasica 103–5
nature (natural) 63, 283–85
Nero
– death of 82
– deeds of 97
– marriage of *77*
– statues of 71–72, 134–35
Num 5:18 65–66
Numa 94–96, 100, 201–2

oath *157*
obsessive-compulsive disorder 217
ordeal of the bitter water (*see* Num 5:18)
Origen 311

patera 143–45
paterfamilias 144, 213, 238–39
Paul
– and divine communication 196–201

Index of Subjects

– authority of 175, 240–41, 291–92
– in paradise 198–99
– thorn in flesh 162–63, 197
– traditions of 244, 246–47, 257, 261, 264, 282, 292
Pastoral Epistles 294–98
Philo 66, 173, 180, 183
piety (or *pietas*) 108–9, 121, 123–24, 128, 130, 149, 214–15, 238–39
Plautus 107
Pliny the Elder 84
Plutarch 83–85, 93, 95–96, 110–11, 214, 219, 254
pneuma (see Spirit)
pneumatikoi (see spirituals)
Pompeii 128, 131, 141–44
Pompey 84
pontifex 101, 103, 121, 153
possession, divine 51, 184–87, 195, 201–2
prayer
– "Abba! Father!" 159
– "Amen" 159
– benediction *159*
– efficacy of 152, 159, 163
– formularies 152, 158
– in Paul 154–63
– lifted hands 96, 100, 123–25, 160, 307
– Lord's 160
– petitionary 154, 156–57
– posture 158–60
– Roman 153–54, 307
– Shema 160
– silent 154
– thanksgiving 154–55, 157–59
– terms for 152
priestly colleges, Roman
– Arval Brothers 83, 139–40
– augurs 114, 119
– *quindecemviri* 114, 119
– *septemviri* 114, 119
prophecy
– and divination 164, 196, 200–201
– and dreams 187, 194–95
– and prognostication 181–84

– and revelation 169, 173–74, 176
– and teaching 165–66
– as accessing divine knowledge 183
– as sign 169–72
– as speech-act 167–69, 175–80
– definition of 164–80
– ecstatic 41, 62
– evaluation of 172–73
– function of 174–75
– oracular 188–89
– terms for 164
propriety 282–83
Pseudo-Clementine Homilies 272
public places 47, 90, 120, 238
pudicitia 255–56
purity 92–93, 102, 182, 214, 219
Pythagorean philosophy 110

Qumran
– angelology 274–75
– divination 194
– prayers 155–56
– theology 155–56

rabbinic material 32–33, 35, 65
rebellion, of women 39
religion, Roman 94, 97, 213–15
revelations 169, 173–74, 198–99, 213
ritual
– and cognition 206
– and routinization 212
– criticism of 108
– definition of 207–11
– gesture 26, 30, 240
– healing 162–63
– performance 26, 220, 240
Ritual Form Theory 216–217
Romans, Paul's letter to the 227, 293–94
Romulus 83, 94

Sallust 84
salutatio 90
Samnite War, First 100
Saturn (deity) 111

Scipio the Younger 85
sexual impropriety 61, 66–67, *162*
shame 267
short hair
– and Gal 3:28 59–60
– on man 31, 59, 260, 285
– on woman *56*, 59–60, 66, 68, 259–61
Sibylline books 114, 189, 197, 202
silence, of women 39, 233–34, 296
social ostracism 222, 239, 241
spies, government 74, 277–78
Spirit 158–59, 280
spirituals (*pneumatikoi*) 45, 175, 200
status, in society 74–76, 115, 247, 263
subjection of woman 31–32, 37–38, 48, 295–96, 315
Sulla 84
superstition 93–94, 99, 112
synagogue 33–35, 227

Tarquinius Priscus (king) 97–98
Tarsus 253
temple
– of idol 232–33, 274
– Roman 47, 236
Tertullian 29, 305–11
Theodotus 301
Tiberius 123, 132–33, 195
Tiberius Gracchus 103–4
Tibullus 50
Titus (emperor) 106, 136
Titus Castricius 90
toga
– and *capite velato* 72, 88, 101, 106
– depiction of 89
– occasions for 90
– symbol of 224
– types of 88–89, 96
tongues (*glossalia*) 167–71
Trajan 136
Trajan's column 136
transvestism 67–70
triumph, Roman 102

uncovered head
– and Gal 3:28 39, 44
– and health 85
– and honor 83–85, 111, 251
– and liberty 37–38, 42
– and lust 33, 37, 43, 272–73, 303
– and sexuality 76
– and shame 43–45, 74, 252, 273, 280, 296
– and weather 85
– and worship 39–40, 111
– as bodily defect 274
– occasions for 34
– on woman 257–59, 262–64, 309–10
– symbolism of 31, 37

Valentinians 298–301
Varro 109
veil
– and marriage 74, 77
– in 1 Cor 11 299–301
– *rica* 109
– symbolism of 39
– terms for *259*
veiling, practice of 33, 42, 53, 301, 303, 309–10, 312–13 (*see also* covered head, head-coverings)
Vespasian 106, 136
vicomagistri 125–28, 202
Virgil 91, 93, 219, 251

Watchers (*see* angels)
wedding, Roman 127
women
– and leadership 250, 296, 312
– and marriage 255–56
– and sacrifice 109
– and wild behavior 50–51
– as writers 312–14
– weakness of 303–4
worship 105
– Roman 47, 75, 238
– emperor 224
– of idols 72–74, 291, 293

Dissertationes Theologicae Holmienses

1. Eurell, John-Christian. *Peter's Legacy in Early Christianity: The Appropriation and Use of Peter's Authority in the First Three Centuries.* DTH 1. Stockholm: Enskilda Högskolan Stockholm, 2021.
2. Mannerfelt, Frida. *Co-preaching: The Practice of Preaching in Digital Culture and Spaces.* DTH 2. Stockholm: Enskilda Högskolan Stockholm, 2023.
3. Appelfeldt, Joel. *Dopet som hantverk: Gudstjänstkreativitet och liturgisk taktik i Svenska kyrkan och Equmeniakyrkan.* DTH 3. Skellefteå: Artos Academic, 2023.
4. Gobena, Abate. *Sanctity and Environment in Ethiopian Hagiography: The Case of Gedle Gebre Menfes Qiddus.* DTH 4. Stockholm: Enskilda Högskolan Stockholm, 2023.
5. Lockneus, Elin. *Kyrkbänksteologi.* DTH 5. Skellefteå: Artos Academic, 2023.
6. Asserhed, Björn. *Gardens in the Wasteland: Christian Formation in Three Swedish Church Plants.* DTH 6. Stockholm: Enskilda Högskolan Stockholm, 2024.
7. Hallonsten, Simon. *Online Small Groups as Sites of Teaching: An Action Research Dissertation into Christian Religious Education in the Church of Sweden.* DTH 7. Stockholm: Enskilda Högskolan Stockholm, 2024.
8. Plantin, Lisa. *Birth Metaphors in the Book of Job: A Blending Theory Analysis.* DTH 8. Stockholm: Enskilda Högskolan Stockholm, 2024.
9. Nõmmik, Aldar. *Robes, Romans, and Rituals in First Corinthians: Paul and the Conflict over Head-Coverings.* DTH 9. Stockholm: Enskilda Högskolan Stockholm, 2025.

www.ingramcontent.com/pod-product-compliance
Lightning Source LLC
Chambersburg PA
CBHW052129010526
44113CB00034B/1127